The Impact of World War II

A note for the general reader

Total War and Social Change: Europe 1914–1955 is the latest honours-level history course to be produced by the Open University. War and Society has always been a subject of special interest and expertise in the Open University's History Department. The appeal for the general reader is that the five books in the series, taken together or singly, consist of authoritative, up-to-date discussions of the various aspects of war and society in the twentieth century.

The books provide insights into the modes of teaching and communication, including the use of audio-visual material, which have been pioneered at the Open University. Readers will find that they are encouraged to participate in a series of 'tutorials in print', an effective way to achieve a complete command of the material. As in any serious study of a historical topic, there are many suggestions for further reading, including references to a Course Reader, set book and to two collections of primary sources which accompany the series. It is possible to grasp the basic outlines of the topics discussed without turning to these books, but obviously serious students will wish to follow up what is, in effect, a very carefully designed course of guided reading, and discussion and analysis of that reading. The first unit in Book 1 sets out the aims and scope of the course.

Open University students are provided with supplementary material, including a *Course Guide* which gives information on student assignments, summer school, the use of video cassettes, and so on.

Total War and Social Change: Europe 1914–1955

Book 1 *Europe in 1914*
Book 2 *The Impact of World War I*
Book 3 *Between Two Wars*
Book 4 *The Impact of World War II*
Book 5 *Retrospect: War and Change in Europe 1914–1955*

Other material associated with the course

Primary Sources 1: World War I, eds Arthur Marwick and Wendy Simpson, Open University, 2000

Primary Sources 2: Interwar and World War II, eds Arthur Marwick and Wendy Simpson, Open University, 2000

Secondary Sources, eds Arthur Marwick and Wendy Simpson, Open University, 2000

Total War and Historical Change: Europe 1914–1955, eds. Clive Emsley, Arthur Marwick and Wendy Simpson, Open University Press, 2000 (Course Reader)

J. M. Roberts, *Europe 1880–1945,* Longman, 2001 (third edition) (Set Book)

book 4

The Impact of World War II

Clive Emsley, Arthur Marwick, Bill Purdue, Tony Aldgate,
James Chapman, Mark Pittaway and Annika Mombauer

Total War and Social Change: Europe 1914–1955

This publication forms part of an Open University course: AA312 *Total War And Social Change: Europe 1914–1955*. Details of this and other Open University courses can be obtained from the Course Reservations Centre, PO Box 724, The Open University, Milton Keynes MK7 6ZS, United Kingdom: tel. +44 (0)1908 653231, e-mail ces-gen@open.ac.uk

Alternatively, you may visit the Open University website at http://www.open.ac.uk where you can learn more about the wide range of courses and packs offered at all levels by the Open University.

For availability of this or other components, contact Open University Worldwide Ltd, The Berrill Building, Walton Hall, Milton Keynes MK7 6AA, United Kingdom: tel. +44 (0)1908 858785; fax +44 (0)1908 858787; e-mail ouwenq@open.ac.uk; website http://www.ouw.co.uk

The Open University, Walton Hall, Milton Keynes, MK7 6AA

First published 2001 by The Open University. Reprinted 2006.

Edited, designed and typeset by The Open University

Printed and bound in the United Kingdom by The Alden Group, Oxford

ISBN 978 0 7492 1695 5

Cover illustration:The snipers and the partisan have spilled their blood for the people of Paris, 1944. Photo from Gallo, M. (1974) *The Poster in History (with an essay on the development of poster art by Carlo Arturo Quintavalle)*, trans. Alfred and Bruni Mayor, London, Hamlyn, p.269.

2.1

385870B/aa312b4prei2.1

CONTENTS

Acknowledgements

Grateful acknowledgement is made to the following sources for permission to reproduce material in this book.

Text

Welch, D. (1983) *Propaganda and the German Cinema 1933–1945,* © David Welch 1983, by permission of Oxford University Press; Seaton, J. (1987) 'Reporting atrocities' in *The Media in British Politics,* Seaton, J. and Pimlott, B. (eds), Avebury, Gower Publishing Company Ltd, by permission of Ashgate Publishing Ltd.; Bédarida, F. (1988) in Marwick, A. (ed.) *Total War and Social Change,* Macmillan. Klessman, C. (1984), *Die doppelte Staatsgründung: Deutsche Geschichte 1945–1955,* Schriftenreihe der Bundeszentrale für politische Bildung, vol. 193.

Tables

Table 21–25.1: Kennedy, P. (1988) *The Rise and Fall of the Great Powers,* ITPS Ltd; *Table 21–25.2:* Ellwood, D. (1985) *Italy 1943–45,* The Continuum International Publishing Group Ltd.

Figures

Figure 21–25.1: Koskinski, L. (1970) *The Population of Europe: A Geographical Perspective,* Longman.

Unit 20 THE NATURE OF WORLD WAR II

CLIVE EMSLEY

Open University students of this unit will need to refer to:

Set book: J. M. Roberts, *Europe 1880–1945*, Longman, 2001

Primary Sources 2: Interwar and World War II, eds Arthur Marwick and Wendy Simpson, Open University, 2001

Course Reader: *Total War and Historical Change: Europe 1914–1955*, eds Clive Emsley, Arthur Marwick and Wendy Simpson, Open University Press, 2000

Maps Booklet

Video 2

INTRODUCTION

This unit is concerned with the conduct and nature of the Second World War in Europe. By the end of the unit you should be able to recognize:

1   the different ways in which the war was waged on land, sea and in the air;

2   the contrast between the conduct of the war in the west and in the east of Europe.

In Britain, probably the immediate impression that people have of the contrast between the First and Second World Wars is that the former was essentially static, with the two sides entrenched in positions which hardly moved for four years, and that the latter was one of rapid movement typified by the *Blitzkrieg* ('lightning war') tactics of the Germans. This, like many first impressions or traditional views, requires qualification. As you will have learned from Book 2, Units 6 and 11–13, the First World War, including the revolutionary conflicts which followed it, was not static in the east; moreover, while there was considerable movement in North Africa involving British, German and Italian armies between 1939 and 1943, nothing could have been more static than the western front involving Britain and occupied Europe from the summer of 1940 to the summer of 1944. On the eastern front, following the German invasion of the USSR in June 1941, the combatant armies swept backwards and forwards over enormous tracts of territory; this was a war of movement, but in no sense was it a 'lightning war'. Before we address ourselves to the detail of *Blitzkrieg* and the war on the western and eastern fronts, it is worth noting the sheer variety of European theatres of war between 1939 and 1945.

The final chapter of Roberts (set book, pp.443–65) gives a broad survey of the war and will provide an introduction to many of the issues that we will be studying in this unit. Read those pages now.

The following listing of European theatres of war between 1939 and 1945 omits the detail of the German–Soviet war and the reconquest of western Europe following the landings of 1944; instead it lists the beginning, end, and some of the key events of World War II in the other European theatres. Study it now, as it will help you when I refer to these theatres later in the unit.

Some of the European theatres of World War II

The Polish war of 1939

1939

23 August: Nazi–Soviet pact, with a secret protocol assigning Estonia, Finland, Latvia and eastern Poland to the Soviet orbit.

1 September: German invasion of Poland. Polish army virtually destroyed by 18 September.

17 September: Red Army invades eastern Poland.

27 September: Warsaw surrenders.

28 September: Nazi–Soviet pact revised; Lithuania included in the secret protocol concerning the Soviet orbit. In October the USSR imposes treaties on Estonia, Latvia and Lithuania requiring Red Army garrisons on their territory; the following summer the three countries are incorporated into the USSR. Finland is asked to exchange territory with the USSR (particularly to assist the defence of Leningrad) but refuses.

The Russo-Finnish war 1939–40

1939

30 November: USSR attacks Finland.

1940

12 March: Peace of Moscow. Finns cede Karelian Islands and Eastern Karelia, and lease Hangö to USSR.

Hitler's successful war in the west 1939–40

1939

3 September: British and French ultimatums to Germany over Polish invasion expire, leading to war.

September 1939–April 1940: 'The phoney war'; little action on the fronts between British and French and German armies.

1940

9 April: Germany occupies Denmark.

9 April–10 June: Germany occupies Norway.

10–15 May: Germany occupies Belgium.

26 May–3 June: British troops evacuated at Dunkirk.

10 June: Italy declares war on Britain and France.

22 June: French sign Armistice.

With the French surrender the war in western Europe was largely over until the summer of 1944, except for limited resistance activity, strategic bombing and occasional pinprick raids by British commando or parachute units.

The war in the Balkans 1939–41

1939

April: Italy occupies Albania.

1940

June: USSR occupies north-eastern Romania.

August: Hungary occupies north-western Romania; Bulgaria occupies south-eastern Romania.

28 October: Italians invade Greece from Albania.

1941

March: British troops land in Greece.

6 April: Germany invades Yugoslavia.

11 April: Bulgaria, Hungary and Italy invade Yugoslavia.

17 April: Yugoslav army capitulates.

27 April: Germans occupy Athens.

May–June: Germans occupy Crete and the Greek islands.

With the defeat of Greece the conventional war in the Balkans was over, although partisan warfare, and in some instances civil war, continued. Hungarian and Romanian troops fought alongside Germans in the invasion of the USSR; Bulgaria declared war on Britain (and subsequently on the United States) but, fearful of the pro-Russian sympathies of the population, the Bulgarian government declined to join the war against the USSR.

The war in Italy 1943–45

On 13 May 1943 'Army Group Africa' capitulated: 252,000 German and Italian troops became prisoners of war and the Allies turned their attention to Italy.

1943

10 July: Allied troops land in Sicily.

25 July: Italian King dismisses Mussolini.

17 August: Allies capture Messina; the campaign in Sicily ends.

3 September: Italy signs Armistice; first Allied landings on the Italian mainland.

12 September: German paratroops free Mussolini, who assumes leadership of the Fascist Republic of Salò in the north of Italy.

3 October: Kingdom of Italy declares war on Germany.

There followed eighteen months of hard fighting as the Allies pushed up the Italian peninsula; there were also bursts of occasional fierce fighting in the rear of the German front between Italian partisans, Germans and Italian Fascists.

1945

28 April: Mussolini captured by partisans and shot.

2 May: German troops in Italy surrender.

The war in the Balkans 1944–45

1944

March: The Red Army begins an advance into the Balkans.

23 August: Coup in Romania; Romania declares war on Germany. Red Army occupies Romania.

25 August: German troops begin evacuation of Greece.

5 September: USSR declares war on Bulgaria.

8 September: Bulgaria declares war on Germany followed by pro-Soviet coup; Red Army occupies Bulgaria.

9 September: Yugoslav Partisans link up with Red Army.

11 October: Hungary makes secret armistice with USSR, but German army in Hungary forces its revocation.

18 October: Yugoslav Partisans enter Belgrade. Greek government returns to Athens supported by British troops. Civil war in Greece between communists and British-backed monarchists.

23 December: Counter-government in Hungary declares war on Germany.

1945

13 February: Budapest falls to Red Army.

1   THE 'LESSONS' OF WORLD WAR I, AND THE *BLITZKRIEG*

World War II is commonly contrasted with World War I as being a war of movement rather than stalemate, a ground war of tanks rather than trenches. Although in some measure this is true, in the Second World War as in the First, there were variations from theatre to theatre, and there was no simple progression from the tank of World War I to the *Blitzkrieg*.

Trench warfare during World War I had prompted much of the discussion of military tactics to concentrate on defence and had led to the construction of sophisticated fortified lines, most notably the Maginot line. Some military experts were keen to develop armoured warfare, but only in the USSR did generals, drawing on their experience of mobility in World War I and the civil war, develop advanced offensive tactics combining the use of artillery, tanks and aircraft; the disappointing performance of tanks in the Spanish Civil War and Joseph Stalin's purges effectively silenced the advocates of these tactics. In Germany tanks were seen as providing mobile defence. Especially after the reintroduction of conscription in 1935, German military planners still thought in terms similar to Schlieffen, and considered large bodies of infantry to be the primary instruments of battle.

Most military planners contemplated linking airpower with ground forces, but in Britain, with a unique air force separate from the army and the navy, the notion of strategic bombing was developed in the belief that this could be deployed to undermine both the morale of an enemy population and an enemy's economy. The principal theorist of strategic bombing, however, was not British but the Italian General Guilio Douhet.

Blitzkrieg, by which armoured columns supported by aircraft punched through an enemy's line, may have had meaning at a tactical level in the German army, but it was not perceived as a military doctrine until after the victories of 1939 and 1940. Moreover, although the German army was successful in these short campaigns, it believed (rightly as it turned out) that it should be planning for a long war and not a succession of short ones.

The success of the *Blitzkrieg* campaigns, especially that against France, can blind us to the true nature of the way that the bulk of Hitler's armies were deployed, fought and received supplies. Most of the German combat troops, indeed most of the combat troops of all nations engaged in World War II, were infantrymen. Panzer tanks could spearhead an attack; railways could transport troops to Germany's frontiers; but after that, for much of the time during campaigns, the infantry walked – and they did not walk any faster than their fathers had done in 1914. Hitler had decreed that his armies should be mechanized; this concentration on providing motor transport for the army in fact led to a decline in railway rolling stock so that, even though it worked out cheaper to use internal railway communications for journeys over 200 miles, there was less railway stock available in 1939 than there had been in 1914. A further problem was that the German motor industry was not sufficiently developed to provide the vehicles that Hitler wanted; and motor vehicles require oil and rubber, both of which had to be imported to Germany – something which was to create serious wartime problems, as considerable funds were siphoned off for the research and development of synthetic oil and rubber. Only sixteen of Germany's 103 divisions were fully mechanized in 1939, and a considerable amount of German transport remained horse-drawn. A lack of marching discipline led to congestion and jams as infantry, lorries and horse-drawn transport shared the same roads; in retrospect, perhaps, this makes the success of the German army's early campaigns even more remarkable.

These successes encouraged the popular impression in Germany that the war was over in the summer of 1940 and again in October 1941; indeed, Hitler himself contemplated running down arms production in both years. German economic production for war did not show a massive increase until after 1942, and this has led some economic historians to develop the idea of the *Blitzkrieg* economy. The most sophisticated version of this has been put forward by Professor Alan Milward in a series of studies of the Nazi war economy. He has argued that the Nazi Party wanted a system that would enable them to wage war without a drastic reduction in civilian consumer standards. Accordingly German rearmament was organized to produce armaments in 'width' rather than in 'depth'; this enabled the Nazis to fight short, relatively limited wars and not to risk internal disorder by inflicting too much privation on the German population. Only with growing pressure on the eastern front and the entry of the US into the war were the Nazis compelled to organize Germany wholly for total war. A key shift was indicated by Goebbels' speech in February 1943 threatening the Allies with '*totalen Krieg*' (total war), but it was still another year before he became Plenipotentiary for Total War.

Exercise   Study Table 20.1 and answer the following questions:

1   When was the greatest percentage increase in German military expenditure?

2   Do the figures in the table suggest any questions about the idea of the *Blitzkrieg* economy? ∎

Table 20.1   Military expenditure, state expenditure and national income in Germany, 1938–39 to 1943–44 (milliard *Reichsmark*, current prices)

Year	Military expenditure	State expenditure	National income
1938–39	17.2	39.4	98
1939–40	38.0	58.0	109
1940–41	55.9	80.0	120
1941–42	72.3	100.5[1]	125
1942–43	86.2	124.0[1]	134
1943–44	99.4	130.0[1]	130

[1] Based on revenue from occupied Europe and the *Reich*.

(Source: R. J. Overy, 'Hitler's war and the German economy: a reinterpretation', 1982, p.283)

Specimen answers   1   The greatest percentage increases in military expenditure are to be found in the years 1939–40 and 1940–41. These are, respectively, 120.9 per cent and 46 per cent. Military expenditure became a much greater percentage of state expenditure between the years 1938–39 and 1939–40, rising from 43.6 per cent to 65.5 per cent; this is a much larger jump than in later years.

2   Since there is no qualitative leap in military expenditure after 1941 and 1942, the figures suggest that the reasons for the increase in war production after 1942 need to be sought in something other than the idea of the *Blitzkrieg* economy.

Discussion   As the figures presented in the table are annual estimates, you might have considered that monthly fluctuations could still add weight to the theory of the *Blitzkrieg* economy. However, if the expenditure went up during the campaigning months to produce those overall annual figures, then surely emergency production for the periods of *Blitzkrieg* must have been far in excess of the steady, continuous production achieved in the period of total war. □

Exercise   Table 20.1 is taken from an article by Richard Overy reprinted in the Course Reader (Chapter 9), which you read in conjunction with Book 3, Unit 17. Turn to that article again now. What is Overy's criticism of the concept of the *Blitzkrieg* economy? ■

Specimen answer   Overy maintains that Hitler was planning for total war during the 1930s, and that his economic planning got out of phase with the events of his foreign policy; in particular, Hitler did not expect war to develop with Britain and France as a result of his Polish adventure. In sum, Overy maintains that Hitler was planning for a long war, not a *Blitzkrieg*.

Discussion   Overy has developed these arguments in subsequent essays, notably 'Mobilization for total war in Germany, 1939–41' (1988, pp.613–39). He argues that while there were plans for total war, for the mass mobilization of the labour force and of all Germany's resources – plans which were technically put into operation in 1939 – they were undermined by poor and diffused leadership. Goering, for example, was not up to the task of the economic management of total war, and though he tried to centralize the war economy in his office whenever and wherever he could, both the civilian and the military economic leadership tried, often successfully, to circumvent his jurisdiction.

Much of the early military expenditure went towards the construction of an industrial substructure of factories and airfields which, as a result of the Treaty of Versailles, scarcely existed for a war economy. Here too there was mismanagement of resources: in 1942 it was reported that 1.8 million construction workers were employed in building new factories, while firms producing for the war effort could not mount second shifts because they were short of 500,000 workers. Decisions about the kinds of weaponry to be produced and how production was to be carried out gave rise to additional problems. The German military demanded a high standard of finish in its equipment and insisted on a flexible, highly trained workforce to achieve this. Their insistence did indeed result in weaponry of a very high quality, but such expensive equipment was not necessarily the best option; the mass-produced, much cheaper equipment that was more speedily produced by the war economies of Britain and, later, the US did the job just as well, and was more easily replaced. In 1940, for example, Germany and Britain spent, respectively, an estimated $6 billion and $3.5 billion on armaments, yet Britain produced twice as many vehicles, over 50 per cent more aircraft and almost as many tanks as did Germany.

Overy's research underlines an argument increasingly accepted by military historians that *Blitzkrieg* was not a planned tactic for quick, limited wars; it became elevated to such only after a succession of victories which were achieved by the imagination of German field commanders and the courage and initiative of their men, together with a degree of luck and a greater number of errors on the part of their enemies.

Overy's research cannot be taken as the last word on the subject, however. David Kaiser has stressed that we still know little about exactly how the German government made decisions on the day-to-day management of economic policy. Both he and Hans-Erich Volkmann have suggested that by 1939, because of labour shortages, a foreign exchange crisis and competing domestic priorities, the Nazis could not have continued peacetime rearmament at the existing pace. The economic clauses of the Nazi–Soviet pact eased the situation, while the victories of 1939 and 1940 gave the Nazis fresh economic resources and additional labour supplies to tap. The war against Russia can be seen, in turn, as an attempt to carve out a self-sufficient empire in central Europe, which would enable Germany to fight a long war against Britain and the US. Kaiser argues:

> Each new war, in short, grew at least partly out of the need to secure additional resources to continue and expand rearmament, and production did expand dramatically from 1940 until 1942 ... the bulk of the existing evidence seems to show that [Hitler] found himself obliged to proceed at least to limited war in 1939 or else to abandon the existing pace of rearmament. Driven by his ideology, he refused even to consider the latter alternative and chose the former. One may also discern an element of self-fulfilling prophecy in Hitler's economic thought. The rearmament which he undertook ultimately to free Germany from dependence upon the world market in itself made it harder and harder for Germany to draw sustenance from the world market, and impelled him to begin the conquest of *Lebensraum* ... sooner than he had anticipated.

(Quoted in Kaiser *et al.*, 'Debate: Germany, domestic crisis and war in 1939', 1989, pp.204 and 205) □

2 THE NATURE OF THE WAR IN THE WEST 1940–45

With the fall of France in the summer of 1940 the British were effectively barred from engaging with German and Italian troops in western Europe. However,

both sides maintained armies in North Africa, and British troops were sent to
assist Greece against invasion in 1941.

Exercise   1   Using your common sense and general knowledge, what main problem do
                 you think is created by having an army hundreds or even thousands of miles
                 from home?

             2   How is this problem to be solved in general? How do you suppose it was
                 solved during the Second World War? ■

Specimen answers   1   The principal problem is that the army has to be supplied with food, fuel,
                         munitions, replacements, etc.

                     2   This can be overcome only by keeping supply lines open. For Britain,
                         Germany and Italy, the maintenance of armies in North Africa required the
                         use of merchant shipping; aircraft simply could not carry the volume of
                         supplies necessary. However, aircraft, together with warships, could be
                         deployed to protect merchant shipping and to disrupt the supply lines of the
                         enemy. □

Exercise   Think back to the conduct of World War I. What other crucial supply routes were
             likely to witness major fighting? ■

Specimen answer   Britain was still an important trading nation and relied on other countries
                    (including the territories of its far-flung empire) for supplies of oil, raw materials
                    and much of its food. During World War I the Germans had sought to cut
                    Britain's supply lines by unrestricted submarine warfare.

Discussion   Unrestricted submarine warfare had contributed significantly to American
               involvement in World War I. Admiral Erich Raeder, the Commander-in-Chief
               of the *Kriegsmarine* (the German navy), recognized the danger of American
               involvement. Nevertheless, he concluded in October 1939:

> no threat by other countries, especially the United States, to come into
> the war – which can certainly be expected if the conflict continues for
> a long time – must lead to a relaxation of economic warfare once it is
> begun. The more ruthlessly economic warfare is waged, the earlier it
> will show results and the sooner the war will end.

(Quoted in John Costello and Terry Hughes, *The Battle of the Atlantic*,
1977, p.42) □

Exercise   Think back to the Treaty of Versailles. Can you suggest any reason, besides the
             principal German desire to starve Britain of supplies and therefore to
             concentrate on attacking its merchant fleet, for there not being any great fleet
             action similar to the Battle of Jutland? ■

Specimen answer   The Treaty of Versailles forbade the Germans from having large warships
                    (specifically ships of over 10,000 tons); while Germany did circumvent the treaty
                    in many respects, it would have been very difficult to conceal the construction of
                    battleships. Although Germany had begun to rearm in the 1930s, it would have
                    taken a considerable time to build a battle fleet capable of challenging the Royal
                    Navy.

Discussion   By agreements between Britain and Germany in 1935 and 1937 the latter was authorized to build up to 35 per cent of the British surface fleet and to achieve parity in submarines. Germany had, in fact, already begun rebuilding its fleet, laying down in particular the *Bismarck* and the *Tirpitz* – battleships more powerful than any others then afloat or contemplated. Raeder had formulated a plan for a large battle fleet, but when war broke out this was abandoned in favour of what were seen as immediate priorities – submarines and the completion of the *Bismarck*, the *Tirpitz* and two heavy cruisers.

British naval strategy had three key aims in the war against Germany: ensuring the safe arrival of supplies to the United Kingdom; preventing enemy landings; and facilitating landings by British forces and supplying these forces on foreign territory. The Royal Navy considered that the best way of achieving these aims was to seek out and destroy enemy ships whenever they took to sea. The German surface fleet was involved in the seizure of Denmark and Norway in 1940, but after this the principal aim of the *Kriegsmarine*, as noted above, was to cut Britain's supply lines using surface raiders, aircraft and, above all, submarines. The aims of the naval war ensured that the focus of the struggle was the Atlantic Ocean. The Battle of the Atlantic, while enlivened by the forays of German warships, notably the *Graf Spee* in the autumn and winter of 1939 and the *Bismarck* in May 1941, was essentially a struggle involving, on the one hand, convoys and their escorts and, on the other, the U-boat 'wolf-packs'. □

Exercise   What German success in 1940 created additional problems for Britain in the battle of the Atlantic? ■

Specimen answer   The fall of France enabled the *Kriegsmarine* to station its U-boats on the Atlantic coast, which had not been possible in World War I. It also made Atlantic convoys vulnerable to air attacks from the French coast.

Discussion   You might have suggested that the fall of France made the French fleet available to the Germans, but in fact Article 8 of the Armistice agreed to by the French specified that, except for those ships required for the maintenance of their empire, the remainder of the fleet was to be immobilized. The British were sceptical and set out to immobilize the French fleet in their own way. The few warships in British ports were seized, while those in North Africa were given an ultimatum: they could join in the war alongside the British, or they could surrender under a promise of repatriation of the crews and the ultimate restoration of the ships; otherwise they were expected to scuttle themselves within six hours of the receipt of the ultimatum, or face attack. The French ships in port at Alexandria, alongside units of the Royal Navy, agreed to surrender and be repatriated. A much larger contingent at Mers-el-Kebir, to the west of Oran on the coast of Algeria, rejected the ultimatum and were shelled by a Royal Navy squadron; the fifteen-minute 'battle' resulted in enormous French losses, but destroyed the potential threat perceived by the British government.

The Battle of the Atlantic swung to and fro for three and a half years (see Tables 20.2 and 20.3). It began with the 'happy time', as the crews of the U-boats called it, when, in the early months of the war, they wrought havoc among the Atlantic convoys. Gradually, during 1940 and 1941, the convoy escorts gained in experience, numbers and equipment: the Royal Canadian Navy was considerably increased in size, and US warships began escort duty in July

1941 as far as Iceland; air cover was developed from land bases in North America, Iceland and the British Isles, as well as from escort carriers; ship radar was improved and given a high priority for convoy escorts. In addition, the British were probably assisted, unwittingly, by Hitler's determination to keep a sizeable U-boat presence in the Mediterranean, thus reducing the number available for the Atlantic.

Table 20.2   British, Allied and neutral merchant ship losses 1939–45

Period	Tonnage of ships lost		Percentage of tonnage lost in Atlantic	Number of British merchant ships lost	
	(all causes)	(U-boats)		(all causes)	(U-boats)
Sept–Dec 1939	755,392	421,156	99.9	95	50
1940	3,991,641	2,186,158	91.6	511	225
1941	4,328,558	2,171,070	76.1	568	288
1942	7,790,697	6,266,215	79.0	590	452
1943	1,218,219	804,277	37.2	266	203
1944	530,510	358,609	63.9	102	67
Jan–May 1945	411,127	270,277	89.2	45	30

(Source: Based on figures in Costello and Hughes, *Battle of the Atlantic*, pp.304–5)

When the US entered the war formally in December 1941 the U-boats embarked on their second 'happy time' since, in spite of appalling losses, the Americans did not establish a convoy system for ships sailing on their east coast and sea lanes until May 1942. In July 1942 the U-boat packs switched to the 'Black Gap' – that stretch of the north Atlantic which could not be patrolled by the long-range, four-engine Liberator aircraft operating from land bases. A crucial incident occurred on 30 October 1942 when a boarding party from a Royal Navy warship managed to retrieve several codebooks from the sinking U-559. These enabled the code-breakers at Bletchley Park in Buckinghamshire to crack the U-boat Enigma cipher 'Shark', the most difficult of Germany's Enigma codes.

The climax of the Battle of the Atlantic came in the first half of 1943; the U-boats had a particularly successful month in March, but a disastrous one in May. At the end of April the Atlantic wolf-packs targeted a slow-moving convoy of forty ships, known as 'ONS 5'. Their initial attacks were successful, but then a thick fog came down. The convoy and its escorts were now invisible to the U-boats, but the U-boats remained vulnerable to ship radar and to the High Frequency Direction Finders (HFDF) of the escorts, which pinpointed them from their radio transmissions. Twelve ships of ONS 5 were sunk, but the escorts destroyed five U-boats, two more collided and sank, and another two were destroyed by air patrols. The total U-boat losses for May 1943 came to forty-one, and they were temporarily withdrawn from the Atlantic. The U-boat war was by no means over, as is demonstrated by the statistics in Tables 20.2 and 20.3.

Table 20.3   German U-boat operations 1939–45

Year	Quarter	Total fleet	Daily average numbers		Sunk	Atlantic theatre	
			Operational	Engaged in Atlantic		New U-boats commissioned	Ships sunk by U-boats
1939	Sept–Dec	57	12	5	9	2	105
1940	Jan–Mar	51	11	5	6	4	80
	Apr–Jun	49	10	7	8	9	75
	Jul–Sep	56	10	8	5	15	150
	Oct–Dec	75	11	9	3	26	130
1941	Jan–Mar	102	20	12	5	31	100
	Apr–Jun	136	25	15	7	53	150
	Jul–Sep	182	30	17	6	70	90
	Oct–Dec	233	35	16	17	70	70
1942	Jan–Mar	272	45	13	11	49	225
	Apr–Jun	315	60	15	10	58	240
	Jul–Sep	352	95	25	32	61	290
	Oct–Dec	382	100	40	34	70	260
1943	Jan–Mar	418	110	50	40	70	200
	Apr–Jun	424	90	40	73	69	120
	Jul–Sep	408	60	20	71	68	75
	Oct–Dec	425	70	25	53	83	40
1944	Jan–Mar	445	65	30	60	62	45
	Apr–Jun	437	50	20	68	53	20
	Jul–Sep	396	40	15	79	50	35
	Oct–Dec	398	35	20	32	67	17
1945	Jan–May	349	45	20	153	93	55
					Total 782	Total 1,133	

(Source: Based on figures in Costello and Hughes, *Battle of the Atlantic*, pp.304–5)

Schnörchel equipment was developed which enabled U-boats to remain submerged while recharging their batteries, and acoustic torpedoes were introduced which homed in on the sound of a ship's propellers. Increasingly, however, the U-boats became the hunted rather than the hunters: in the last year of the war the average life expectancy of a U-boat was reduced to one and a half sorties. □

In addition to that established in the Atlantic, a convoy system was employed from the summer of 1941 to transport goods from Britain to the USSR. The ships were routed through Arctic waters around Scandinavia and through the Barents

Sea to Murmansk or Archangel. U-boats played a role in German attempts to destroy these convoys, but the merchant ships on this route also had to run the gauntlet of naval bases and airfields in both Germany and Nazi-occupied Norway. The significant battle here was fought by surface vessels. At the end of 1942 British destroyers protecting convoy JW 51 B by a mixture of skill, luck and the last-minute arrival of a covering squadron of cruisers, beat off an attack by German warships in the Battle of the Barents Sea. As a result of the battle Hitler concluded that Germany's surface fleet was not worth maintaining; Raeder resigned in disgust as Hitler decommissioned the bulk of the fleet.

The Mediterranean was the third area of significant naval operations in the European war. Mussolini had dreamed of mastery over the Mediterranean and had built up the *Regia Marina* in consequence. But this fleet was rather more impressive for its size than for the weight and equipment of its ships. While the four new battleships built since 1933 were as good as, or even better than, their British counterparts, overall the Italian navy was inferior. At the outset of the war its fleet of 113 submarines was, with the probable exception of the USSR, the largest in the world; but these submarines were primitive and in particular were slow to dive and vulnerable to depth-charge attack. There were no aircraft carriers, and since co-operation between different sections of the Italian armed forces was poor, the proposed reliance on the *Regia Aeronautica* provided no real substitute, even in waters close to Italy. Italy's shipbuilding industry, with its limited raw materials and financial resources, was considerably less developed and less able to replace lost ships than that of Britain; and while during the interwar period the Italian aircraft industry had seemed to be in the forefront of innovation, the lack of financial resources and raw materials meant that any such innovations were rarely transferred into military development and production. The British and Italian fleets fought a succession of engagements in the Mediterranean before the Italian fleet surrendered in 1943. British historians have tended to speak of the Royal Navy's 'moral superiority' over the *Regia Marina*, although a reappraisal by James J. Sadkovich suggests that a double standard has been applied and that it would be more just to consider the conflict as a draw ('Re-evaluating who won the Italo-British naval conflict, 1940–2', 1988). First, Sadkovich stresses that the Italians succeeded in maintaining a battle fleet which continued to present a threat to the British. While this might not seem, on the face of it, a success, it must be remembered that the Italians could not offer battle unless sure of an advantage, since they did not have the industrial base easily to replace lost ships. Second, Sadkovich emphasizes the overall Italian success in protecting their convoys to Tunisia, Libya, the Aegean and the Balkans.

German warships constituted the first targets of RAF Bomber Command during the war when a raid was mounted on ships in the Kiel Canal on 4 September 1939. There was considerable concern about the effects of the bombing of civilian targets and, while Warsaw had been hit by the *Luftwaffe* in September 1939, there was a general avoidance of bombing civilian populations in the west until May 1940. The turning point came as a result of two accidents. On 10 May 1940 three German bombers mistakenly bombed the German town of Freiburg-im-Breisgau instead of an airfield by the French town of Mulhouse; the British suspected a German plot to justify the future bombing of civilians and warned that they would take appropriate action. Four days later the *Luftwaffe* bombed Rotterdam, killing nearly a thousand people and starting huge fires – not because incendiary bombs were used but because the oil from a margarine factory caught fire and because the bombing destroyed the main water-supply system. The raid was designed to break Dutch military resistance in the city; the Dutch in fact agreed to surrender while the German attack planes were in the air, but only just under a half of the hundred German bombers received the recall message. Technically, since Rotterdam was resisting a military ground attack and since the aircraft had been called in to neutralize Dutch artillery, the raid could not be termed a terror attack on civilians; yet it was precisely in the latter terms that the raid came to be seen, and it was for this reason that it was raised during the Nuremberg war crimes trial. On 15 May RAF Bomber Command was authorized to attack industrial targets east of the Rhine, and that night ninety-nine bombers raided oil refineries and railways in the Ruhr. This raid can be seen as the beginning of the strategic bombing offensive against Germany. (For a comparison of tonnage of bombs dropped during World War II see Table 20.4.)

The first major air 'battles' following the fall of France were fought over Britain and the English Channel. In July and August 1940, as a prelude to Operation *Seelöwe* (Sea-lion) – a seaborne invasion – the *Luftwaffe* attacked radar installations and fighter airfields in the south of England. Wrongly estimating the effects of the attacks, and in response to British bombing raids on Berlin, early in September Goering switched the attack from the airfields to London. This decision, probably a mistake given the pilot losses which RAF Fighter Command had suffered (there was no similar shortage of planes), signalled the beginning of the 'Blitz' of British cities, especially London. The *Luftwaffe* attacked London incessantly from September to November 1940; there were only ten nights of the sixty-eight between 7 September and 12 November when it did not mount what it called a 'major raid' (i.e. dropping at least one hundred tons of high-explosive bombs) on the city. According to Matthew Cooper, 'This was an ordeal that, for its continuity (though not for the severity of destruction) was never to be approached by either side for the rest of the war' (*The German Air Force*, 1981, p.165). The Blitz on London, as well as on other cities, notably Coventry, continued less frequently until May 1941.

Exercise Turn now to Video 2 and watch item 1, 'All in a Fighter's Day's Work' (7 October 1940), item 2, 'Coventry – The Martyr City' (21 November 1940) and item 3, 'Reprisal Interviews' (1941).

1   What do you consider is illustrated by the items?

2   Is there a contrast between the attitude and portrayal of the British fighter pilot in item 1 and the civilians in item 3, and might this account for the way in which the film was ultimately used?

3   What arguments can be drawn implicitly or explicitly from this film to justify the strategic bombing of Germany?

4   What other arguments could have been used to justify the bombing of Germany? ∎

Table 20.4   Comparative bombing statistics

Target	Number of raids	Tonnage of bombs dropped
(a) German raids		
Rotterdam 14 May 1940	1	94 (high-explosive)
London (Blitz) 7 Sept 1940– 10 May 1941	86	19,141 (high-explosive) (also 36,568 incendiary canisters each holding 72 incendiary devices)
Coventry 14 Nov 1940	1	503 (high-explosive) (also 881 incendiary canisters)
(b) RAF raids		
Berlin (main raids only) 16 Jan 1943– 24 Mar 1944	24	49,400 (plus incendiaries)
Hamburg ('Battle of') 24–29 July 1943	4	7,196 (plus incendiaries)
Dresden 13 Feb 1945	1	2,978 (plus incendiaries)

(Source: Compiled from Matthew Cooper, *The German Air Force*, 1981; David Irving, *The Destruction of Dresden*, 1963; Max Hastings, *Bomber Command*, 1979)

Specimen answers   1   In broad terms these films illustrate the war in the air over Britain between 1940 and 1941, first showing fighter pilots involved in the Battle of Britain, then one of the most notorious incidents of the Blitz – the raid on Coventry – and finally what at least some of the victims of bombing thought about it.

2   There is, I think, a significant contrast between the stiff-upper-lip fighter pilot who, having shot down a Messerschmitt, is off for a cup of tea, and the vindictiveness of the civilians in the third piece of film. The latter is, of course, understandable, but it may also explain why the film was not incorporated into a newsreel; the commentaries accompanying the first and second items are patriotic and uplifting, and with the images and interviews they contribute to a positive note and perhaps also to a positive image of Englishness or Britishness in the face of adversity. It would be rather difficult to create such a positive commentary to accompany the attitudes expressed in the third item, though perhaps these attitudes better reflect those of the civilian population.

3   In the heat of the war it could be, and was, argued that the strategic bombing of Germany was merely retaliation for the bombing of Britain, though politicians were not quite as blunt as the civilians interviewed in the third item here.

4   The strategic bombing could also be justified on the grounds that it would disrupt the German economy and weaken German morale (though it should be remembered with reference to this claim that the British insisted that their own morale had not been weakened by the Blitz). Also, after the fall of France, bombing was one of the few means that Britain had of striking at Germany.

Discussion   Each of the arguments noted in questions 3 and 4 were deployed by different advocates of strategic bombing during the war, and have been re-emphasized in response to the moral condemnation of the campaign after the war. Air Vice-Marshal Arthur Harris, who commanded Bomber Command from February 1942 until the end of the war, was one of the first military officers to publish justifications for his actions after the war:

> The surest way to win a war is to destroy the enemy's war potential. And all that I had seen and studied of warfare in the past had led me to believe that the bomber was the predominant weapon for this task in this war.

> (Sir Arthur Harris, *Bomber Offensive*, 1947, p.31)

It could also be claimed to the USSR that the Allied strategic bombing offensive was the equivalent of a second front against Germany after the invasion of Russia in June 1941. □

After the Battle of Britain and the Blitz, the forces of the air war switched to the skies of continental Europe, though the *Luftwaffe* continued to mount raids against Britain, and in 1944 the first 'V' weapons were launched (the V1 flying bomb and the V2 rocket). The strategic bombing offensive went through a series of phases and 'battles'.

May–August 1940. There were attempted 'precision' attacks on German targets largely by day; they were made under the assumption that bombers had little difficulty in finding and hitting their targets.

Autumn 1940–summer 1941. 'Precision' attacks were continued generally by night. In August 1941 a government-commissioned report, having analysed the photos of the RAF Photographic Reconnaissance Unit, confirmed that these attacks were not precise and estimated that of 4,065 aircraft sorties which claimed to have hit their targets, only one-third had bombed within 5 miles of the aiming point. The government, concerned among other things with the war in the Atlantic and the threat to the Suez Canal, resolved to shelve plans for a force of 4,000 heavy bombers to win the war.

Autumn 1941–March 1943. Since precision bombing had failed, a new policy of 'area' bombing was introduced, by which whole towns were to be attacked and brought to a halt. Professor F. A. Lindemann, one of the academics employed to advise on bombs and bombing, estimated that the area bombing of the working-class districts of the fifty-eight German towns with a population in excess of 100,000 could break the enemy's spirit. Lindemann reckoned that it should be possible to make one-third of the German population homeless between March 1942 and the middle of 1943. Although his estimates were challenged in some quarters, the policy was adopted.

March 1943–March 1944. This was the period which Harris termed 'the main offensive'. It drew its authority from instructions drawn up by Winston Churchill, Franklin Roosevelt and their chiefs of staff; the Casablanca Directive of January 1943 declared the overall aim of the bomber offensive to be:

> the progressive destruction and dislocation of the German military, industrial and economic system, and the undermining of the morale of the German people to a point where their capacity for armed resistance is fatally weakened.
>
> (Quoted in Sir Charles Webster and Noble Frankland, *The Strategic Air Offensive against Germany 1939–1945*, vol.iv, 1961, p.153)

The offensive was now divided into two. The United States Army Air Force (USAAF), operating from bases in Britain, made precision raids by day particularly on economic targets. RAF Bomber Command carried out area bombing on a massive scale by night; in particular they hit several key targets in a succession of raids which became characterized as 'battles' – the Battle of the Ruhr (March–July 1943), the Battle of Hamburg (July–August 1943) and the Battle of Berlin (August 1943–March 1944). The first two were counted as 'victories' in as much as they devastated vast areas, though they did not halt the Nazi economy. The Battle of Berlin petered out after very heavy losses inflicted on Bomber Command during a disastrous raid on Nuremberg on 30 March 1944; ninety-six of the 795 aircraft which embarked on the raid failed to return, and another twelve were damaged beyond repair.

Overall losses in aircraft and aircrew were high, especially for the USAAF on their daylight raids. Behind the scenes a sophisticated technological struggle developed as Allied researchers produced electronic equipment to blind the German defences and to find and hit targets more effectively, while German researchers sought to counter these. Bigger and 'better' bombs were developed and aircraft technology was refined. American losses were greatly reduced when a long-range fighter, the P51 Mustang, was introduced to accompany daylight bombing raids in February 1944.

March 1944–May 1945. Early in 1944 the Allies began to achieve superiority in the air. Much of the spring and early summer of 1944 witnessed the bombers preparing the ground for the invasion of Europe. In mid April and late May there was very heavy bombing of the railway lines in France, particularly in the north around Lille and the Belgian border and around Paris. Attacks were also directed at communications and German oil production. However, Bomber Command continued the area bombing of German cities, and this policy culminated in the devastating raid on Dresden in February 1945. This raid involved three enormous waves of bombers, the first two made by night by Bomber Command, the third in daylight by the USAAF. The full horror of the resulting fire storm, with its gale-force winds and temperatures of perhaps 1,000° Celsius, was not realized by the Allies until after the war. However, what was known of the scale and impact of the raid caused considerable disquiet among ministries, legislatures and even the populations of the Allied powers.

Nine months before the raid on Dresden, Allied armies had landed in northern Europe, inaugurating the final phase of the war in the west – the liberation of the occupied countries of western Europe and Scandinavia and the invasion of Germany from the west. The fighting in north-west Europe was not marked by any new tactics. As the Allied armies advanced, however, civilians were caught up in the fighting; its disruptive effects (there was starvation in parts of Belgium and the Netherlands in the winter of 1944–45) were on a scale unknown in 1914–18 and 1939–40. The final campaigns of the war in the west are probably most notable for the sheer volume of men and *matériel* amassed against Germany. Operation Overlord, the Allied landings in Normandy, was the largest seaborne invasion ever mounted; it was also the most thoroughly planned. For eighteen months before the first troops hit the landing grounds and the beaches in June 1944, military planners had worked on the problems and the logistics of the operation. Their solutions were marked throughout by conservatism and caution, underestimating what might be achieved by determination and improvisation. Of course, men's lives and the outcome of the war were at stake, but in his important and pioneering analysis, *Supplying War: Logistics from Wallenstein to Patton* (1977), Martin van Creveld writes disparagingly of the 'war of the accountants'. When problems began to mount on the Normandy bridgehead, for example, the supply officers and planners revised all of their estimates with gloomy foreboding. One American field commander, General George Patton, ignored the planners and broke out from the bridgehead, with the armies of the American General Hodges and the British General Montgomery in his wake. The three armies crossed the Seine and had cleared its western banks on 24 August 1944, eleven days ahead of the schedule which the planners said could not be met.

3   THE NATURE OF THE WAR IN THE EAST 1941–45

Operation Overlord was the largest seaborne invasion ever mounted; Operation Barbarossa, the German invasion of Russia in June 1941, was the largest single military operation of all time. Almost 3.5 million men were deployed by the Germans. In addition, the Finns began a second, brief 'instalment' of their war against the USSR; Romania launched two armies over the River Prut towards the Bug and Odessa; and Hungarian, Italian and Slovakian troops were also engaged on the German side. The invasion force was divided into three army groups driving respectively from East Prussia and Poland towards Leningrad (Army Group North), Moscow (Army Group Centre), and the Ukraine and Crimea with their wheatfields, coal and oil (Army Group South) (see map number 7 in the *Maps Booklet*). The distances which these armies were expected to cover were enormous and made the problems of supply phenomenal, the more so because of the shortages of rubber and oil in Germany which combined with the few and generally poor roads in Russia to militate against German vehicles running at optimum efficiency. Hopes of using the Russian railway system as it was captured were complicated by German locomotives and railway stock being of a different gauge; *Eisenbahntruppen* (railway troops) were deployed with the invaders, but in insufficient numbers to solve all the difficulties of changing gauges and water stations.

Exercise

How might the concept of *Blitzkrieg* have solved the potential problems faced by the Germans in invading Russia? ■

Specimen answer

A 'lightning war' which speedily and totally destroyed the Red Army would have solved the problem of supply over long distances with bad roads and unsuitable railways, and over a long period of time.

Discussion

In his Directive No.21, issued on 18 December 1940, Hitler ordered his armed forces to be prepared 'to crush Soviet Russia in a quick campaign'. Of course, it is easier to issue such directives than to carry them out. The plan was to push ahead with the Panzer units and envelop the Russians before they could withdraw into the east. The problem was that the distances to be covered were so much greater than in the west, where, as noted earlier, *Blitzkrieg* was as much due to accident and luck as to any forward planning or development of the concept; furthermore, there was a severe shortage of mechanized transport. Captured British and French vehicles were brought into service and large numbers of lorries were purchased in Switzerland. Consequently the German army embarked on Barbarossa with 2,000 different kinds of vehicles, leading to nightmares for those responsible for organizing spare parts. Much of the equipment for the infantry columns behind the Panzers was horse-drawn, and seventy-five infantry divisions were each issued with 200 *panje* wagons (peasant carts) for equipment and supplies. In his discussion of the logistic preparations and assumptions underlying Barbarossa, van Creveld concludes that 'the German General Staff seemed to have abandoned rational thought' (*Supplying War*, p.151).

Yet Barbarossa appeared to begin well. The Panzers of Army Group North covered 200 miles in five days; those of Army Group Centre reached Minsk after four days; and those of Army Group South, driving south of the difficult terrain of the Pripet Marshes, found themselves in ideal tank country in the Ukraine. Gradually, though, progress slowed as heavy summer rain and continual traffic turned poor roads into quagmires, and as the Panzers had to wait for the infantry. At the beginning of December, Army Group Centre was halted some 50 miles from Moscow, the furthest east that the two northern Army Groups were to penetrate. By the end of the year the Russians had suffered enormous losses: lost territory meant the loss of industry – 63 per cent of pre-war coal production, 60 per cent of aluminium, 68 per cent of steel and 71 per cent of pig iron had gone; half of the Red Army of 4.7 million men had also been lost. But the Germans had lost 830,400 men, and for them this was potentially even more serious.

Although checked in the north, the Germans launched a new offensive in the summer of 1942. Army Group South was reorganized into Army Groups A and B, and a deep thrust was made into the Caucasus. The Germans were halted at Stalingrad, in September. There followed four months of savage fighting for the city which ended with the remnants of the German 6th Army – surrounded, lacking food, fuel, ammunition, warm clothing for the winter, medical supplies – being forced to surrender. Precise figures are unknown but perhaps as many as 60,000 Germans died in the Soviet encirclement and another 120,000, Germans and their allies, were taken prisoner. It was a massive disaster. An abortive advance was attempted around Kursk in July 1943, but following the surrender at Stalingrad the German armies were to be continually on the defensive in the east. Hitler insisted that they hold on to 'fortified positions'; the Russians, usually deploying far superior numbers of four or even six to one, simply encircled such positions and annihilated their defenders.

Much of the key to Soviet success was to be found in its industrial potential. The stubborn resistance of pockets of the Red Army in the summer of 1941 enabled the withdrawal of 10 million people and 1,523 plants of varying size. Even though much of the old industrial heartland was under German occupation, fresh coal and ore deposits could be, and were, opened up in the Urals and West Siberia, and factories were relocated here or newly built.

The pre-war weighting towards armaments production and the strict state supervision of industry probably facilitated the industrial reorganization, but there were other elements also working in the Russians' favour. There was a general standardization of equipment and parts in the Red Army, and while the Russians had two types of armoured fighting vehicle, the Germans had twelve. Moreover the Russians were acquainted with and equipped for their winters; when German vehicles and guns seized up because of the cold, most Russian equipment continued to function. □

Exercise Thus far the struggle in the east may look similar to the land war in western Europe, but I want you now to read Documents II.1–II.3 in *Primary Sources 2: Interwar and World War II*, and then answer the following questions:

1   How do these documents direct German soldiers to behave in Russia?

2   How are German troops to be punished for any offences committed against civilians?

3   How, according to Halder, did Hitler intend that Soviet Commissars were to be treated?

4   What, according to Halder, was the generals' response to the latter (the 'Commissar Order')? ∎

Specimen answers 1   The orders authorize the troops to terrorize the enemy into submission, and any enemy civilians guilty of offences against the German army are to be subject to prompt punishment without even the necessity for military courts.

2   Punishment for such offences is declared to be 'not obligatory', and Section II.2 of the 13 May 1941 order argues that Bolshevik attacks on Germany and National Socialism should be borne in mind whenever such offences have to be judged.

3   They were to be shot.

4   The generals were outraged by the order.

Discussion Directives and orders such as these played a prominent part in the prosecution case at the war crimes tribunal at Nuremberg. Among the army officers who testified in those trials was Field Marshal Erich von Manstein, who had commanded an armoured corps in Army Group North during 1941. With reference to the 'Commissar Order', he told the court:

> It was the first time I found myself involved in a conflict between my soldierly conceptions and my duty to obey. Actually I ought to have obeyed, but I said to myself that as a soldier I could not possibly co-operate in a thing like that. I told the Commander of the Army Group

> ... that I would not carry out such an order, which was against the
> honour of a soldier.
>
> (Quoted in William L. Shirer, *The Rise and Fall of the Third Reich*, 1964,
> p.993 note)

Similar arguments have been used by many German army veterans of the
eastern front, as well as by historians. What happened, in this version, was that
the *Wehrmacht* fought the war as ordinary, honest soldiers fighting for their
country, but in their wake came the *Einsatzgruppen* (task forces) who rounded
up Jews, Gypsies, communists and other 'undesirables' or *Untermenschen*
(sub-humans). Units of the *Einsatzgruppen* (*Einsatzkommando* or
Sonderkommando) either murdered their victims then and there, or transported
them to the death camps; the army was thus not involved and generally ignored
the 'Commissar Order'. However, younger historians who grew up after the war
have challenged this version. The subtitle of Omer Bartov's book is indicative of
their interpretation of the conflict in the east: *The Eastern Front 1941–1945:
German Troops and the Barbarisation of Warfare* (1985).

Bartov made a detailed study of three combat divisions which served on the
eastern front for the duration of the war. He suggested that the terrible physical
and mental hardships – including long marches, poor food, lack of leave, battle
fatigue and enormous casualties – may have contributed to the brutalization of
the men and a blunting of their moral and ethical sensibilities. But he also noted
that most of the officers in these divisions had grown up under the National
Socialist government and appeared highly susceptible to Nazi influences.
Moreover, perhaps partly because of the strain of the campaigns, it seems that
the majority of the rank and file, whatever they thought of the Nazi Party, were:

> firm believers, almost in a religious sense, in their Führer and, by
> extension, in many of the ideological and political goals quoted in his
> name. It ... seems that political indoctrination did achieve two essential
> purposes: it stiffened the determination of the soldiers at the front and
> played an important role in preventing disintegration and breakdowns
> among the ranks of the German army in the East; and at the same
> time it legitimised and enhanced the barbarisation of warfare in Russia
> which, coupled with the brutality emanating from the nature of the
> war itself ... led to the terrible destruction of western Russia by the
> German army.
>
> (Bartov, *The Eastern Front*, p.149)

Whatever Manstein said at Nuremberg, many other senior officers, even non-
Nazis, saw the war as ideological. General Erich Hoepner, commander of a
Panzer group in Army Group North, had openly opposed Hitler in 1938 and was
to be executed for his part in the July bomb plot of 1944; but in May 1941 he
wrote:

> The war against Russia is an important chapter in the struggle for
> existence of the German nation. It is the old battle of the Germanic
> against the Slav peoples, of the defence of European culture against
> Moscovite-Asiatic inundation, and the repulse of Jewish Bolshevism.
> The objective of this battle must be the destruction of present-day

Russia and it must therefore be conducted with unprecedented severity. Every military action must be guided in planning and execution by an iron will to exterminate the enemy mercilessly and totally. In particular, no adherents of the present Russian-Bolshevik system are to be spared.

(Quoted in Jürgen Förster, 'The German army and the ideological war against the Soviet Union', 1986, p.18)

The documentary evidence used by Bartov, Förster and others shows that many of the troops in the field had little compunction about executing commissars or following their 'Guidelines for the Conduct of Troops in Russia', which called for 'ruthless action' (*rücksichtslos vorzugehen*) against 'Bolsheviks, agitators, guerrillas, saboteurs and Jews'. 'Ruthless action' was generally translated into shooting or hanging; and many ordinary German soldiers appear to have accepted the idea of the struggle in the east as a race war (*Rassenkrieg*).

Commissars, communists and Jews were weeded out from Red Army prisoners of war as soon as they were taken. But even if ordinary Russian prisoners were not singled out for 'ruthless action', their chances were slim. You will have noted Halder's reference to the problem in Document II.3 discussed above. In the early months of the war so many Russians were captured that the German army simply could not cope; in September 1941 the mortality rate in some of the prison camps was running at 1 per cent per day. Prisoners were sent to labour camps, and some were experimented upon. Ten thousand Soviet prisoners of war arrived in Auschwitz in September and October 1941, of whom at least 900 were gassed in experiments with Zyklon B. Of the 5.7 million Russian prisoners taken between June 1941 and February 1945, 3.3 million died, often from starvation, or were killed. Christian Streit, in his detailed study of the treatment of Soviet prisoners (*Keine Kameraden: Die Wehrmacht und die Sowjetischen Kriegsgefangenen, 1941–1945*, 1978), concluded that the attitude of the *Wehrmacht* to these prisoners, its preparedness to assist *Einsatzgruppen* by identifying Jews and communists among them, as well as its assistance in identifying and arresting civilian Jews, contributed to the Nazi decision to implement its 'Final Solution' policy in the summer of 1941. The Nazis, Streit argues, had been uncertain about how the army would react to the policy; there had been murmurings and even criticism by army officers when the Polish élite was exterminated after the invasion of 1939. The *Wehrmacht*'s attitude to Soviet prisoners and its preparedness to obey the Commissar Order convinced the Nazis that there would be no opposition. Of course, such an argument has not gone unchallenged. Jürgen Förster, for example, does not think it credible that the 'Final Solution' was unleashed because the feared opposition of the army did not materialize; he insists that the decision to exterminate the Jews of eastern Europe was taken in conjunction with the plan for Barbarossa, and was set in motion in the early days of the invasion of Russia when early success suggested that the Soviet Union was heading for rapid defeat. But whatever the precise relationship, if any, between the systematic mass murder of millions of Jews, Gypsies and others, and Barbarossa – and we will return to this in section 6 – it is clear that the Germans fought the war in the east in a different way from the war in the western theatres. □

You may be wondering at this point about how the Russians fought the war; was barbarization only to be found on one side? The question has not been systematically studied with reference to the treatment of Germans in Soviet hands, though it appears that they fared little better than Russians in German hands. About 95 per cent of the NCOs and other ranks captured at Stalingrad died before they were released; and it was only in 1955 that the Soviets released the last 9,600 German prisoners of war whom they described as 'convicted war criminals'. It is also apparent that the Soviet authorities used the opportunity created by war in a brutal and ruthless way in Poland. While the Nazis set about liquidating the Polish élite in their half of the country, so the Soviets pursued a rather similar policy in their zone (the western Ukraine and western Belorussia). Indeed, the purges were such that Nazi repatriation commissions looking for ethnic Germans to repatriate from these regions found themselves deluged with requests from non-Germans and most notably (and tragically) from Polish Jews. In April 1943 German troops found mass graves in Katyn Forest near Smolensk, an area from which they had driven the Red Army. Stalin and other Soviet leaders insisted that the Nazis were responsible for the murder of the several thousand Polish officers in these graves; the evidence always pointed to Soviet guilt, however, and in the Cold War thaw of the late 1980s Mikhail Gorbachev finally acknowledged the Soviets' responsibility for the massacre. In addition, beginning in February 1940, the Russians deported some 1.5 million people from Poland, out of a population of 13 million, and they deliberately played on racial and social divisions in the territory they occupied. Ukrainians and Belorussians were encouraged to seek out and kill Polish settlers, described as 'gentry'; peasants were encouraged to murder landlords and seize the land.

The Soviets also conducted massive purges of their own ethnic groups at the end of the war. Thousands of Cossacks, Ukrainians and others were forcibly returned to the USSR, sometimes by those very Allied troops whom they had looked to for protection. They were either executed or disappeared into labour camps, branded as collaborators; some had fought on the German side against the Red Army, but by no means all, and many of those who were returned in this way were simply refugees. But the treatment of these people was not necessarily the result of the barbarization of war. During the interwar years Stalin had pitilessly persecuted *kulaks* (peasant proprietors) and other 'enemies' of the regime. The destruction of wartime 'collaborators' can be seen as a continuation of Stalin's paranoia and his determination to liquidate those whom, often for little reason, he perceived as a potential threat.

4 PARTISAN WARFARE

You will have noticed that among those against whom 'ruthless action' was authorized by the 'Guidelines for the Conduct of Troops in Russia' were 'guerrillas' and 'saboteurs'. On 3 July 1941 Stalin broadcast over Soviet radio, calling upon the people to rise up against the invaders; two weeks later instructions were issued for the organization of partisan units in Russia focused on local institutions such as factories or else on villages. It took time for the Russians to organize effective partisan activity. There could sometimes be friction where the most able guerrilla leader in a district was first and foremost an army, rather than a party, man; but there were also sensible political commissars, like Nikita Krushchev in the Ukraine, who recognized the importance of the soldier's skills and knowledge over party conformity in matters of military tactics. Soviet historians probably overemphasized the spontaneity of the partisans; they have also played down the stupidity of the Germans, first in not seeking to build on anti-Soviet feeling in captured territory like the Ukraine, and second in alienating this feeling by savage reprisals on the civilian population after partisan raids. As the war dragged on, and as more and more men and weapons could be infiltrated behind the lines, the partisan problem became an increasing threat to the German armies in Russia. Nor was this threat only to be found in Russia; most armies of occupation commonly have difficulties with those whom they are occupying, and at the peak of its power Nazi Germany and its allies occupied a considerable part of Europe (see the map entitled 'Europe at the height of German domination, Nov. 1942' in the *Maps Booklet*).

No country in western Europe burst out into spontaneous resistance and partisan warfare following defeat and occupation in 1940. For one thing there was the obvious demoralization caused by defeat, and for another, potential resistance groups could not always agree politically and tactically among themselves. The political factions most used to the tight-knit, secretive organization required by resistance were the communist parties, and a few of their leaders had experience of guerrilla warfare from the Spanish Civil War. But until the German invasion of Russia the European communists remained aloof from the struggle between capitalist powers. When the communists did get involved from the summer of 1941, resistance movements generally became better organized, stronger and more aggressive; such was the case with the *Front de l'Indépendence* in Belgium, the *Borgerlige Partisaner* in Denmark and the *Front Nationale* in France. All of these groups had non-communists in their ranks, though the party sought to maintain overall direction. As was inevitable in such a situation there were problems of reconciling or subordinating political hostilities to a common end, especially when the disciplined communists joined the resistance. It took Jean Moulin, as a representative of de Gaulle's Free French in London, fifteen months of negotiation to forge resistance unity in France and to establish the *Conseil National de la Résistance* in April 1943.

Resistance in western Europe involved collecting intelligence, aiding escaped prisoners and air-crew who had been shot down, propaganda and, occasionally, sabotage. Most of the latter was directed from London and often carried out by Special Operations Executive (SOE) agents on the ground. Resistance in the west did not involve much in the way of guerrilla fighting until Allied troops had landed. Partisan groups began fighting in the north of Italy following Mussolini's fall in the summer of 1943; in a few instances they were joined by Allied prisoners of war liberated after the demise of fascism or co-ordinated by soldiers of the British Special Air Service (SAS) or American Office of Strategic Services (OSS). Italian partisans ranged across a political spectrum from communists to liberals to ardent royalists, with consequent internal friction and mutual suspicion; the majority of the partisans, however, were drawn from either the liberals of centre or the communists. In France, which until November 1942 was divided between the occupied zone in the north and west and Vichy, it was

German labour policy which alienated many of the young men who took to the forested hills around the River Rhône and formed the nucleus of the *maquis* (guerrilla fighters). In the summer of 1942 the Germans demanded 50,000 Frenchmen to work in Germany; the following March this number was increased to 400,000. But the *maquis* did not constitute a major threat to Vichy and the German army before the invasion of 1944. Even then the most successful guerrilla activities were generally those organized by SAS units of the Free French or British armies, or those directed by the uniformed Jedburgh Teams of Allied soldiers organized specifically to liaise with and co-ordinate partisan activity. About 3,000 *maquisards* attempted to fight a conventional battle with German troops on the plateau of Vercors to the west of Grenoble in June and July 1944; they were annihilated.

Exercise   The biggest and most effective partisan armies were to be found in the east and south-east of Europe. Turn now to Video 2 and watch item 4, an extract from the film *The Nine Hundred*. This was a short documentary made in 1944 about an airlift to Yugoslav Partisans by Allied units based in Italy; the film itself was shot by cameramen of the Mediterranean Allied Army and Airforces (MAAF). As you watch the sequences, ask yourself what they tell you about the Partisans and about their strength. ■

Specimen answer   Perhaps the first thing to strike you was that the Partisans contained men, women and children. Second, the film is called *The Nine Hundred*, and whether or not there are 900 Partisans in these sequences, there clearly were a significant number. Third (and this point may not have occurred to you), setting up a sequence involving a large number of people zig-zagging down terraced slopes may be artistically satisfying, but it must also have taken a considerable amount of time. The fact that this could be done in broad daylight by Allied military cameramen in 'occupied' Yugoslavia, demonstrates in itself the hold which the Partisans could have over different parts of territory at different times. It is a classic example of the unwitting testimony that can be got from film. □

The fighting in Yugoslavia between 1941 and 1945 was not as simple, however, as a single army of Partisans against the various occupying and puppet Yugoslav forces (see the map entitled 'The partition of Yugoslavia' in the *Maps Booklet*). Yugoslavia contained a mixture of ethnic groups – Croats, Montenegrins, Serbs and Slovenes among others – and religions – Christian (Catholic, Orthodox and Protestant) and Muslim. The German conquest in 1941 gave the opportunity for right-wing Ustashi (*ustasa*) to set up, under Axis aegis, the Independent State of Croatia (usually known as the NDH after the initials of its designation, *Nezavisna Drzava Hrvataskas*). The Ustashi were Croat nationalists, generally Catholics but with some Muslims. Once in power they embarked on their 'final solution' to the 'Serbian problem'. Several hundred thousand Serbs were killed during the three and a half years of the NDH. The precise number is uncertain, and the figure of 700,000 given by the post-war Yugoslav regime has been questioned. Many died in the ghastly death camp at Jasenovac where victims were beaten to death, boiled alive, even beheaded with saws. The Serbs met violence and massacre with violence and massacre; in some instances German and Italian troops felt compelled to intervene to stop the butchery. In addition to this fratricidal conflict there were two different groups of guerrilla fighters against the Axis, the *chetniks* and the Partisans.

The *chetniks* (literally members of military companies – *ceta* – though the term also referred back to guerrilla bands in Serbia who had fought against the Turks and to a World War I veterans' association) were divided into several different groups. Some of those in the Italian district of occupation were initially armed by the Italians to fight the Partisans, but the most famous *chetnik* bands were those under the leadership of Colonel Dragoljub-Draza Mihailovich. Mihailovich's aim was the creation of a 'Yugoslav Home Army', a secret body led by officers of the old royal army which would work in conjunction with the Yugoslav government in exile and with the Allies, to prepare the way for the restoration of the monarchy. The second large group of resistance fighters was the communist-led army generally known as the Partisans. Initially there appeared to be the chance of co-operation between Mihailovich and Josip Broz, better known as Tito, the Partisan leader. However, Mihailovich, conscious of his role as the representative of the exiled royal government, counselled lying low so as not to provoke German reprisals. Tito did the opposite, and provoked German attempts to terrorize the people into submission. On 16 September 1941 Hitler ordered that for every German soldier killed by guerrillas, 100 Yugoslav hostages would die, and for every German soldier wounded, 50 Yugoslavs would die. In the following month, following a Partisan attack which left ten Germans dead and twenty-six wounded, the Germans massacred 7,000 men and boys from the town of Kraguyevats. This was only one, perhaps the most notorious, of such reprisals in Yugoslavia, but it was typical of the war in the Balkans and in Russia. There was only one equivalent massacre in the west, at Oradour-sur-Glane, near Limoges, in France in June 1944 – which might be taken as an indication of resistance performance in the west as compared with the east, but might also be taken as an indication of the Germans' racial attitudes to western Europeans and to Slavs. The different resistance policies of *chetniks* and Partisans eventually led to open warfare between the two, especially as Mihailovich's men became branded as collaborators because of the links which some *chetnik* bands had with the Italians. At times the Partisans directed the bulk of their efforts towards the struggle with the *chetniks* and, as the Serbian historian Veselin Djuretic revealed in a sensational book published in 1985, at one point in March 1943 this even led them into negotiations with the Germans.

Britain had begun sending aid to the *chetniks* shortly after the German invasion. Rumours of the Partisan campaign and of the fighting between *chetniks* and Partisans gradually filtered through to the British government, but there was uncertainty about who the Partisans actually were and about the identity of Tito.

> One school of thought refused to believe that he existed at all. The name, they said, stood for *Tajna Internacionalna Teroristicka Organizacija*, or Secret International Terrorist Organisation, and not for any individual leader ... the more romantically inclined claimed that Tito was not a man, but a young woman of startling beauty and great force of character.
>
> (Fitzroy Maclean, *Eastern Approaches*, 1949, p.225)

In 1943 Churchill dispatched a military mission to Yugoslavia under Fitzroy Maclean 'to find out who was killing the most Germans and suggest means by which we could help to kill more' (Maclean, p.227). Maclean contacted the Partisans and was greatly impressed by them and their leader. As a result of his analysis of the situation on the ground, British aid to Mihailovich dried up and was diverted to Tito. King Peter acquiesced in the transfer of aid and accordingly changed the composition of his government in exile.

Exercise   Turn now to *Primary Sources 2: Interwar and World War II* and read Document II.4. This is a series of extracts from the wartime memoirs of Milovan Djilas, one of Tito's most dependable lieutenants in the Partisan war. Djilas was editor of *Borba* (*The Struggle*), the newspaper of the Communist Party in Yugoslavia. The Partisans tried to publish *Borba* weekly when possible during the war; in addition, the editorial group under Djilas published other periodicals, directives and Marxist theoretical pamphlets. Read the extracts from his book now, and answer the following questions:

1   What were the Partisans' goals in the war?

2   What kind of appeals did the Partisans make to the peasants during the war?

3   What policies, in addition to the pursuit of the war, did the Partisans try to carry out in the field? ■

Specimen answers   1   The Partisans fought the war with both nationalist and revolutionary aims.

2   The Partisans do not seem to have appealed to the peasants in theoretical Marxist terms. Rather, with reference to the inevitability of proletarian revolution, when Djilas was called upon to address a group of peasants he appealed to Yugoslav patriotism and, in addition to the contemporary situation, he made reference back to the struggles against the Turks and to folk epics.

3   Djilas describes the Partisans as trying to neutralize the extremism that had led to massacres and reprisals among the different groups within Yugoslavia. He also describes the Partisans as trying to win over the peasants by punishing looting and recompensing victims, and as seeking to bring education and good order to the villages through which they moved.

Discussion   You may have wanted to take all of this with a very large pinch of salt, recognizing that, as Djilas was responsible for publishing the Communist Party newspaper, he might have been painting a rather too rosy picture of the Partisans. Of course, he may have been stressing the heroism and attractiveness of the Partisans, yet neither here nor elsewhere does he deny that they shot prisoners; he reports 'requisitioning' from peasants when the Partisans were in need, and he shows considerable sympathy for the rank-and-file *chetniks* as their depleted forces were hounded to destruction by the Partisans and some surviving bands of Ustashi early in 1945. The Partisans did urge ethnic and religious tolerance, often against the feelings of local Partisan groups as they moved through their lands. This tolerance seems to have helped them to survive their epic long march across Montenegro and Bosnia during the summer of 1943. The march culminated in the declaration of a provisional government at Jajce on 29 November, which divided the country into a federation of six provinces (hoping thus to eliminate ethnic hostilities), denied the authority of the royalist government in exile, forbade the return of the King, and put off a decision on the future of the monarchy until the full liberation of all territory would enable the people to decide freely. In addition, especially in those areas which the Partisans controlled for any length of time during the fighting, they set up people's committees, drawing on people of ability without reference to their political affiliation and without necessarily any previous administrative experience; these committees then ran their allotted districts, though Communist Party officials always sought a supervisory role. □

Partisan fighters in Greece were divided in much the same way as those in Yugoslavia, but the outcome of the struggle there was very different. The largest guerrilla army in occupied Greece was ELAS (the National Popular Liberation Army). It was the military wing of EAM (the National Liberation Front), a union of several radical and socialist groups, which became increasingly dominated by the communists. The acronym ELAS was pronounced in the same way as 'Ellas' – i.e. 'Greece' – which made it particularly effective in focusing on the patriotic aspect of the war. ELAS was based in the mountains, and sweeps by German and Italian troops, as well as collaborating Greek gendarmes, led to villages being destroyed and executions in the search for the partisans. These punitive raids sometimes strengthened the partisans by bringing new, vengeful recruits to their ranks, but the raids appear also to have had the effect of alienating some peasants from the partisans, especially as fighting between the partisan groups at times seemed to take precedence over fighting the army of occupation. Nicholas Hammond was a British liaison officer with ELAS, and he recalled that:

> [during] the first year the peasants were all in support and one was absolutely safe moving amongst peasants in Thessaly ... In the later stages, when the five months of civil war had caused great loss of life and terrible distress to the peasant population [things were different] ... I was in a village where the ELAS HQ was and there were executions every morning, mainly civilians – there was a great fear of all of the Resistance movements towards the end.

(Quoted in Marion Sarafis, *Greece: From Resistance to Civil War*, 1980, p.112)

As the Germans withdrew from Greece in October 1944, ELAS claimed to control most of the countryside. The second-largest guerrilla group, EDES (the National Republican Greek League), had survived the onslaught of ELAS and was dominant in the remote north-west. EDES was originally republican, but increasingly it was dominated by supporters of King George II and the Greek government in exile. But what eventually tipped the balance in favour of the restoration of the monarchy was the deployment of British troops in Athens against ELAS in December 1944. The use of British troops against former allies led to disquiet in both Britain and the US, but Churchill, who seems to have felt some personal obligation towards King George for rallying to Britain in 1940–41, was determined that Greece should not 'go communist'. Tito's Partisans gave some assistance to ELAS, especially as the fighting in Greece developed into a full-scale civil war (1947–49), but a crucial blow to the communists was Stalin's refusal to become involved, acknowledging the division of Europe agreed between himself and Churchill in October 1944.

5   THE IDEOLOGICAL NATURE OF THE WAR

Diplomacy and international negotiations do not cease when war begins. The leaders of belligerent states still have to deal with neutrals and with their allies, and they commonly seek to justify the belligerence of their states by appeals to general principle. Already in this unit, and elsewhere, we have touched on the kind of ideology deployed by the Nazis to justify (and perhaps also impel) their involvement in war. Nazi ideology was intent on creating a New Order in Europe, while the looting of captured territories and the exploitation of their industrial resources would, it was believed, contribute significantly towards paying for the war and increasing German autarky. In this section I want to concentrate particularly on the anti-Axis coalition and what its leaders claimed to be fighting for.

In August 1941 Churchill met the American President Roosevelt on board ship in Argentia Harbour off Newfoundland. Britain had recently enjoyed some success in North Africa, but had been driven from Greece and Crete, while war against Japan in the Far East appeared increasingly likely. The US was not yet a belligerent, but was providing considerable military assistance to Britain under the Lend-Lease Act which had been passed by Congress in March 1941, and which authorized the lending or leasing of equipment to any nation 'whose defense the President deems vital to the defense of the United States'. Churchill and Roosevelt concluded the meeting by issuing a statement, subsequently known as the Atlantic Charter.

Exercise   Read the Atlantic Charter, which is Document II.5 in *Primary Sources 2: Interwar and World War II*, and then answer the following questions:

1   What do the two leaders consider to be the principal threat to the world?

2   What kind of world order do they wish to see emerge from the war?

3   Given its position as an imperial power, can you see any problems for Britain in creating this new world order? ■

Specimen answers   1   The main threat to the world is identified as military aggression, and Nazi Germany is singled out and named as an offender.

2   They seek a world order based on the abandonment of aggression and force as a means to achieving political ends, a world in which all people have the right to choose their government, and in which a liberalized world economy will bring about an end to fear and want.

3   If all people had the right to choose the form of government under which they lived, how could the British Empire survive? And was Britain's economic policy of imperial preference compatible with the proposed international economy?

Discussion   The Atlantic Charter is, as you probably noticed, a vague document. In some ways this was deliberate, as no one wished to repeat the embarrassments that had resulted from some of President Wilson's very specific Fourteen Points. Yet some things were inserted deliberately with a positive purpose in mind. The British War Cabinet, for example, persuaded Churchill to include the reference to social security specifically for home consumption. Churchill himself understood 'free peoples' to mean those European peoples who were to be liberated from Nazi and fascist oppression: in his Mansion House speech in 1942 he pointedly declared that he had not become Prime Minister 'in order to preside over the liquidation of the British Empire'. □

The continuation of European empires was just one area of disagreement between Britain and the US, though as far as possible it was kept discreetly in the background. There were other disagreements between them over relationships with other members of the anti-fascist, anti-Nazi alliance. The US maintained diplomatic relations with Vichy France until the Anglo-American landings in North Africa in November 1942; even then it was Vichy which broke off relations rather than the US. Nevertheless, President Roosevelt was reluctant to recognize General de Gaulle as spokesman for France; he feared that de Gaulle was a potential dictator, but he also had his suspicions about France, which he saw as a power typical of a decadent Europe with a corrupt political and social system and espousing an exploitative colonialism. Relations between Britain and de Gaulle were prickly, but the British considered a strong, restored France as essential to their own post war security. They never had relations with the Vichy regime and, in spite of recurrent reservations about, and dislike of, de Gaulle, they continued to press his suit with the Americans. Even so, it was not until a month after the D-Day landings that Roosevelt extended recognition to the General and his Free French.

While Roosevelt was suspicious of the French, Churchill was suspicious of Italy. The Italian invasion of Ethiopia in 1935 had posed a threat to British imperial interests, and Churchill and his colleagues wanted to ensure that no such threat would arise again. The US, with its large Italian minority (many of whom voted for Roosevelt and the Democrats), did not share such concerns. After the fall of Mussolini, Britain and the US recognized Italy as a 'co-belligerent', even though this meant dealing with a monarch, Vittorio Emanuele, and a prime minister, Marshal Pietro Badoglio, who were both tainted by fascism. In January 1944 representatives of the anti-fascist *Comitati di Liberazione Nazionale* (Committees of National Resistance) met in Rome and resolved that the King should abdicate and his heir delegate all his powers to a body which would, in turn, appoint a new cabinet made up of all parties in the resistance. Churchill was furious when the Allied authorities in Italy accepted the proposal; he fumed that the anti-fascists were not representative of the Italian people, and he publicly declared his support for the monarchy. A compromise was reached whereby the King did not abdicate but retired from public life, and his son became Lieutenant General of the Realm. The following June the anti-fascists engineered Badoglio's resignation and replaced him with a socialist. Again Churchill protested, but the Americans refused to support his demand that Badoglio be reinstated. From Badoglio onwards the Italian governments sought a change in their status from 'co-belligerent', a subordinate position subject to strict controls established under the Armistice of September 1943, to full ally. As a part of this aspiration to equality, and to demonstrate their independence as a sovereign nation, the Italians shocked and surprised Britain and the US in March 1944 by agreeing to a formal exchange of diplomatic representatives with the Soviet Union. The Soviet Union, though a full member of the anti-Nazi alliance, had been excluded from any effective say in the running of liberated Italy.

Exercise   Document II.6 in *Primary Sources 2: Interwar and World War II* is an extract from a speech made by Stalin on the 25th anniversary of the October Revolution (6 November 1942). Read it now and then answer the following questions:

1   What argument does Stalin contest in this extract?

2   Can you see any way in which the programme of the Allies, as presented by Stalin, differs seriously from that presented in the Atlantic Charter? ∎

Specimen answers   1   Stalin challenges the idea that 'an organic defect' within the Anglo-Soviet–American alliance will undermine it; this supposed defect he identifies as the differing ideologies and social systems of the Allies.

2   In my opinion, there is no essential difference between the programme outlined in the Atlantic Charter and that given in the third paragraph of the extract.

Discussion   Stalin was not present at the Argentia Conference, but the Soviet Union subscribed to the Atlantic Charter when, in January 1942, its principles were embodied in the Declaration of the United Nations signed by all governments at war with the Axis powers. In May 1943 Stalin sanctioned a specifically anti-revolutionary move when he authorized the Communist International to dissolve itself. The International (Comintern), founded in 1919 and based in Moscow, had sought to direct the communist parties of different countries during the interwar years. Admittedly it had not been a great success, yet its dissolution was perceived, by Stalin at least, as a gesture to his allies in the struggle against Hitler. However, at the same time, Stalin was putting a very loose interpretation on the principles of the Atlantic Charter and the Declaration of the United Nations, particularly when he asserted Russia's intention to restore its 1941 frontiers. □

Exercise   In what way do you think that the restoration of the 1941 frontiers of the Soviet Union might be said to be against the spirit of the Atlantic Charter? (You might find it useful to refer back to the chronology at the beginning of this unit.) ∎

Specimen answer   The Baltic states had been incorporated into the USSR in 1940 and would therefore come into Russia's 'restored' frontiers; so too would much of eastern Poland, occupied by the Soviet Union in 1939 – and, of course, it was Polish independence that had been the reason for Britain going to war in the first place.

Discussion   The Russians could claim that all of these territories had been lost to them as a result of World War I, the Revolution, and the war against Poland in 1920; at the conclusion of the latter the Poles had pushed their frontier many miles east of the proposed Curzon Line (you can refresh your memory on this by looking at Roberts, p.266). The Polish government in exile, based in London, was incensed by the Russian claim to the 1941 frontiers, and was disappointed and frustrated when, at the Tehran Conference in November 1943, Churchill and Roosevelt agreed to Stalin's demands on the Polish/Russian frontiers. Churchill attempted to build bridges between the Poles in London – who controlled the bulk of the Polish Home Army (the resistance army in Poland) – and Stalin, who was endeavouring to build up the Polish Communist Party into a significant resistance organization. The London-based Poles were reluctant to make any rapprochement with Stalin, especially after the discovery of the graves in Katyn

Forest; their suspicions of Stalin appeared confirmed (at least in their eyes) when the Red Army halted on the banks of the Vistula in early August 1944 and failed to assist the insurrection of the Polish resistance in Warsaw. The Red Army insisted that it was compelled to halt for sound military reasons; the non-communist Poles insisted that the Red Army halted so as to see them defeated and discredited. □

Exercise   The 'big three' (Churchill, Roosevelt and Stalin) met for the last time at Yalta in the Crimea in February 1945. The concluding declaration of the conference is reproduced as Document II.7 in *Primary Sources 2: Interwar and World War II.* Read it now and then answer the following questions:

1   How would you say this declaration differs from the Atlantic Charter?

2   How is the Polish problem to be resolved?

3   Which state is to be invited to share in the occupation of defeated Germany?

4   This invitation was largely at the insistence of the British. Can you think of any reasons why they suggested this? ■

Specimen answers   1   The aims of the two documents are similar, but the Crimea Declaration contains much more precise detail on certain issues. This was possible because the Germans were in retreat on every front and the end of the war was in sight.

2   The Polish problem is to be resolved in Stalin's favour, with the Curzon Line being taken as the frontier; the Poles are to be appeased with territory in the north and west, at the expense of Germany.

3   France.

4   In the aftermath of World War I the US had withdrawn into isolation. A French presence in occupied Germany following the defeat of the Nazis meant that, if the US withdrew again, Britain would not have to bear the burden of administrating the west of Germany alone. Moreover, although defeated in 1940, France still had pretensions (especially under de Gaulle) to being a great and an imperial power like Britain; both states were liberal and democratic, in contrast to the power advancing into the east of Germany: the Soviet Union.

Discussion   There were ideological aspects to the 1939–45 conflicts in Europe. On the Nazi side there was the ideology of racial superiority, the need for *Lebensraum* and security, and the concept of war as a vital element in the development of a successful racial group. The opponents of Hitler did not seek to engage in debate on these grounds, and very little was said during the war about the evil of Nazi racial policy and the systematic attempts at exterminating peoples and social groups. Much of this was due to the fact that the true nature of these policies was probably not understood until Allied troops began overrunning concentration camps and extermination camps towards the end of 1944 and at the beginning of 1945. The extreme propaganda of World War I might also have created a resistance to 'evil Hun' stories. The members of the anti-Axis coalition claimed to be fighting for democracy and a more secure world, but each had very different interpretations of democracy and of what constituted their own security. These interpretations were based partly on their ideological differences, shelved for the duration of the war against Hitler yet reappearing from time to time, especially as victory came closer. Particularly worrying in the eyes of men like Churchill was the fact that the best organized and most efficient resistance groups were often dominated by communists (Poland was the great exception here). Spheres of influence were drawn up by the anti-Axis coalition as victory seemed certain. As noted in section 4, Stalin acknowledged that Greece lay outside his sphere of influence and, apparently as a result of this, he left the Greek communists to fend for themselves in the civil war. Yugoslavia was supposed to be split 50/50 between east and west influence; the victory of Tito's Partisans seemed to throw Yugoslavia into the Soviet camp, but Tito's independent line, especially when Partisans clashed with British troops over Trieste in the summer of 1945, infuriated Stalin. The 'people's democracies' of eastern Europe that emerged in the aftermath of the war were expected to follow the lines laid down in Moscow. There is controversy over the extent to which, if indeed at all, Washington exerted, or sought to exert, a more veiled hegemony over western Europe. □

6   THE HOLOCAUST

World War I has a claim to being called the first industrialized war in the sense that, for the first time, the full power of industrial technology was deployed in concentrated ways on the battlefields. During the Second World War, what might be termed industrialized mass killing was employed for the first time – not on the battlefields but in specially designated areas behind the battle fronts. The perpetrators were directed by educated men, little different socially from the bureaucrats in other European states proud of their 'civilization'. The firms that competed for contracts to build the extermination plants and supply the killing gas were, in the run of things, ordinary businesses, but the specifications to which they worked and their bills of lading reveal that they knew clearly in what they were involved. The victims were non-combatants selected primarily because of their racial origin. European Jewry was the principal target of this killing; however, the Nazis also used their killing machinery against Gypsies and Slavs, and they murdered others regarded as mentally defective or deviant and who, in consequence, were considered a threat to the 'Aryan race' (see Table 20.5 for estimates of the numbers killed).

The Holocaust, as the destruction of European Jewry is commonly known, and the broader mass killing pose many questions both for this course and for our understanding of the development of European civilization during the twentieth century. I cannot hope to answer these questions here, in so few pages. When you have finished the section, however, you should have:

1   a perception of the enormity of the events under discussion;

2   a recognition of the kinds of ideas and incidents which may have prompted them;

3   an awareness of the historical arguments surrounding the Holocaust;

4   an awareness of the relationship between the Holocaust and the war.

Table 20.5   The genocide of Jews by the Nazis (minimum and maximum estimates)

Country	Jewish population	Estimates of number of Jews killed		
		Lowest	Highest	% of Jewish population
Poland	3,300,000	2,350,000	2,900,000	88
USSR	2,100,000	700,000	1,000,000	48
Romania	50,000	200,000	420,000	49
Czechoslovakia	360,000	233,000	300,000	83
Germany	240,000	160,000	200,000	83
Hungary	403,000	180,000	200,000	50
Lithuania	155,000		135,000	87
France	300,000	60,000	130,000	43
Holland	150,000	104,000	120,000	80
Latvia	95,000		85,000	89
Yugoslavia	75,000	55,000	65,000	87
Greece	75,000	57,000	60,000	80
Austria	60,000		40,000	67
Belgium	100,000	25,000	40,000	48
Italy	75,000	8,500	15,000	26
Bulgaria	50,000		7,000	14
Denmark		(less than 100)		
Luxembourg		3,000		
Norway		1,000		
Total	[8,388,000]	4,194,200	5,721,000	68

(Source: Tim Kirk, *The Longman Companion to Nazi History*, 1995, p.172)

Precursors?

Exercise From your own general knowledge, and from what you have read earlier in this course, do you consider the Holocaust to have been a unique event? ∎

Specimen answer Earlier units have discussed the Turkish massacres of Armenians during the First World War. There were also massacres of Greeks and Turks by opposing sides during the Turkish–Greek War of 1921–22; Serbs were reported to be imposing their dominance in the new Kingdom of the Serbs, Croats and Slovenes by killing ethnic and religious rivals. Earlier in this unit, I mentioned the Ustashi massacres of Serbs, the Serb massacres of Croats and the Soviet massacres of Poles. However, what we might term the 'industrial plants' of Auschwitz-Birkenau, Belzec, Chelmno, Sobibor and Treblinka were designed to manufacture death. They used modern technology to mass-produce killing, unlike the grisly, primitive barbarism of the Ustashi death camp at Jasenovac. And I think it is justifiable to say that they constituted a qualitative and quantitative jump in massacre and genocide.

Discussion   The question I posed here takes us to the heart of issues surrounding the Holocaust. Is it unique? If so, what makes it unique? And, of course, why did it happen as and when it did? In 1981 Tim Mason suggested a major division between historians of the Holocaust: the 'intentionalists', who stress Hitler's ideology and leadership, and point to a programme of policies which the Nazis sought to implement from the beginning; and the 'functionalists', who put less emphasis on individuals and their ideas, and more on the institutional and social structures of Nazi Germany (Mason, 'Intention and explanation: a current controversy about the interpretation of National Socialism', 1981). There are also arguments over the extent to which the German people as a whole were to blame; were they, as Daniel J. Goldhagen has argued, 'Hitler's willing executioners' (1996)? And to what extent should the Holocaust be seen either, in essence, as a 'war' against the Jews, or as one element of a much broader denial of human value to a whole clutch of individuals and social groups – Gypsies, homosexuals and others, as well as, most significantly in terms of numbers, Jews. Although in the mass killings of the Holocaust this denial reached its most horrifying manifestation, the science on which it was based was not unique to Nazi Germany. □

Anti-Semitism was not an invention of the twentieth century, nor was it simply a German phenomenon. In the years before 1914 violent pogroms were directed against Jews, who were made scapegoats for the problems of the Russian Empire. The flight of Jews from the east, first to escape the violent prejudices unleashed periodically in Tsarist Russia and then to escape the upheavals in the aftermath of World War I, sharpened the anti-Semitism which was already to be found in the west of Europe. The Jewish population of Paris had risen from 24,000 in 1870 to 150,000 sixty years later. In 1882 a Catholic priest established a newspaper whose title, *L'Anti-sémitisme*, advertised its content; four years later a young journalist, Édouard Drumont, published a deeply unpleasant but very successful book with a similar message, *La France juive*. The fact that Captain Alfred Dreyfus was a Jew contributed significantly to the hostility directed towards him when he was accused of spying for Germany in 1894; according to *La Croix*, a newspaper which spoke on behalf of the zealous Catholic Assumptionist Order, his trial became 'a duel between the army and the Jewish syndicate'. In France Jews were blamed for the economic recession of the 1930s. In Britain anti-Semitism and fear of alien Jews from the east who did not appear to seek assimilation fed into the Aliens Restriction Acts of 1905 and 1919. It was to be seen in British fascism, but it could be found also in non-political, everyday life. When, terrified by the Blitz, the proprietor and his wife of a coffee shop directly opposite a Metropolitan Police section-house sought refuge in the section-house shelter, the police officers, who frequented the coffee shop, objected that 'We don't want Jews in here' (H. Daley, *This Small Cloud*, 1986, p.174). But anti-Semitism, like any other form of racial or religious prejudice, does not automatically lead to mass murder.

Just as anti-Semitism was not unique to Nazi Germany, neither were ideas of racial superiority or attempts to create a society peopled by 'better' human beings. Politicians, scientists and social commentators in many European countries expressed concern about the 'degeneracy' of their respective 'national stock' in the years before World War I. Sir Francis Galton – scientist, anthropologist, cousin of Charles Darwin and inspired by his work – had coined the word 'eugenics' in 1883. Eugenics was to be 'the study of the agencies under social control which may improve or impair the racial qualities of future generations physically and mentally'. In 1912 the first International Congress of Eugenics was hosted by London University. Heated arguments took place over whether measurable human characteristics could be used to assess laws of human variations, and whether the strong might mate with the physically attractive but feeble-minded to produce satisfactory offspring. The slaughter of World War I accentuated the concerns about 'national stock' and impelled many governments to encourage repopulation and to 'improve' and 'reinvigorate' their citizenry. Eugenics appealed to politicians and thinkers of both the left and the right. On the positive side its influence resulted in the development of housing and welfare policies and the encouragement of physical fitness in schools and elsewhere. But the question of what to do with 'degenerates', 'inferior types', the 'mentally deficient' and the 'ineducable' produced what was often an unpleasant, negative side. In Britain the solution to this question was generally seen to be incarceration; thus, for example, many young women who gave birth to illegitimate children were labelled as 'mentally deficient' and shut away in asylums for an indefinite period. Elsewhere sterilization was seen as the answer. Nazi Germany led the field here, with over 200,000 sterilizations by 1937, but was by no means alone. Sweden began a similar policy in the mid-1930s, and it continued for forty years. In 1939 Nazi Germany progressed from sterilization to the killing of the inmates of asylums as part of its 'euthanasia' programme; around 70,000 were killed before the programme began to be run down in 1941 following protests from the public and church leaders.

Moreover, if Nazi Germany stands out for pursuing brutal eugenics policies before the implementation of the so-called 'Final Solution [*Die Endlösung*] of the Jewish question', there were others in influential positions elsewhere who, before the start of the Second World War, were advocating violent policies to restrict the rights of minorities and/or to remove alien ethnic groups from their national territory. In 1919, for example, the new Hungarian state set limits on the number of Jews who could enter university. These restrictions were tightened in 1921, and in 1939 legislation was introduced that banned Jews from white-collar occupations. Vaso Cubrilovic was the youngest of the group of Serbs whose assassination of Archduke Franz Ferdinand had triggered the events leading to war in 1914. Released from prison on the collapse of the Austro-Hungarian Empire, he went on to become a distinguished historian and philosopher at the University of Belgrade, and eventually served as a minister under Tito. In 1937, in the midst of his academic career, he published a pamphlet which urged the use of 'the brute force of an organised state' to make life intolerable for Albanians living in the Yugoslav province of Kosovo and to drive them out either to Albania or Turkey.

Nazi ideology and anti-Jewish policies

In Unit 17 you touched on the anti-Semitic policies of Nazi Germany. I want now to rehearse and extend that earlier discussion. Anti-Semitism was central to Hitler's world view and to that of most Nazi activists. Hitler considered Jews to have been foremost among profiteers and racketeers during World War I; they engineered the 'stab in the back' of November 1918; they were hand-in-glove with Bolshevism. In August 1919 Hitler was an instructor at a military camp at Lechfeld, near Augsburg. His task was to inject nationalist and anti-Bolshevik ideas into the men in the camp, many of whom were recently released prisoners of war. Anti-Semitism was a major feature in Hitler's addresses to the men, and this led to him being consulted by his superiors on 'the Jewish question'. The consultation led, on 16 September 1919, to his first recorded written statement on the matter. This looked forward to the removal of rights from the Jews and, eventually, to 'the removal of the Jews altogether' (quoted in Ian Kershaw, *Hitler, 1889–1936: Hubris*, 1998, p.125). With hindsight it is tempting, and perhaps satisfying, to draw a line from Hitler's attitudes in 1919 to the death camps – but does such an 'intentionalist' perspective provide a satisfactory explanation for developments and contingencies over twenty-five years?

An analysis of Hitler's writings and speeches from the origins of the Nazi Party through to the outbreak of World War II suggests that he shifted his language to suit changing audiences and changing priorities. From late 1922 and through 1923, for example, ferocious anti-Semitism gave way to extreme anti-Marxism with little or no reference to, or linkage of this with, Jewry. Ian Kershaw (*The 'Hitler Myth'*, 1987, p.231) has suggested that this was part of a conscious attempt to appeal to a wider audience; anti-Marxism had a bigger appeal than anti-Semitism. Verbal attacks on the Jews were not a main theme of the electoral campaigns of the early 1930s, and even after the Nazis had achieved power Hitler avoided personal association with attacks on Jews, though he publicly supported 'legal' discriminatory measures.

Hitler's government was sworn in on 30 January 1933. On 28 March all Nazi Party organizations were urged to carry out a boycott of Jewish businesses and professionals on 1 April. The exhortation came from 'the Party Leadership' and claimed that the boycott was in response to the lies spread in the foreign press by Jewish emigrants; in reality, though, it was an attempt to impose some discipline on the freelance, anti-Semitic vandalism and violence of Nazi activists (especially the SA) in the light of the Party's political dominance. The German population as a whole did not show itself to be particularly sympathetic to the boycott, and it was called off as an organized, nationwide event after one day. Over the next two and a half years, while some local Nazi activists continued to rant against the Jewish 'menace' and, on their own initiative, assaulted or intimidated Jews, little was said or done publicly by the Party hierarchy. Then, on 15 September 1935, in a speech to the *Reichstag* assembled at the Party rally in Nuremberg, Hitler announced 'defensive actions'. He declared that these were necessary as calming measures because of plots and boycotts which had been engineered against Germany by Jews abroad. These 'actions' became known as the Nuremberg Laws. The 'Citizenship Law' led to the division of the population into 'subjects' and 'citizens'; Jews became mere 'subjects' and lost legal equality. The 'Law for the Defence of German Blood and Honour' forbade marriage and sexual relations between Jews and 'Aryans'. At the same time Jews were banned from raising the German flag and employing non-Jewish female servants or staff under the age of 45. An additional thirteen decrees supplemented these laws over the next few years; the Protection Law, for example, was extended to include Gypsies and 'Negroes'. Most of the new decrees, however, were concerned with removing Jews from influence and authority within the *Volksgemeinschaft* (the national community); thus the licences of Jewish doctors and lawyers were revoked, Jews were issued with new, distinct passports, and so forth. There was some negative reaction to this legislation – from a few businessmen who feared an adverse effect on the economy, and from churches, liberals and ideological opponents of the regime – but most ordinary German people appear to have accepted it, or at least turned a blind eye. But again, for a long period, there was little public comment from the Party hierarchy, and little public debate.

Exercise On 7 November 1938 the Third Secretary at the German Legation in Paris was assassinated by the 17-year-old son of a deportee. The Nazi response was the organized pogrom of the night of 9–10 November, *Kristallnacht* – 'Crystal Night', or 'the Night of Broken Glass' (some now prefer the less euphemistic term *Reichspogromnacht* – pogrom night). You have already read an account of this written by the American Consul in Leipzig (in Book 3, Unit 17). Now read Documents II.8, II.9 and II.10, in *Primary Sources 2: Interwar and World War II*, which are extracts from other reports of the event.

1   What is the origin of each of these reports?

2   Might you expect the origin of each document to affect how the events are reported in it?

3   In the light of your answer to question 2, can you detect from these reports a general picture of the reaction of the German people to *Kristallnacht*? ■

Specimen answers 1   Document II.8 is a report smuggled out of Germany by socialists or socialist sympathizers; Document II.9 is a police report; Document II.10 is a report from a senior local government official.

2   Whatever document we are looking at, we have to be aware of who wrote it and for what purpose. We might, therefore, approach each of these documents with some reservations. Might the socialists have had an axe to grind? Might they have been tempted to couch their account in ideological terms, or in terms which their audience would have found generally encouraging about the direction events in Germany were taking? Similarly with the police and the local government official: how far might they have been writing what they knew their superiors wanted to read?

3   What is interesting is that, even given these differences of origin and ideological baggage, the reports tell roughly the same story – *Kristallnacht* was not universally well received by the German people.

Discussion Historians of Nazi Germany, whose conclusions are, of course, based on many more than three documents, generally agree that the destruction and violence of *Kristallnacht* prompted widespread criticism. Some of this may simply have been concern about violence on the streets; note, for example, the comments made by the *Regierungspräsident* towards the end of his report. Moreover, as the SOPADE report suggests, the reaction to the event – and to the persecution of the Jews in general – appears to have varied from place to place given the numbers of Jews present in the community, the extent of intermarriage and local traditions of anti-Semitism. □

Hitler made no reference to *Kristallnacht* in his speeches at the time of the event. Less than three months later, however, on 30 January 1939, he gave a two-hour address to the *Reichstag*. The speech focused principally on the international situation but contained the 'prophecy' that a new war would bring about 'the destruction [*Vernichtung*] of the Jewish race in Europe'. The 'prophecy' was singled out in newsreel coverage of the speech, yet neither the official reports on the impact of the speech nor the SOPADE reports comment on this section in their assessment of its impact. What people appear to have been most interested in was Hitler's discussion of the chances for peace or war.

By the outbreak of World War II, Jews in Germany had been deprived of citizenship. In addition they had been the victims of boycotts, intimidation, physical violence and brutality, some of which had been organized by Nazi Party officials, some of which was the work of local Nazi thugs acting on their own initiative. With hindsight we know that the situation was to get infinitely worse, but, prophecies about 'the destruction' of European Jewry aside, was there anything yet to suggest the creation of death camps and genocide?

The treatment of the Jews between 1933 and 1939 was one aspect of a policy which sought the creation of a racially homogenous, focused, national community – the *Volksgemeinschaft*. Other countries which emerged out of the First World War with multi-ethnic populations also looked for ways of dealing with their minorities, and few of these were particularly generous or pleasant – remember Cubrilovic's plan for the Kosovo Albanians quoted earlier. There are two things which stand out about Nazi Germany, however: the ethnic minorities within the territory of Germany were relatively few in number; and Nazi policy during the 1930s set out to incorporate into the *Reich* many of those territories occupied by ethnic Germans outside the frontiers of 1918 – Austria, the Sudetenland, and so on. The mystic utopia of the *Volksgemeinschaft* required that all its members be centred on the same goal, dedicated to hard work and prepared for self-sacrifice. Those who would not fit in – the 'asocial', the 'workshy', homosexuals, political opponents – and those who could not fit in – 'aliens', the 'ineducable', the 'incurable' – had to be excluded, even eradicated. Anthropology, biological sciences and eugenics were deployed to identify both these groups of outsiders and even to suggest 'treatment'. As noted above, the treatment of the 'insane' and 'incurable' was more violent in Germany than elsewhere and, from 1939, involved murder. Furthermore, in Nazi thinking Jews were not merely people who practised a particular religion; they were a 'race'. Given thinking that was not unique to interwar Germany, the Nazis believed that as a 'race' Jews could be identified scientifically. The Nazis did not only present the Jew as someone who could be identified biologically; they also put forward a series of artificially constructed manifestations of the Jew as an enemy of the *Volksgemeinschaft*. In the words of Detlev Peukert, one of the most authoritative commentators on everyday life in Nazi Germany:

The very diversity of actual modern Jewish experience was taken to point to the existence of the mythical hate-figure of the essential 'Jew' lurking behind the most disparate surface appearances. The intellectual, culturally assimilated Jew stood for detested modernity; the religious Orthodox Jew matched the traditional hate-image of Christian anti-Semitism; the economically successful Jew stood for 'money-grubbing capital' and liberalism; the Jewish socialist represented abhorrent 'Bolshevism' and 'Marxism'; the 'Eastern Jew' from the alien culture of the ghettos was a suitable target for the aggression and arrogance of the civilising and colonialist missions of the imperialist era.

(Peukert, *Inside Nazi Germany*, 1987, p.209)

Exercise   Many, indeed most, of these images were not confined to Nazi thought. Can you suggest why, in the context of Nazi Germany, they may have formed the basis for genocide? ■

Specimen answer   It is, of course, a truism to say that the Nazi regime was ruthless and brutal; it had demonstrated itself as such both in the treatment of some of its own (Röhm and the SA for example), and in the treatment of the 'insane' and 'incurable'. While the abstract image of the 'Jew' was not specifically German, it constituted an all-encompassing opponent of the *Volksgemeinschaft*, the Nazi utopia. It might be argued that, having created this ubiquitous monster, ultimately only an all-encompassing 'solution' to the problem would suffice. Moreover, once Germany had embarked upon war, and once therefore the *Volksgemeinschaft* had to be fully focused and prepared for determined effort and self-sacrifice, the removal of any internal 'alien' threat – especially this threat – became all the more imperative.

Discussion   That answer relies heavily on Peukert's analysis. You may have come up with something very different. When Peukert gave a conference paper arguing that the Final Solution was 'a systematic, high technology procedure for "eradicating" or "culling" those without "value"' he was criticized for refusing to afford primacy to the attempt to exterminate European Jewry – the Jews were, after all the principal victims of the mass killing – and for seeming to reduce Nazism to 'biological politics' (T. Childers and J. Caplan, *Reevaluating the Third Reich*, 1993). Explaining mass murder is not easy. The point to note, I think, is that there was a change in the Nazi persecution of the Jews during the war, and it is to this change that I want now to turn. □

War and the Final Solution

The term 'Final Solution' (*Die Endlösung*) was a euphemism. Himmler was fully prepared to talk about killing to his immediate subordinates (see Document II.11 discussed below), but much of the Nazi killing machine was shrouded in bureaucratic euphemism. The doctors and administrators charged with murdering 'incurables' were the 'Public Ambulance Service Ltd' (*Gemeinnützige Krankentransport GmbH*); the motorized death squads which first went into action in Poland in 1939 were 'task forces' (*Einsatzgruppen*); the massacre of nearly 34,000 Jews in the ravine of Babi-Yar after the capture of Kiev in September 1941 was a 'major operation' (*Gross-Aktion*). People identified for extermination in official Nazi documents were listed as those to be given 'special treatment' (*Sonderbehandlung*), sometimes abbreviated to 'SB', and from roughly mid-1943 the term 'special lodging' (*Sonderunterbringung*) was also used.

The occupation of western Poland after the brief campaign of 1939 gave the Nazis *Lebensraum* to colonize with ethnic Germans, some of whom were soon to be repatriated to the *Reich* (and thence, often reluctantly, to the newly annexed provinces of the Warthgau and Danzig) by new conquests. But the preparation of these provinces for the colonists necessitated the expulsion of a million Poles and Jews, who were driven east to the Nazi-controlled satellite of Poland known as the *Generalgouvernement* (General Government). In the autumn of 1939 plans were prepared for a Jewish reservation in the vicinity of Lublin. It was estimated that some 3 million German, Austrian, Czech and Polish Jews would have to be moved east. As part and parcel of these expulsions Jewish elders were murdered, together with several thousand Polish notables (academics, national and local leaders) who, it was feared, might become the leaders of a Polish resistance. At the same time, linked with the euthanasia programme, about 10,000 patients in psychiatric hospitals, both Jews and Poles, were murdered by shooting and gassing; this was so that accommodation and transit camps could be created for the ethnic German settlers being brought in at this stage from the Baltic states and that part of Poland occupied by the Soviets. However, the policy of genocide does not yet appear to have been on the agenda. The Jews were shut up in ghettos, most notoriously in Warsaw and Lodz, to await resettlement. Himmler himself dismissed extermination in a memorandum of May 1940, preferring the option of shipping Jews off to a colony in Africa or somewhere similarly distant: 'this method is still the mildest and best, if one rejects the Bolshevik method of physical extermination of a people out of inner conviction as un-German and impossible' (quoted in Browning, *The Path to Genocide*, 1992a, p.17). For a few months after the fall of France there were serious discussions about using the island of Madagascar in such a way; the number of Jews to be thus 'resettled' grew to about 4 million with the addition of those from France, Belgium, the Netherlands and other conquests. The failure to defeat Britain created a major problem for the implementation of this plan.

While discussions about the Madagascar plan continued, the situation in the ghettos deteriorated. There had been no clear policy from Berlin about confining the Jews in the ghettos; local Nazi authorities were left to improvise on what everyone appears to have regarded as a temporary expedient. Whatever else they were, the ghettos were not the intended resettlement reservations. The Jews rapidly spent their money and sold their valuables so as to purchase food from the Nazi administration and from those outside the ghettos. They began to starve, and epidemics started; possibly as many as 500,000 Polish Jews died as a result of the increasingly appalling conditions in the ghettos. Some Nazi administrators were unconcerned, but the majority sought to facilitate the creation of systems whereby the ghettos could become self-sufficient, with the Jews being put to work but kept separate from 'Aryans' and others.

Around the beginning of 1941 the Madagascar plan was finally abandoned; while the Nazis had no qualms about killing Jews and others, they appear still to have been thinking in terms of removal and using the fittest as slave labour. In

March 1941 Reinhard Heydrich, the head of the *Reich* Security Head Office (*Reichssicherheitshauptamt*, RSHA), was discussing plans for a new deportation of Jews further to the east of Poland. Much of the precise detail remains unclear, but it appears that the intention was to separate the Jews by gender, possibly even sterilizing the women; the fit would then be used as slave labour, to build roads and drain marshes, while the remainder would be put into 'death reservations'. It was also accepted that many would die while marching east for the resettlement.

Exercise   Two simple questions:

1   What was east of Nazi-occupied Poland?

2   On what would this new resettlement depend? ■

Specimen answers   1   Soviet-occupied Poland, and then the USSR.

2   On seizing and occupying Soviet territory.

Discussion   Heydrich's new round of planning coincided with the preparations for Operation Barbarossa and depended on German victory over the USSR. In consequence it coincided also with the preparation of the Commissar Order. Historians, and others, have argued about the precise point at which the final decision to murder European Jewry was taken, but there does appear to be some tie-in with the brutality unleashed in the invasion of Russia. The problem is a lack of precise documentation. Much was destroyed on Himmler's orders in the closing stages of the war; other documents appear to have been destroyed as a matter of course as events progressed; and much is also obscured by the use of weasel words and euphemism. There are arguments for seeing a significant shift in policy towards the Jews during the preparations for Barbarossa in the spring of 1941, in Goering's instruction to Heydrich of 31 July 1941 to prepare 'a comprehensive solution to the Jewish question'; in the increased exterminating fury (that is, killing women and children in equal numbers to men) among the *Einsatzgruppen* during the euphoria of the initial success against the USSR in August 1941; in Heydrich's meeting with government ministry representatives at the Wannsee Conference of 20 January 1942. But the German historian Götz Aly has argued that the search for an 'order' or a 'decision' essentially ignores the way in which the Nazi state bureaucracy worked (and, indeed, how any state bureaucracy works).

> Political decisions generally are not made in a day, nor are they carried out in linear fashion; and they are not exclusively positively determined ... [T]he course of political opinion formation – even under the conditions of the Nazi dictatorship – can be viewed as a more or less open process. The transitions between planning, decision-making, and practice were fluid, the boundaries between the participants and interested institutions permeable ...

> A Führer order was not needed ... Hitler took part in building the consensus, made demands, and let the implementors know that they did not need to conform to any traditional norms; rather they could carry out any type of 'solution' at all ...

The ongoing linkage between practice and planning was characteristic of the attempts to deport the Jews right from the start. Even in their first weeks on the job, the bureaucrats in Himmler's 'resettlement' institutions had resorted to mass murder. For their immediate purposes, they had patients in Pomeranian, Polish, and West and East Prussian psychiatric hospitals 'cleared out' to 'accommodate' ethnic Germans ...

With the start of the Russian campaign, a second important practice joined the almost two years of practical experience of murder: the mass executions of Soviet prisoners of war, Jews, and suspicious civilians on the eastern front.

(Aly, *'Final Solution'*, 1999, pp.253–4) □

The *Einsatzgruppen* followed the army into the Soviet Union, massacring Jews and Russians with their guns and their gas vans; but, as discussed in section 3 above, the evidence suggests that the members of the German army too were fully prepared to become involved in the killing of a 'race war' (*Rassenkrieg*). In August 1941 the 6th Army headquarters, at the news that some off-duty soldiers had volunteered to help with executions, or had gone along to watch or to take photos, instructed that men should not participate in such executions unless ordered by a superior officer. Two months later Field Marshal von Reichenau, the 6th Army commander, backed by Field Marshal von Rundstedt, issued an order to his men explaining what made the war in the east different.

In this eastern theatre of war, the soldier is not only a man fighting in accordance with the rules of war, but also the ruthless standard-bearer of a national ideal and the avenger of all the bestialities perpetrated on the German peoples. For this reason the soldier must fully appreciate the necessity for the severe but just retribution that must be meted out to the subhuman species of Jewry.

(Quoted in Beevor, *Stalingrad*, 1998, pp.56–7)

Mass shootings by soldiers and *Einsatzgruppen* and the use of the mobile gas vans took time and energy. There was concern about the effects on the morale of the men involved. Towards the end of 1941, even before the Wannsee Conference, the Nazis had begun building camps in Poland that incorporated large gas chambers for the mass production of death. Belzec was the first to come into operation in February 1942, killing people with carbon monoxide first released from bottles and subsequently produced by a conventional internal-combustion engine. But the bureaucrats responsible for the killing found that the procedures were still not quick enough to cope with the numbers of those who were to be given 'special treatment'. The problem was exacerbated after Himmler's order of 19 July 1942 that all Jews in the General Government of Poland, with the exception of a few who might be put to work, should be exterminated before the end of the year. The gas chambers were enlarged, but problems began to be experienced as a result of the enormous numbers of corpses that had been buried, and were putrefying in the vicinity of the camps. The bodies were consequently exhumed and burned. From the end of 1942 and through 1943 the first extermination camps were gradually run down. The bulk of the killing was switched to Auschwitz, where people had been killed since

September 1941. Four massive buildings known as crematoria (incorporating gas chambers which used the hydrocyanic acid gas Zyklon B, as well as ovens for the incineration of corpses) were completed at Auschwitz-Birkenau in the spring of 1943. Precise records of how many were murdered in Auschwitz-Birkenau do not exist; roughly two-thirds of the arrivals at the camp were classified as 'unfit for work' and were marched straight to the gas chambers. It seems that there were at least 1,334,700 victims: 1,323,000 Jews; 6,430 Gypsies; 1,065 Soviet prisoners of war; 3,655 others, mainly Poles (Kogon *et al.*, *Nazi Mass Murder*, 1993, p.173 note). One of the crematoria was put out of action by a prisoners' revolt in October 1944. In January 1945 all four were dynamited by the SS, and attempts were made to destroy camp documents in the panic generated by the Russian advance.

Ordinary men? Ordinary Germans?

Exercise   Read Document II.11, *Primary Sources 2: Interwar and World War II*, Himmler's speech to the *Gauleiter* (leaders of the territorial divisions of the Nazi Party) of 6 November 1943, and answer the following questions:

1   What, according to Himmler, have been the advantages of the extermination policy?

2   What have been the difficulties with it?

3   How do you think he portrays the killing and the killers? ■

Specimen answers   1   Himmler speaks in terms of the removal of 'a plague' which was destroying the people, and argues that this has enabled Germany to survive the pressures of war, particularly aerial bombardment.

2   He suggests that there have been several difficulties, all of which have been overcome. First, there has been the assumption by some – even Party members – that there were 'decent Jews' who might be spared. It is implicit in what Himmler says here, though not developed in any way, that such notions are quite wrong-headed. Equally wrong-headed, in his estimation, was the notion that women and children might be spared; this, he insists, is 'unjustified' since it would leave the potential for future avengers. Finally, he notes concerns about the extreme pressures on the people responsible for the killing, and the fear that they might be seriously distressed or psychologically damaged.

3   Himmler portrays the killers as heroes carrying out an unpleasant, but necessary, task. There seems to me to be an element of the 'stiff upper lip' here when he talks of the killers stoically bearing their responsibility in silence.

Discussion   The speech has an internal logic, but it is a perverted one. It shows the extent to which Himmler and the Nazi élite had internalized the idea of the Jews as being subhuman; they were simply 'a plague' which had to be destroyed for the good of all. It was unpleasant work, but someone had to do it; it was also a noble task, and the men who were involved had to be strong and silent. The question then has to be posed: is this what the killers themselves believed? □

Exercise   Read Christopher Browning's article 'One day in Jósefów: initiation to mass murder', which you will find in your Course Reader (Chapter 10), and answer the following questions:

1   Who were the killers discussed by Browning?

2   What offer did Major Trapp make to his men, and what happened to the men who accepted it?

3   What were the effects of Jósefów on the men of Reserve Police Battalion 101?

4   What does Browning note as having been significantly ignored in the judicial interrogations of the 1960s and 1970s? Can you think of any ideology which is not much mentioned, but which ultimately inspired the killing? ■

Specimen answers   1   The killers came from two major sources. There were men from former prisoner-of-war camps, generally Ukrainians, Lithuanians and Latvians, who had been trained by the SS. These men usually did the brutal work of driving Jews from their dwellings to the railway stations and shooting on the spot those too old, too young or too sick to make the journey. A few hundred of these men subsequently went to the death camps, where they outnumbered the German staff by four to one. Then there were police units, like Reserve Battalion 101, which drew its NCOs from career policemen and young men who had volunteered for the Order Police before the war, sometimes to avoid conscription. The rank and file of these units were civilian conscripts generally considered too old for front-line military service. In passing, Browning also mentions 'the desk murderers' – the bureaucrats who never got their hands (or uniforms) bloody, but who worked in a routinized way at a distance from the killing.

2   Trapp ordered that anyone who did not feel up to the killing could fall out. Some of those who refused to participate were subsequently given tough, unpleasant tasks; for others there appear to have been no repercussions.

3   Some men could not cope with the killing; they avoided it and/or broke down during it. Those who carried on, which was the majority, appear to have become desensitized during subsequent actions, though on these later occasions they tended to form cordons, leaving the 'dirty work' to the 'Hiwis'.

4   Browning notes that anti-Semitism was virtually ignored both by those asking the questions and by the men who were being interrogated. Browning also only touches on Nazi ideology in passing, and he remarks that the men of the battalion mostly came from 'one of the least Nazified cities in Germany' (Hamburg), and 'from a social class that in its political culture had been anti-Nazi'. □

Browning developed his work on Police Battalion 101 into a book, *Ordinary Men: Reserve Police Battalion 101 and the Final Solution in Poland* (1992b). The same material was subsequently used, and reinterpreted, by Daniel J. Goldhagen for *Hitler's Willing Executioners: Ordinary Germans and the Holocaust* (1996). Goldhagen points the finger of blame for the Holocaust precisely at Germany. The Holocaust was, he stresses, a German phenomenon, and he argues that it built on what he detects as 'an eliminationist form of anti-

Semitism' already present in nineteenth-century Germany. Of course, it was Hitler and the Nazis who unleashed the mass murder; nevertheless, Goldhagen maintains, they succeeded with such frightening ease because of the way in which ordinary Germans had long regarded Jews. The debate has been furious. Goldhagen's book was, initially, poorly received – particularly so by German academics. The main criticisms focused on three main areas: the extent to which such 'eliminationist' anti-Semitism existed; the fact that Goldhagen was making a special case for the treatment of Jews when Slavs, Gypsies and others were also being massacred; the fact that much of the killing was actually done by non-Germans, such as the Latvian Auxiliary Security Police (*Arajs Kommando*). This particularly appalling group tortured and raped their victims, sometimes literally wading in blood and drunk on vodka. But Goldhagen has also had his strong supporters, who stress that, when all is said and done, it was the Germans who began the mass murder. They also point out that, even if the Germans did not commit all of the killing, they nevertheless administered it, and very few ever spoke out against it (unlike, for example, the euthanasia programme, which had been publicly criticized). The arguments can be followed up in, for example, Robert R. Shandley, *Unwilling Germans? The Goldhagen Debate* (1998). For two particularly ferocious critiques of Goldhagen, which challenge the way in which he has both interpreted documents and constructed his argument, see Norman J. Finkelstein and Ruth Bettina Birn, *A Nation on Trial: The Goldhagen Thesis and Historical Truth* (1998).

Let me now turn briefly to the response of some of Germany's allies to Nazi anti-Semitism and the Final Solution. The Hungarians were latecomers to the killing of Jews, but when they became involved in 1944 their police and administrators appear generally to have acted with an unpleasant enthusiasm for the enterprise. Vichy France introduced anti-Semitic legislation early on. The Statute of Jews of 3 October 1940 barred French Jews from holding responsible positions in the public service, from teaching and from the news media; it also prohibited them from entering the *département* of the Allier, where the town of Vichy itself was situated. Over the next two years there was increasing discrimination as Jewish businesses were expropriated and as quotas were introduced in the professions. Non-French Jews – those who had fled from the east in the aftermath of World War I or from Nazi persecution in the 1930s – were handed over to the Germans first. While there may be something in the argument that this was done to protect those Jews who were French citizens, the three men appointed, successively, to head Vichy's department of Jewish affairs were all noted for their anti-Semitism, and even French Jews were handed over in the end. Some of Vichy's behaviour was clearly to appease the Germans, though it can also be said to have built on the long-standing tradition of anti-Semitism in France. It should also be noted that there were French people who resisted these policies, notably Protestants in the Cévennes who established escape routes for Jews, and for the first time a section of the French clergy came forward during Vichy to denounce anti-Semitism.

Mussolini's Italy began an anti-Jewish campaign in 1937 and a succession of anti-Jewish laws was passed in the following year, coinciding with *Kristallnacht*. Foreign Jews were to be deported; Italian Jews were forbidden to marry 'Aryans', to run businesses employing more than 100 workers, to own more than 50 hectares of land, to work for the civil service or in teaching. It is difficult to account for the laws. The Fascist movement was racist, particularly with regard to Africans, but, while some Fascists were anti-Semitic, this was not a key tenet of the creed and there were relatively few Jews in Italy. Nor is there any evidence of Nazi pressure. The anti-Jewish policies appear to have been the result of concerns about loyalty during a future war; however, they were generally unpopular among the conservative élites which had supported Fascism, as well as among ordinary people, who began to wonder where aggressive foreign policy was leading and who generally disliked the Germans. Italian army officers seem to have had no qualms about handing Serb partisans over to the Ustashi, yet they did not hand Jews over to their German allies when requested. And if the tiny 'Italian Social Republic' established for Mussolini in September 1943 pursued anti-Semitic policies, this can be put down principally to the fact that the Germans – notably the ambassador Rudolf von Rahm and SS General Karl Wolff – had the real power.

Legacy

In the wake of the Soviet armies during 1944–45 came police units. In Poland the communist Office of State Security (*Urzad Bezpieczerstwa Publicznego*, UB) refilled former Nazi camps and prisons with civilians, many of whom were Germans innocent of any offence other than that of being German. Somewhere between 60,000 and 80,000 died as a result of UB behaviour in the camps and prisons; victims were beaten, tortured, starved, killed. One of the only researched UB units is that which operated in Upper Silesia, particularly around the town of Gliwice, about 50 miles north of the Czechoslovak border; the town had formerly been in Germany, and had been known as Gleiwitz. All of the commanders of this UB unit were of Jewish origin, as were three-quarters of their men. John Sack, who drew particularly on the oral evidence of Jews, Germans and Poles from the region, called his bleak study of Gliwice *An Eye for an Eye* (1993). Even recognizing that the Jews were 'provoked', Sack, himself a Jew, found it painful to acknowledge that Jews were responsible for the deaths of 'not Nazis ... but German civilians, German men, women, children, *babies*, whose "crime" was to be Germans ... I suspected that some Jews would ask me, "How could a Jew write this book?" and I knew the answer must be "No, how could a Jew not write it?"' (pp.x–xi).

I am conscious that the preceding paragraph might be taken as an attempt at relativizing the Holocaust. This has been one of the classic techniques of some of those engaged in Holocaust denial; they have sought to minimize Nazi atrocities by listing them alongside the British concentration camps of the Boer War, the terror bombing of German cities during World War II and, perhaps most effectively, the purges and Gulags of the Soviet Union under Stalin. When, during the 1980s, the eminent German historian Ernst Nolte suggested that the Third Reich was a symbiotic product of Soviet terror and that the atrocities it perpetrated might be typical of certain modern states experiencing massive internal reconstruction and expansion, he unleashed an international furore. Yet Nolte never denied the events of the Holocaust, as some individuals on the political right have sought to do, and, as in the high-profile case of David Irving, with the trappings of academic history. The Nolte incident can be situated in the context of German historians trying to come to terms with the enormities of the

Nazi regime and confronting the problem of how to interpret the course of modern German history – where did it all go wrong? But interpreting events – questioning why the Nazis came to power and why the Holocaust happened – is quite different from denying that those events ever happened or arguing that the events themselves are merely interpretations.

In interwar Europe ethnic Germans had been in an overwhelming majority in the populations of both Germany and Austria. In addition, the two largest minorities spread across the states of interwar Europe, and particularly the states of the centre and east, had been Germans and Jews. The war and the Holocaust produced 'solutions' to the questions of both minorities. The Jews of central and eastern Europe who survived were often unwilling to return to their former homes; indeed, many of those who did return home found their property destroyed or occupied by others who would not give it up. Thousands of them moved westwards; and thousands more moved westwards from Poland, from Hungary, and from elsewhere following a wave of anti-Semitic pogroms in 1946 which left many dead. But the states of western Europe were reluctant to absorb these Jewish refugees, and those who sought to travel to Palestine were prevented by the British, who held the territory under a League of Nations mandate. The creation of Israel in 1948 finally opened the door to them, but led, in turn, to the displacement of Palestinian Arabs. The Holocaust and its aftermath did not eliminate Jews from Europe, but it resulted in the continent being far less a central focus of the life of the Jewish people.

German minorities in eastern Europe also fled westwards in the aftermath of the war; 5 million went in 1944–45. Over the next three years the governments of Czechoslovakia, Hungary, Poland, Romania and Yugoslavia expelled another 7 million. Rather than being Hitler's dream of empty land for German settlers, central and eastern Europe, which had witnessed most of the Holocaust, now became empty of Germans as well as Jews.

References

Aly, G. (1999) *'Final Solution': Nazi Population Policy and the Murder of the European Jews*, Arnold.

Bartov, O. (1985) *The Eastern Front 1941–1945: German Troops and the Barbarisation of Warfare*, Macmillan.

Beevor, A. (1998) *Stalingrad*, Viking.

Browning, C. J. (1992a) *The Path to Genocide: Essays on Launching the Final Solution*, Cambridge University Press.

Browning, C. J. (1992b) *Ordinary Men: Reserve Police Battalion 101 and the Final Solution in Poland*, HarperCollins.

Childers, T. and Caplan, J. (eds) (1993) *Reevaluating the Third Reich*, Holmes and Meier.

Cooper, M. (1981) *The German Air Force: An Anatomy of Failure*, Jane's.

Costello, J. and Hughes, T. (1977) *The Battle of the Atlantic*, Collins.

Creveld, M. van (1977) *Supplying War: Logistics from Wallenstein to Patton*, Cambridge University Press.

Daley, H. (1986) *This Small Cloud: A Personal Memoir*, Weidenfeld and Nicolson.

Finkelstein, N. J. and Birn, R. B. (1998) *A Nation on Trial: The Goldhagen Thesis and Historical Truth*, Henry Holt.

Förster, J. (1986) 'The German army and the ideological war against the Soviet Union' in Hirschfeld, G. (ed.) *The Politics of Genocide*, Allen and Unwin.

Goldhagen, D. J. (1996) *Hitler's Willing Executioners: Ordinary Germans and the Holocaust*, Alfred A. Knopf.

Harris, Sir A. (1947) *Bomber Offensive*, Collins.

Hastings, M. (1979) *Bomber Command*, Michael Joseph.

Irving, D. (1963) *The Destruction of Dresden*, Kimber.

Kaiser, D., Mason, T. and Overy, R. J. (1989) 'Debate: Germany, domestic crisis and war in 1939', *Past and Present*, no.122, pp.200–40.

Kershaw, I. (1987) *The 'Hitler Myth': Image and Reality in the Third Reich*, Oxford University Press.

Kershaw, I. (1998) *Hitler, 1889–1936: Hubris*, Allen Lane.

Kirk, T. (1995) *The Longman Companion to Nazi History*, Longman.

Kogon, E., Langbein, H. and Rückerl, A. (eds) (1993) *Nazi Mass Murder: A Documentary History of the Use of Poison Gas*, Yale University Press.

Maclean, F. (1949) *Eastern Approaches*, Cape.

Mason, T. (1981) 'Intention and explanation: a current controversy about the interpretation of National Socialism' in Hirschfeld, G. and Kettenacker, L. (eds) *Der 'Führerstaadt': Mythos und Realität*, Klett-Cotta.

Overy, R. J. (1982) 'Hitler's war and the German economy: a reinterpretation', *Economic History Review*, second series, no.xxxv, pp.272–91.

Overy, R. J. (1988) 'Mobilization for total war in Germany, 1939–41', *English Historical Review*, vol.ciii, no.408, July, pp.613–39.

Peukert, D. J. K. (1987) *Inside Nazi Germany: Conformity, Opposition and Racism in Everyday Life*, Penguin.

Sack, J. (1993) *An Eye for an Eye: The Untold Story of Jewish Revenge against Germans in 1945*, Basic Books.

Sadkovich, J. J. (1988) 'Re-evaluating who won the Italo-British naval conflict, 1940–2', *European History Quarterly*, vol.18, no.4, pp.455–71.

Sarafis, M. (1980) *Greece: From Resistance to Civil War*, Spokesman Books.

Shandley, R. R. (1998) *Unwilling Germans? The Goldhagen Debate*, University of Minnesota Press.

Shirer, W. L. (1964) *The Rise and Fall of the Third Reich*, Pan.

Streit, C. (1978) *Keine Kameraden: Die Wehrmacht und die Sowjetischen Kriegsgefangenen, 1941–1945*, Deutsche Verlags-Anstalt.

Webster, Sir C. and Frankland, N. (1961) *The Strategic Air Offensive against Germany 1939–1945*, 4 vols, HMSO.

Units 21–25 THE IMPACT AND CONSEQUENCES OF WORLD WAR II

ARTHUR MARWICK, BILL PURDUE, TONY ALDGATE AND
JAMES CHAPMAN

Introduction and sections 'Economic performance and theory' to
'Political institutions and values' by Arthur Marwick; section 1 to
'Social geography' by Bill Purdue; section 3 by Tony Aldgate and
James Chapman

For the purposes of your study time Unit 22 comprises section 1 to 'Economic performance and theory', Unit 23 the section on 'Social structure' to 'Social reform and welfare policies', Unit 24 the section on 'Material conditions' to 'High and popular culture' and Unit 25 'Political institutions and values' to the end of section 3.

Open University students of this unit will need to refer to:

Set book: J. M. Roberts, *Europe 1880–1945*, Longman, 2001
Primary Sources 2: Interwar and World War II, eds Arthur Marwick and Wendy Simpson, Open University, 2000
Secondary Sources, eds Arthur Marwick and Wendy Simpson, Open University, 2000
Audios 1, 2, 3 and 4
Video 2

INTRODUCTION

In these units Bill Purdue, Tony Aldgate, James Chapman, and I discuss the geopolitical, social and cultural effects of the Second World War, rather as Bill Purdue and I did in Book II for the First World War. We shall again be attempting to estimate the significance of the war experience in comparison with the many other forces which led to change; we shall try to distinguish between the immediate impact of the war and its more enduring effects. Just as it was important to be clear about the nature and levels of development in the different European countries as they were in 1914, so also we will now have to bear firmly in mind all that you have learned about the different kinds of countries as they developed in the 1920s and 1930s. If, for example, a condition which can reasonably be described as 'mass society' came into being in these years, then one would not be able to argue that the experiences of World War II 'created' mass society (though they might result in extensions of the facets of that society to new areas – rural ones, for instance – or to new countries; they might result in the further development and exploitation of the artefacts of mass society).

When assessing the effects of World War I it was very important to make contrasts between autocratic and liberal-democratic societies, and between developed industrial and less-developed, largely agricultural societies. I want you to spend much of your time in this introduction reflecting on:

1   the main differences between the societies that went to war with each other in the period 1939–45;

2   how the likely effects of total war might be influenced or constrained by these differences.

I have already suggested that in explaining the relationship between war and social change (if and where there is one) it is necessary to look for what happens in a society at war that does not happen in a society not at war. Already the notion has arisen once or twice (Unit 3) that in total war we get the *participation* of groups which in time of peace have not been very highly regarded. This is the third of four processes that, I suggest, come into play during war. As you may have picked up from Ian Beckett's article, 'Total war' in the Course Reader (pp.24–41), I have suggested elsewhere (Marwick, *War and Social Change in the Twentieth Century*, 1974) that the other three processes that come into play during war are:

- the destruction of resources and the disruption of existing patterns of life (resulting, for instance, in people being projected into new work situations, but also, conversely, there is often a great emphasis toward reconstruction);

- the testing (and therefore frequent modification) of existing social and political institutions and ways of doing things;

- the engendering of intensified emotional states (including enhanced loyalties to one's own communities – national, racial, or class – and considerable psychological stresses).

The exact way in which these 'processes' (or 'modes' or 'dimensions of war', as I have variously termed them) are expressed is not very important – and indeed no effort is being made in this course to stress this particular approach.

However, it is possible that, now that you have had time to find your bearings amid all the arguments and counter-arguments involved in a course of this sort, you may find the above four headings useful. In doing outside reading, making notes, etc., it is always helpful to have headings and issues ready in mind. The latest statement of my own approach is to be found in the introduction and conclusion to *Total War and Social Change* (Marwick, 1988), a collection of essays based on an Open University conference, and in the introduction to *The Deluge: British Society and the First World War* (Marwick, 1991).

Much more central to the whole course is the question of whether, and how, one can single out war as a cause of change from all the other potential causes. With respect to this conundrum, World War II raises some of the same issues as World War I, but it also embroils us in some rather different debates. To move towards the heart of one of these debates, you will find it extremely useful to read, as part of the next exercise, the contribution on Germany which Mark Roseman made to the conference 'Total War and Social Change' which I have just mentioned.

Exercise   Turn now to the chapter in the Reader by Mark Roseman, 'World War II and social change in Germany' (pp.238–54). You will find this article most helpful for several of the aspects of social change which will be discussed later in these units. While you are reading the article, and making notes on the issue I raise below, I therefore suggest that you also make notes on 'social structure and class', 'social welfare', 'material life and living conditions', 'the role and status of women' and 'institutions and values', or at least make annotations in the margin which will later remind you where information on these topics can be found. You may find it useful to apply some of my headings relating to the four processes mentioned above that (I argue) are touched off by war.

The particular issue I want you to address at this stage, and to which I would like you to write down answers, is the following. In contrasting Germany with Britain, Roseman (apart from all the other vitally important ideas and information that he provides) indicates two critical circumstances which severely limit the possibility of identifying the war experience in itself as a separate cause of social change. Write several sentences indicating what (in Roseman's view) these circumstances are, and bringing out the way in which he sums up the issue. Please read Roseman's article now with great care; it is far more important that you concentrate on Roseman's expert analysis than on my attempt to summarize it. ∎

Specimen answer   The first circumstance concerns the nature of the Nazi regime. Germany was *already* experiencing many of the developments which in Britain only came with the actual advent of war. Germany's 'total peace' entailed the mobilization of society and economy. Labour was already controlled in the way that other countries endeavoured to control it in time of war. There was a 'peacetime war economy', involving a substantial modification (with respect to economic change) of both investment activity and raw material allocation and (with respect to social change) of occupational structure. The Nazis had already disrupted many aspects of the traditional class structure, had at least made some pretence at giving enhanced status to labour, and had tried to create a kind of national unity through an 'authoritarian corporatism'. The transition from peace to war, Roseman argues, was not a sharp one. (As you know, Richard Overy has challenged the notion of Germany merely waging a *Blitzkrieg* war, but this does not, I think, substantially invalidate Roseman's main point.)

The second circumstance is that, rather than the experience of war or the responses to the needs of war shaping the development of German society, the decisive influences were those of the occupying powers. The Soviet Union 'totally reorganized society and economy' in East Germany, while West Germany was essentially recreated in the image of the United States.

Roseman sums up these, as he sees them, distinct circumstances (distinct from the British experience) in the phrase 'political discontinuities': that is, the Nazi take-over in 1933, and the Russian and American take-overs in 1945. Because of these, 'total war does not stand out as a revolutionary impulse in the way that it perhaps does in some other countries'. It is evident, says Roseman, 'that "total war" is not an independent cause of social change. Its influence on German society was shaped decisively by the nature of the regime which waged it and that of the regime which followed it' (p.252).

Discussion   In these phrases Roseman shows one of the great historical skills, that of expressing the essence of a problem in a few pithy sentences. In your reading you should be developing the skill of getting into the heart of the arguments being made. The three paragraphs of Roseman's final section (p.252) make a most effective summing up, and the first of these paragraphs is a splendid summary of the two circumstances I asked you to identify in the exercise. Of course, the final selection is of no use to you unless you have mastered the arguments that have led to it.

I hope that (whatever other points you noted down for future use) you did get from Roseman the same two circumstances that I did. Before moving on, do be sure that you really have understood his arguments. Of course, he does also give important instances of the way in which the war experience *did* have effects, but these are to be seen within the general framework of the natures of the regime that waged the war, and the regime (Roseman puts it in the singular because in his conclusion he concentrates purely on West Germany) that followed it.

Roseman's article further pays its way in that it keys us into two general debates of great importance. First, it suggests that in analysing the war we may be able to discriminate between societies that are more or less like Britain (and, incidentally, the US) and ones that are more or less like Germany. Second, in giving considerable weight to the American and the Russian occupations, he ties in with an important line of thought that has been followed by those belonging to the tradition which likes to generalize about, or build models relating to, historical explanation. This is that the major determinant of social change in the aftermath of World War II was the division of Europe into an American sphere of influence and a Russian sphere of influence; thus, for western Europe 'Americanization' is seen as a fundamental characteristic of social development. Personally, I challenge this view, believing that the roots of social development are much more complex, and that, in particular, the influence of Americanization, as against indigenous Italian, French, British, etc. influences, has been grossly overstated. On this issue we hope to help you arrive at informed conclusions of your own.

For the purpose of this introduction I want now to concentrate on the first issue. □

Exercise   1   What major countries, apart from Germany, could be seen as being affected by 'political discontinuities making it particularly difficult to single out the war as an independent cause of social change' (no one could ever say, of course, that war was ever a *completely* independent cause of social change)? Which country went through one, rather than two, discontinuities?

2   This is a slightly different point, but let's deal with it here. Roseman concludes by stressing the importance of American and Russian occupation policies. But, of course, the war itself was accompanied by occupation policies which had very profound, if not necessarily long-lasting, effects on several countries. What am I referring to here? ■

Specimen answers   1   Italy is the country which went through discontinuities broadly analogous to the German ones. You might wish to maintain, however, that in so far as Italy was less 'revolutionized' than Germany, there was more scope for the war to have a strong impact. Italy was not subject to occupation in quite the same way, but the same arguments about the salience of an American sphere of influence can be advanced. The other country is Russia, which obviously had been 'revolutionized' before the war; clearly it was not subject to any kind of discontinuity and external influence at the end of the war (on the contrary, it extended its own influence).

2   *German* occupation of a number of European countries – touched on by Roseman from the first paragraph on p.242 to the end of section II. As you know from Unit 20, occupation policies in Denmark, the Netherlands, France and Italy were not on the same scale of bestiality as they were in the east.

Discussion   Those who maintain that the nature of social change after World War II depended upon whether a country fell within the influence of Soviet communism or American capitalism, rather than on the experience of war itself, would seem to have a particularly good example in the case of Poland. Yet Norman Davies, Britain's leading authority on Poland, has maintained almost the exact opposite:

> The changes brought about by the War were deep and permanent.
> Seven years of slaughter refashioned the state, nation, and society
> more radically than a century of endeavour beforehand or three
> decades of communist rule afterwards.
>
> (Norman Davies, *God's Playground: A History of Poland*, vol.2, 1981,
> pp.488–9)

This is perhaps, for rhetorical effect, slightly overstated, but it is certainly not a summary that can be ignored. Perhaps it might be truer to say that some of the more fundamental effects of the war were concealed by communist rule, but that, after 1989, the ways in which Poland was a vastly different country from what it had been in 1939 became more apparent. (The individual points made by Davies will be discussed in these units under the appropriate headings.)

It may be that from all this we are left with Britain as a unique example, occupied neither by the Germans during the war, nor by the Americans or Russians after the war (though many academics would, not without reason, still apply the Americanization thesis to Britain). Hardach is far from the only historian to argue that generalization from the British experience gives a totally wrong impression of there being a connection between total war and desirable social change. Yet, for analytical purposes, it might be worthwhile putting France into the same category as Britain, as a country which on the eve of the war was a western liberal democracy.

There has been much discussion of the longer term effects of the destructive aspect of war. F. C. Iklé, in his *The Social Impact of Bomb Destruction* (1958, p.121), has pointed to a distinction between 'passive morale', which shows itself in personal bearing and in private relations and which, as a result of bombing, was generally low, and 'active morale', concerned with public and job activities, which was not adversely affected. In my *War and Social Change in the Twentieth Century* (1974) and elsewhere I have suggested that the destruction of war may have some of the same effects on human communities as natural disasters such as earthquakes, and in this connection I have referred to the collection *Man and Society in Disaster* (1962) edited by G. W. Baker and T. E. Chapman. The notion is that bomb (and other destructive) attacks may in fact strengthen morale, creating a determination not just to survive but to rebuild and to reconstruct.

The paradigm of the (aerial) blitz in the early stages of the war was that of London. The citizens of Moscow, in late 1941, initially feared that they might suffer a similar blitz (though, as we shall see, the destruction and loss of life in Britain was tiny compared with what was later to be suffered in many other countries). Some of the most devastating bombing of all took place on Germany in 1943 and 1944. Albert Speer, in his visits to arms factories and from his 'contacts with the man in the street', derived an impression of 'growing toughness'. Christabel Bielenberg, an Englishwoman domiciled in Nazi Germany, wrote:

> I learned when I was in Berlin that those wanton, quite impersonal killings, that barrage from the air that mutilated, suffocated, burned and destroyed, did not so much breed fear and a desire to bow before the storm, but rather a certain fatalistic cussedness, a dogged determination to survive, whatever their policies, whatever their creed.

> (*The Past is Myself*, 1969, p.127)

I would now like you to look at two documents relating to the bomb attacks on Germany. □

Exercise   Turn to Document II.12 in *Primary Sources 2: Interwar and World War II*, 'Extract from the report by the Police President of Hamburg on the raids on Hamburg in July and August 1943'. When you have read it, write down answers to these questions:

1   What three German air-raid protection services are mentioned?

2   Where does the Police President draw parallels with natural catastrophes? What difference was there in the Hamburg situation?

3   Where is there a suggestion of such destruction having a 'reconstructive effect'?

Before I suggest answers to these questions, I would like you to look at the second extract from Document II.13 in *Primary Sources 2: Interwar and World War II*, 'Extracts from *I Lived Under Hitler*', by Sybil Bannister.

4   What indications are there of 'reconstruction' and social change? ■

Specimen answers and discussion

1   The organizations are: Self Protection, Extended Self Protection, and Works Air Protection Services. On the whole, the Nazi air-raid precaution services seemed to have worked reasonably effectively (though, of course, they were completely overwhelmed by something like the Hamburg fire storms); however, it was a feature of Nazi society to have such services divided up into different organizations.

2   There are references to fires in Tokyo, Hamburg (1842), Chicago and the Paris Opera House, and to the 1906 earthquake in San Francisco. The difference is that these all came unexpectedly, whereas the people of Hamburg were expecting the raids – but they were still overwhelmed.

3   In the last phrase: 'an irresistible will to rebuild'. Of course, this is only an opinion, and an opinion which it was in the interests of the Police President to express. I am not trying to identify some universal truth here: I simply want you to consider the possibility that destruction in war can produce reconstructive effects.

4   Despite the appalling destruction, people have 'started afresh', and 'much reconstruction' has been done, etc. With regard to social change, one might detect evidence of 'social levelling' (though that would not necessarily be lasting): prosperous shops are now shacks, one of Hamburg's wealthiest merchants is living in a garage. Again these are hints picked up from only one piece of evidence, but much of historical writing consists of putting together such hints. □

In most of the remainder of these units Bill Purdue, Tony Aldgate, James Chapman and I look at the question of the relationship between war and social change under the series of headings for social change which was introduced at the beginning of the course in Book I, pp.6–10. This should be convenient for you, but it runs the risk of misrepresenting the nature of the interaction between war and society. In 'society at war' (as distinct from society not at war), a complex of direct and indirect responses, interaction and cross-action is touched off: changes in one area will often produce consequent changes in other areas. In my own books, as already explained, I have tried to express this complex by speaking of war as simultaneously bringing about destruction and disruption (with, possibly, the reconstructive effects I have just been discussing), operating as a 'test' of and 'challenge' to existing institutions (the French capitulation in 1940 was often seen as a sign that existing French élites had failed the test of war), creating new opportunities for participation, and involving whole populations in an enormous psychological experience. This is only one way, and not necessarily the best one, of expressing complex processes. The point is that you should have a sense of many different effects and counter-effects taking place together in the enormous catastrophe of war.

As in Book 2, Bill Purdue starts off with the geopolitical implications of World War II and then goes on to examine the first two of the areas of change on which we have decided to concentrate in this course. I then take up the topics of social structure, national cohesion, social welfare, living conditions, customs and behaviour, the role and status of women, high and popular culture, and institutions and values, concluding with a document exercise. A specific, and very important, aspect of popular culture – the mass media – is then taken up by Tony Aldgate and James Chapman.

1 INTERNATIONAL AND GEOPOLITICAL CHANGE

The war in Europe and the world war

When, in September 1939, Britain and France declared war on Germany, they did so to prevent the German domination of Europe. Notions that their purpose was a crusade against fascism are born of retrospective myth making. The aim was not the total defeat and surrender of Germany but to achieve by war what diplomacy had failed to achieve, a European settlement, one that would leave intact much of the revision of Versailles that had taken place, while limiting Germany's expansion to areas contiguous to the Reich and inhabited by Germans.

The essential war aim of placing limits on German power and expansion was, thus, broadly the same as in 1914, and to most of the British and French population it seemed that the war, which appeared to have ended in 1918 had begun again. However, the general consensus in the years immediately after 1945 was that the Second World War was a separate war, unique in its causes and character. More recently, as you know from Unit 19, the view of a long European civil war, embracing both the First and Second World Wars, has once more become influential. The principal interpretative divide on the causes of World War II remains that between those who see it as separate from World War I and those who stress a continuum between the two wars.

I personally agree with the 'long European civil war' thesis when it comes to the reasons for the war which broke out in 1939, but it is obviously true that as World War II continued it developed a momentum of its own: the aims of the original participants changed (or, some would say in Germany's case, were revealed), some participants were defeated and new combatants drawn in, and the ferocity and scale of the war with its many atrocities hardened attitudes and raised stakes, while the war became global in a way World War I had never been. World War I (there is much to be said for its earlier appellation, the Great War) was essentially a European conflict, though the extra-European interests of the participants resulted in fighting outside Europe and the US eventually joined in, while World War II, though it began in Europe, became a global struggle, which justified the adjective 'world'.

We can discern three distinct stages in the development of the war:

1 A war fought after the defeat and partition of Poland by the allied powers of Britain and France against Germany, joined tardily by Italy. This war saw Germany triumphant in the west, France defeated and most of western Europe under German control directly or indirectly. Britain, however, continued to fight on.

2 A widened European war consequent upon Germany's invasion of the USSR.

3 A world war, consequent upon Japan's attack on Pearl Harbor and Germany's and Italy's declarations of war upon the US. This war was fought in the Far East as well as in Europe.

Our course is one which centres upon European history but it is justifiable to query how far we can consider World War II's effects upon the international, geopolitical structure of Europe without full reference to the progress of the war outside Europe and its effects on the political geography of areas far from Europe. We must be aware of the interaction between the war in the Pacific and the war in Europe. Although the US adopted the policy of giving priority to the war in Europe, the number of American troops, planes and ships that could be brought into action in the European sphere was necessarily limited by the need to fight in the Pacific as well. Japan's early successes exposed the weaknesses of the British, French and Dutch empires and was an important factor in hastening the demise of these empires. So far as the shape and nature of post-war Europe itself is concerned, however, the only really important extra-European factor is the wartime strategy of the US and the influence of American foreign policy at the end of the war and during the immediate post-war years.

World War II was in reality two fairly discrete wars – one in Europe (though it spilled over into North Africa and the Middle East) and the other in the Pacific – linked by Britain's and America's involvement in both. It is significant that historians do not always use the term 'Second World War' when referring to the war in the east, instead often using the terms 'Pacific War' or 'Far Eastern War'. Clearly the fortunes of war in the Far East had their effect on Anglo-American strategy in the west and on their military effort in that sphere. But Germany and Japan were at best nominal allies, joined more by the imagination of Joachim von Ribbentrop than anything else, and strategic co-operation between them was minimal; the influence of Mussolini on the Japanese high command was, to say the least, underwhelming. Things might, of course, have been very different if Japan had chosen to seriously attack the Soviet Union rather than the United States. When the Japanese Foreign Minister, Matsuoka Yosuke, was in Berlin in April 1941 Hitler told him nothing about his plan to attack Russia, and Matsuoka accordingly went on to Moscow and signed a neutrality pact with Stalin. The puzzled Matsuoka said to the Japanese cabinet in June: 'I concluded a neutrality pact because I thought that Germany and Russia could not go to war. If I had thought they would go to war ... I would not have concluded the Neutrality Pact' (Ian Nish, *Japanese Foreign Policy 1869–1942*, 1977, p.242). As it was, the Soviet Union only entered the war against Japan at the last moment in order to safeguard its post-war position in the Far East, and was thus enabled to occupy Manchuria and North Korea and to pick up Sakhalin and the Kuriles Islands.

Britain, alone among the major combatants, had a continuous involvement in both spheres and, indeed, it is impossible to understand British foreign policy in the 1930s without an appreciation that 'appeasement' resulted as much from the weakness of the British position in the Far East as from a diagnosis of Europe's problems. Some commentators have seen the US's involvement in the European war as a natural and inevitable progression from concern at Germany's early successes combined with a protective attitude towards democracy which led, via lend-lease, to Roosevelt being able to bring American public opinion around to the point where entry on Britain's side was possible. However, without Germany's declaration of war on the US after Pearl Harbor, would the US have entered the European war?

Exercise   Read Roberts, pp.440–42, and then answer the following questions:

1   What does Roberts have to say about the pact of 28 September 1940 between Japan and Germany and Italy?

2   What is his assessment of Hitler's action in declaring war on the US on 11 December 1941? ■

Specimen answers   1   He sees the pact as being designed to discourage the US from continuing its gestures of support for Britain.

2   He considers it a 'fatal mistake' and an illustration of the irrational origins of Hitler's foreign policy. In the eyes of the Japanese the virtue of the 1940 pact was that it seemed to prevent strong American action in the Pacific. By late 1941, however, American economic embargoes had made Japan decide that war with America was inevitable. But as Roberts says, 'America was not at war with Germany and might well have turned her back on Europe to fight Japan. This possibility was thrown away by Hitler' (p.442). □

Once in, America's impact on the war in Europe was colossal and probably decisive, but the impact was akin to that of some mighty *deus ex machina* which threw its power into the European sphere with the sole aim of defeating Germany. The origins of the war in Europe were domestic to the continent while all the European participants had war aims moulded by tradition, geography and self-interest, whereas the United States had no settled convictions as to the geopolitical shape of post-war Europe. That the military success of American armies had an enormous influence on the *de facto* maps of Europe that emerged in the summer of 1945 is certain, but it was not a politically purposeful influence, for alone among the Allies, the US allowed the strategic consideration of the war to be paramount over considerations of post-war advantage.

The view of the closing stages of the war and its immediate aftermath as marking the divided hegemony of two extra-European powers over a diminished Europe is flawed, so far as America is concerned, in that it reads the period from the Cold War perspective of 1948. So far as the Soviet Union is concerned, its flaw is the categorization of Russia as somehow not a European power, which would have been news to Metternich. Indeed, far from being a totally novel end to European war, the situation in 1945 has some similarity with that of 1814–15, with Russian armies penetrating deep into central Europe, though the main countervailing influence is not a semi-detached Britian but its fully extra-continental ex-colony, the US.

The role of ideology

The view that it was ideology that produced the opposing alliances, the war aims of the combatants and the shifting changes to the European political map between 1939 and 1945 is problematic. Were Hitler's and Stalin's war aims determined by the theories of national socialism and communism respectively, or did they correspond to the traditional aims of German and Russian leaders, so that they would have made perfectly good sense to many of their predecessors? Was Britain's and France's intervention in 1939 born of concern for the independence of small nations, a vague anti-fascism, or simply national self-interest and concern for the balance of power in Europe?

Exercise   What development at the beginning of the war and during its earlier stages constitute the biggest single argument against ideology being the dominant consideration? ■

Specimen answer   The Soviet–German Non-Aggression Treaty of 23 August 1939, which was
and discussion   followed by Soviet–German co-operation over the division of Poland between them, together with the attempts of the two powers to reach an agreement over spheres of influence, which continued until late 1940. The existence of an understanding or of co-operation between two ideologically opposed powers does not, of course, mean that their respective ideologies were unimportant to them, but it does point to ideology being a less than omnipresent motive for their actions.

From the early 1920s both Germany and the Soviet Union were revisionist powers with ambitions in east and central Europe which they were determined to pursue, whether as allies, enemies or independently. At different times they investigated the possibilities of alliance (as with von Ribbentrop's plan for a Eurasian alliance made up of Germany, Italy, Japan and the Soviet Union), sought to co-exist and fought. Ideological considerations and the theoretical commitment of the Soviet Union to world revolution did put difficulties in the way of the option for France and Britain of an understanding with Russia, similar to that reached before 1914, to balance Germany's strength. However, they did not prevent Anglo-Russian and American–Russian co-operation after 1941, any more than they prevented the Soviet–German treaty of 1939. Ideology could make alliances difficult and could be used as a justification for territorial ambitions and gains and as propaganda for them, but the alliances entered into, the moves made by the powers, their territorial ambitions, and even the post-war territorial adjustments are all readily comprehensible within the framework of conflicting and traditional national aims pursued as opportunity offered. □

East and central Europe

It was in east and central Europe that the origins of the war were to be found, that Russia and Germany had major territorial ambitions, that almost every smaller power had designs on its neighbours' territories, and that the war resulted in major territorial changes.

It is not only with the aid of hindsight that we can see the political geography of east and central Europe that had emerged by 1922 as ephemeral. The writ of the Versailles Settlement had not penetrated far into eastern Europe, but neither the provisions it did make for that region nor its provisions for central Europe were ever as securely imprinted as those from western Europe. The Treaty of Locarno had seen the powers guarantee the frontiers of France and Belgium with Germany, but not Germany's eastern frontiers. Further east, as we saw in Book 2, Units 7–10, frontiers had been set – not by Versailles, but by the fighting that had continued between 1918 and 1922 and by separate treaties. A month before the Treaty of Tartu in 1920, by which the Soviet Union recognized 'unconditionally' and 'forever' the total independence of Estonia, Lenin wrote: 'The borders of these new states are fixed only for the time being.'

The territorial settlements of 1918–22 had left Europe divided between those states committed to their preservation, and revisionist states determined to see them modified.

Exercise 1 Which states were revisionist and which were relatively satisfied with existing frontiers?

2 What changes to the territorial arrangements of 1922 had already taken place before the outbreak of World War II? ■

Specimen answers and discussion 1 Revisionist: Germany, USSR, Hungary, Bulgaria and Italy. Upholders of the existing order: Britain, France, Czechoslovakia, Yugoslavia, Estonia, Latvia, Lithuania, Finland, Romania, Belgium and Albania. Poland comes into a category of its own, being a state created by the peace settlement and by its own military success in the war with Russia. But Poland still had territorial ambitions. A. J. P. Taylor has commented that Poland's problem was that it believed it was a great power but wasn't.

2 Czechoslovakia had, of course, disappeared from the map: the Sudetenland had been incorporated into Germany; Bohemia and Moravia had been declared German protectorates; Poland had taken Teschen; Hungary had taken southern Slovakia and Ruthenia; and the rest of Slovakia had become a dependent state.

Germany's war in the west gave the Soviet Union the opportunity to strengthen its position in eastern Europe beyond the understanding of the Non-Aggression Treaty. That treaty had provided both for a division of Poland and for Latvia and Estonia to be Russian spheres of influence, while Lithuania was to be under German hegemony. A new German–Soviet treaty of 28 September 1939 gave Germany a somewhat larger share of Poland but assigned Lithuania to the Russian sphere of influence. By the late summer of 1940 the Soviet Union was not only digesting its Polish gains but had fought a winter war with Finland (which, if it brought little glory to the Russian army, did result in territorial concessions by the Finnish government), annexed the Baltic republics and incorporated the Romanian province of Bessarabia. The frontiers of the USSR were now almost commensurate with those of tsarist Russia in 1914.

It remained an open question during late 1939 and 1940 whether or not Soviet and German expansionist aims were compatible. Could accommodations be made and spheres of influence be allocated that would keep the two powers apart or even bring them into alliance? If one sees Germany's decision to invade Russia in 1941 as the inevitable outcome of Hitler's long-standing ambitions or as an atavistic manifestation of an age-old German drive to the east, then the answer must be firmly in the negative. But there are good reasons and considerable evidence for believing that the situation was fluid and that Germany seriously investigated the possibility of accommodation. □

Exercise   Why do you think Germany should have wished to accommodate rather than fight Russia in 1940? ■

Specimen answers   1   Germany's campaigns to the west had been enormously successful, but Britain, though weak, was not defeated. The familiar problem of a war on two fronts was to be avoided if possible.

2   Germany had made considerable territorial gains and occupied vast areas; it needed time to consolidate.

3   The German economy had not been prepared for a long war.

4   The USSR was in 1939–41 providing Germany with large consignments of essential raw materials. Germany didn't need to go to war to gain these raw materials.

None of the reasons ruled out a strike against Russia, but together they provided strong grounds for avoiding it unless absolutely necessary. □

Exercise   I would now like you to read the article by H. W. Koch, 'Hitler's "Programme" and the Genesis of Operation "Barbarossa" ', which is reproduced in *Secondary Sources* (pp.102–31).

1   How would you summarize Koch's general thesis?

2   What alternatives to an attack on Russia did Germany consider in 1940?

3   What is Koch's interpretation of Russian policy? ■

Specimen answers   1   The German government was considering a number of policy options during 1939–40, and it would have preferred an accommodation with Russia. It was the realization that Russian aims were centred on eastern Europe and the knowledge of the threat they posed to Germany that persuaded Germany that war with Russia was inevitable.

2   A Euro-Asian alliance including Germany, Italy, Japan and the USSR and the offer to the USSR of a path to expansion in Asia that would give that country control of Iran and then divert towards the Persian Gulf in India. This would enable Germany to get on with the job of finishing off Britain. Germany wanted peace with Britain, but if Britain was not prepared to come to terms, Operation Sea-Lion would have to be undertaken.

3   Essentially Koch sees Russian expansionist aims as being focused in eastern Europe. Russia had gone beyond the agreement over spheres of interest agreed to in the Russo-German agreements, and the further extension of Russian influence, especially in Romania where Germany needed to maintain control of the oil fields, threatened German interests.

Discussion   Both Koch and Roberts see November 1940 as the month in which Hitler made up his mind that Russia had to be dealt with. Roberts writes: 'Now Hitler decided to settle accounts with Russia. But just at that moment he was distracted by the need to send forces to help Italy' (p.440).

The failure of the talks between Molotov and the German leaders in Berlin in November 1940 demonstrates that the USSR's main interests and ambitions lay in east and central Europe. Stalin instructed Molotov to demand as primary requirements that Finland, Romania, Bulgaria and the Black Sea Straits be allocated to the Soviet sphere of influence, but there is evidence of a list of ultimate demands: the allocation of Hungary, Yugoslavia, Sweden and western Poland to the Russian sphere, with a greater share for the USSR of the Baltic Sea outlets (see Paul Johnson, *A History of the Modern World*, 1983, p.373). As Johnson comments, Stalin's demands, added up, 'are not so very different to what Stalin demanded and in most cases got, as his share of victory at the end of the Second World War. The Molotov "package" testifies to the continuity of Soviet aims' (ibid.).

Like Napoleon before him, who had similarly tried to persuade Tsar Alexander to turn his attention to India and the Persian Gulf, Hitler now determined to attack Russia. An ex-Soviet general staff officer, Victor Suvorov, who defected to the west, has argued that the reason Stalin dismissed rumours of an imminent German attack was that the Russians themselves were in the final phase of deploying 183 divisions on Russia's western frontier, a move which could only have led to a Russian attack. Suvorov's argument, developed in his book *Icebreaker: Who Started the Second World War?* (1990), is that Stalin welcomed the coming to power of Hitler in Germany because he saw him as a profoundly destabilizing influence, the 'ice-breaker' bringing a new fluidity to international relations and giving the Soviet Union and communism their opportunity for expansion. The result of the Nazi–Soviet Pact had been to give Germany and the Soviet Union common frontiers, thus greatly facilitating a surprise attack by either power. Stalin's determination to deny Germany control of Romania, and thus of the Romanian oil fields, was only part of a wider plan to destroy Germany and conquer western Europe. The seizure of Bessarabia alerted Hitler to Russian intentions, and Germany, according to Suvorov, launched *Barbarossa* just before Stalin intended to launch its equivalent.

Were the two powers both seeking the right moment to launch their attacks, making their troop movements and reacting to each other's movements? The evidence is conflicting and the debate heated. It is fair to say that the most widely accepted version of events and that held by eminent experts (see Gerhard Weinberg, *A World at War: A Global History of World War II*, 1994) is still that Stalin had no intention of attacking Germany and was taken by surprise when *Barbarossa* began. Just why Stalin, not normally the most trusting of men, should have remained purblind to Hitler's intentions has never, however, been satisfactorily explained.

What seems increasingly clear is that even after the war between Germany and Russia had begun diplomatic initiatives were not exhausted. It has been suggested that as the German armies advanced on Moscow in October 1941 Lavrenti Beria, the Soviet Union's Chief of Secret Police, acting on Stalin's orders, approached the Bulgarian Ambassador in Moscow to act as a go-between with Hitler. Fearing defeat, Stalin was prepared to conclude a peace treaty on the lines of Brest-Litovsk. Even before the collapse of the Soviet Union, this suggestion was made by Dimitar Peyev, editor of the Bulgarian newspaper *Orbita* in the late 1980s and during the war a junior diplomat, and by the Soviet military historian General Nicolai Pavlenko writing in *Moskovskiye Novosti* and cast new light on the fluidity of Soviet policy and the fragility of the alliance against Germany. □

Indeed, it now seems evident that, as late as 1943, Stalin approved tentative communications with Hitler. Effectively, however, the German–Soviet war became a fight to the finish.

The entry of the Soviet Union into the war immensely strengthened Britain's military position. Britain had lost one 'continental sword' with the defeat of France but found another in the Soviet Union. However, the Soviet alliance brought complications for Britain so far as war aims were concerned. Having gone to war, at least ostensibly, to protect Poland, Britain was now allied to a power that had partitioned Poland with Germany. The entry of the US into the war was to have similar consequences, ensuring not just British survival but probable ultimate victory, while limiting her opportunities to shape the results of that victory.

Eastern Europe moves west

The initial successes of the German armies enabled all the east and central European losers of 1919, whether states or simply subject nationalities, to make gains under German hegemony. The fortunes of 1919 were almost everywhere reversed. The revisionist states of Hungary and Bulgaria extended their frontiers. Romania, though a victor at Versailles, had been divested of most of its gains but joined the alliance against Russia in the hope of regaining lost territory and even of making further acquisitions. Hungary, like Romania, joined in the war against Russia, although Bulgaria did not. The Slovaks and Croatians, dissatisfied in 1919, attained a limited sovereignty under German supervision. Those who had gained most at the end of World War I – the Czechs, the Serbs and the Poles – had had their states dismembered. Some other winners in the immediate post World War I period who had lost all to Russia in 1940 – Latvia, Estonia and Lithuania – retained governments in exile in London, though many of the population supported the German war effort. Finland, having fought a desperate war with Russia, joined combat again on the side of Germany.

The question of who would have won the war in eastern Europe had it not been for American intervention is debatable. The German advance was checked and then reversed by the Soviet army and by the grim efforts of Russian civilians, though the British and then Anglo-American campaign in North Africa drained German resources. Without allied supplies and without the Italian campaign and the Normandy landings, however, a decisive Soviet victory in the east would still have been in doubt. The Red Army that advanced westwards from 1943 did so in American jeeps and tanks, while much of the technology which enabled the Soviet Union to produce aircraft capable of seizing command of the air from the Germans came from the US. It is instructive to compare the furthest limits of the German advance in 1942 (see 'Europe at the Height of German Domination, Nov. 1942' in the *Maps Booklet* or Map 8 in Roberts) with Germany's position at the time of the Treaty of Brest-Litovsk in 1917. Germany had got a little, but not much, further in the second round, and the new order of 1942 bore some striking similarities to the situation in 1917. This order was to be ephemeral, and that which emerged in 1945 was to be its mirror image, a Russian hegemony.

Should or could the Soviet Union's western allies have done more to modify the effects of a Soviet victory in the east on the shape and political complexion of east and central Europe?

From the beginning there were differences between Britain and America on the one hand and the Soviet Union on the other as to both strategy in the war against Germany and a post-war settlement. There were also differences between the two western allies themselves. Stalin repeatedly pressed the western powers for an invasion of occupied Europe via the French coast, and did not consider the Anglo-American invasion of North Africa and Southern Italy in 1942 and 1943 as sufficient substitutes. For their part, both America and Britain still feared in 1942 that the USSR and Germany might make a separate peace.

Relations between Britain and the US, the latter increasingly the senior partner in the alliance, bore some similarity to those between the US and its west European allies in World War I. In 1941 Roosevelt had put forward a loose concept of a post-war world based on the rights of all peoples to self-determination, and had secured Russian and British association with it. Such a concept recalls the views of Woodrow Wilson, but Roosevelt was conscious of the post-war repudiation of Wilson's policies by the American public, caused in part by the gap between Wilsonian idealism and the more self-interested aims of the European powers. Roosevelt was determined to avoid Wilson's fate, not by cutting back on the idealism but by disassociating himself and America from any carving up of Europe into spheres of interests which might recall the secret treaties concluded among the Allies during World War I.

Roosevelt was both opposed to the British Empire and suspicious of Britain as a practitioner of a worldly approach towards international relations involving spheres of influence and considerations such as the balance of power. He had no illusions that the USSR's twin preoccupations with its security and world communism would make it a satisfactory partner in implementing a world order based on self-determination, but placed high hopes on the establishment of a close relationship between Stalin and himself, a relationship he hoped to make closer by expressing his distrust of British policies. Roosevelt's own policy, so far as Europe was concerned, was to content himself with a lofty moral conception of the future, to concentrate on winning a war against Germany, and largely to ignore the question of the future territorial and political arrangements for east and central Europe, even as that question became steadily more pressing. He hoped that the Soviet Union would be contained, not by arrangements in east and central Europe but by the United Nations, on whose Security Council Russia would be in a minority, and by US military might, together with an Ango-US monopoly on the atomic bomb.

American lack of concern for the post-war political balance of Europe and distaste for making agreements as to future frontiers and spheres of influence led to both strategic and political disagreements with Britain. Roosevelt was always more sympathetic than Britain to Russian demands for an invasion of France and less interested in alternative strategies which might strengthen the western position in east and central Europe. Even after D-Day Churchill supported General Alexander's plan for an operation eastwards from the Allied positions in Italy to cross the Rivers Po and Piave, seize Trieste and the Istrian Peninsular, and march through the Ljubljana Gap, threatening Vienna. The plan, code-named Armpit, was brusquely turned down by Roosevelt and the American Chief of Staff. Harold Macmillan, Alexander's political adviser, wrote in his memoirs that it:

> might have altered the whole political destinies of the Balkans and eastern Europe ... But apart from Roosevelt's desire, at that time to please Stalin at almost any cost, nothing could overcome the almost pathological suspicions of British policy, especially in the Balkans.
>
> (Quoted in Alistair Horne, *Macmillan*, vol.1, 1988, p.220)

Macmillan was convinced that the war could have ended 250 miles east of where the Iron Curtain eventually divided Europe, with Vienna and Prague firmly in western hands. Even in the last weeks of his life Roosevelt did nothing to encourage Eisenhower to push towards Berlin, Vienna and Prague as the British wanted. General Montgomery wrote that 'The Americans could not understand that it was of little avail to win the war strategically if we lost it politically.'

By the end of 1942 the only firm decision that had been reached among the Allies as to the shape of post-war eastern and central Europe was that Austria should be re-established as an independent power. The Tehran conference of December 1943, however, saw a discussion of the future Polish frontiers. Churchill agreed to the Curzon line of 1920 for Poland's eastern frontier, thus depriving Poland of the territory won from Russia in 1921; he also accepted that Poland should be recompensed with German territory east of the Oder River. Poland was to prove the most contentious issue dividing Britain and the Soviet Union. After all, Britain had ostensibly gone to war for Poland as constituted in 1939, and the Polish government in exile was based in London. The Soviet Union had not only invaded Poland in 1939 but had behaved with great barbarity there. That there was little to choose when it came to barbarism between the Soviet Union and Nazi Germany was largely ignored after 1941 by Britain and the US, who preferred to represent Stalin as an avuncular figure and the Soviet Union as a courageous ally. But even under the blanket of wartime propaganda, news of the massacre at Katyn of 4,510 Polish officers by the Russians was brought to light by an investigation by the International Red Cross. When asked where these officers and another 9,000 Polish officers and NCOs were, the Russians lied: 'perhaps they fled across the Manchurian border?' (Hugh Thomas, *Armed Truce*, 1986, p.353). Nevertheless, Britain, because of wartime expediency and because it could exert little influence on Stalin's determination to impose a compliant regime on Poland, and also nudged by the US, was steadily to move towards what can only be regarded as a betrayal – both of its ostensible reason for going to war, Poland, and of the Polish forces fighting with Britain.

As Roosevelt rejected Churchill's urgings that there should be Anglo-American negotiations with Stalin in order to set limits to Russian control of eastern Europe as Russian armies 'liberated' it – negotiations which would stand a better chance of success while the Soviet Union was still dependent on western assistance – Churchill attempted to play a lone hand. The so-called 'Percentage Agreement', worked out virtually on the back of an envelope between Churchill and Stalin in Moscow in October 1944, gave the Soviet Union effective control over Romania, Bulgaria and Hungary, Britain and the Soviets joint influence in Yugoslavia, and Britain a free hand in Greece. That Stalin to some extent honoured this agreement in the immediate aftermath of the war suggests that had the US lent its greater weight towards a wider but equally cynical type of agreement, the eventual Soviet hegemony in eastern Europe might have been modified.

Britain was playing with an ever weaker hand as allied victory grew closer. As Chamberlain had realized, Britain's major problem since 1918 had been how to manage decline so as to save as much of substance as possible. The Second World War accelerated decline and weakened Britain's independent management of her fortunes. America's intervention in the war resulted in an Anglo-American alliance in which Britain had increasingly to bend to the will of the ally, which provided the preponderant military and economic strength. This was less clear in 1942 before American forces had arrived in Europe in large numbers, but from mid-1943 Britain's influence on major decisions waned as her junior position became apparent.

Churchill, Stalin and Roosevelt met at Yalta in February 1945 to discuss the future of Europe on the eve of Germany's defeat. The very imminence of that defeat had already robbed Britain and America of much of their influence over the Soviet Union. The powers accepted the agreements that their officials had previously arrived at in respect of Germany's division into military zones, although, at Churchill's insistence, France was allocated a smaller zone of its own. It was also decided to set up a four-power military council in Berlin, itself to be divided into four military sectors. A supposed compromise, which in reality was a Soviet victory, was reached over Poland: the two western powers agreed that the Soviet-backed Polish Communist Committee based at Lublin in Soviet-occupied Poland should form the nucleus of a Polish provisional government, with a few members of the London-based government in exile given ministerial posts. Stalin promised that there would be free elections in Poland after the war, and the lines of the territorial arrangements sketched out at Tehran were confirmed (though Roosevelt refused to agree publicly to these). The USSR had already ensured – by the murder of so many of the Polish officer corps and by allowing the Germans to crush the Warsaw ring in 1944, while Russian armies paused a few miles away – that the anti-communist forces in Polish society would be much weakened. The Yalta agreement was thus a blueprint for a Soviet-dominated post-war Poland. In return for these western concessions on Poland, Stalin was free with words and signed a three-power declaration which included an acknowledgement of 'the right of all peoples to choose the governments under which they lived'.

Stalin's achievement at Yalta was considerable. As Michael Dockrill has written:

> He believed that the west had accepted Soviet control over Poland and eastern Europe, although he realised that this would have to be achieved behind a façade of self-determination. Roosevelt had said nothing at Yalta which disabused the Soviet leader of this impression. Stalin was willing to pay lip-service to western principles by encouraging the formation of so-called 'people's' democracies in eastern Europe whereby communists formed coalition governments with anti-Nazi left and centrist parties. In countries under Red Army control real powers of course rested with the Communists.

(*The Cold War 1945–1963*, 1988, p.22)

The major factor in determining the political arrangements of post-war Europe was not the decisions of plenipotentiaries at peace conferences but the extent of the Red Army's advance at the end of hostilities. By the spring of 1945 Russian troops were in control of all of Poland, the Baltic states, East Prussia, the Karelian peninsular (previously Finnish territory), east Germany, north and east Austria (including Vienna), Hungary, Romania and Bulgaria. The Soviet Union was also a dominant influence, via indigenous communist forces in Yugoslavia and Albania, but it was to prove important that these countries had not been 'liberated' by Soviet forces.

Britain had gone to war in 1939 to prevent the alarming expansion of German power, but if the war had been successful in fulfilling that aim, it resulted in a situation just as threatening to Britain and the other western European powers. The defeat of Germany had brought Russian power right into the centre of Europe, and the countervailing power of Germany no longer existed. There was eastern and there was western Europe, but the centre had collapsed and the line between east and west was where the Allied armies had met.

Exercise   Let us return to the questions we posed previously:

1   What could the western Allies have done during 1942–45 to curtail the developing hegemony over east and central Europe?

2   Why did they do so little? ■

Specimen answers   1   They could have:
and discussion

(a) used their position as the suppliers of aid and war materials to gain more influence over Soviet policy and to extract firm agreements from Stalin on the shape and character of the regime of post-war Europe;

(b) come to a realistic understanding with the USSR on a *quid pro quo* basis as to spheres of influence;

(c) aligned their military strategy so as to pre-empt Soviet control in east and central Europe;

(d) encouraged forces within Germany, especially within the *Wehrmacht*, to overthrow the Nazi regime and conclude an armistice, separately from the Soviet Union if need be, with a new German government.

2   Because the US under Roosevelt was not prepared to recognize the problem, at least in public. Determined to avoid the fate of Woodrow Wilson, Roosevelt felt that American public opinion would not wear agreements, secret or otherwise, over post-war territorial arrangements or spheres of influence. He also distrusted the British, disliked the British Empire, was preoccupied with the Pacific war, and trusted that the post-war international organization (the outline of the United Nations Organization had already been agreed at Dumbarton Oaks in 1944) would be able to curtail Soviet actions. □

Churchill's 'Percentage Agreement' with Stalin, combined with the British willingness to use British troops in Greece and northern Italy to safeguard western interests, showed what could be achieved by a combination of options (b) and (c). It was British initiatives that largely preserved the Mediterranean from Soviet influence, but British power was severely limited and Churchill's actions were disapproved of by the US State Department, though Roosevelt himself seems privately to have been more sympathetic.

Option (d) may be considered a purely theoretical course of action. America and Britain had bound themselves to unconditional surrender at Casablanca in 1943, though whether that had been wise is doubtful. There is some evidence, however, that the British Cabinet had contemplated a negotiated peace with Hitler in 1940, so, logically, an armistice with a putative anti-Nazi regime which had overthrown him should not have been impossible in late 1944. The intellectual climate of the time did, however, probably rule out such an armistice.

The Potsdam Conference of the three powers produced little in the way of constructive agreements but succeeded in temporarily papering over the cracks between east and west – cracks which were widening as Truman, who had succeeded to the presidency on Roosevelt's death on 12 April 1945, became aware of Russian intentions in eastern Europe. The main decisions of Potsdam concerned the future of Germany. It was agreed: that eastern Germany be considerably reduced from its pre-war frontiers; that Poland be expanded westwards at Germany's expense; that the Soviet Union receive half of East Prussia; that authority in Germany be exercised by the Commanders-in-Chief, controlling their own forces and acting together in a control council; and that Germany should be treated as a single unit. This latter decision marked the formal abandonment of the plans for the dismemberment of Germany that had been mooted in 1942 and 1943, but the differences between the western Allies and the USSR were soon to result in the effective separation into two Germanies.

As in 1919, the major changes to frontiers occurred in east and central rather than in western Europe (see 'Europe 1945' in the *Maps Booklet*). The frontier between France and Germany remained much as in 1919, while there were only minor rectifications to the Italian–French frontier, and that between Austria and Italy was also unchanged. The Italian Yugoslavian frontier was a matter of considerable contention, and Italy lost most of its post First World War gains; indeed Italy, without the presence of British troops in northern Italy, would almost certainly have lost more. The status of Trieste continued to be disputed until 1954. Hungary and Bulgaria were reduced to their pre-1938 frontiers, save that Bulgaria retained southern Dobruja. Romania recovered Transylvania from Hungary, but its loss of Bessarabia and northern Bukovina to Russia was confirmed. Finland had to yield to Russia the territory it had lost in the 'Winter War', plus some additional territory that gave Russia a common frontier with Norway. Austria was restored to its pre-*Anschluss* frontiers, and even Czechoslovakia had to give up some territory to Russia, losing Subcarpatho Ruthenia. Like Hungary, Czechoslovakia now had a border with the Soviet Union. These common borders would greatly assist Soviet control of both countries. Although peace was not made with Germany, 'temporary' arrangements were treated by its eastern neighbours as final. In accordance with Potsdam, East Prussia was partitioned between Poland and the USSR: the USSR received the northern half of Königsberg. Poland gained territory up to the Oder–Neisse line but, as has been noted, lost land to the east of the Curzon line to Russia. The Baltic states were incorporated in the Soviet Union.

A feature of the post-1945 settlement, if settlement is not an inapposite term, was the brutal displacement of population. Whereas in 1919 the attempt had been made to make frontiers coincide with ethnic divisions, the less civilized world of 1945 saw the device of making ethnic divisions fit frontiers. In particular, millions of Germans were expelled from East Prussia, from the German territory ceded to Poland and from the Sudetenland, while there were parallel movements of Poles from the territory ceded to Russia into that gained from Germany.

Such movements, which we will return to below, were both part of and symbolize the general westward momentum of eastern Europe. The eastward momentum of Germans over many centuries was instantly reversed, and the westward social, political and cultural inclination of the old Habsburg Empire was abruptly ended. *Mitteleuropa*, or central Europe, was, for several decades at least, to be eastern Europe.

2   SOCIAL CHANGE

Social geography

The effect of World War II on the size of the population within different countries and on the distribution of population in Europe was enormous, and the consequences are still being felt. The war resulted not only in a colossal loss of life but in the intra-European migration of vast numbers of people, both during the war and because of the victories and defeats of armies, and at its end because of the realignment of frontiers and the desire of many to escape new uncongenial regimes.

Exercise   Do you suppose that the loss of life in World War II was greater or less than in World War I? ■

Specimen answer and discussion   The loss of life in World War II was far greater, and this was largely due to the very high war losses in east, central and southern Europe. Two new factors were the many deaths due to bombing and those due to the deliberate extermination of civilians. As with World War I, one must consider the impact on fertility and mortality as well as losses directly due to the fighting. It would be understandable if you got the above answer wrong, for the losses of World War II are not seared in the British memory in the way that those of World War I are. British and, indeed, French losses were far fewer. Consult the war memorial in your own town or village and the servicemen commemorated on it for having died in World War II will be much fewer in number than those who fell in the Great War. Of course, British civilian casualties were far greater than in the previous conflict (30,000 were killed during the Blitz, and the total for civilian casualties during the war was approximately 60,000, while until September 1941 the enemy had killed more civilians than combatants), but by the end of the war Britain with some 260,000 victims of war and France with 620,000 had both suffered far less than in World War I.

One estimate is that European military losses were about 14 million and that civilians killed amounted to about 27 million (Norman Davies, *Europe: A History*, 1996, p.1328). The loss of life in central and eastern Europe was enormous: Poland lost more than 20 per cent of its total population and Yugoslavia 10 per cent, while around 5 million Germans died. The Soviet Union's overall military losses were over 8 million and Davies's figures for Russian civilians killed in the war are between 16 and 19 million. □

Russian figures are much disputed in large part because census figures are of dubious accuracy, not just because of difficulties in collecting them but because they were adjusted for political reasons. Estimates of wartime deaths range from excess deaths (i.e. the number of deaths above the pre-war norm, taking the death rate of 1940 as the base) of 26.6–35.8 million. Military losses were probably greater than the estimate of the Soviet army of over 8.5 million, and Norman Davies's figures of 16–19 million are close to V. I. Kozlov's estimate of 15–20 million losses. It must be remembered, however, that such figures include 'the missing', prisoners who did not return and those who died from wounds, illness and accidents. Excess deaths among civilians are generally agreed to have been over 15 million. It must also be remembered that wartime deaths came on top of an abnormally high pre-war death rate due to famine, forced collectivization, purges, prison camps and internal exile. A recent careful study considers that 'the total number of excess deaths in 1927–38 may have amounted to some 10 million persons' (S. G. Wheatcroft and R. W. Davies, 'Population', 1994, p.77).

As with World War I, estimates of the effect of the war on the populations of individual countries are made difficult by changes in frontiers; for instance, the Soviet Union grew enormously in size, incorporating 360,000 sq km of new territory from other countries, and the three Baltic states with a combined population of 5.7 million.

Leszek Kosinski, in his *The Population of Europe* (1970), refers to the estimate of League of Nations demographic expert G. Frumkin that, excluding Albania and the European parts of the Soviet Union and Turkey, the population of Europe fell by 7.9 million between 1939 and 1945, a decline caused by 15.1 million direct war losses. These losses contributed to an excess of deaths over births of 3,160,000 and the removal of 4,770,000 prisoners of war outside Europe.

Figure 21–25.1 indicates percentage changes of population between 1940 and 1950 based on the territorial map of c.1970; it is taken from Kosinski's book. The figures, Kosinski admits, do not provide a fully satisfactory solution to the problem of getting accurate figures after the population transfers and boundary changes. Because he excludes all of the Soviet Union, the eastern boundaries of his Europe have all been changed by the war. However, it does demonstrate certain broad trends.

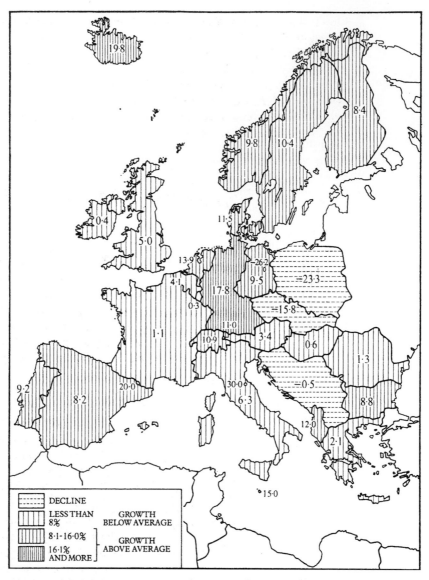

Figure 21–25.1 *Percentage changes of population 1940–45, based on the territories of countries as they were in 1970. The relevant changes since then are the re-unification of Germany and the fragmentation of Yugoslavia.*

(Source: Kosinski, *The Population of Europe*, 1970)

Exercise Look at Figure 21–25.1. What significant variations in population change do you detect? ■

Specimen answer 1 The decline or low rate of growth of central and east European countries with certain exceptions such as Albania and Bulgaria.

2 The relatively high rates of growth of neutral countries or those which were fought over for only short periods.

3   The highest rate of growth is achieved by West Germany. This last factor should alert us to the great migrations of population that accompanied and followed the war. □

The movement of population

The Nazi 'New Order' in east and central Europe saw an ambitious attempt to change ethnic maps of east and central Europe between 1939 and 1944. Basically this *Generalplan Ost* consisted of the expulsion of Czechs, Poles and Slovenes from lands incorporated into the expanded Germany and their replacement by some 1.5 million Germans either from areas of eastern Europe or from the interior of Germany. At the same time there was a movement into Germany of foreign workers recruited and forcibly mobilized to take the place of German workers drafted for military service. In 1944 this foreign workforce was estimated to be about seven or eight million, including five million civilians and two million prisoners of war.

With Germany's defeat in the east came a general westward movement of German civilians, but this left large numbers of Germans in Poland, Czechoslovakia and Hungary and, of course, in the eastern provinces of Germany which at the end of the war were incorporated into Poland.

The number of Germans transferred to within the new frontiers of occupied Germany between 1945 and 1949 was about six million. The German minority in Poland was thus much reduced, and only tiny numbers of Germans were left in Hungary and Czechoslovakia.

During 1939–40 there were large movements of population to and from the lands and countries incorporated in the USSR: some 485,000 Finns, for instance, were evacuated from the territory ceded by Finland and about 2.5 million Russians were settled in ex-Polish territory. By the time of Stalin's death 10 per cent of the population of the Baltic republics of Estonia, Latvia and Lithuania had been removed by several waves of deportations, with the population of Estonia being a quarter smaller than it had been at the time of the Russian occupation. The place of the indigenous population was to be taken by Russians brought in to work in new factories and to help secure Soviet control of the territories.

Germans were pushed westwards and their place was taken by Poles and Czechs; Poles and Czechs were in their turn pushed westwards and their place was taken by Russians. There were exchanges of population between Czechoslovakia and Hungary and between Hungary and Yugoslavia. Well over 200,000 Italians left territory gained by Yugoslavia, while 103,000 Hungarians were repatriated from Romania.

Macro-demographic trends

Prior to the war the rate of growth of the European population had been falling, with the west European rate slowing spectacularly and even the east European growth rate beginning to slow down. The west European growth rate had been 9 per cent in the period 1920–30 and 7 per cent over the ten years 1930–40. Between 1940 and 1950, however, the west European growth rate was to be the highest in Europe (8.1 per cent) and this trend continued for another two decades. Part of the west European increase can be attributed to a higher marriage rate followed by higher fertility in the post-war period. Even France overcame its long-term problem of low fertility. This trend should not automatically be seen as a result of the war, since the populations of neutral countries such as Ireland and Sweden saw similar increases. But the major factor for the high growth rate for western Europe was immigration into the region, particularly into West Germany but also into France and Switzerland. An important cause of the lower rates of population growth in eastern Europe in the years after the war was the constant decline of the population of East Germany until the building of the Berlin Wall in 1961, as migration to West Germany proceeded apace.

World War II thus had a very considerable impact, at least in the medium term, on the social geography of Europe. Though the loss of life was colossal, the shift of populations as a result of frontier changes and ideological pressures was probably the more significant factor. Movement of more than 25 million people took place. The importance of the German migration can be demonstrated by the fact that, excluding the Soviet Union, Germany with its pre-war frontiers had in 1939 the largest population in Europe, with 69.6 million people; the UK was second with 48.0 million. By 1950 the UK had the largest population with 50.3 million and West Germany was second with 47.8 million. But by 1966 West Germany was to head the list with 59.5 million and the UK was second with 54.7 million. Even today a stream of migrants from isolated German (*Volksdeutsche*) communities in Russia are making their way to their homeland of Germany.

Over the longer term it is doubtful whether the war's impact can be compared to the well-documented tendency towards a lower birth rate in technologically sophisticated societies, where children are not considered as an economic advantage. Thus Europe's population increase in the post-war decades was modest in comparison with that of Africa and Asia. The increase in eastern and southern Europe slowed from its already decreasing pre-war levels, but by the 1950s it was higher once more in southern than in northern Europe. Save for the haemorrhage of emigration to the west, it would also have been higher in eastern than in western Europe during that decade.

Urbanization

The term 'urbanization', like 'industrialization', becomes increasingly imprecise when we consider recent history. One sense in which urbanization is now often used is to describe the spread of an urban way of life into the countryside; in that sense rural areas of western Europe can be considered urbanized. Even if we take a yardstick such as population density, there may be no firm divide between town and country such as we could discern in much of nineteenth-century Europe, but a spectrum moving from densely populated towns or cities, through suburbia, to a more thinly populated countryside, with that spectrum disrupted by new towns. In considering cities and their respective sizes we are confronted with problems of definition. Do we go by legal and administrative definitions of cities, or do we consider conurbations?

The increased percentage of the urban population of Europe, despite a variety of definitions of urban (some legal, some based on population density, and some based on economic activity), was a major phenomenon of the post-war decades. The lead taken by western Europe in the process of urbanization continued to be reflected in post-war statistics. Only one of the ten most urbanized countries in Europe in 1960 was in east or southern Europe, namely

East Germany, while of the ten countries with the highest percentage of population employed outside agriculture, only two – East Germany and Czechoslovakia – were outside western Europe (Kosinski, *The Population of Europe*, 1970, p.102). But if western Europe was more heavily urbanized, parts of eastern Europe were rapidly moving in the same direction. The socialist regimes of eastern Europe pursued policies of deliberate urbanization creating new cities surrounded by dreary industrial factories. Poland, for instance, despite the destruction brought by the war, had eleven cities with populations over 100,000 in 1931 and twenty-three (with 25 per cent of the population) in 1966. The incredible case of Leningrad demonstrates how even a city reduced to a garrison at one stage in the war and unfavoured by central government in the post-war years nevertheless managed by the late 1950s to surpass its pre-war population level, while the proportion of the Russian population living in an urban environment passed the 56 per cent mark in the 1960s.

It was in western Europe that the polycentric urban systems identified by geographers as the most modern phase of high-density urban development became apparent in the immediate post-war decades. The four largest European conurbations by the early 1980s were London, the Rhine–Ruhr region, Paris and Randstad Holland. The Ruhr area was well established by the early twentieth century as a major zone of industrial/urban development, but its expansion into the major European conurbations – consisting of the areas of the Inner Ruhr (Essen–Dortmund–Duisberg), Hamm, Krefeld–Mönchen–Gladbach–Rheydt–Viersen, Düsseldorf, Wuppertal–Solingen–Remscheid, Cologne and Bonn – was the combined result of the German 'economic miracle' of the 1950s and the resettlement of German immigrants from East Germany and the *Volksdeutsche*.

Economic performance and theory

The haunting image of a Europe in ruins, a wasteland, pervades most accounts of the state of the European economy in 1945 and 1946. Walter Laqueur comments that, 'All visitors to central Europe reported a feeling of unreality: lunar landscapes dotted with enormous heaps of rubble and bomb craters, deserted and stinking ruins that had once been business centres and residential areas' (*Europe Since Hitler*, 1972, p.16). Richard Mayne refers to Europe, above all central and eastern Europe which had seen so much of the fiercest fighting, as:

> a land laid waste. In the cities, the skyline was jagged with destruction: amid the ruins and craters, rubble and wreckage blocked the streets ... Much of the countryside was charred and blackened. Mutilated trees, burned bushes, and fields ploughed by tank tracks marked the site of battles.
>
> (*The Recovery of Europe*, 1970, p.24)

You will notice that the titles of both the books from which I have quoted point towards the successful expansion of the European recovery from the nadir of 1945–46. Silver linings must have been pretty hard to find in the summer and autumn of 1945, but within a few pages of the quotation above, Laqueur is writing 'The preconditions for a spectacular recovery existed in 1945 but were hidden beneath the surface; not even the most sanguine expected rapid economic expansion' (p.7). Well, yes, sanguinity must also have been in short supply along with food, housing and clothing. Again, though, Laqueur is clearly correct in that a sustained recovery of the European economy, to say nothing of the social structure, was to take place in a very short period. By 1950 European output of almost everything was to be substantially above pre-war levels.

World War II and the years immediately after the war highlighted two economic developments: the European economy relative to the world economy had declined in its strength and importance from the position it had held earlier in the century; however, in absolute terms it not only remained dynamic and sophisticated but had considerable potential for expansion. The performance of the wartime economies of the European powers is instructive on both counts.

The wartime economies

Prior to the war, the more optimistic British politicians and commentators were inclined to point to weaknesses in German military preparedness and to cast doubts on Germany's ability to fight a war lasting any length of time. The success of German arms between 1939 and 1942 and Germany's ability to sustain its war effort for over five years would appear to have proved them entirely wrong. Yet there were weaknesses in the German military position in 1939: although the army was spearheaded by well-armed mobile divisions, much of the reserve was under-equipped and in the process of being trained, while munitions stocks were low; the surface navy was greatly inferior to the Royal Navy, even if U-boats were being produced in large numbers; and the *Luftwaffe*, although it outclassed the British and French air forces, also suffered from a lack of reserves. More importantly, given that it is the strength and the production power of the economy that are held to determine the potential military strength of a modern state, Germany's rapid rearmament had strained and overheated the economy, and had exposed the shortcomings of the administration and management of the economy within the national socialist state. Germany was also highly dependent upon imported raw materials, so there was some sense in the view that Germany was not in a good position to fight a long war.

Germany's success in the first stages of the war and its ability to withstand greatly superior odds for so long between 1942 and 1945 can be attributed in large part to a non-economic factor, the calibre and the operational doctrine of the German army. The use of tank formations and motorized infantry by Guderian in the French campaign of 1940 is an outstanding example of German operational doctrine, but throughout the war German training emphasized decentralized commands and maximum flexibility on the battlefield. To a considerable extent, therefore, German military ability was able to compensate not only for the fact that they were usually fighting an enemy numerically superior in men and tanks, but also for the shortcomings of the German economy and armaments production.

Another factor in Germany's early successes was that many of the problems facing the economy were able to be solved, at least in the short term, by the state's expansion. It has been suggested (see, for example, Tim Mason's 'Some origins of the Second World War', 1971) that the whole logic of German economic development under national socialism pointed towards the plundering of power and materials by wars of conquest. The answer to a heated economy and shortage of raw materials was found first in Czechoslovakia and then in the 'New Order' in east-central Europe. Germany was thus able to gain labour, raw materials and new productive capacity from its advance to the east. At the same time failings in the German economy and disadvantages in Germany's position against enemies actual and political were disguised by the nature of the 'phoney war' and by the pact with the Soviet Union which permitted Germany to take imports from eastern Europe without interference. Thus it was, according to Mason, that until 1942 Germany was able to do without the imposition of a total war economy – unlike Britain and, indeed, unlike the Soviet Union, whose economy was geared to war well in advance of the war.

Exercise You are already familiar with the article in the Course Reader, 'World War II and social change in Germany' by Mark Roseman (pp.238–254). Say how and why Roseman thinks Germany avoided a total war economy. (Pages 240–2 give you the outline of his arguments.) ■

Specimen answer and discussion For the first two years of the war Germany was able to fight a type of war suited to 'its state of half preparedness'. The Nazis were unwilling to impose too many sacrifices on the population. Competing authorities and interest groups made mobilization of the economy difficult. There was a reluctance to involve women in war work (here Roseman rather sneeringly refers to the 'traditional cosy bourgeois view on women's place at the hearth', though I personally can't see why either 'traditional' or 'cosy' should be considered pejorative words; the working classes have always been as attached to this idea as the middle classes). The exploitation of the occupied territories also served to protect the German population from the hardships resulting from a total war economy.

Here, it is suggested, is one of the great paradoxes of the war. The state which had been taken as virtually the model totalitarian state and the rhetoric of whose leaders was full of words like 'planning', 'corporation' and 'autarky' in fact allowed its business interests, its workers and its consumers to enjoy more 'business as usual', to take a phrase current in Britain at the beginning of World War I, than any other European participant.

But is Roseman correct in his analysis? Another article in the Reader with which you are familiar – 'Hitler's war and the German economy: a re-interpretation', by Richard Overy (pp.142–64), attacks the '*Blitzkrieg* economy' concept put forward by Roseman. ☐

Exercise Where does Overy disagree with Roseman? ■

Specimen answer and discussion Overy accepts the shortcomings of the German armaments programme in the early years of the war and agrees that before 1942 the German government did not restrict the civilian sector in favour of military production. This does not, of course, mean that there were plentiful consumer goods. He does not, however, think this was because the regime planned only to fight a short war or a number of short *Blitzkrieg*-type wars, nor that it was reluctant to impose sacrifices upon the civilian population. (In another article, 'Mobilization for total war in Germany' in the *English Historical Review* (1988), Overy has challenged the notion that the Reich made little use of female labour in the early stages of the war, asserting that a greater percentage of the female population was employed in Germany than in Britain.) According to Overy, Hitler planned a major war of conquest which he believed could last for a decade. However, he did not expect war to break out in 1939 with any of the great powers, and thus foreign policy and the economic preparations for war got out of step, 'a dislocation that was exacerbated after 1939 by a combination of poor planning, structural constraints within German industry, and weaknesses in the process of constructing and communicating policy'. As with so many issues relating to World War II, we come back to the central question of Hitler's plans and motives.

A successful mobilization of the German economy for total war only came with the appointment of Albert Speer, who became Minister of Munitions and Armament in February 1942, and with the realization of the desperate situation Germany was in, once the *Wehrmacht* had failed to knock out the Russians and the Americans had entered the war. Speer established a centralized machinery of control, the Central Planning Board, and by 1943 he had complete control of the economy. The production of armaments and munitions soared. This German economic miracle was based on a combination of centralized planning and a belated embargo on the production of luxury commodities, together with the intensified exploitation of occupied territories, the plundering of their raw materials, and the conscription of foreign labour, though Overy insists that the main factor was simply that under Speer existing resources were used better. Despite British and American concentration on destroying Germany's production capacity by bombing, Germany attained its highest levels of munitions production in August 1944, of aircraft in September 1944, and of weapons production in December 1944 (William Carr, *A History of Germany 1815–1945*, 1987, p.388).

The approach of the Soviet Union was very different. Indeed, one might say that for most of its history the Soviet Union has had, whether in war or peace, a war economy. During the 1920s the Soviet Union devoted some 12–16 per cent of the state budget to armaments (estimates from within the Soviet Union put the 1989 share at between 25 and 34 per cent), and although the percentage fell during the early 1930s, the years after Hitler's succession to power saw an accelerated armaments programme. But a concentration on armaments *per se* only gives us a partial picture, for the Soviet Union's potential strength as a military power lay in the fact that private consumption's share of Gross National Product (GNP) had already been driven down to an abysmally low level, and the resources of the state had been directed to heavy industrial production; such industrial production both supported an armaments industry and could quickly be redirected to concentrate upon it. Thus despite weaknesses in the Russian army due to the purging of nearly all its generals and colonels and the obsolescence of so many of its tanks and aircraft, the Soviet economy could move to a ruthless concentration on the production of armaments with greater ease than other European powers, and by 1940 the share of the state budget directed to armaments had increased to 32.6 per cent.

Table 21–25.1 shows the armaments production of the powers between 1940 and 1943, and illustrates a number of facets of the balance in military might between the powers. □

Exercise   What conclusions do you draw from Table 21–25.1? ■

Table 21–25.1 Armaments production 1940–43 (in billions of 1944 dollars)

	1940	1941	1943
Britain	3.5	6.5	11.1
USSR	(5.0)	8.5	13.9
US	(1.5)	4.5	37.5
Total of Allied combatants	3.5	19.5	62.5
Germany	6.0	6.0	13.8
Japan	(1.0)	2.0	4.5
Italy	0.75	1.0	—
Total of Axis combatants	6.75	9.0	18.3

Note: brackets indicate that these countries had not yet entered the war.

(Source: Paul Kennedy, *The Rise and Fall of the Great Powers*, 1988, p.355)

Specimen answer and discussion   The table clearly illustrates the large discrepancy between the opposing sides in terms of armaments production. It also reveals the massive part played by the US in that discrepancy. We can see a shortfall between German and Russian production in 1941, bearing out the view expressed previously that on its entry into the war Russia was already running a war economy. By 1943, although the USSR had greatly increased its production, Germany under Speer's direction had virtually equalled Soviet levels of production. The tremendous stride made by Britain between 1941 and 1943 is also revealed.

Clearly, had it not been for US involvement in this war, the sides would have been much more evenly matched, although even if we take Japanese and half of the American armaments production out of the picture in order to see the European sphere more clearly, Germany and Italy in 1941 and Germany alone in 1943 were failing to match Britain and the USSR, and were falling well short of Britain, the USSR and the US. □

Roberts comments that 'England and Russia achieved the greatest subordination of economy and society to the war effort' (p.445). As we have seen, this was scarcely surprising in the Russian instance, where both Russian history and communist doctrine supported the subordination of civil society to the state, and where everything had been subordinated to industrial production and armaments under a system of state planning before the war. But why and how did Britain, with its liberal and individual traditions, impose such a subordination of economy and society to the war effort and achieve such a startling leap in armaments production?

As Roberts suggests (p.445), 'the experience of the Great War was there to be drawn on'. Britain had gone a long way in the direction of 'war socialism' in the previous war, and the Lloyd George coalition had, in particular, identified itself with the idea that civil liberties, private property and consumers' needs and desires should be subordinated to the war effort. The legislation and planning machinery that had been prepared for the event of war was based on the assumption that a similar approach would be required for the next war. Britain thus went to war with the assumptions of 1918 rather than those of 1914, and these had been strengthened by the widespread popularity of 'planning' during the 1930s among centre and left political circles. The rearmament programme of the Baldwin and Chamberlain governments must, however, be given some credit for Britain's ability to expand its production lines so rapidly, especially as regards aircraft production. New factories rather than the immediate production of aircraft were the aim, and by1941 the efficiency of this approach was making itself felt.

The renewed emphasis on central planning in Britain during the war was endorsed by the economic section of the Cabinet and given maximum scope by the fact that Churchill left so much of the 'home front' to Labour ministers like Ernest Bevin at the Ministry of Labour, Herbert Morrison at the Home Office and, later on, Hugh Dalton at the Board of Trade. The government moved in a corporatist direction as Bevin attempted to enlist the support of trade union leaders for the direction and allocation of labour. An equality of hardship was imposed as rationing was introduced on clothes as well as food, and income tax rose to ten shillings (50p) in the pound; by 1941 personal consumption was 14 per cent less than in 1939. The coal mines, shipping and the railways came under government control. More and more of the population were working for the state in one way or another – 49 per cent by 1941 – and more of them were women as the government implemented conscription of the female population. This siege economy was in part supported by high taxation and a high level of personal savings, but above all it was based on the sale of Britain's dollar assets and financial aid from the US.

Britain's wartime controlled and planned economy was perceived by contemporaries as a great success, and it has been argued that this perception of the success of a state-controlled economy did much to ensure the Labour Party's victory at the 1945 general election. Britain, it was thought, had won through by harnessing the skills of its people and its resources by intelligent planning and with a beneficent egalitarian ethic which had melted class and industrial antagonisms. It was not just that the production figures were so impressive; there were the major technological and scientific innovations that the war effort had produced – penicillin, jet-propelled aircraft, radar, the deciphering techniques that cracked enemy codes, major innovations in photographic equipment and, of course, Britain's contribution to the atomic bomb. Britain's success in the war was to be hailed as demonstrating the advanced state of its science and technology, the resilience of its manufacturing capability, and the miracles wrought by planning, collectivism and the generous participation of all classes in the war effort.

A rosy picture? Or was it a mirage? Was the true picture much bleaker, as Correlli Barnett has argued in *The Audit of War: The Illusions and Reality of Britain as a Great Nation* (1986)? It is true, argues Barnett, that the war produced some specialized products such as highspeed cameras and Rolls-Royce engines and a major advance for one industry, chemicals, but otherwise the war found Britain wanting in every branch of second industrial revolution technology. The much vaunted effects of wartime controls and planning resulted in low productivity per person. The image of the enthusiasm and dedication of shipyard workers returning to yards unused since the 1920s – presented by the wartime propaganda film *Tyneside Story* (Video 2, item 17) – can be contrasted with the rigid adherence to craft demarcations and the over-manning insisted upon by unions. Far from a 'people's war' with everyone working for a common cause, the figures for strikes and absenteeism during the war reveal a home front in which the trade unions and workforce simply took advantage of wartime full employment. The impressive figures for war production can be seen as being possible only because of lend-lease and sterling area credit, which relieved Britain of any need to export.

Certainly, Britain's life-support system came in the shape of American dollars. The great economic phenomenon of the war, and the one that had the decisive impact in the European sphere as in the Pacific, was the astonishing growth of the US economy. The war revealed the degree to which during the Depression the US economy had been ticking over below its capacity. Stimulated by war expenditure, the American GNP measured in 1939 dollars grew from 38.6 billion in 1939 to 135 billion in 1945, by which time the value of the dollar stood much higher. Industrial expansion in the period 1940–44 grew by over 15 per cent a year, and the physical output of goods rose by over 50 per cent. Alone among the combatants, the US was able to expand the production of goods that were not part of the war effort, so that civilian standards of living were able to rise. By the end of the war the US not only possessed two-thirds of the world's gold reserves, but its economy produced a third of the world's goods of all types (figures taken from Paul Kennedy, *The Rise and Fall of the Great Powers*, 1988, pp.357–8), while at the same time its aid buttressed its European allies.

As the war moved towards its close, the dictum that economic strength combined with manpower would prevail in modern war was being fulfilled. The efforts and ingenuity of Speer and Germany's industrial managers and workforce enabled Germany to produce 17,800 tanks and 39,807 aircraft in 1944, but these totals must be compared with those of the Allies. In the same year the US produced 17,500 tanks (29,500 in 1943), Russia 29,000 and Britain 5,000, the US produced 96,318 aircraft, Russia 40,300 and Britain 26,461 (figures again from Kennedy; as Kennedy points out, the fact that the Anglo-American figures include a large number of heavy bombers disguises the even greater strength of Allied air power). It became clear also that the end of the war would witness (a) a German economy which, although it had reached its production peak in the war's penultimate year, would be severely damaged and dislocated by the final months of the conflict; (b) a Soviet Union capable of sustaining great levels of war production but with the rest of the economy in an abysmal state; (c) a Britain over-strained and over-stretched by its military and economic effort; and (d) an American economy in a position to dominate the post-war world.

We need now to consider what plans the Allied powers had made for the European economic crisis that was bound to follow the end of hostilities and whether the individual economic ambitions of the powers and their hopes for the economic shape of a post-war Europe were compatible.

The economic ambitions of the big three

The views of the three Allied powers, the US, the USSR and Britain, as to how to refashion the economic structure of the post-war world were, inevitably, conditioned by a mixture of their self-interest, their political and economic philosophies, and their relative strengths and weaknesses, together with their analysis of the failings of the world economy as it had existed in the 1930s. Just as inevitably, economic and political ambitions faded into each other.

Exercise What sorts of differences were likely to divide the Allies? ■

Specimen answer and discussion The USSR was a communist state and the ruble had never been a convertible currency, so one might well have expected that the Soviet Union would not be as eager as the western powers for the re-establishment of the international capitalist economy. In particular it would much prefer to keep capitalism well away from its own frontiers and wished to impose socialist economies on its east and central European neighbours. The sheer strength of the US economy, the economic powerhouse of the alliance against Hitler, was an invaluable asset to the Soviet Union during the war but could inspire Soviet fears that it would be overwhelmingly influential after the war, especially as the USSR, with the devastation heaped on it by the war, would be in poor condition to compete.

However, the situation was more complex than this, for there was no clear community of interests between the US and Britain any more than between the two western powers and the Soviet Union.

Since 1900 it had become increasingly obvious that the US was the dominant economic power in the world. If after World War I the US had withdrawn into political isolation, it had not withdrawn into economic isolation, and the implications of its actions and its fortunes had been profound, whether as the underwriter of agreements over German war reparations via the Dawes and Young plans or as the catalyst for the Depression as the effects of the Wall Street Crash reverberated around the European economies. American economic policy towards the outside world since the late nineteenth century had combined a demand for 'open doors' for American goods with a readiness to impose protective tariffs wherever American industries were threatened.

The 1930s had been a period of protectionism during which most states had sought to protect their native industries against foreign goods, with adverse consequences for the international economy; the United States had been no exception. Yet the New Deal had not been very successful in taking the American economy out of depression – far less successful than Hitler's economic policies for Germany – and it was essentially the effects of World War II and the need for armaments that gave the US full employment and got its industries humming. Even the vast US home market was arguably insufficient to absorb the State's productive capacity on a peacetime basis. By the early 1940s not only was American political policy moving away from isolationism, but American economic policy was becoming posited on a belief in international free trade, which would open up the world to American goods. Like Victorian Britain before it, the US, coming into its prime, believed that a free trade dominated by the most successful economy, itself, was not only in its own best interests but a positive moral good which would both lead to prosperity and bring liberal values in its wake.

The post-war world was almost certain to see an American economy, untouched by bombing or by fighting on its own territory, suffering from problems of over-capacity and in search of markets, and a Soviet economy, devastated by war and disabled by inefficiencies endemic to its system, suffering from problems of under-capacity. The Soviet leadership, not surprisingly, did not welcome the prospect of seeing the Soviet Union drawn into a world economy dominated by the US and the dollar, although it might have made Soviet society more prosperous. Though prepared to accept American aid in the short term, the Soviet Union was determined to keep its own economy, those of its neighbours in eastern and central Europe, and as much of Germany as possible out of a future world economy dominated by the US.

Britain, the free trading power *par excellence* in the late nineteenth and early twentieth centuries, was also threatened by US economic ambition. With many world markets closed because of protectionist policies, Britain in the 1930s had increasingly relied on the empire and the sterling area for its exports and imports. From the time of the lend-lease agreement onwards, the US was bent on exacting as the price for its aid the end of the sterling area and imperial protection. As Wilfred Loth has written:

> Negotiations with the British Allied partner which were conducted from Washington at a very early date on account of the economic importance of Great Britain in the pre-war world, turned out to be an endless series of American demands for liberalisation, British refusals, American threats of the most brutal nature and eventual British capitulation out of their concern for the indispensable support of the Americans.
>
> (*The Division of the World*, 1988, p.24)

Neville Chamberlain's fear that another war would mean the end of the British Empire and the further decline of Britain's economic position was being fulfilled.

On strictly economic grounds Soviet and British fears of a world economy dominated by the US and the dollar were probably unjustified. It can be argued that the world economy works best when dominated by a single power and a single economy – Britain and sterling before World War I and, as events were to show, the US and the dollar between 1945 and 1970. It also seems true, as Paul Kennedy (1988) argues, that, just as political dominance contains within it the seeds of decline as the dominant power taxes its strength and its worldwide military commitments, so the corollary of economic supremacy, the possession of the strongest currency, has effects which are by no means entirely to the benefit of the possessor. The stimulation of the west European economy by the US after 1947 was, for instance, to be as economically necessary to the US as it was politically desirable. But neither Britain nor the USSR were thinking purely of the long-term economic effects of the emerging US-controlled world economy; they were more concerned at the effects of such a development on their political and strategic positions. □

The problems of Germany

Although the Allied powers had their economic ambitions and fears for the shape of the world and European economies after the war, they were muddled and even individually inconsistent as to policies for the immediate economic problems that Europe would face at the end of hostilities. The defeat of

Germany and its east and central European allies was bound to leave an economic hole in the centre of Europe. From the late 1930s the *Reichsmark* regime of east-central Europe had increasingly become an economic unit dependent upon Germany. This *Reichsmark* area had indeed prospered up until 1942, and Austria and much of eastern Europe had rapidly industrialized. In many ways the economic effects of the Nazi New Order were beneficial, with rises in real wages in Bohemia–Moravia and mini-booms in Slovakia, Hungary and Romania. Soviet policy at the end of war was clearly to reverse the direction of these economies towards the Soviet Union, while the Anglo–American aim was to co-opt these states into a multilateral free trade system. But what of Germany itself, the strongest economic power in continental Europe since the early twentieth century?

Exercise   Bearing in mind what had happened after World War I, what do you think was the Allies' view as to what should be done about the German economy? ■

Specimen answer   They could have adopted one of two contradictory views:

(a) They could have gone along with the Keynesian analysis of Versailles and seen reparations and the desire to punish Germany as having led to a German economic weakness in the early 1920s which had had deleterious repercussions on the whole European economy, as well as fuelling German desires for revenge.

(b) They could have taken the view that Versailles was in fact 'too lenient for its own severity', as Tony Lentin has described it, and argued that the German economy should be permanently weakened. □

Their initial view was close to that of (b), but from 1946 on, the Allies increasingly favoured the reconstruction of the German economy.

Such views could not, of course, be disassociated from plans for Germany's political future. The decision to demand unconditional surrender from Germany ensured that Germany (and most of central Europe) would have its economy temporarily destroyed, while the eventual agreement to divide the state into four zones of occupation resulted in four very different policies towards the economies of those zones. The most important difference was to be between policy in the Soviet zone and that in the rest.

The most explicit plan for the permanent destruction of Germany's capacity for industrial production was that put forward by the US Secretary of the Treasury, Henry Morgenthau, who demanded that all but the lightest of German industries be dismantled and that the country be made 'primarily agricultural and pastoral in character'. For a time such ideas interested Roosevelt: 'If I had my way, I would keep Germany on the breadline for the next twenty-five years.' Furthermore, he stated, 'We have either to castrate the German people or ... treat them in such a manner ... that they just can't go on reproducing people who want to continue in the way they have in the past.' Churchill's response was that the result of such a plan would be that 'England would be chained to a dead body'. 'I'm all for disarming Germany', he said, 'but we ought not to prevent her living decently.' Even Churchill departed from this magnanimity for a while, arguing for the destruction of the principal industries of the Ruhr and the Saar, although by 1945 he had returned to his previous moderation. Roosevelt and his successor, Truman, distanced themselves from the Morgenthau plan. Yet its influence can be discerned in the directive JCS/1067 drawn up by the US Joint Chiefs of Staff to guide their occupation authorities. By this, 'no steps looking forward to the rehabilitation of Germany, or designed to maintain or strengthen the German economy should be taken'. Between a Soviet Union which at Yalta had demanded that Germany pay 20,000 million dollars' worth of reparations in the form of plants, goods and labour, and a US which seemed destined to leave the German economy in whatever parlous state it was in at the end of the war, the future of the economic heartland of Europe did not seem good.

The economic wasteland

The economic crisis that awaited Europe at the end of the war was by no means to be confined to Germany and its allies, and there can be little doubt that the victorious powers had made inadequate plans for dealing with it. The Soviet Union was essentially concerned to salvage its own ailing and war-stricken economy by exacting resources from Germany and east-central Europe, while what plans the western Allies made were based on colossal underestimates of how great the economic crisis would be.

Early in the war, Churchill had pledged British relief to continental Europe, and the decision to set up the United Nations Relief and Rehabilitation Administration (UNRRA) in 1943 followed this spirit. UNRRA was to do a good deal in countries such as Italy, Poland, Austria and Greece by dispensing food, clothing, raw materials and even machinery, but, largely because the US government feared that Congress would frown upon long-term assistance to future industrial competitors, none of its aid was supposed to go to the long-term rehabilitation of economies. Nor was aid supposed to go to ex-enemy countries, though in practice Austria and Italy came to be admitted, and to a lesser degree Finland and Hungary. A means test was imposed on potential recipients, so that those who had means of foreign exchange were disbarred. This excluded the greater part of western Europe, and Britain, France, Belgium, the Netherlands, Luxemburg, Norway and Denmark did not apply for aid.

What was available to such countries up until the end of the war was lend-lease. Originally designed to provide defence equipment to the recipients, the principle of lend-lease became widely interpreted by Roosevelt: 'Success in restoring the countries we free will be a powerful factor in shortening the war and giving the liberated peoples their chance to share in the victory' (quoted in Mayne, *The Recovery of Europe*, 1970, p.68). But lend-lease ceased immediately on Germany's surrender; even ships carrying lend-lease goods turned around and began to unload in American ports. Although Truman quickly rescinded the order for the discontinuance of lend-lease made in May 1945, the programme was finally cancelled five days after the end of the war in the Far East. It ensured that a devastated Europe and a near-bankrupt Britain were without any effective form of US aid.

The extent of that devastation must now be briefly investigated. It was such that many experts thought that economic recovery could take many decades. Not only was the loss of human life due to World War II much greater than that caused by World War I, but material losses were also much greater.

Exercise Which areas of Europe and which countries do you suppose suffered the most extensive devastation? ∎

Specimen answer and discussion Central Europe was particularly badly affected because there the German army, which had battled for every mile on all fronts, was accompanied in its retreat by many civilians as the advancing Russians looted and ransacked. But every part of Europe where there had been fierce fighting exhibited its wounds: Poland and Russia, Yugoslavia and Greece, Italy and northern France, Belgium, Holland, Germany, Austria, Hungary and Czechoslovakia. Britain might have seen no land battles, but air raids had done damage enough. Warsaw and Berlin were almost completely destroyed, and virtually every major city in the countries involved in the war had suffered extensive damage, with only Paris, Prague, Brussels and Rome among capitals escaping large-scale destruction. The scorched earth policies adopted by the Russians and the Germans in their respective retreats had left millions homeless and had destroyed not only industry but also farms and crops; to the west, the invasion of France by the Allied forces had resulted in enormous destruction to the coastal and northern region, while in Holland large areas had been flooded.

The devastation was much more general than that which had been caused by World War I. That many wondered whether reconstruction in some areas was even possible is illustrated by the case of Berlin:

> Ninety-five per cent of its urban area lay in ruins. There were three thousand broken water mains, and only twenty-five stations out of eighty were in operation. 149 of the city's schools had been demolished, and not one of its 187 Evangelical Churches was untouched. In the streets were over 400 million cubic metres of rubble: one estimate reckoned that if ten trains a day with fifty wagons each were used to remove it, the process would take sixteen years.

(Mayne, *The Recovery of Europe*, 1970, p.30) □

The pressing economic problems that were either pan-European or affected much of Europe were formidable:

1 Most basic of all there was a widespread shortage of food. Immense tracts of arable land had been laid waste and nearly 40 per cent of Europe's livestock was gone. There were shortages of seed, fertilizers, pesticides, draught animals and agricultural machinery. Hunger was therefore a common problem and malnutrition a threat. The countryside was not always eager to supply the towns and be paid in inflated currency, so peasants ate better than urban dwellers and black markets flourished. A United Nations report suggested that in 1946 140 million Europeans were receiving fewer than 2,000 calories a day and 100 million of them less than 1,500 (quoted in Mayne, p.74).

2 Industry, where it had not been damaged by enemy action, was beset by shortages of machinery, raw materials and power. Coal production outside the Soviet Union was down to two-fifths of its pre-war level and electricity supplies accordingly found it difficult to cope with demand. Production capacity was therefore almost everywhere greatly below pre-war levels.

3   Communications problems were caused by paralysed transport systems: roads and bridges were closed or impassable, vast numbers of vehicles had been destroyed, canals and rivers were unnavigable, and long stretches of railway tracks were out of commission.

4   War is an expensive business: bombing and shelling destroys fixed assets, military expenditure diverts money from investment in civilian industrial production, and most governments find it necessary to sell assets and get into debt. As in World War I, Britain, faced with greatly increased expenditure and with many export markets closed, was forced to liquidate overseas investments (worth £1,118 million) and borrow heavily from the US. All European participants on the Allied side were recipients of lend-lease, but when that ended Britain, France, Belgium and the Netherlands found it necessary to raise US loans.

5   Inflation affected most European countries and was worst in Belgium, Bulgaria, Czechoslovakia, Finland, France, the Netherlands, Norway, Spain and Turkey. In Greece and Hungary the currencies collapsed completely, while Germany became a barter economy with cigarettes the main means of exchange.

Certain features were common to most of the European economies in the immediate post-war years. Almost everywhere the standard of living fell *after* the war. Victorious powers like Britain and France were dismayed to find that there were few fruits of victory. Rationing intensified in Britain: bread, which had never been rationed during the war, was rationed in 1946. In France all goods were scarce, inflation soared, and an enormous black market defied attempts at regulation. It was no great comfort to the British and French to know that things were incomparably worse in defeated Germany and in east and central Europe, where the individualist looting by Red Army units paled in comparison to the looting by the Soviet government of the raw materials and the factory machinery from the countries it controlled.

Reflecting a general political shift towards the left, the tendency in the immediate post-war years was for a move towards statism and collectivism in the European economies. The process of war elevates the state and results in a diminution of the individual's economic and political rights. Societies emerged from war accustomed to look to the state for decision making. Shortages resulted in demands for government intervention in the interests of 'fairness'. The great nostrum of the centre-left during the inter-war period had been central planning. Now, with the immensity of the task of post-war reconstruction before them and accustomed to government direction during the war, many European societies turned towards major extensions of public welfare and public ownership.

British historians are, not unnaturally, divided about the effects of the post-war Labour government's shift towards central planning and increased social welfare. For Kenneth Morgan, the record shows that 'deliberate government policy' was able to 'significantly influence the geographical spread of new industry and employment', and the welfare state 'offered an essential base for future social advance (*Labour in Power 1945–51*, 1984). For Corelli Barnett (*The Audit of War*, 1986), the Labour Party in power were the architects of future decline. Grossly overestimating the success of collectivism and planning during the war, which had largely been paid for by American loans, Labour made a decrepit economy pay the price for a romantic social vision: 'By the time they took the bunting down from the streets after VE-Day and turned from the war to the future, the British ... had already written the broad scenario for Britain's post-war descent' (ibid., p.304).

State directives and controls were the order of the day, whether in Britain, France, the Netherlands, Italy or Germany, via the controls established by the Allies, to say nothing of eastern Europe as it was pushed increasingly towards the Soviet model. For a while such controls seemed to succeed well in reconstructing European economies.

We began this section with Walter Laqueur, who pointed to the fact that the preconditions of a European recovery existed but were 'hidden beneath the surface in 1945'. The infrastructure of the European economy had been damaged but not destroyed by the war and, if the last years of the war had destroyed industrial capacity, the early years of the war had actually seen it increase. The potential, especially strong in the western zones of Germany, remained, awaiting enlightened economic policies to release it. The possibility of agricultural innovation and the intensified use of agricultural machinery, which would release vast numbers for industrial production, was only beginning to be realized in continental Europe.

It may also be the case that the experience of war and the scientific and technological changes that came with it were to have some beneficial effect on the post-war economy. Besides the obvious benefits of medical advances associated with the war (sulphonamides, penicillin and anti-infection agents) and the discoveries and innovations which clearly demonstrated a potential for peacetime uses (more sophisticated photographic equipment, radar, the jet engine and the atom bomb) the challenge of war production had resulted in important changes in methods of production. Productive technology improved, more machine tools were used, and the organization and management of factories changed radically. The European combatants moved towards a more American model of industrial production which would allow the post-war German economy in particular to build on the experience of war.

Most of the preconditions for industrial recovery did indeed exist bar one – perhaps the most important, dollars. Many of the European countries' currencies were grossly inflated and their overseas assets had disappeared or were shrinking fast. Even trade between European countries was difficult, for a fistful of francs or lira was of dubious worth to the recipient, and a quasi barter system was resorted to. Exports were well below pre-war levels, and by 1947 Europe's current account deficit with the dollar area was 7,000 million dollars. In 1947 Europe's industrial production and its farm yields were still considerably below peacetime norms, and western Europe could no longer rely on food and raw materials from eastern Europe or the Far East. European governments urgently needed to import capital goods and farm machinery as well as food and raw materials, but lacked the money to pay.

The loans made by the US government since the war (650 million dollars to France, 3,750 million to Britain) had been inadequate and were quickly used up by 1947. Europe was living on capital and imports it could no longer afford. The American Congress showed little enthusiasm to make further loans.

The bad harvest of 1946 and the harsh winter of 1946–47 brought the crisis to a head, a crisis which appeared to imperil not only Europe's economic but also its social and political stability. It also affected Britain's ability to continue with its world political role.

Yet the crisis of 1947 was largely a financial or, more narrowly, a shortage of dollars crisis than the more general social and economic crisis it is made out to have been. The reconstruction of the European economy was bound to involve massive imports of capital goods from the US, and it was as much in America's as in Europe's interests that arrangements should be made to facilitate such imports and that this sensitive phase in European recovery be put in the past.

The US reaction to the European crisis was, however, not primarily determined by the needs and ambitions of the US economy. It was in large part determined by the fear of Russian and communist expansion. The US response and its economic and political repercussions will be considered in Unit 26.

Social structure

The central debate in considering social structure or class is over whether or not the experiences of World War II involved what is usually referred to as 'social levelling'. The phrase is in many ways an unsatisfactory one. The notion of class, whether Marxist or non-Marxist, involves a sense of social aggregates existing in some kind of hierarchy – of being inferior, or superior, to each other. If classes were 'levelled' (that is to say, brought to the same level), that would in effect mean the end of classes – that a 'classless society' had actually been achieved. (Indeed, many of those who use the phrase 'levelling' have in mind the idea of some kind of progress towards a classless society.) Since the article which I am going to ask you to read in a moment, 'The "levelling of class"' by Penny Summerfield in the Course Reader (pp.198–222), explicitly reacts to some writing of my own, I would like to make it clear that I do not myself anywhere speak of war as 'levelling' social classes. My book *Class; Image and Reality in Britain, France and the USA since 1930* (1990), to which Summerfield specifically refers, firmly concludes that Britain and France were still manifestly class societies in the 1970s. Mark Roseman, you may remember, in his article 'World War II and social change in Germany' (Course Reader, pp.238–54), did perceive some changes in the nature of class in West Germany between the Weimar Republic and the German Federal Republic, though he put as much weight on Hitler and the Americans as on the war itself. (Now is the time to bring to hand the notes you took, or the annotations you made on this article – see the exercise at p.54.) The debate, then, should be about how far there were changes – in the nature of class, in the social structure itself, in relationships between the classes, in attitudes about class in general and about individual classes; whether there were such changes, and what part, if any, the war experience played in them. Class, as we are all by now aware, is one of those topics in which the general approach one follows, the way in which one defines one's terms, can be significant in the answers one comes up with. Penny Summerfield's article is a splendid example of careful, meticulous research which deliberately avoids all easy generalizatons and places great emphasis on detailed quantitative analysis. You will find that you have to concentrate very carefully, but I think that if you do so you will feel the pleasure of joining with Summerfield in trying to tease out precise answers to precise questions. Regretfully, I do have to comment that since Summerfield concentrates on only one chapter of quite a large book, she misses the fact that I do, at the beginning of the book, make very clear what my own definition of class is. However, for present purposes it is much more important to be clear about the way in which Summerfield is defining class. Her article is extremely useful to us here for two main reasons. First, it gives a vivid insight into some of the detailed methodological problems inherent in trying to discuss class, and brings us into contact with the concrete realities of actual earning and expenditure which are so often obscured in wider generalizations. Second, it gives us an intriguing start to our comparative study of changes in class across Europe: if (allegedly) 'exceptional' Britain went through so little change, won't there be even less change in all of the other countries? Or, on the contrary, can we expect the more catastrophic events on the continent to have brought about much more significant change? It might be added that the article is a model of forensic skill, of how to develop an argument: in essence it takes in turn the arguments that have been made, or could be made, in favour of the thesis that there was 'levelling' because of the war, and rebuts each one in turn. As you read the article I want you to follow the careful stage-by-stage way in which the overall argument is built up; that in fact forms the purpose of the main exercise I am about to set. However, there are some other issues as well: for instance, the article is not, as Summerfield readily makes clear, a complete treatment of its subject.

Exercise   I suggest that you read once carefully through the entire article by Penny Summerfield in order to get a complete sense of its scope and structure, then go back through it noting down answers to the following questions.

1   How does Summerfield define class? What two aspects does it have? One of these aspects is deliberately omitted from this article: in what ways might one tackle that aspect? Entailed within this definition, what is taken to be a significant indicator of belonging to, or joining, the middle class?

2   What alternative way is there of defining class, and what criticisms of Summerfield's approach would it involve?

3   Now the main question. I want you to prepare a table in which you set out on the left-hand side each argument in favour of the 'levelling' hypothesis that is being discussed, and then on the right-hand side each answer made by Summerfield. ∎

Specimen answers   1   Class is an economic relationship, 'whether in terms of income, occupation
and discussion   or ownership of capital'. The two aspects are (a) stratification with respect to these economic categories, and (b) class consciousness and activity, or 'political identity of separate social classes'. To analyse the latter, one would presumably have to look at voting figures (to establish correlations between belonging to a particular class and voting for a particular political party), and membership of specific political or industrial organizations (political clubs, professional associations, trades unions). The indicator of middle classness is saving, or the 'accumulation of capital' (see, for example, the last sentence of the second paragraph on p.206).

2   An alternative definition would see class as involving more than an economic relationship (for example, lifestyle – where you live, what you eat, recreational activities, etc., what class you think you belong to, what class others think you belong to, whether your occupation, whatever the level of pay, is manual or not, etc.). It would query the automatic association between saving and middle classness (what class is a butcher, a bookmaker, a publican, in a working-class area?). Above all, it would query the notion of class consciousness as an indicator of class (arguing, for instance, that a man can be manifestly working class while having absolutely no political opinions, or, indeed, being a Conservative voter). It is possible to envisage a manual worker moving into a middle-class occupation, for instance bank clerk, without ever accumulating any capital.

3   My table looks like this:

Argument	*Rebuttal*
D. C. Marsh's argument, based on tax returns, that the gap between rich and poor had narrowed.	Tax returns are inaccurate, ignore those below taxable levels, and also the hidden income of the rich. They refer to individual, not family, income, and do not take account of inflation. In short, they do not deal with *real* incomes, and thus greatly exaggerate 'levelling up'.
Seers, Cole, and Westerguard and Resler all showed that there had been a 'levelling' of real incomes, partly because of the overall rise in the GNP during the war, and partly because of taxation and food subsidies. Change in taxation and subsidies polices after the war meant that the 'levelling' trend was short-lived.	Even so, the amount of levelling during the war may still have been over-stated. The figures dealt with overall growth in working-class incomes, rather than with growth in individual incomes. Also, the distinctions made between middle class and working class may not have been accurate (some of the growth may actually have been among middle-class incomes). Even if there was levelling up of incomes, a possibly more important question is that of the distribution of property. In fact, the investigations of Charles Madge showed that only a tiny minority of workers were saving towards the accumulation of capital.
Numbers in paid employment rose during the war, and average earnings rose by 80 per cent. Averages suggest that full employment made manual workers better off than they had been before the war.	But these are just averages. There were great differences between different groups within the working class, and there was no levelling between these groups: indeed (first paragraph on p.205) 'differentials widened'.
A small minority of men did have exceptionally high wartime earnings.	However, they did not use these earnings to save, and thus be assimilated into the middle class. Furthermore, their conditions of work, and their job security, was totally different from that of middle-class earners.

There was some improvement in conditions for working-class earners, and some deterioration for some middle-class earners. For some manual workers there were greater opportunities for promotion.

Government departments would have liked to have seen a levelling of income among manual workers.

But all that this adds up to is greater variety within the working class, without any automatic levelling up for the higher paid manual workers.

In fact, those in 'essential' industries did very well, but not those in 'non-essential' industries. Thus 'the war had the opposite effect on manual workers' earnings to 'levelling'. [One might possibly argue here that in moving from levelling between classes to levelling within the working class, Summerfield obscures an important point: she does seem to be admitting that *some* workers were levelled up; however, I suppose she could respond that she has already explained the limits upon that.] Arguments about general levelling are controverted not just by the variations in available income per head between families (large families being worst off), but also by the different practices of husbands in giving money to their wives.

Undoubtedly women's earnings made a significant contribution to family incomes in wartime.

But this did not amount to a general redistribution: it simply meant that there was more paid employment among wives of lower income than higher income husbands.

There was social mixing among women workers.

In fact, only a very tiny minority of women who took paid jobs in wartime came from the higher social classes (such women tended to prefer to go into voluntary work).

Women's wartime employment contributed more to the working-class share of the national income than to the middle-class share.

But the effects of this depended very much on the number of mouths to feed, other items needed, etc.

There was a levelling in the services.

Servicemen's wives were the 'new poor' of the war. In fact the service hierarchy was very energetically maintained, outside as well as inside the services.

The rise in the working-class share of the national income meant for that class (or a substantial part of it) a process of permanent 'levelling up', either between the working class and the middle class or within the ranks of the working class.

Probably the permanent levelling up affected only a tiny group of self-denying savers, while the war probably increased differentials rather than diminished them.

The relative fall in the middle-class share of the national income meant a permanent 'levelling down' for them. As Seers put it, 'the real net incomes of the working class had risen over nine per cent, and those of the middle class had fallen over seven per cent'.

In fact, Guy Routh's analysis of average earnings over a longer period than that of the war itself revealed that while lower-middle-class groups had done quite badly, some higher groups had actually improved their position. The picture 'was not one of overall levelling, but of differing fortunes for different groups'.

The shortage of manual labour in the munitions industries and the enhanced power of the trade unions narrowed differentials between middle-class and working-class occupations.

But, as Routh stated, the changes were only partly caused by changes in the pay of individual occupations, and were also caused by fluctuations in the numbers in different occupations. Some of the reduction in middle-class incomes could be explained by the substitution of female for male labour. Summerfield cites figures to indicate that there was indeed a great influx of women into white-collar work. Relative to the jobs done, women were even worse paid here than in the working-class jobs they took on.

There was a growth of a 'cross-class' group of low-salaried workers and better-paid manual workers, leading to a breakdown of all the class distinctions.

On the contrary, there is a good deal of evidence that mixing of social classes and other groups creates social friction.

Levelling of consumption (because of rationing, etc.) suggests a 'levelling of class'.

In fact, many middle-class families were making up for this, and in fact maintaining their positions by saving.

Discussion   I hope you were able to identify the main stages in argument and counter-argument, though you may not always have linked up the points on the right-hand side as I have done. Also, I have made the points on the left-hand side more extensively and repeatedly than Summerfield (who after all is writing a polished article, not producing a schematic table).

The general conclusion is that there was little in the way of social levelling, and possibly some trends in the other direction. I hope you noted the other major points made by Summerfield.

1   She describes her conclusions as 'tentative', and presents her article as 'an antidote to a focus entirely upon images and attitudes'. (The approach of my book on class does explore images and attitudes very fully, though it seeks to integrate these with statistical information.) It is not altogether clear whether Summerfield (given her very firm Marxist, or perhaps Weberian, definition at the beginning) feels that further light could be thrown by paying attention to images and attitudes. Anyway, that is what I shortly propose to do.

2   Summerfield usefully identifies the 'three camps' in the debate over war and class (this is in the second paragraph of p.199): 'those who believed that levelling took place in World War II and was permanent; those who argued that by some criteria levelling can be seen to have taken place but that it was

not necessarily permanent; and those who concluded that no levelling took place at all'. Keep these categories in mind for our discussion of the other European countries.

3   The argument contained in the last sentence of the first paragraph on p.212. You may well not have thought this sentence worthy of any special attention. I want you now to consider its significance. □

Exercise   Here is the sentence:

> It is almost irresistible to conclude (with Madge) that most male members of the working class were drinking and smoking their wartime 'excess incomes' rather than using them as a means by which to 'level up' socially, because for the majority such a shift in class position had very little meaning.

If this is true, what significance does it have in the debate on the 'levelling of class'? ∎

Specimen answer and discussion   Well, I do sympathize if you don't quite see what I am getting at. What is being said is that most of the working class weren't interested in moving up the social scale, in 'levelling of class' in that sense. Thus there is perhaps little point in worrying over whether the working class, or substantial numbers of them, did move up the social scale. What was presumably of importance to members of the working class was whether, within a basically unchanged class structure, their conditions, their job security, etc., improved. That is what I have argued took place; note, however, that the Summerfield article is most effectively questioning even that.

If Summerfield is correct, that would certainly throw serious doubt on the validity of the whole participation argument. It is my contention, Summerfield's excellent article notwithstanding, that the indispensable contribution of the working class to the war effort – whether in the forces or on the home front – the absolute necessity for keeping working-class morale high, and its strong market position, did produce clear gains over the condition of the working class in the 1930s, though these were within a broad class structure which (I have never maintained otherwise) did not significantly alter. I would make four points:

1   While I agree that Penny Summerfield is absolutely right in bringing out the variegated detail behind the broad averages, that some families were much better off than others, and that there were pockets of relative deprivation, she cannot escape the overall fact that working-class real earnings did steadily rise throughout the war and that (this is the really significant point which her article does not explore) these formed a platform for long-term change when immediately after the war new agreements on wages and hours ratified and perpetuated the broad 50 per cent gain in real earnings that had been made. If we are looking at the working class as a class, then we have to look at the aggregate figures relating to the class as a whole. The point Summerfield makes about the experience of individual families – particularly about women's earnings – is very important. But she leaves out of her account the fact that a significant section of the working class, as it was to be in the post-war years, was serving in the army and was not therefore included in the figure she quotes: what was important from the

longer-term point of view was that when these men came back they took up employment at the new enhanced wage rates. Certainly there were many difficulties and contrary cross-currents during the war, but there was a general upward movement in earnings levels once the war had ended. Without doubt, an important factor was the control on the cost of living exercised through food subsidies. Though these were removed in the post-war years, this did not necessarily have a serious adverse effect, since, in a time of high demand for labour, wage rates continued on the steady upward movement that (in contrast to the inter-war years) had been established. Average weekly earnings, standing at 53s 3d in October 1938, rose 30 per cent (while the cost of living rose 26 per cent) to 69s 2d in July 1940, and 80 per cent to 96s 1d in July 1945 (when the cost of living was only 31 per cent about 1938). □

Exercise   Turn to Document II.14 ('Wages and the cost of living in the United Kingdom, Germany, France, Italy and Serbia *c.* 1910–1955' in *Primary Sources II: Interwar and World War II*)

1   What happened year by year to real earnings throughout the war?

2   What was the overall gain in real earnings?

3   In what ways do overall changes in the period of the Second World War differ from those in the First World War?
Look carefully at all three columns. ■

Specimen answers   1   Compared with 1938, they had risen quite significantly during 1940. They
and discussion   then fell back very slightly in 1941, rising slightly above the 1940 figure in 1942. There was a very sharp rise in 1943, a considerable rise in 1944, and then a slight fall back in 1945 (though the figure was still above that of 1943). There was a further fall back in 1946, to just below the 1943 figure, then a rise in 1947 (though still below the 1944 figure), a fairly steady (with slight fluctuations) year-on-year series of rises.

2   If we compare 1938 with the average figure from 1946–50 there is an overall gain of 30–40 per cent.

3   The most striking comparison is that the cost of living rose much more sharply during the First World War than it did during the Second. Thus real earnings throughout the war, until 1918, were actually lower than they were in 1913. Thereafter, real wages do on the whole continue to rise, with some down-turns, but till 1926, they are only around 15 per cent up, and only reach over 25 per cent in 1930, compared with the 30 per cent at the end of World War II – which has gone on rising quite considerably up to 1955.

Wartime changes were ratified in 1946 when there were general reductions in the working week from 47–48 hours to 44 or 45. □

Continuing with my 'four main points':

2   That the workers were in a strong market position as against the employers, and a strong moral position as against the government, is shown in the way in which, despite the national emergency, and despite the overwhelming commitment of everyone to the defeat of Hitler, strike action was successfully resorted to. At the height of the war crisis in 1940 and 1941 there was a slight drop from the 1939 figures in the number of days lost due

to strikes, but thereafter there was no shyness on the part of local labour leaders over using their power to press their claims, and the number of days lost due to strikes steadily mounted throughout 1942, 1943 and 1944, dropping slightly in 1945, when it was still double that of 1939. Summerfield is absolutely right that workers in 'essential' industries did best; but my main point remains valid.

3   Attitudes towards the working class on the part of other sectors of society changed. I have to be careful here, having already talked about the prestige and status which the working class gained due to its participation in World War I. What essentially happened was that the working class became more homogeneous, the marginal elements of Edwardian times becoming established within the working class. The place of the working class in society was clearly recognized, but members of the working class were expected to stick very firmly in that place. A 'statutory working class' was clearly singled out in social welfare legislation as being the sole class to which such legislation applied. (This point is developed in my *Class: Image and Reality in Britain, France and the United States since 1930*, 1990, and summarized in my *A History of the Modern British Isles 1914–1999: Circumstances, Events and Outcomes*, 2000). While not utterly alone in suffering from the slump, it was the class which could expect nothing in the way of job security in the face of economic vicissitudes. Expressions of opinion, if unrelated to any actual action, do not count for much; yet if attitudes generally do change among a significant number of people, that is a change. Vested interests and entrenched attitudes do not change overnight; indeed, they often do not change at all. The balance between stirrings of change and a determination to retain the existing structure of relationships is well brought out in the history of a Ministry of Labour memorandum of September 1942 on industrial morale. The first draft was drawn up within the ministry, and depended upon reports sent in from all over the country by regional controllers, industrial relations officers, labour supply inspectors, all of whom were well qualified to present an authentic view of what was happening in the realm of industrial relations. Their draft provided a neat and true encapsulation of how the participation dimension of war was modifying the class relationship between employers and workers:

> Many employers still cherish the right to discipline their workers and to manage labour in their own way and resent the alleged curtailment of managerial rights. Management are slow to realise that times are changing and that their relationship with their work people must change also.

Yet a small committee of senior civil servants insisted on redrafting the passage in a manner which brings out well the resistance to, and total unwillingness to accept, any change in relationships between employers and workers:

> Many employers still consider it important that they should have the right to discipline and manage their workers in their own way, and dislike curtailment of managerial rights.

(Drafts from the Bevin papers, Churchill College, Cambridge)

But the Federation of British Industry had declared in respect of the London blitz, 'So great a people deserve the best', and was arguing two years later: 'we are on the threshold of a new world, and the theories and practices of the past cannot be taken for granted in the future'. 'It is hard', wrote Constantine Fitzgibbon, 'to persist in looking down upon or resenting a man who night after night is sharing the same dangers and doing exactly the same work as yourself' (*The Blitz*, 1957, p.118). The practical implications show themselves most obviously in government social policy at the end of the war, which would take me to the topic of social welfare. But if one simply concentrates on the literature associated with the establishment of the welfare state which poured out from the government presses after the war, one can see a complete change in tone from that of the official attitude towards the working class in the 1930s. Photographs, drawings and histograms proliferate: there is a clear intention to communicate in a civilized and friendly fashion with a wide audience, to be accessible to all.

4   The obverse of this point is that one can detect within the working class a greater self-confidence, a greater assertiveness. When, in his chairman's address to the 1941 conference of the Transport and General Workers' Union, Harry Edwards, a docker, expressed his conviction that this war was a 'people's war', he was echoing a sentiment which was remarkably widespread, as can be seen from the secret reports the government itself compiled on civilian attitudes, from letters sent abroad, which naturally passed through the hands of censors, and from private letters and diaries. Henry Penny, a London bus driver who wrote a diary on scraps of paper during the long nights in his air-raid shelter, noted in the early stages of the blitz: 'we are all in the "Front Line" and we realise it'. Throughout, his diary is marked by a tone of reasoned self-confidence, of pride in himself and his fellow working men, and by an acceptance of the established order of society and Churchill's leadership. A Methodist minister reported on his encounters with soldiers on leave: 'Most of them are thinking of a world where there will be better opportunities for everyone, and more economic security than there has been since the early ages of mankind.' (Reports on morale are filed with the Cabinet in the Public Records Office; the private papers are in the Imperial War Museum.) The mood continued in the post-war years. Here is a Transport and General Workers' conference chairman, Edgar E. Fryer, in 1949: 'Let there be no mistake about it, we have made substantial progress in working-class conditions during the lifetime of this government.' Here is a plumber interviewed in 1951:

> there is now so much work to be done and so little unemployment, so if the boss rattles at you or threatens you with the sack you can just up and leave. There is no poverty anymore so that makes a lot of difference. The working people are better off and the bosses have lost a lot of their grip.

> (Documents in Modern Records Centre, University of Warwick, and in Josephine Klein, *Samples from English Cultures*, 1965)

Labour politicians with manifestly proletarian attributes, such as Ernest Bevin and Herbert Morrison, were, and were seen to be, important members of the wartime government.

Whether or not the figures are used to support the idea of growing class consciousness (in Summerfield's sense, though this would cut across her main argument), they certainly do demonstrate an increased confidence and assertiveness. More workers than ever before voted Labour in 1945, which is one of the reasons for Labour's election victory; and trade union membership rose over the war period from 6 million in 1938 to 8 million in 1944.

Summerfield is right to be scornful of notions of 'social mixing' during the war. In the chapter from *Class: Image and Reality* to which Summerfield refers, I quote from the diary of a spinster who on the second day of war (somewhat prematurely one might think) remarked: 'there is one thing, and one only, about this war – it is an instant and complete leveller of "classes"'.

Throughout the war, and after, there was much talk in this vein: of the war 'breaking down' the social structure, 'levelling' or 'mixing' social classes, and creating class unity. To talk of levelling or breaking down the class structure might be to imply the differences between classes, in power, wealth, life-styles, and so on, were so reduced as to lose almost all significance, so that everyone was left on the same social plain. More often what was probably meant (the war did tend to provoke the exaggerations of genuine self-delusion as well as those of interested intent) was that significant reductions in class differences did indeed take place, but within a class structure which basically remained unchanged. Likewise with social mixing: this could imply that there was so much mobility, such a startling elevation of the material conditions of those lowest in the old hierarchy (the working class) and such an accretion of power to them, so many instances of miners hobnobbing with top civil servants, bank clerks issuing orders to barristers, and duchesses bunking down with dustmen, that the old class reference points had become meaningless. Or again mixing could simply mean that, within the recognizable continuance of the old structure, there was more mobility, and that, in greater numbers than ever before, members of different classes were associating with each other – 'mixing', indeed. Most of those who spoke of class unity were in fact recognizing the continued existence of classes: they did not usually mean that the nation was being united into one homogeneous class, but rather that the middle and upper classes were showing greater sympathy for, and understanding of the working class, and a greater willingness to support improvements in working-class conditions.

That is indeed what they meant, and that it did indeed coincide with what was really happening is what I endeavoured to show in that particular book. □

During the war itself, much was made of the experience of the evacuation of the country's children from urban areas likely to be bombed to safer rural areas. This was said at the time to have amounted to a 'social revolution' and to have aroused the conscience of the better-off in sympathy with the terrible plight of the products of the country's urban slums. Probably the ultimate wisdom has been pronounced in Travis L. Crosby's *The Impact of Civilian Evacuation in The Second World War* (1986): evacuation aroused as much bitterness between the classes as it did sympathetic responses on the part of middle-class individuals; it intensified working-class aspirations, and contributed to working-class determination to vote Labour in 1945. Cross-class encounters through air raids, and through evacuation, have been given too much attention. Where they did occur consistently throughout the war was in the voluntary activities almost exclusively undertaken by upper- and middle-class women. Summerfield is right to remove the majority of such women from alleged mixing in the factories, but she fails to allow for the 'social mixing' of voluntary air-raid, ambulance and canteen work.

There is certainly no need to weep over the fate of the various groups that make up the middle classes. But the fact is that taxation levels in the post-war years did remain far higher than would have been acceptable in the interwar years. That persistent upper class of which I have spoken several times continued to maintain its position (indeed, several leading members of the post-war Labour government, and almost all leading civil servants, belonged to it). In the upheavals of war this class recruited even more actively from below than previously (D. N. Chester – Sir Norman Chester – made his way up through being a wartime civil servant; Edward Heath through active service in the Royal Artillery). Broadly speaking, for the older established middle-ranking professional middle class, real disposable income was reduced. The research organization Mass-Observation, which in pre-war days had concentrated its attention on the working class, felt it worthwhile in 1949 to carry out two investigations into 'The London middle-class housewife and her food problems' and 'The London middle-class housewife and her expenditure'. In the previous year it also collected interview material which makes a fascinating source for 'images and attitudes'. A woman civil servant aged 50–60 declared:

> I definitely think of myself as middle-class. It is difficult to say why. I had a typical middle-class education (small private school and secondary school). I have a middle-class job and I live in a middle-class district. But none of these things would make me middle-class in themselves. If I had been clever enough to get a higher post or profession, or rebellious enough to choose a more attractive manual job, I should not thereby have changed my class. Nor should I change it by living in a different district. Besides, my education and job and residence (to a certain extent) were determined by the fact that my parents were middle-class, so it is like the old riddle of the hen and the egg. Income has something to do with it but is not in itself a deciding factor nowadays, as many working-class people get higher pay than the lower-middle class, and many upper-class 'new poor' get less.
>
> I suppose it is rather a question of being born into a family and social group with particular customs, outlook and way of life – a group, that is (in my case), in which it is normal for the children to go to a secondary school; which usually chooses 'black coat' or professional careers, but which cannot afford university education or the higher professions; which has a certain amount of leisure and culture and expects to have time for such things as books, music and social activities, but does not go in for extravagant

entertainment, expensive dinners and hotels, and so on; which chooses theatres in the balcony or pit rather than the stalls or gallery; which lives, generally, in dining room or lounge rather than in the kitchen or in various rooms for different times of the day; which speaks and writes generally correct English, and is, generally speaking, thrifty And so on!

(Mass-Observation archives, University of Sussex, file 3073)

My argument is that while the contemporary phrases 'levelling' and 'social mixing' are over-dramatic, they do refer to something which, in a rather limited way, did actually happen. The working class in general gained in living conditions and in self-confidence; it was treated less contemptuously by members of other social classes. While the class structure itself did not appreciably alter, much of the middle class relatively lost. The upper class remained mainly unchanged, but recruitment from below into the various élites expanded. Summerfield's case is that nothing changed. (My views about the positive effects of the Second World War – also presented in *The Home Front: The British and the Second World War* (1976) – are supported in Paul Addison, *The Road to 1945: British Politics and the Second World War* (1975), strongly opposed in Angus Calder, *The People's War: Britain 1939–45* (1969) and H. L. Smith (ed.), *War and Social Change: British Society in the Second World War* (1986), and *Britain in the Second World War: A Social History* (1996) and treated critically in Stephen Brooke, *Labour's War: The Labour Party during the Second World War* (1992) and Kevin Jefferys, *War and Reform: British Politics during the Second World War* (1994).

France

Let us see how these thoughts and counter-thoughts apply to the experience of France. Let me start once more with the notion of participation. Using this line of argument, one would expect social gains to be made by those who participated in the Resistance, in the Free French, and in the Liberation – particularly since a Liberation government was in power in the closing stages of the war. It is here that we should look for evidence of 'levelling' and 'mixing'. Associated with this approach is the idea that since the groups and classes that dominated in the interwar years had failed, their position in the social hierarchy would be adversely affected. This whole approach, then, contrasts the Vichy and collaborationist regime with that of the Liberation: participants in the former lose out; participants in the latter make gains. However, that view was challenged over forty years ago by the American historian Stanley Hoffmann in an article to which the much over-used adjective 'seminal' may properly be applied. For the moment, I just want to get at the essence of the Hoffmann thesis.

Exercise   Turn to Hoffmann's article 'The effects of World War II on French society and politics' in the Course Reader (pp.177–97). Just concentrate for the moment on reading the second paragraph. In discussing social change in France, how does Hoffmann relate the war to the 1930s, and how does he relate Vichy to the Liberation? ∎

Specimen answer and discussion   Hoffmann believes that the social system that had flourished since 1878 began to change in 1934 (and thus not with the war – here we have a curious parallel with what Roseman was saying about Germany), though the changes which amount to 'death blows' for the old system come with war itself. In this summary Hoffmann is not making any distinction between the Vichy regime and the Liberation: the changes began with Vichy in 1940, not with the Liberation in 1944.

Before attempting to sum up where all this takes us with regard to the effects of the war on class in France, let us see what the Resistance experience suggests in the way of levelling or mixing. □

Exercise   Turn to Documents II.15, II.16 and II.17 in *Primary Sources 2: Interwar and World War II*, the interviews with former resistance workers carried out by historian Rod Kedward in the early 1970s and printed in his *Resistance in Vichy France*.

1   As sources, what are the strengths and weaknesses, collectively and individually, of these documents?

2   What in them would tend to suggest that there was little or no levelling or mixing of classes?

3   What in them suggests that there was mixing or levelling of classes?

4   Which do you find more impressive, the evidence for question 2 or the evidence for question 3? ■

Specimen answers and discussion

1   Collectively, these documents have the strength that they are accounts by individuals who participated directly in the circumstances they are describing. (Also, the interviews were conducted by a highly qualified historian.) Even these three documents give us a range of social backgrounds and attitudes. (Kedward printed eighteen 'profiles' altogether; I shall mention some of the others shortly.) It is a strength of oral history that it can provide us with details that simply would not be available in any other sources. (Resistance workers did not have time, nor would it have been prudent, to keep diaries, and they certainly could not speak of their activities in letters, given the nature of the German censorship). The collective weakness of this oral history is that it was recorded thirty years after the events took place and thus depends on possibly fallible memories. There might always be a temptation for individuals to exaggerate their own roles. Clearly each individual had his or her own class and political viewpoint, which may have affected his/her perception. Malafosse call himself a patriot. He was rich (but this perhaps enhances the value of his testimony about the role of a working-class figure). Pestourie is a Communist Party member, Chauliac a pacifist socialist.

2   Wittingly, Pestourie would seem to be indicating an absence of 'mixing' when he says 'our Resistance was a class struggle' (on the other hand, in so far as this was successful, it could be held to be achieving 'levelling'). Chauliac brings out the point that the Resistance was not a movement of the people till August 1944: if it only involves a tiny minority, it can perhaps have little effect in mixing and levelling. Malafosse notes that 'we recruited mainly among workers', which would seem to suggest that there was not a lot of social mixing, though on the other hand it could have the effect of raising the status of those workers.

3   You have noted how, in giving answers to question 2, I felt bound to indicate points which more properly answer question 3. This is all part of the complexity of historical source material, which frequently does not point unambiguously in any one direction. For all his insistence on class struggle, Pestourie reveals that he did work with those whose concern was purely the liberation of the country and with 'good republicans'; he also admits that Gaullism (which was based on a notion of class unity) 'spread much faster than we did'. Chauliac states quite straightforwardly: 'there were all types of people in the Resistance. There was a great fraternity of different jobs and different political backgrounds.' Malafosse clearly is mixing 'downwards': as a barrister he defended Communist Party members – 'I was also a patriot, and more and more of a democrat.'

4   You can see the way in which the evidence can be read in different ways. For myself, I do think there is clear evidence of social mixing, of unity in a common purpose. But we do have to bear firmly in mind that until 1944 resistance was very much a minority activity (involving perhaps 4 per cent of the population). □

Note that Chauliac says that he never thought Pétain was playing 'a double game': this phrase is often used by supporters of the Vichy regime, and refers to the argument that, while pretending to collaborate with the Germans, Pétain was really looking after the best interests of the French people. This is not a part of the Hoffmann thesis, except in so far as Hoffmann says that Vichy felt it better to set up its own institutions of social and economic reorganization rather than have the Germans impose them. Kedward also interviewed an aristocratic landowner who traced his inheritance back six hundred years, declared himself 'a man of the Right, a man of order', an opponent of the Popular Front 'because it was revolutionary', and an upholder of the 'cardinal virtues' of *patrie* and *famille*.

> There were all types of people in the network by the end, though at the beginning it was the humble people who were most easily recruited. As Jaurès said, and Socialists do say something true occasionally, 'The fatherland is the only wealth of the poor'. No cottage door was ever closed to me in the Resistance.
>
> (*Primary Sources 2: Interwar and World War II*, Document II.17)

Another Kedward interviewee was a university-educated engineer in a small factory, who was a member of the main trade union confederation CGT. He noted signs of the Resistance as a social leveller:

> Within the Resistance, prejudices tended to disappear, since people were united by something essential – the defence of liberty, justice, dignity, and the fatherland. For myself Resistance was the direct continuation of my pre-war ideas. I had always dreamed of revolution, the remaking of the economic and political structure, and the movement towards a peaceful world of people united in a common cause. Resistance was a sense of Utopia, and it is always necessary to envisage Utopia, even though serious-minded people at the time saw this Resistance as mad and ridiculous.
>
> (*Primary Sources 2: Interwar and World War II*, Document II.16)

The needs of the Nazi war machine did, in a crude, ambivalent and strictly circumscribed way, confer a certain power on labour: there could be no concealing the essentiality of labour to the war effort, nor of the possibilities which labour had of sabotaging that effort. During the Liberation period a famous film, *La Battaille du Rail (The Battle of the Railways)* was made which symbolized the unique power that railway workers had to sabotage the Nazi war effort, and which celebrated their heroic participation in the national resistance.

With regard to the working class as a whole, I would say that the effects of World War II in the longer term were very similar in France to what they were in Britain. The working class did not change its position in the hierarchy, but it benefited from the social legislation introduced after the war, in accordance with the Liberation programme (see Document II.18, 'Programme of the CNR'). The experience of the Popular Front had shown how much resentment of, and contempt for, the relatively small and isolated working class existed throughout middle-class France. The way in which the working class was now integrated into French life is symbolized by the treatment of Léon Blum in the French newsreels: mocked in the 1930s, he is treated as a returning hero in 1945.

There is no need to embark on a controversy over wartime wages, such as is featured in the article by Summerfield (Course Reader). Workers in vital industries did have preferential rations, but in general during the war people suffered lower standards and much deprivation. Harsh conditions continued in the immediate post-war years, but in the long run wage standards after the war were relatively much better than they had been in the 1930s. However, this was due more to a world-wide upsurge in demand than to any participation in the war effort.

The one social group who were able to do quite well during the war were the peasants, as they could eat their own produce or make it available through the black market. Gérard Walter, in his *Histoire des paysans de France* (1963), argued convincingly that the war did substantially change and improve the lifestyle of the peasants (as industry continued to expand, the proportions of those working on the land declined sharply in the post-war years, but that does not negate the argument that those who remained enjoyed high living standards). Nevertheless, François Bédarida, in his contribution to the Open University conference on total war and social change, not only argued that the effects on the peasantry were temporary, but saw little other change in class relationships:

> From the point of view of relations between the classes, the war endorsed and accentuated the existing state of affairs, save with respect to one area, the relationship between town and country. As a result of the widespread shortages the peasants, the producers and purveyors of foodstuffs, acquired the dominant and privileged position, and they benefited greatly from inflation and the black market. Here we do have a reversal of a pre-war trend, but a temporary reversal, directly related to immediate circumstances, and one which disappeared towards the end of the 1940s when the food supply situation returned to normal. Apart from this temporary phenomenon, social mobility changed little, while class divisions tended to sharpen.

Bédarida does recognize that, 'Incontrovertibly there was a shift within the political élites'.

> New men, fresh from the clandestine struggle, now occupied the corridors of power. They were the ones who directed the government and held the ministerial portfolios in place of the figures of the Third Republic (Daladier never recovered from Munich; Reynaud was destroyed by the events of May to June 1940; Herriot was all but a shadow after the war ...). In the parliamentary assemblies, the phenomenon was no less marked: deputies and senators from the Third Republic had for the most part been cleared out and largely replaced by men (and some women) from the Resistance. The numerical importance of *Résistants* among those elected to the assemblies was to be one of the characteristics of the Fourth Republic throughout its entire existence, even if many notables in the localities survived all changes of regime.
>
> (Bédarida, 'World War II and social change in France', in A. Marwick (ed.) *Total War and Social Change,* 1988)

Bédarida also speaks of a 'profound regeneration both in business enterprises and in administration' and of 'the formation of a modernizing élite which took control of the commanding heights of the economy, here through new men taking positions of power, there through amalgamation with directors from former times.' Does this amount to a change in class composition? As with Britain, it amounts to changes *within* the upper class, much greater recruitment from below, and perhaps quite far below compared with Britain, taking into consideration the strongly working-class composition of the Resistance.

Italy

As in World War I, many Italian workers were subject to quasi-military discipline, and the Fascist regime was in any case very restrictive of workers' rights. However, after October 1939 representatives of the Fascist syndicates were sent into the main engineering factories to settle individual grievances and smooth over potential unrest. As always, workers' participation in vital national production had some pay-offs. Wages held up reasonably well until 1943, and workers secured extra unrationed food in factory canteens. But from the point of view of social change, the most important factor was the failure of the government to rise to the challenge of war: opportunities were thus created for workers, and political groups, to show their hostility to the Fascist regime. In October 1941 a Committee of Action was founded, bringing together liberals, republicans and liberal socialists, as well as communists and socialists; on 1 July 1942 *L'Unità*, the communist paper, reappeared as a clandestine monthly. In April 1943 came the United Freedom Front, which provided the essential basis of the collusion between Catholics, communists and socialists which carried through the reform policies of the post-war Italian republic. Allied bombing raids, against which defences were particularly ineffective, also helped to stir up discontent.

Document II.19 in *Primary Sources 2: Interwar and World War II*, the Committee of Action poster, shows how the disruption of bombing could be exploited by the Committee of Action both to denounce Mussolini, and to offer assistance itself during air raids. As we have seen, there are debates about the effectiveness and consequences of bombing. Partly because of the inherent weakness of the regime, the bombing of Italian cities did produce definite results with respect to disruptions in production, the shattering of morale, and causing people to flee from the cities. Workers in industrial plants were particularly vulnerable. By the end of 1942, 25,000 buildings had been wrecked in Turin and 500,000 people had left Milan. The government was forced to grant what was called the 192 hours evacuation allowance (that is to say, an extra month's wages). The government's subsequent decision that only heads of families who could prove that they had in fact moved house were to receive this allowance was one of the grievances which provoked the celebrated 'internal strikes' that began in Turin on 5 March 1943 and spread to other industrial centres in Piedmont, Milan, Bologna and Florence. The strikes took the form of downing tools for relatively short periods. But in a desperate war situation they were extremely effective, and on 2 April the government secured a return to work on the basis of a pay increase. Martin Clark, in his *Modern Italy*, 1996, p.289), has commented that: 'The strikes were the first mass protest demonstrations in Axis Europe; they revealed how weak the Fascist regime had become by March 1943.'

I now want you to read document II.20 in *Primary Sources 2: Interwar and World War II, L'Unità*'s report on the strike of 100,000 Turin workers, relating it to the information I have just given you. Later in these units I will set an exercise on this primary source.

It is a moot point whether (mainly non-violent) resistance to Mussolini, or the military resistance to the German occupation which took over in the north of Italy in September 1943 (see document II.21, the statement issued by Field Marshal Rommel) were more important in stimulating social change at the end of the war. Given that armed resistance was largely confined to the north of Italy – the Committee of National Liberation of northern Italy was formed on 17 October 1943 – while the Allies were advancing up through the southern half of Italy, it is probably true to say that the critical factor was the inadequacy of the Italian regime in face of war, rather than participation in resistance activities, though these contributed to the general reformist atmosphere at the end of the war. The popular rising of the ordinary people of Naples against the Germans in the 'four Days' at the end of September 1943 did bring some prestige to the working class in the south, while the great strike of March 1944 in the north again drew attention to the special role of the working class.

As elsewhere, then, the story is of general working-class gains (though intense privation after 1943) within a basically unaltered class structure. Wartime conditions were again favourable for the peasants who, as in France, could keep their food to themselves or put it on the black market. In the words of Martin Clark, 'As in 1915–18, many peasant families became relatively prosperous. They began buying land, and inflation soon reduced their mortgages. Sensing their chances, they simply ignored the regime: it was in the countryside, not the towns, that the Fascist system first collapsed.' Peasant resistance activity also, as Tannenbaum has stressed (*The Fascist Experience*, 1972, p.323), contributed to bringing them into the mainstream of Italian life.

Germany

I hope that you took the opportunity earlier to take notes from, or make annotations on, Mark Roseman's article on Germany in the Reader.

Exercise   What are the main points made by Roseman with respect to changes in class and the relationship of the war to these changes (we are talking here of outcomes in *West* Germany)? ■

Specimen answer   Roseman's first point is that the pre-war Nazi regime had already brought
and discussion   changes in class relationships, particularly with respect to mobility from manual to white-collar positions, upward mobility through Nazi organizations, and the abandonment of traditional working-class dress. The war maintained and, as Roseman says, increased the already high level of geographical and social mobility. This had long-term significance for rural communities and also substantial sections of the working class. With reference to the extension of working-class cultural horizons, note Roseman's phrase about 'war as the continuation of tourism by other means'. Both economic mobilization and the army itself offered opportunities for upward social mobility: 'in practice a good war career proved advantageous at most levels of the post-war job market.' Furthermore, the influx of foreign forced labour created 'a form of collective upward mobility for German workers.' Many German employees found themselves elevated to positions of overseers and foremen; from interviews, Roseman tells us, we know that many workers did perceive their new responsibilities as a sort of promotion. Roseman also sees war conditions as fostering harmonious relations between employers and workers. Again and again, though, Roseman returns to the importance of the pre-war period, throwing out more neat formulations:

> In general we can say that the war undermined the Nazis' own appeal while reinforcing many of the social changes which they had initiated in the 1930s ... Yet through isolation and terror, through collective and individual mobility and through the forging of new loyalties and solidarities, the war confirmed the Nazis' assault on class traditions ... Of greater long-term significance for the German working class were the subtler changes to perceptions, behaviour and relationships, above all the weakening of traditional class identities and antipathies which had been wrought by fascism and war.

Roseman also refers to the effect of the Allies in preventing 'the bitter conflicts between labour and capital that had resulted after 1918 and would otherwise probably have resulted after 1945.' Personally I am dubious about this reference to the influence of the Allies: Roseman seems to me to have already adequately explained the development in working-class attitudes. But that is yet another issue for you to think about. What is certainly beyond dispute is the emergence of a 'hard-working, consumer-orientated, sceptical and unpolitical working class'. As Roseman neatly adds, a strong suspicion of the bosses co-existed with the feeling that labour's status had collectively improved: 'The boom economy of the 1930s with its possibilities for individual advancement and the toughening experiences of soldiering and surviving the hardships of the Occupation years had encouraged in many workers a confidence in their ability to stand up to those in authority and to profit from the capitalist system.' □

It would be naive, I think, to take the view that the class structure that emerged in post-war West Germany was simply imposed on it by the Americans. Clearly some of the features of East Germany were determined by the Russian occupation, but Professor Ralf Dahrendorf, in his study of *Society and Democracy in Germany* (1969), brought out that in East Germany 'a society with its own peculiar structure has emerged'. In general, it was a society in which political élites replaced the upper and middle classes as they had developed in the early twentieth century. Specifically, there were major land reforms which brought a final ending to the pre-eminence of the Junker landowners, many of whom fled to the west. There was a working-class rise in status in that they were guaranteed social and economic rights in the form of full employment and welfare benefits. Dahrendorf has offered this comparison between the German Democratic Republic in the east and the Weimar republic:

> In the Weimar republic the role of the citizen was formally guaranteed to all, but this offer was undermined by the absence of the social preconditions of its realisation. In the DDR [German Democratic Republic] the preconditions are at present, but the realisation is made impossible by numerous formal restrictions on the citizenship rights that are part and parcel of the constitution of liberty. De facto, there is no universal, equal, free and secret suffrage, no liberty of the person and of political activity, no equality before the law; but there is a society that would enable its members to make effective use of these liberties, if only they had them.

The two Germanies after the war are discussed fully in Unit 27.

Russia

Russia suffered greater destruction and devastation, and greater loss of human life, relative to its population than any other country involved in World War II, save for Poland (see section 2.6 below). Yet such was the firm grip of the Soviet regime as it had established itself by the late 1930s, that it has been argued that far less in the way of change in the social structure took place there than in the other countries we have been discussing. The American analyst, Edward L. Keenan, put the matter this way in an article published in 1986:

> The very fact that this devastating war, more costly for Russia in human and economic terms even than the first, produced so few significant changes in the structure or political culture of Soviet society is, in my view, the most eloquent evidence that the society had become restabilized, and its political culture 're-knit', before the outbreak of the war. Evidence of long-term economic and social processes bears this out: the fundamental and dramatic processes of social change – industrialization, urbanization, the creation of the new élites – although they had not entirely run their course, were slowing by the beginning of the 'forties, and had already established the basic patterns and relationships that were to be reconstituted and redefined in the post-war period.
>
> (Keenan, 'Muscovite political folkways', *The Russian Review*, 45, 1986, pp.167–8)

Paul Dukes, who quotes the above passage from Keenan in his contribution to *Total War and Social Change*, links up with a debate which I identified in my Introduction in discussing Germany: he had suggested that Russia's relationships with the outside world in the 1940s imposed profound constraints on social change. In particular, the Cold War put a stop to any modifications in Soviet society which might have developed out of the war.

What evidence is there of change in social structure? It can be argued, and it has been argued by Susan J. Linz in her introduction to *The Impact of World War II on the Soviet Union* (1985), that in the Great Patriotic War internal war gave way to a new social cohesion. The effect of war service in broadening horizons was encapsulated in Roseman's phrase about 'war as tourism by other means'. Dukes has an even finer phrase to express that same idea: 'It was difficult to keep them down on the collective farm now that they had taken Berlin'.

The evacuation of industry eastwards (see Document II.22 in *Primary Sources 2: Interwar and World War II*) created an expansion in industrial employment. However, the extensive application of compulsion, the appallingly cramped accommodation, the generally low wages, meant that there were no gains for the working class. There was some talk during the war of improvements for the peasants (who suffered desperately at the hands of the Germans) but in fact in the post-war years very harsh quotas were imposed on the collective farms. It was, as Alec Nove has put it, 'as if Stalin was determined to make the peasants pay for the necessary post-war reconstruction' (*An Economic History of the USSR,*1972, p.298). The currency reform of December 1947 was in part meant to hit at black marketeers and those who had managed to hoard savings, but it failed to curb inflation, while the turnover tax payable by everyone was scarcely kind to the least well-off. There were no structural changes in the political élites, 'the new class', but Dukes has indicated that there were qualitative changes here (perhaps comparable with the kind of changes that took place in the upper class in western countries):

> Allowing for those dismissed from the Party, a guarded estimate indicates that about 75 per cent of the membership in 1952 had joined since the outbreak of war in June 1941, and that roughly the same percentage was under 45 years of age. While the bulk of the new recruits were of peasant and worker origin, they appear to have risen for the most part to managerial level. The educational level had gone up, too, the percentage of those having completed secondary education having climbed from less than 15 per cent in 1941 to about 20 per cent in 1947. In 1952, nearly 12 per cent had experienced some degree of higher education.
>
> (Dukes, 'The social consequences of World War II for the USSR', 1988, pp.54–5)

Other east European countries

With regard to the social structures of the other east European countries, the question that arises is this: is the critical factor their position within the Soviet sphere of influence, or are there any significant internal developments springing out of the experience of war? A number of issues need to be clarified:

1   We are now moving from the detailed study of relatively limited (though, I would maintain, still significant) changes within the major countries to a broad comparison taking Europe as a whole. Rather than taking the separate aspects of social structure, we are essentially taking social structure together with political systems and values. Just as one could ask whether the First World War contributed materially to the division in the interwar years between one-party dictatorships and liberal democracies, so now we are considering whether the Second World War contributed to the broad division of Europe between one-party communist states and liberal democracies.

2   We have to be clear about the distinction: is it really true to say that, with regard to the particular question of class and social structure, the two groups of societies are very different in terms of the position and status of the working class, the nature of the 'upper class', etc? Is one group more 'classless' than the other – has levelling proceeded further in one than in the other? Actually there were some structural changes which outweigh the ideological and political division of Europe, the most noteworthy being the acquisition of coalfields and industrial areas by the new westward-shunted Poland (although it lost agricultural areas): thus, for the first time Poland had the basis for a large, skilled industrial working class.

3   We have to be clear about when exactly the division of Europe came about. As hostilities ended, there was certainly an occupation of the two halves of Europe by, respectively, Soviet and western forces. But for a few years after 1945 there were coalition governments of various sorts, as well as forms of democratic government, in several of the countries later to fall within the eastern bloc.

4   How far is the division essentially a function of Russia's emergence as a world power (very definitely, of course, a consequence of the war) and how far, if at all, is it related to internal developments within the various countries, in particular with reference to occupation and resistance during the war?

5   It may be that, compared with the brute facts of the physical presence of Russian military power, all other issues are drained of significance. However, it would be worth looking at the nature of the various east European regimes and social systems as they were on the eve of war, with a view to asking whether, under the impact of war, they might have undergone some transformation even if Russia, after the war, had exercised a restraint not usual in great powers. Few east European regimes in the 1930s were full liberal democracies on the western model (Czechoslovakia is the noteworthy exception, but after 1938 it was in effect absorbed into the Nazi system.) Where there was manifestly Nazi or Fascist influence in pre-war regime, did that mean that oppositional impulses (which, as in Italy, might gain new opportunities in war) would be towards the Soviet system or the western one?

'Divided Europe' is a topic that is discussed in Unit 26.

In discussing the differences in social structure and class relations between eastern and western countries as they finally emerged, it is difficult to steer clear of overtly political judgements. Perhaps the extract I quoted from Dahrendorf with respect to East Germany is as good a basic proposition as any. There is, as in Russia, the problem of the particular nature of Stalin, and of the insecurities bred by the Cold War; might the east European societies otherwise have come closer to realizing the nobler aspects of Marxist philosophy? We know that these societies, while clearly not offering political liberties to their citizens, failed (even after allowance is made for the desperately destructive effects and after-effects of war, including the reparations exacted by Soviet Russia) to provide them with decent living standards. With regard to the other issues I have raised, let me conclude with a few questions which you should be able to answer on the basis of your reading in the course so far, including Roberts.

Exercise   1   Which east European country achieved a one-party socialist form of government and social system almost exclusively through the efforts of its own liberation fighters? Which foreign country provided most assistance?

2   Which east European country, left to its own devices, would have been most thoroughly opposed to any form of Soviet socialist system? Explain your answer.

3   In which country was there the greatest welcome for the Russians as genuine liberators from a detested previous regime? Explain your answer. ■

Specimen answers   1   Yugoslavia. Britain provided most assistance. (See Roberts, p.458–9; see also
and discussion   Document II.23 in *Primary Sources 2: Interwar and World War II*, the letter from Tito to the Italian command – I will discuss the context of this document later.)

2   Poland. Poland had been divided up between Russia and Germany at the beginning of the war (there is a catalogue of further Polish grievances against the Russians which I don't need to go into here). (See Roberts, p.458.)

3   Czechoslovakia. The western powers had failed to support Czechoslovakia's liberal democracy in 1938, the country in fact (in two stages) being handed over to the Nazis. (See Roberts, p.458–9.) □

National cohesion

In our discussions of the origins, causes and consequences of World War I, nationality was a prominent issue. In the eyes of idealists, World War I was in part fought over, and in part succeeded in, securing the rights of the different nationalities to their own independent nation-states. The question of nationality had featured most prominently with respect to the Austro-Hungarian Empire, but it was an issue which affected central and eastern Europe in general. Before the war, Russia figured largely in western eyes as the champion of all Slav populations; that Russia was itself a multinational empire only became more obvious in the later stages of the war. By the time of World War II, questions of nationality and race were being stridently emphasized in a rather different way.

Exercise   1   Which country was most outspoken on matters of nationality and race? Write a few sentences on this issue.

2   Which major power had very genuine nationality problems? Where else was nationality a significant issue immediately before or, more important, during the war?

3   What overall effect did the war have on nationalities? ■

Specimen answers and discussion

1   Germany. There are two, or perhaps three, aspects to the issue. A particularly obnoxious feature of Nazi philosophy was the emphasis on 'racial purity', involving anti-Semitism in particular. This led before the war to policies designed to expel Jews from Germany and, during the war, to their extermination. Associated with this was the notion of the *Herrenvolk* (the superior race), which entailed the deplorable treatment of perceived *Untermenschen* (sub-humans) such as the Slavs. At the same time there was the drive to unite all Germans, scattered as they were throughout central and eastern Europe, in one great German empire.

2   Russia (the problems had not gone away). As noted earlier by Bill Purdue, there were pockets of Germans throughout Europe: some had been dispersed for centuries, some found themselves included in a foreign country (for example, Poland or Belgium) because of the way in which the Versailles frontiers had been drawn. In Czechoslovakia, apart from the German minority in the Sudetenland, there was the problem of national rivalries between Czechs and Slovaks. There were Hungarian minorities in Romania and Poland. But the country I particularly hope you thought of is Yugoslavia, where the Germans and Italians were able to exploit the national rivalries between the Croats and the Serbs (remember from Unit 20 the setting up of the puppet kingdom in Croatia).

3   The two main points, which I hope you got, were that the war both induced great movements of population and also resulted in the redrawing of frontiers. The ultimate expression, as in so many other spheres, was Poland. After 1945 Poland was, for the first time in history, a homogeneous nation-state. Though its boundaries had been shunted westwards, the people within them, following the mass transfers of Germans, were exclusively Polish. There are rather more subtle, and perhaps more problematic, possible consequences. It is probably true that in some cases unity was forged in the face of the common German enemy (see Roberts, p.453). At the same time, given that the upheavals of war bring into question the legitimacy of certain states, and given that (as I have suggested) wars tend to stimulate communal feelings, there could be encouragement of national self-expression within established states. Both forces, I think, are true with respect to the growth of Flemish sentiment within Belgium, and the latter is important with respect to the growth of Scottish nationalism within the UK (where there were also particular grievances, such as the conscripting of Scottish girls to work in English factories). One point that you almost certainly will not have thought of is that with the dreadful destruction of male lives in the war, women, if they were to have a husband at all, often took one from outside their own national group. It has been argued that this was a factor in producing greater cohesion between the nationalities in Russia. □

One of the most tragic consequences of World War II was the destruction of European Jewry. In Germany, where Jews in the past had contributed so much to national culture, there was now a Jewish population that was only one-tenth of that of 1933. The post-war settlement left a number of areas of friction, those resulting for Russia and Poland moving westwards being ones I have already alluded to. The boundary between Italy and Yugoslavia was a matter of contention in the post-war years. A result of the settlement was the considerable transfer of populations. In many cases what people feared was not an alien national regime, but an alien form of government. On the whole it could be said that the general movement which had accelerated earlier in the century towards each nationality having its own nation-state was consolidated in the aftermath of World War II. If you turn to Document II.24 in *Primary Sources 2: Interwar and World War II*, 'Extracts from *Protocol of the Proceedings of the Potsdam Conference*', you will see that great transfers of German populations were envisaged, with only a rather cursory reference to these being carried out in an orderly and humane way.

In discussing the aftermath of World War I, Bill Purdue stressed the continuing, and perhaps even intensifying, role of religion in fostering divisions within societies. Generally (I'll touch on this again later in this unit), the experience of World War II – joint participation, shared suffering – brought greater tolerance, greater co-operation between religious denominations, a greater sense of common European/Christian heritage. The great exception was Ireland. While Protestants in the north were swept up in patriotic British sentiment and intense hatred of the Germans, much of that hatred was directed against the Republic, which remained neutral, and, therefore, against all Catholics.

Social reform and welfare policies

Two documents have long been taken as symbolizing the aspiration that World War II should result in a world in which there would be better social conditions and better social provision for the ordinary people: the Atlantic Charter (the statement of common aims subscribed to by Churchill and President Roosevelt in August 1941, four months before the US's entry into the war) and the Beveridge Report (formally the report of a committee appointed to 'undertake ... a survey of the existing national schemes of social insurance and allied services ... and to make recommendations', the report being published in December 1942).

Exercise   Turn to Document II.5 in *Primary Sources 2: Interwar and World War II*, 'The Atlantic Charter'. As you will quickly see, it is not basically concerned with issues of social policy. However, it is a good illustration of the notion of participation, in so far as it was the Labour members participating in the Churchill coalition who insisted that a clause be inserted referring to the better world to be created after the war. Which clause is this? ■

Discussion   I can't believe that you need an answer to that one, though I will mention the clause number later just to make sure that no one has gone off on the wrong track. Because of this single clause the Atlantic Charter did come to represent that psychological reaction to war which produces the argument that all the destruction and sacrifice must be for something better. We find it being mentioned in Resistance literature, and Beveridge himself, in a radio broadcast of 2 December 1942, said of his plan: 'It's the first step, though it is one step only, to turning the Atlantic Charter from words into deeds.' The Beveridge Report also suggests the validity of the participation thesis, since the committee was, in the first instance, set up at the behest of British trades union leaders whose co-operation was, of course, essential to the war effort. □

Exercise   In this exercise, for once, I shall be doing most of the work. I want you to have beside you the extracts from the Beveridge Report which are printed in *Primary Sources 2: Interwar and World War II* as Document II.25. I propose to talk you through this very famous and very important document, clause by clause, with just a few preliminary general questions for you to answer.

1   Where does the document, in the very strongest terms, express the view that the war is in itself a time of change, and that it is a time when there must be plans for further change?

2   What specific aspect of social policy is this report basically about?

3   Where is it stated that this aspect is not in itself enough? What other aspects of social policy are advocated in the report? ∎

Specimen answers   I shall now comment paragraph by paragraph, with the answers to these
and discussion   questions emerging clearly in my commentary.

It is evident from the first paragraph that we have come in about half-way through the report, and that up to this point the report has consisted of a survey of the existing system, prior to the making of recommendations. It is the second paragraph which, in its last two sentences, contains what I was referring to in my first question above. The general sentiment is an important one and was much quoted, thus helping to add to this sense that there must be a better world after the war, particularly since, thanks to the efforts of the British Ministry of Information, the contents of the Beveridge Report were widely known across the world. However, we must be cautious. One trap which earlier, and unthinking, commentators on the relationship between war and social change often used to fall into was to take phrases of this sort at face value, to assume that because someone like Beveridge said that the time was right for revolutionary change, revolutionary change therefore took place. In discussing programmes put forward in wartime, it is essential always to continue into the post-war years and see whether they were actually put into practice.

The specific reference to 'sectional interests' is to the various bodies who gave evidence, particularly the insurance companies and to a lesser extent employers' organizations and trades unions. In the existing social insurance system, as originally set up by Lloyd George (remember Document I.12 in *Primary Sources 1: World War I*), the private insurance companies (known as the 'approved societies') had a part in running the system. Beveridge is giving a warning here that whatever the companies may think, they will be cut out of his system which will be administered directly by the state.

The next paragraph is the one which helps to answer my second question, and provides the main part of the answer to the third question. Although this document is specifically concerned with the narrow aspect of social insurance,

Beveridge also wants there to be 'a comprehensive policy of social progress'. Then comes the Dickensian language of the five giants (actually taken from the opening pages of *A Tale of Two Cities*). The meaning may not be very clear to you; want is loss of income, to be dealt with by social insurance; disease stands for all kinds of ill-health and physical incapacity, and is to be dealt with by a National Health Service; ignorance means inadequate education, and is to be dealt with by a new Education Act; squalor basically means poor housing, and it is to be dealt with by a Housing Act; idleness signifies unemployment, and it is to be dealt with by policies directed towards the avoidance of high unemployment. Thus we see what Beveridge means by a comprehensive policy, though in fact education and housing are not again dealt with in the report. Nevertheless, in that the Beveridge Report was widely taken as the blueprint for what was already in some circles being spoken of as a welfare state (to contrast with Hitler's warfare state), that welfare state was taken to embrace positive policies on all of these matters.

Beveridge was a Liberal. Like Margaret Thatcher four decades later, he believed that individuals should be encouraged to take action to provide for themselves – this idea is embodied in his 'third principle' of co-operation between the state and the individual. The post-war Labour government which was responsible for implementing the Beveridge proposals aimed actually to provide benefits above the mere subsistence level which Beveridge recommended, though in practice these benefits quickly fell behind inflation. Certainly Labour policies did not aim to encourage private insurance coverage as Beveridge had hoped: that is the basis of the Thatcherite accusation that a 'dependency culture' was created.

The next paragraph gives the full and explicit answer to my second question. The report is essentially concerned with the 'limited contribution' of an immediately achievable plan of insurance. The next paragraph sets out what social insurance is seen as covering: interruption (for example through unemployment or sickness) and destruction (through permanent disability or retirement) of earning power, and also special expenditures arising from birth, marriage or death. The six fundamental principles are very important: they contain the essence of the Beveridge view – many were not followed in continental European plans, and many have been abandoned in Britain in more recent times. The term 'flat rate' is a key one: everybody was to pay the same level of contribution, and everyone, whatever their ordinary earnings, was to receive the same level of benefit. (This contrasts with earnings-related schemes, where the better-off pay more, but then get higher benefits.) The various British social insurance schemes (we took an overview of them in Book 2, Units 7–10) had continued to grow in piecemeal fashion; Beveridge's idea (spelled out later) was that there should be one Ministry of Social Security to bring everything together in one united scheme. Benefits were to be genuinely of subsistence level, but, as already noted, it was expected that through private provision individuals would build on these. 'Comprehensiveness' is another key word, sometimes rendered as 'universality'. In my discussion of class, I mentioned that social security and other services prior to World War II were essentially and explicitly aimed at the separate working class. The new idea, which it was hoped would genuinely create a more united society, was that this social security scheme would bring in everyone, rich as well as poor. The exact meaning of 'classification' is spelled out in (ii) below – it is a functional classification and one which cuts right across the conventional notion of social classes. 'National assistance' figures again later in the document. Because the Beveridge scheme depended, like that of Lloyd George, on insurance stamps being bought, there were inevitably people not covered by this scheme; hence the need for national assistance, for which contributions were not required, but which for many working-class people had overtones of the old Poor Law and the dole of the 1930s. If we look ahead to what actually happened after the war, we find that while national assistance featured quite prominently in the post-war years, voluntary insurance (or private provision) did not play a great part for ordinary people. Several socialists argued, unsuccessfully, that the insurance principle should be abolished, and that all benefits should be made available to anyone in need without the distinction between contributors and non-contributors. Nevertheless, the aim of the plan 'to make want under any circumstances unnecessary' is a noble one, and expresses well the noble side of the aspirations engendered by war.

I now come on to the individual points (i) to (xii):

(i)   This spells out the 'comprehensiveness' or 'universality' principle. The idea of 'different ways of life' is not related to social class, but to the classification spelled out in (ii).

(ii)   The basic classification is between I, employees, and II employers and the self-employed. That this is scarcely a class distinction is clarified when one realizes that I included top professional people 'under contract of service', while II could, for example, include a self-employed window-cleaner. III obviously covers all social classes, while IV includes both the idle rich and those unable to secure employment. V simply means children, and VI, of course, is those who have qualified, or now will qualify, for some kind of old-age pension.

(iii)   Retirement pensions of a sort had existed since before the First World War, but the idea of children's allowances, or family allowances as they were actually called when introduced by the Churchill coalition in 1944, was something new (though long agitated for). Paid on the universalist principle, this, as child benefit, survived all Thatcherite reforms. The 'appropriate' conditions relating to the other four classes are spelled out in the next two sub-sections, (iv) and (v).

(iv)   The critical points here are that employed persons will have a contribution from their employer, thus creating for themselves a higher entitlement to benefits. The self-employed and non-employed will simply have their own contribution. Housewives do not make any contribution, it being part of the assumptions about the nature of the family of the time that the benefits they can receive will be covered by the contributions that men have to make for that very purpose (bear in mind Summerfield's figures for the earnings for men and women in the Course Reader).

(v)   This sub-section spells out the wider range of benefits available to employees (with their higher total contributions) than the other classes. Again we see what housewives are to get, by virtue of their husbands' contributions.

(vi)   The means test was a hated symbol of the 1930s, and it was the intention of the Beveridge plan, and its Labour and trade-union supporters, that this was now to be abolished. However, a form of means test would remain for national assistance (see below).

(vii)   In the post-war years the 'limited number of cases' proved not to be quite so limited, though many were deterred from claiming national assistance because of the overtones of means test. It should be said that the whole spirit in which needs were assessed in the post-war years differed totally from the viciously inquisitorial means test of the 1930s.

(viii) This was not, strictly speaking, part of Beveridge's brief, but is one of the items he felt to be essential to 'a comprehensive policy of social progress'. Already, to meet the expected needs of war, there was in existence an Emergency Hospital Scheme which could form the basis for a future National Health Service. The Churchill coalition government was responsible for a separate white paper, *National Service for Health*, which recommended the establishment of a National Health Service after the war. Again the principle is that of universality ('all citizens').

(xii)   In fact a Ministry of Social Security was not set up (until the 1960s and the advent of supplementary benefits), so the system created by the post-war Labour government was less unified than Beveridge had envisaged. The phrase 'social security' did not come into general usage: instead there was a Ministry of National Insurance, and an autonomous National Assistance Board.

The next paragraph, in perfectly clear language, sums up the essentials of the Beveridge insurance scheme. It picks up the point about social insurance in itself not being enough, and returns to the notion of 'a concerted social policy', which, in so many ways, was what made the Beveridge Report famous. Three particular assumptions relating to 'a concerted social policy', the paragraph is saying, are essential for the implementation of the social insurance scheme. The first assumption is the institution of family allowances (as they were actually called in the 1944 Act). The Beveridge Report does not state who these are to be paid to, but in fact by 1944 feminist sentiment was strong enough (or at least the fear that husbands would waste the money was) for it to be enacted that the family allowances were to be paid direct to mothers. Family allowances expressed the universalist principle in its fullest form: as the next paragraph makes clear, they are not to depend on insurance contributions, but are payable to everyone and are financed out of taxation. The second assumption (or assumption B, as Beveridge calls it elsewhere in the document, not in your extract) is that there will be a National Health Service. This too involves a very full statement of universalist principles. It was in fact decided that a portion of the cost of the National Health Service (which began in 1948 under the terms of the Labour government's National Health Service Act of 1946) would be met from insurance contributions made by those who paid them, but this is a minor detail since the service was to be completely open to everyone. Its administration was also to be totally detached from social insurance, and it was in fact the responsibility of the Ministry of Health in England and Wales, and of the Department of Health of the Scottish Office in Scotland. If one looks at the rather tentative and fragmented proposals that were being made for health provision before World War II, then I think a good argument can be made that the war experience (particularly the nationalization of hospitals in the Emergency Hospital Scheme) did make a significant contribution towards the comprehensive National Health Service that finally emerged (this at least is the argument of my article 'The Labour Party and the welfare state in Britain', 1967). The phrase 'prior to any other consideration' is worth noting; this means that treatment should be provided whether or not a patient had money or insurance cover, considerations which loom large in societies which do not have a comprehensive National Health Service.

Britain after the war became, for a considerable period, a full-employment society: that, indeed, is one of the crucial differences between conditions before the war and conditions after the war. The Beveridge Report, in assumption C, expresses a commitment to the maintenance of employment. In intention, the Labour government went even further, though the most important influence was the high level of world demand after all the destruction of resources during the war. It is important to note that Beveridge did not expect, and did not call for, full employment. As you will see as you work through the paragraph, he expected an average unemployment rate of 8.5 per cent, though he does immediately express the hope that unemployment might be reduced to below that level. The report does not explain how maintenance of employment is to be achieved; Beveridge, on his own initiative, wrote a separate report on this, while the government published its famous *Employment White Paper,* which announced the aim of avoidance of mass unemployment. What all had in mind were Keynesian policies of managing total national expenditure so as to keep up demand in times of potential recession. Beveridge does not expect it to be possible to control 'completely the major alternations in good trade and bad trade'; in fact Keynesian policies were fairly successful in this respect throughout the 1940s, 50s and 60s. Beveridge expects some short-term unemployment: the evil he is concerned to eradicate is long-term unemployment for the same individual. His implication is that a fair amount of labour mobility will enable an unemployed man to find another job within about twenty weeks.

The penultimate paragraph again brings out the essence of Beveridge's liberal principles. Unlike traditional socialists, he does not believe that the main kind of redistribution of wealth and income required is that between land, capital, management and labour (in the direction of the last, of course). He believes that the main problem is within classes, between those earning and those not earning, between those with large families and those with no families. He then rests much of his case on better administration, which he believes will eliminate waste. Clearly he would be worried by the creation of a 'dependency culture' – he intends that this plan will not have a depressing effect on incentives. In the final paragraph he is saying that want could have been abolished before the war. The phrase 'abolition of want' is very much a phrase of the 1940s, and very much a concept which like the Beveridge Report itself, achieved international circulation. His key-note now is that it should be regarded as a post-war aim capable of early attainment. In saying this he was anticipating the criticisms of people like Churchill, who did not want any discussion of such post-war aims to distract from the prime task of getting on with the war. Churchill was also to warn at the end of the war that the country was too impoverished for radical social schemes. □

That ends my detailed textual commentary, which you will find very useful should you, in a TMA or exam, have to write a commentary on an extract from the report. There remains the question of what it all adds up to: what is the ultimate historical significance of these extracts from the Beveridge Report? As I have indicated from time to time, the basic provisions were adopted in the post-war Labour government legislation which is usually seen as establishing the British welfare state. The Beveridge Report, to put in summary form what really should be spelled out in a little more detail, forms a vital link in any chain joining the war experience to the enactment of social legislation. It also had symbolic significance when resistance fighters and progressive elements in other countries discussed the kind of society there should be after the war. (The leading authority on Beveridge, the Beveridge Report, and social reform generally, is José Harris, author of *William Beveridge: A Biography* (1977) and a large number of articles to be found in the many collections on recent British history now available in bookshops. She is unusually cited as one of those – like Summerfield – sceptical about war's effects in bringing about social change, yet I don't think her accounts conflict with the version given here.)

In this course we have tried to avoid placing too much emphasis on Britain, but with the Beveridge Report it really is a case of the British document being a seminal one. I want to keep it in mind as we turn to the relationship, if any, between war and social welfare in some of the other main countries. Let me see whether, on the basis of what you already know, you can make any connections.

Exercise

Let us consider France, Italy, Germany and Russia. Remembering their differing experiences of war, occupation, resistance, and so on, say which of these countries you think would have been most susceptible to the influence of Beveridge's ideas on welfare, and which would have been least. Briefly explain your lines of reasoning. Don't struggle too long with this one if it seems beyond the bounds of your present knowledge, but try at least to set down a few odd thoughts. You may find it easiest to start with the country where the influence of Beveridge would be least. ■

Specimen answers and discussion

With respect to that last helpful sentence, I hope you immediately thought of Soviet Russia, where the liberal–capitalist ideas of Beveridge would be unlikely to have much appeal. In any case, we have already seen that there were severe limits on the extent to which change was permitted to take place in Russia at the end of the war. You may then have found it very difficult to say which of the other three countries was most 'susceptible'. During the war, France, because of the contacts between the British government and the French Resistance, was most open to ideas from Britain, and certainly it is in French Resistance documents that we see the clearest signs of the influence of Beveridge. I'll come back to this again in a moment. Next (this may surprise you) I would actually put Germany. Britain, remember, was an important occupying power at the end of the war and (we'll also look at this in a moment) it was under the Allied occupation that various reformist ideas from the west could be put forward. In Italy there were no immediate comprehensive social welfare reforms as there were in France and Britain. Although some older British traditions had some influence in post-war Italy (for instance, with respect to the nature of independent, non-political newspapers), there was no effective mechanism for such 'new' ideas as those of the Beveridge Report to make a great impact. In fact, while there was a definite commitment to social welfare on a better scale than ever before, post-war Italian social welfare, very much in the spirit of Christian Democracy, depended heavily on voluntary and local organizations. □

I'm going to end this section by encouraging you to take a detailed look at France, followed by a briefer one at Germany.

I want you now to return to Hoffmann's article on 'The effects of World War II on French society and politics' in the Course Reader. Forgetting Beveridge and the Resistance for a moment, note down the extent to which, according to Hoffmann, the development of welfare policies was initiated by the Vichy regime.

Exercise   Note down the main relevant points made by Hoffmann. ■

Specimen answer   Here is my own summing up (some of the points I make are less directly relevant to social welfare than others).

Hoffmann lists four types of new organization set up by the Vichy regime: 'organization committees' within the world of business, on which the post-war *Conseil National du Patronat Français* was modelled; the Vichy government's Peasant Corporation, which provided the structure for the Liberation's *Confédération Générale Agricole* (established in reaction against the Peasant Corporation) and the leadership of the *Fédération Nationale des Syndicats d'Exploitants Agricoles* of post-war years; the workers' groups established within the Vichy Labour Charter, which continued to flourish in the post-war years; and finally the various professional organizations of lawyers, doctors, and so on, which were also preserved and consolidated in the post-war period. In theory at least, the Vichy Labour Charter recognized the just needs of the working classes, and the regime made much of its main contribution to social insurance policy, the institution of old-age pensions for retired workers. The new Vichy organizations, Hoffmann claims, were put in the hands of a dynamic new generation of businesspeople (partly, indeed, as a result of pressure from the Germans, who were anxious to squeeze as much out of France as possible). One of the top figures he especially singles out for mention, Jean Bichelonne, is important in respect of economic planning, rather than social welfare, but Pierre La Rocque, one of the main drafters of the Law of August 1940 which set up Vichy's business committees, later, according to Hoffman, 'built ... the social security system of the Liberation'.

Hoffmann, I think, overstates his case. However, his thesis does bring out the 'neutral' pressures of war, which has significance, rather than the ideological commitments of groups, parties or governments. Several Resistance organizations put forward programmes which went far beyond social welfare of the Beveridge type, but rather envisaged a complete social and economic reorganization of society. □

I want now to look at some of the French Resistance organizations and the sorts of programmes for economic and social reform that they proposed. France's greatest authority on World War II from the older generation is Henri Michel. This is an invaluable collection of documents which he compiled with Boris

Mirkine-Guetzovitch, in which he sought to draw attention away from 'sabotage and para-military activities' to 'social and political policies' (*Les idées politiques et sociales de la Résistance, 1954*). Questions that we would have to ask are: were these policies put into practice, and, if so, was this due to the Resistance? (Or would they have been put into practice anyway?) In April 1942 Jean Moulin parachuted into France to group together the various Resistance organizations, and set up a General Committee to draw up political and social policies for the Liberation. In a main report of 1943 the committee declared that 'the working masses expect from the Liberation the birth of a new world where everyone can develop to the full without constraint'. At the same time a Catholic Resistance journal insisted: 'the working class is the most important. It has the right to speak and the right to responsibility.' Of course, the various statements I am quoting here are of relevance also to our earlier discussion of class; however, I put them here because they are really dealing with future policy rather than with changes in class structure actually taking place. Many of them, indeed, seem to be spoken *for* the working class, rather than *by* the working class. The non-socialist Resistance group *Défense de France* published an important statement in March 1944:

> The governing class had abdicated. The bourgeois class is shown to be incapable of directing by itself the destiny of the country. It senses obscurely the arrival of a new social structure and, while its best elements devote themselves already to trying to establish and to promote its main features, the rest weep for a dead past and whine uselessly over the uncertainties of the time.
>
> The moment is propitious to ratify anew the social unity of the nation, destroyed by the birth of large-scale industry and by the accompanying birth of a capitalist bourgeoisie and of a proletariat of mechanical beings, whose work, tears, clothiers and even the quarters to which they are relegated, separate them from the rest of the nation. The revolution must consist of re-integrating all classes of society into the nation, thus giving to the workers [*travailleurs*, meaning all workers, whether by hand or brain] the place which must be returned to them.

> (Quoted in Michel and Mirkine-Guetzovitch, *Les idées politiques et sociales de la Résistance,* 1954, pp.376–7; trans. Arthur Marwick)

Trade unions, the statement said, have improved the material conditions of the workers, but there is still a chasm between 'proletarians' and 'non-proletarians'. The very condition of being proletarian must be suppressed (and this will not be done through the empty rhetoric of the Pétain regime). There must be an end to the 'absolute dependence in regard to terms of employment, to the perpetually re-born fear of tomorrow, of the deprivation involved in an immense mechanistic organization in which the worker [*ouvrier*, industrial worker], an anonymous peon, is buffeted around at the whim of sovereign and mysterious forces'. Having long since achieved its political, administrative and territorial unity, France is now, in the Resistance, 'forging its moral unity'. Next it must establish its 'social unity'. To achieve this social unity, liberal capitalism would have to be abolished:

It will be necessary to institute an economic structure in which all Frenchmen can participate both in prosperity and in common set-backs. It will be necessary to re-make 1936, with different methods and a different spirit, suppressing not only the hostility of the Right towards the leaders of the popular masses, but also the efforts of the 'revolutionary' to avoid real revolution, and the 'socialists' to save capitalism. It would be necessary to put the economy at the service of the nation. Then, having eliminated the material cause of the chasm between our children, France can hope to re-find her internal coherence and to march in harmony towards a better future.

(Ibid., p.378)

Certainly we seem here to be a long way from the ideology of Beveridge. The programme of the Lyon region of the *Movement de Libération Nationale* (into which *Défense de France* was merged) stressed the need for the whole war experience to yield benefits for the working class and the peasants (*cultivateurs*). *Organisation Civil et Militaire* (OCM) suggested that the companies of private capitalism might be replaced by 'groups of workers' brought together to carry out a common labour and using the help of capitalists; collective agreements would unite together the enterprises and those working in them. Many Resistance organizations supported 'the politics of the family' very much along Vichy lines (here is a point in favour of the Hoffmann thesis). OCM wanted a Ministry of Social Life to deal with abandoned mothers and children, and to rehabilitate criminals, prostitutes and beggars. The *Défense de France* statement announced that every man and every woman should feel 'the obligation to transmit life'. Calling for the equal distribution of the charges involved in bringing up children, it declared that 'an important part of the increase in salaries should be granted in the form of an increase in family allowances accompanied by marriage loans, tax relief, and a battle against abortion'. So one can see that many traditional considerations were mixed in with what seem like revolutionary utterances. Bearing these various quotations in mind, and also a further observation by Henri Michel that 'in politics, economics and in democracy, the members of the Resistance were constructing a new France' (p.17), I want you to turn to Document II.18 in *Primary Sources 2: Interwar and World War II*, the programme of the CNR (National Resistance Council) (you worked on a brief passage from this in Book I, Unit 1).

Exercise   First, I want you to work your way carefully through the document, indicating:

1   which paragraphs merely deal with the immediate circumstances created by the war;

2   which paragraphs indicate, in very broad terms, the idea of a complete break with France as it was in the 1930s;

3   which paragraphs deal (a) with proposed political reforms and (b) with proposed economic reforms;

4   which paragraphs deal with matters that were also central to the Beveridge Report. What proposal mentioned by Beveridge does not feature at all in this programme?

5   There is a long list of proposed social reforms of other types: what particular aspects of French life do they reflect?

When you have completed this preliminary exercise, which is useful in helping you to grasp the content of the document, try these two more wide-ranging questions:

6   In two or three sentences say what this document suggests about the relationship between the war experience and social welfare legislation.

7   What indication is there in the document that the proposed legislation will be implemented once the war is over? ■

***Specimen answers
and discussion***

1   Paragraphs 1–3. In paragraph 1 it is stated that the Provisional Government will re-establish the independence taken from France by Germany; the other two paragraphs concern traitors, profiteers, the actions of enemy citizens, etc. Paragraph 5(b) talks of compensation for war victims. In other places, as for instance where 5(b) talks of the 're-establishment' of trade union freedoms, there is the suggestion that what is being dealt with is the evil wartime situation.

2   I think it can be seen that with each point there is the suggestion of going further and introducing better conditions, more rights, etc., than existed in the 1930s. This is made most explicit in the final section where, in addition to references to the 'vile' Vichy regime, there is also reference to 'the organs of corruption and treachery' that existed *prior* to the surrender to the Germans.

3   (a) Paragraph 4, though note that this deals with political *rights* rather than any precise proposals for institutional reform; (b) paragraph 5, which we discussed in Book I, Unit 1.

4   (a) 'A complete social security plan', etc. (b) 'Security of employment', though the devices mentioned differ from the regulation of the trade cycle envisaged by Beveridge; also the paragraphs on education and 'retirement pensions'. There is no mention of a national health service.

5   The other proposals reflect the relative weakness of French trade unions and the comparative lack of legislation on hours of work, etc. (and probably also the long hours of work enforced during the war); the instability of the franc over the period of the First World War and again in the Second World War, and its general decline in value in the 1930s; and the great importance in French life of the agricultural community. You should be able to pick out for yourselves the different proposals which relate to these issues.

6   First, this is the programme of the body which brings together the various Resistance organizations, and is also linked to General de Gaulle, leader of the Free French: it is the document of a body brought into existence only by the need to carry on the war against the Germans. We have already seen how individual Resistance organizations related their policies to the idea that surrender to the Germans demonstrated the inadequacies of the old system, which now must be reformed. This document, as we have just seen, links together proposals that will create a better society. Both at the

beginning and the end of the document the sense of unity in national resistance is stressed, a unity to be perpetuated in a fairer and more equal society.

7   The fact that this document unites not just the Resistance organizations, but also major political parties and General de Gaulle and his supporters. □

Provided, then, that the Germans were indeed defeated (as, of course, we know they were), one could expect this document to have practical consequences. To see what exactly did happen, I turn to the leading authority, Jean-Pierre Rioux, whose two volumes on *The Fourth Republic* have now been translated into English (1987). In the original French, the appropriate section was entitled *Le 'New Deal' social*, which might suggest an American influence, though I don't think there was on this French legislation. Rioux in fact begins with the ordinance of 22 February 1945, dealing with the issue of workshop delegates and workers' rights – issues featured in the CNR programme. Rioux says that this ordinance also built on the Popular Front legislation of 1936, and the Vichy Labour Charter. The demands in the CNR programme relating to the agricultural community were met in the statute of 13 April 1946.

The 'New Deal', Rioux continues, was finally cemented by a new concept which should transform the condition of the worker – social security: 'The 'revolution' so often promised passed, this time, into the daily life of a large proportion of the French people' (p.111). Two ordinances of 30 December 1944 established social security contributions. Further ordinances of 4 and 19 October 1945 brought together all the old piecemeal insurance schemes under one single organization and brought all wage and salary earners within the social security system. Benefits referred to the same areas as identified in the Beveridge Report, with a special emphasis on family benefits. There was no separate national health service; instead the French social security scheme included provision for reimbursement of 80 per cent of all medical expenses. A law of 22 May 1946 extended social insurance to some of the self-employed. Maurice Larkin (in his *France Since the Popular Front*, 1988, p.128) has declared that 'it is arguable that the reforms of the brief liberation era were a more significant advance on the past than Labour's creditable six-year record in post-war Britain'. The pre-war baseline is the crucial element in such a judgement. In absolute terms the British welfare state was indisputably more effective and more comprehensive.

Germany

First, something about the responses of the National Socialist government. Here is a brief extract from a speech made on 15 September 1940 by Dr Robert Ley, who was responsible for planning old-age pensioner schemes:

> The German people are going to be rewarded for their wartime sacrifices with an old age free from cares.
>
> In eighteen years Germany will not be recognisable. A proletarian nation will have become a master nation.
>
> In ten years' time the German worker will look better than an English Lord.
>
> (Quoted in Jeremy Noakes *Nazism 1939–1945*, 1998, p.298)

Note the long time-scale, ten years, and even eighteen years. The language is also fascinating: 'proletarian' is a socialist term; the reference to 'an English Lord' reminds us of the German fascination with the British aristocracy. The idea of a 'reward' for wartime sacrifices is one that runs through this course: it is a good point, related to the participation theme, but, of course, everything depends on what actually happens at the end of the war. Then, neither Hitler nor Dr Robert Ley were there to carry out promises: none the less it is worth thinking about whether post-war, German governments didn't feel some obligation to reward the workers for their sufferings.

Post-war governments were, in fact, dominated by the newly formed Christian Democrat Party (remnants of the old Centre Party, but with Christian protestants as well). This new, united, Christian Party was to be quite a strong force in favour of implementing social reforms.

Now, back to the Beveridge Report, guided by the article by H. G. Hockerts, 'German post-war social policies against the background of the Beveridge plan', 1981. That the Beveridge plan should be under consideration in post-war West Germany was partly because of the British presence as an occupying power. Hockerts shows that the Americans also had an interest in it, but that the main pressure for its application came from the German trade unions. In fact, particularly from the German Christian Democrats, there was a considerable resistance to such a unified state-sponsored plan. Hockerts has a neat formulation, reminiscent of points made by Roseman:

> In Britain the war experience had engendered a sense of national solidarity and confidence in state intervention and had thus prepared the ground for the Beveridge reform; in Germany, by contrast, the experience of Nazi misuse of power had provoked opposition to any form of any government-imposed centralisation or collectivism.

Furthermore, the Germans were proud of their own indigenous tradition of social insurance, which went back well before the Lloyd George reforms in Britain. Addressing a mass rally of the Christian Democrats in August 1946, their leader Konrad Adenauer, the dominant figure in the first years of the West German Federal Republic, declared:

> We must hold on to this social insurance. We are proud of it. And as for the proposals Beveridge has recently made in Hamburg [the occupying authorities sent Beveridge on a tour of West Germany] I can only say we Germans have already had such things these past thirty years.

(Quoted in Hockerts, p.172)

Between 1949 and 1953 there was in fact a reconstruction of what was very largely the traditional structure, embodying different, and much more favourable, conditions for white-collar workers compared with manual workers (this, incidentally, is a significant piece of evidence that West Germany was very far from being a classless society in the years after 1945). The Child Allowances Law of 1954, however, was very much in the Beveridge tradition. Germany's big pensions reform came in 1957 when, in effect, it set the pattern for breaking from the Beveridge flat-rate principle by introducing earnings-related pensions. Hockert's general summing up is as follows:

For the instances cited here, the Beveridge plan had provided some important initial ground work. Even if some of the proposals no longer seem to provide entirely convincing solutions, hindsight nevertheless shows how momentous the new ideas generated by his plan have proved to be.

(ibid., p.186)

Our concern, of course, is not specifically with the Beveridge Report. I simply started with it, because it is, without doubt, a key document in the study of war and social change. But what my discussions have brought out is the complicated series of interrelationships involved in any study of war and social change: the direct effects; the indirect effects; the cross-currents; the 'feedback'; the interaction between unguided forces, direct responses to war necessities, and the guided actions of major political powers; the forces of tradition; and the desire for innovation, often part of the psychological response to war.

Finally, what about the countries which fell under Soviet influence? These, in theory, abolished unemployment by providing a job for everyone, and offered a free and universal welfare state. In practice there was usually a system of supplementary fees payable for medical and social services. On the whole, however, the result of the war and associated events was the spread of welfare systems on a more thoroughgoing basis than ever before.

Material conditions

The Summerfield article we have already studied in the Course Reader gives a general idea of the relative scale of material conditions in Britain: whether or not wages overall improved for the working class (as I would maintain), we are certainly not talking about conditions of starvation, the terrorization of civilian populations, and so on. The blitz of 1940–41, sporadic later raids, and the V1 and V2 attacks of 1944 were frightening enough. In all, 60,000 civilians were killed in bomb attacks: this is a significant figure in that it amounts to about one-fifth of the total number of combatants killed in action, but it is of course small compared with the immense civilian losses in other parts of Europe; the French, it may be noted, lost almost exactly the same number of civilians through British and American bombing raids. Life in Britain was strictly regimented during the war, some goods disappeared altogether, and there was rationing of all basic commodities, save bread and vegetables. But the result was a fairer distribution than ever before, involving, for many families, higher nutrition standards than had obtained before the war. In a country which was not occupied, did not have a regime imposed on it by an external power, had a government which, whatever the exigencies of war, was mindful of the principles of liberal democracy, material conditions were sometimes unpleasant and even worse, but one can, not unreasonably, speak over the longer term of a desirable redistribution.

At the opposite extreme were Poland and Russia, which experienced war as destruction in its most unmitigated form. Poland, as Norman Davies has put it, 'became the killing-ground of Europe, the new Golgotha' (*God's Playground: A History of Poland*, 1981). Altogether 18 per cent of the Polish population was killed; the figure for Russia is 11.2 per cent, and for Yugoslavia 11.1 per cent. This can be compared with 7.4 per cent for Germany, and 0.9 per cent for Britain. In Poland the Russians exterminated those whom they regarded as class enemies, the Germans those they regarded as race enemies. From 1941 Poland was in the grip of Nazi terrorism, the selective executions of 1939–40 giving way to indiscriminate shootings and hangings. Poland, again in the words of Norman Davies, 'became the home of humanity's holocaust, an "archipelago" of death-factories and camps, the scene of executions, pacifications and exterminations which surpassed anything so far documented in the history of mankind' (p.10). In the countryside hundreds of Polish villages were razed to the ground, their populations massacred. In the towns, prisoners and suspects were shot out of hand. 'In Warsaw, hardly a street corner did not witness the death of groups of citizens by the score and the hundred' (p.11). As German power began to collapse in 1944–45, 'hundreds of thousands of underfed slave-labourers of both sexes and every conceivable nationality were marched back and forth, from project to abandoned project, amidst the endless retreating convoys and demolition squads of the defeated *Wehrmacht*'. The Germans had segregated the Jewish population in the winter of 1939–40. Even had they wished to do so, there was little that the Polish population at large could do, circumstances in Poland, as Davies puts it, bearing 'little relation to the relatively genteel condition of occupied Denmark, France or Holland'. Anyone caught sheltering, feeding or helping Jews was liable to bring instant execution upon his or her entire family.

From June 1941 the horrors of the German 'barbarisation of warfare' (to quote part of the title of the analysis of Omer Bartov) were visited upon Russia. Bartov quotes documents (see Document II.26 in *Primary Sources 2: Interwar and World War II*, 'Orders issued by General Lemelsen') to show that barbarity was practised from the very beginning.

Exercise   Turn now to Document II.26 and answer the following questions.

1   Bartov points out that the German commanders were not opposed to Hitler's orders, nor to shootings as such, but that they were worried by disorderly activities among their troops, and about their soldiers' actions encouraging frenzied desperation in the opposing Russian forces. What in this document would tend to support these points?

2   What role is Lemelsen envisaging for non-Bolshevik, non-Jewish, non-partisan Russians? ■

Specimen answers   1   The last sentence of (a), and the references in (b) to 'Bolshevism', ' Jewish
and discussion   and criminal group', and 'instruction of the Führer' indicate Lemelsen's support for his orders. The phrases in (b) about ' an irresponsible, senseless and criminal manner' and 'only by order of an officer' suggest the worry about disorderly conduct. The last phrase of (b) indicates the worry about stimulating further Russian resistance.

2   To serve as labour for the German army. In fact such labour was exacted under the most inhumane conditions, with masses of deaths from exhaustion and starvation – even populations which might well have welcomed the Germans as liberators from Russian rule were, as Roberts points out, treated in this way. □

Bartov suggests that even the apparently slightly more restrained attitudes of commanders like Lemelsen were effectively blank cheques for the mass killings of civilians that took place on the faintest of pretexts.

Within the appalling general situation of horror and barbarity, there were individual episodes that have become particularly well known, most notably the siege of Leningrad (which lasted well over 300 days). The winter of 1940–41 was appalling beyond description, with deaths from starvation running as high as 50,000 per month. Loss of one's ration card meant certain death. Any offence against the food regulations was punished by summary execution. Desperate, hunger-crazed citizens resorted to murder to gain food and ration cards, and to cannibalism. Frozen corpses were to be seen everywhere. Conditions lightened only slightly in the spring, when it was possible to evacuate about a million of the survivors. The remaining population, about 1 million out of a pre-war total of 3 million, settled down to face the second winter of blockade. Now, though conditions were still desperately hard, better order was maintained. The streets had been cleaned up, and some of the trams were running again. Yet in July and August 1943, with the population down to a select, proud and still near-starving 600,000, there came the worst shelling of the whole war. New street signs went up: 'Citizens: in case of shelling this side of the street is most dangerous'. The military success which finally broke the siege did not come till January 1944. At least a million Leningrad citizens had died of starvation, another 200,000 or so from bombing and shelling.

Leaving Leningrad to starve, in October 1941 the Germans were rapidly advancing on Moscow. On 16 October many top Moscow citizens took to flight. However, Stalin remained; and Moscow, in fact, did not fall. Moscow's winter was not as desperate as that of Leningrad, but, to quote Alexander Werth, Russian-born British correspondent there, 'many individual stories were grim – stories of under-nourishment, of unheated houses, with temperatures just above or even below freezing point, with water-pipes burst, and lavatories out of action; and in these houses one slept smothered – if one had them – under two overcoats and three or more blankets' (*Russia at War*, 1964, p.370). As in all major cities, there was food rationing: 800 grams of bread a day for workers, 600 for office staff, and 400 for dependants and children; 2,200 grams of meat a month for workers, 600 for dependants and children. In June 1941 bread was selling on the open market in Moscow at 150 rubles a kilo (£1.50 a pound). Milk, sugar, fats and tobacco were all very hard to come by. Cabbage and other vegetables had disappeared, having been commandeered either by the German or Russian armies. Werth noted 'a peculiar form of profiteering which had developed in Moscow during the spring, when the owner of a cigarette would charge any willing passers-by 2 rubles [normally equivalent to the then British shilling] for a puff – and there were plenty of buyers'. Werth reported further:

> People in the Moscow streets looked haggard and pale, and scurvy was fairly common. Consumer goods were almost unobtainable, except at fantastic prices, or for coupons, if and when these were honoured. In the big Moscow department stores strange odds and ends were being sold, such as barometers and curling tongs, but nothing useful. In the shopping streets like the Kuznetsky Most, or Gorki Street, the shop windows were mostly

sand-bagged and, where they were not, they often displayed cruel cardboard hams, cheeses and sausages, all covered with dust.

There were other deplorable shortages. In dental clinics – with the exception of a few privileged ones – teeth were pulled without an anaesthetic. The chemists' shops were about as empty as the rest ...

Moscow itself was very empty, with nearly half its population still away.

Only half a dozen theatres were open in June, among them the Filialé of the Bolshoi, and tickets were easy to obtain. In the buffet, all they sold, for a few coppers, was – glasses of plain water. The Bolshoi itself had been hit by a ton bomb, and was out of action. There was a good deal of other bomb damage here and there, and the sky was dotted with barrage balloons.

(pp.218–19)

I referred earlier to Document II.22 in *Primary Sources 2: Interwar and World War II* (*Pravda* report on a factory moved from the Ukraine to the Urals) and the relocation of Russian industry. We may count this a positive long-term consequence of the war, but conditions for workers at the time were dreadful:

In most places, living conditions were fearful, in many places food was very short, too. People worked because they knew that it was absolutely necessary – they worked twelve, thirteen, and sometimes fourteen or fifteen hours a day; they 'lived on their nerves'; they knew that never was their work more urgently needed than now. Many died in the process. All these people knew what losses were being suffered by the soldiers, and they – in the 'distant rear' – did not grumble much; while the soldiers were risking so much, it was not for the civilians to shirk even the most crippling, most heart-breaking work. At the height of the Siberian winter, some people had to walk to work – sometimes three, four, six miles; and then work for twelve hours or more, and then walk back again, day after day, month after month.

It is impossible to work out a balance-sheet between material conditions, physical suffering, risk to life, and the moral aspects of life. In German puppet regimes, as in Hungary, Romania and Bulgaria, the material basis of life was perhaps a little more secure than in the countries we have been discussing. (I shall come to Czechoslovakia in a moment.) Yugoslavia was divided between the puppet regime in Croatia, areas effectively controlled by the Germans or the Italians, and the area centred on Montenegro where most of the Partisan activity took place. Elements of the nature of life in this region are apparent in Document II.23 in *Primary Sources 2: Interwar and World War II*, the letter from Tito to the Italian commander. The context of this document is that the Italian occupying forces had learned that Tito had moved his Partisan headquarters to Varanjak, but that by the time they got there Tito had already moved on. The Italians then took out their frustration on the inhabitants of Varanjak and the neighbouring village of Drenova. The officer and the other soldiers had been captured in an ambush on 3 December, and interrogation, the Partisans claimed, had revealed him as being a Fascist Party member. Tito's letter of protest was forwarded from the garrison in Prijepolje to General Giovanni Esposito, commander of the 'Pusteria' Alpine Division at Pljeulja. Esposito addressed a reply to 'Signor Commander of the Partisans' requesting release of the officer. The request was refused, provoking Esposito into sending a second letter full of threats, this time addressed to 'Bandit Commander'.

Exercise   Turn now to Document II.23 in *Primary Sources 2: Interwar and World War II* and answer these questions:

1   What are the most significant points that emerge from it (I think there are two)?

2   What other points need explanation or elaboration? ■

Specimen answers   1   The significant points, I think, are (a) the evidence of brutality of the Italian
and discussion   occupation forces, and (b) the evidence of the power possessed by Tito and the Partisans. With regard to (a), one might also comment on how the document indicates the escalation in the circle of violence – something, of course, which would bear heavily on the ordinary population (previously, according to the letter, captives had been exchanged or set free).

2   The reference in the final paragraph is to the Battle of Moscow and the Russian counter-offensive which began on 6 December and which started the German retreat, with the Germans sustaining heavy losses. However, 'turning point' or not, victory for Tito was still some way off. □

In Czechoslovakia conditions were determined by Hitler's intention to exploit the material and human resources of the country to the greatest possible extent, but without driving the Czechs to such desperation that he risked guerrilla warfare in his rear. At the same time Hilter's policy was one of ruthless Germanization, and he believed that 'by firmly leading the Protectorate, it ought to be possible to push the Czech language, in about twenty years, back to the importance of a dialect' (see Gotthold Rhode, 'The Protectorate of Bohemia and Moravia 1939–45', 1973. Against intellectuals a policy of terrorization and liquidation was followed, while some concessions were offered to the working class in order to maximize productivity. Bouts of terror were particularly associated with Reinhardt Heydrich, who effectively was in control from September 1941. The men who succeeded in assassinating Heydrich on 27 May 1942 were parachuted in by the Czechs in exile, and protected by the Czech underground. Nazi retaliation took the form of the destruction of the villages of Lezhaky, where thirty-three male inhabitants were shot, and Lidice, all of whose male citizens were shot, whose women were sent to concentration camps, and whose children were dispersed. One measure of the differences between the treatment of Czechoslovakia and the treatment of Poland and Russia was that the Germans officially publicized these measures, whereas the atrocities in Poland and Russian simply proceeded as a matter of course. Altogether the Czechs lost to German reprisals and punitive actions between 360,000 and 500,000 citizens; 250,000 were killed in bomb attacks and military operations.

What, then, of Germany itself?

You should have notes from, or annotations on, the article by Roseman to refer to here. I have particularly referred you to the sixth and seventh paragraphs in section IV, and also the fifteenth and sixteenth paragraphs in that section. Note also the paragraph in section II which refers to the way in which state terror became an increasing part of everyday life. You should refer to Document II.13 in *Primary Sources 2: Interwar and World War II* (extracts from *I Lived Under Hitler* by Sybil Bannister) for the food situation in May 1943, and for the reduced housing circumstances of one of Hamburg's wealthiest merchants in January 1945. For the truly horrendous effects of the Hamburg fire raids in July and August 1943, which created the housing situation described by Sybil Bannister in 1945, turn to Document II.12, the extract from the report by the Police President of Hamburg. Probably the most instructive comparisons are with Italy, where conditions began to deteriorate very badly in 1943 (a year earlier than in Germany) and were desperate by the last stages of the war. The general trend is well indicated in figures given by David Ellwood in his *Italy 1943–45* (1985, p.130) (see Table 21–25.2). Martin Clark (*Modern Italy*, 1996, p.290) gives a horrendous summary. In 1945 prices were at twenty-four times the 1938 level, even after a freeze on gas, electricity and rents. Over 3 million houses had been destroyed or badly damaged, as well as most of the railway stock, lorries, bridges and ports. Industrial output in 1945 was about one-quarter of the 1941 figure, and about the same as 1884; the gross national product was about the same as that of 1911; and income per head was lower than in 1861. In July 1946 the average Italian was taking in only 1,650 calories per day, compared with 2,650 before the war.

Table 21–25.2 Percentage of food available and price index, Italy, September 1943 and July 1944

	Sept. 1943	July 1944
Percentage of food available in:		
Rationed market	10.9	3.4
Free market	23.5	22.6
Black market	65.6	74.0
Price index in:		
Rationed market	100	127.6
Free market	100	397.8
Black market	100	465.0

(Source: D. Ellwood, *Italy 1943–45*, 1985, p.130)

As I keep emphasizing, we have to distinguish between the immediate effects of war and long-term effects. Almost everywhere recovery was remarkably quick, largely because of the new levels of demand engendered by the war, and by the destruction of war. Roseman refers to malnutrition disappearing in Germany after 1948, and to the high standards achieved by 1955. After referring to the harsh conditions of wartime, Alan Milward, the distinguished economic historian, continues:

> Nevertheless the basic economic circumstances of a high and increasing demand for labour did change the conditions which had long prevailed for most employees in most industrial countries. These changes were effected more through the altered aspirations of labour than through substantial increases in real earnings ...
>
> The history of labour during the war was not simply a history of a factor of production, it was the history of most human beings involved in the war. The big changes in their economic circumstances which took place inevitably expressed themselves in important shifts in social aspirations

and political opinions. And these went far towards making the post-war economic world a very different one from that of the 1930s.

(War, Economy and Society, 1977, p.244)

Customs and behaviour

I have suggested that a major outcome of World War I was the full development of 'mass society' – in both the liberal democracies and one-party dictatorships. Here I will confine myself to a few general points. In discussing the effects of the First World War, I suggested that it was in the more 'backward' countries that one could expect to find the greatest upheavals in customs and behaviour induced by war. With the further developments in mass society of the interwar years there was less scope for change as a result of World War II. Yugoslavia was probably the country brought most forcibly into further contact with western ideas. In general, one might expect the war to have influenced customs and behaviour in two main ways: through the upheavals of population and the alterations in class relationships already discussed; and through the damage to civic morality caused by violence, terror tactics, and all the dodges and subterfuges to which people had to resort in order to survive. On the former point, it would be broadly true to say that there was less formality, less sense of hierarchy in most countries (possibly Britain remained the stuffiest in this sphere). On the second point, civic norms were in fact established remarkably quickly: there was no substantial general increase in criminality, though the behaviour of dissident youth in the post war years was often related back to the dislocations of war. Once again the extreme circumstances of Poland draw attention to themselves. I have already mentioned the geographical shift and the need for rebuilding on a massive scale. Polish cities were meticulously rebuilt, but with subtle modifications which reflected Russian influence. At the same time Poland continued to be more open to western popular culture than Russia. Poland was both terribly new, and not new at all. The French philosopher/writer Jean-Paul Sartre, writing in 1960, found Poland 'the world of perfect absurdity' (quoted in N. Davies *God's Playground*, 1981, p.9).

One question often raised, and one that I've already mentioned, concerns the extent of Americanization in the aftermath of the US encroachment on the European continent. As we shall see later, there was something of a flowering in the war years of, for example, both Italian and British film-making, which acted as a counterpoise to the Hollywood influence already there in pre-war days. For all European countries the major spectator sport was association football, a pastime totally resistant to all American forces. Among some groups in Paris there was a fad for certain things American, including jazz, but this scarcely adds up to widespread Americanization. What a number of commentators have signalled out, perhaps rather surprisingly, is the question of developments in religion. I shall make some further comments about these – I've already referred to the connection between Christian Democracy and social cohesion and social welfare, and I'll say more under the heading 'Values and Institutions'. Then I'll conclude this section with what I take to be one of the most important developments of the war, the passing of a further critical stage in the bringing of mass communications directly into the home.

A significant feature of the immediate post-war world in southern and western countries was the political role of Christian Democracy, which was particularly important in West Germany and Italy, but also apparent through the MRP (Popular Republican Movement) in France. The various crises of war had forced Catholic organizations into involvement in, and taking up positions favourable to, moderate social reform. In his paper to the Open University conference on total war and social change, François Bédarida argued that during the war there was a considerable transformation in the connection between religion and society:

> Not only was a new brand of secularism introduced, allowing Catholics to be reintegrated into public life, but Catholicism suddenly pervaded the whole civil society. It is true that French Catholicism was then undergoing a process of renewal, theological, pastoral and liturgical. At the same time it was the war which gave birth to the experience of the worker-priests. It was in the middle of the war that the famous book, *France, pays de mission?*, which sounded the alarm over the depth and extent of the decline in Christianity, was published. It was in face of the great crisis of conscience provoked by the war and the immediate post-war period – and in spite of the support given to Vichy by most bishops – that the most advanced wing of Catholicism affirmed its position (*Témoignage Chrétien, Temps Présent, Esprit, Jeunesse de l'Eglise,* etc.). Whether in the political realm, with the creation and rise of the Movement Républicain Populaire [Popular Republican Movement], the trade union sphere with the CFTC [Confederation of Catholic Unions], the domain of youth and culture with the JOC, the JEC, the JAC [Catholic Youth Organizations], in the media (in particular the press), in economic modernisation, in intellectual life, everywhere could be seen the vitality of a Catholicism which was to pervade everyday life, and the entire social fabric.
>
> ('World War II and social change in France', 1988, p.91)

That there should be comparable developments in the Soviet Union may seem still more surprising, yet this is the case convincingly argued in an article by William Fletcher in the Linz collection which I referred to earlier (*The Impact of World War II on the Soviet Union*, 1985). This development (as in France) comes largely under what I would term the psychological dimension of war. For Russia, the Second World War was the 'Great Patriotic War', in which older traditions of Russian society were appealed to, as well as more recent ones. In particular, as Fletcher brings out, a bargain was struck between Church and state: the Church gave the state political support, and in return the Church was granted the right to exist as an institution in Soviet society. The Russian Orthodox Church, in short, at the expense of limiting itself to a purely spiritual mission, won for itself during the war a legal, as distinct from an underground, existence in society. Furthermore, in the areas that were under German occupation during the war, the populations were both freed from Soviet restrictions and greatly in need of the traditional comforts of religion: thus, argues Fletcher, a 'Bible belt' of firm religious belief and practice grew up in western sectors of the Soviet Union. Although no bargains were struck, it could also be argued that the horrific experiences and upheavals in Poland served to consolidate sentiment behind a

Polish Catholic Church which came to stand for the independent spirit of the people.

During the war peoples everywhere, and often peoples who had hitherto shown little interest in national or world news, became heavily dependent on radio communication. When Tito boasted of Russian victories to the Italian commander, that news would have come to him by radio. In occupied Europe, resistance groups everywhere depended on news broadcasts from London, as a counter to the propaganda and misinformation broadcast by the Germans. The crucial point about radio is that it brings news (and entertainment) directly into a person's own home; there is no need to go out, as with the purchase of a newspaper, or visit to a cinema (where, of course, newsreels also had a special importance). Today we speak of the information technology revolution which is making the home the basis for everything – work as well as entertainment. This process is associated with television and visual display. Yet I believe there is a strong case for seeing World War II as a turning point in so far as it brought a new salience to radio, and a notion of news and entertainment in the home at the touch of a button – what television, of course, also brings in a more elaborate way.

The role and status of women

In *Primary Sources 2: Interwar and World War II* (Document II.13) I have included extracts from the wartime reminiscences of Sybil Bannister; I have also referred to the reminiscences of Christabel Bielenberg. Now both of these women were in slightly unusual circumstances, in that they were English women domiciled in Germany. What we learn from them, and from other sources, is the manner in which women had to cope with the appalling upheavals and great reversals in fortune while continuing always to *manage* their own lives and those of their families. One of the best sources I know is the diary of an Englishwoman, published as *Nella Last's War*, which brings out most effectively the way in which, through both organizing a family and doing a great deal of invaluable national work through the Women's Volunteer Service, Nella comes to realize that she is a much stronger and much more capable person than her husband. Women's work in the auxiliary military services and, even more, in the European resistance movements, is legendary.

The battle lines in the historiographical debate over whether or not the experiences of World War II broadened the roles and improved the status of women in society are familiar ones. Those for whom the overriding issue is the continuing inferior status of women today argue that, accordingly, the war cannot have had much effect, that even when women seemed to be doing new jobs they were always kept in an inferior position to men, and that if there were any changes these were due not to the war but to long-term structural forces. Certainly images of woman as potato-peeler or as pin-up were not suddenly obliterated; in some ways they were strengthened. But overall I would stand by the position I took in *War and Social Change in the Twentieth Century* – though my comments there were made in reference to the US, I consider them to be applicable generally:

> the conclusion is inescapable that the Second World War offered women opportunities normally unavailable in peace time to improve their economic

and social status, and to develop their own confidence and self-consciousness. In many cases these opportunities were firmly grasped; whether they would be extended depended very much on women themselves, for, without doubt, old attitudes, overpoweringly strong in 1941 [or 1939], were still influential in 1946.

                                                                    (1974, p.175)

I lay particular stress on changed opportunities for married women, and the weakening of the prejudices against married women taking jobs (often only part-time jobs, but still, by the account of many women themselves, liberating). My arguments, with particular reference to Britain, have been challenged by Harold L. Smith in his own chapter in his edited collection, *War and Social Change* (1986). In her paper to the Open University conference, Penny Summerfield, by examining in great detail the statistics of married women's employment, has on the whole confirmed my view against that of Smith (Marwick, *Total War and Social Change*, 1988). Summerfield, more recently, has adopted the gender studies, postmodernist approaches about which, as you will know by now, I am thoroughly sceptical. But make up your own mind, and, if you can find the time, read Penny Summerfield, *Reconstructing Women's Wartime Lives: Discourse and Subjectivity in Oral Histories of the Second World War* (1998).

Exercise   I want you to read, in the extract below, what François Bédarida said to the Open University conference on the subject of the effects of the war on French women. Then answer the questions which follow.

> The changes brought to the condition of women by the second world conflict have been greatly exaggerated, both at the time and during the immediate post-war period. People have been too quick to interpret the Resistance as a demonstration of progress towards equality of the sexes. On the other side we perhaps have a tendency today to under-estimate the changes. Within the workplace changes in employment were qualitatively real, though quantitatively slight. If the female working population increased both absolutely and relatively from 1936 to 1946 (an increase of 560,000 individuals), the figures have to be corrected, because they include agriculture where they were over-estimated. If agriculture is left out, the proportion of women in employment only rises from 20.6 per cent to 22 per cent.

> On the other hand, to the extent that the Resistance served as a channel for social promotion, one well might think that women, who played an irreplaceable role, would also benefit from this. But all studies on this theme have illuminated how far in reality they became the 'forgotten people' of history. Besides, even in their clandestine activities, women were for most of the time confined within their traditional roles, above all carrying out subordinate secretarial or social service work. Here for example are the terms in which a leading figure described the work of one of his female collaborators: 'Like all her female comrades, she had the worst job, typing letters, fetching and carrying mail, putting people in touch with each other, taking part in secret rendezvous, emptying our letter boxes, clandestine and

under surveillance, seeking out meeting places, and, whenever that became necessary, doing the shopping with genuine or forged ration books.' And he concludes that if 'the women of the Resistance had their place, their important place in all the networks,' in the end 'they were the Marthas of the clandestine movements.'

One must not minimise to the same extent the progress made, in particular with regard to the acquisition of the vote, a right which suffragist women, in spite of all their efforts, had not been able to gain between 1919 and 1938 in particular because of the opposition of the Senate dominated by the Radicals. Again in 1944, when the Conseil National de la Résistance wanted to include votes for women in its programme, the Radical party tried to obstruct this, but without success, for the text adopted on 15 March 1944 recognised the feminist claim: to become citizens. At the same time, and on the same subject, de Gaulle in a speech on 18 March 1944 declared: 'to establish democracy renewed in its institutions and above all in its practices, the new regime must be based on representatives elected by all men and all women of our country'. Consequently, the ordinance drawn up in Algiers in April 1944 by the Comité Française de Libération Nationale on the constitutional organisation to be set up at the Liberation specified: 'Women are voters and candidates under the same condition as men.' The new right was exercised for the first time in the municipal elections (29 April), then at the time of the referendum and the legislative elections for the constituent assembly (21 October).

This revolution in basic principles was fully achieved in the Declaration of Rights placed at the head of the Constitution of 1946. While the first article declared, 'All men, and all women are born and live free and equal before the law', the second clause added, as a result of a campaign orchestrated by the Union des Femmes Françaises, a para-Communist organisation, 'The law guarantees to women equal rights to those of men in every domain.' But the familial vocation of women was explicitly recalled by article 24 which tried to reconcile equality of the sexes with specifically feminine characteristics: 'The nation protects all mothers and all children through appropriate legislation and institutions. It guarantees to woman the exercise of her functions as citizen and worker in conditions which permit her to fulfil her role as mother and her social function.' One can see here how potent the traditional mould remained and how slowly the relations between men and women evolved.

('World War II and social change in France', 1988, pp.89–90)

1   Is Bédarida saying that women did or did not make gains? How would you characterize the tone of the passage with respect to this issue?

2   Turn to Document II.18 in *Primary Sources 2: Interwar and World War II*, the programme of the CNR, and identify the place where the 'old feminist claim: to become citizens' is recognized.

3   Can you think of any other reasons for article 24 than mere traditionalism? ■

1   Bédarida clearly wants to caution us against exaggerating the amount of
change, but on the other hand he does recognize that important changes did
take place. I would say that the tone is very much in the fashion of today
('shilly-shallying' would be too unkind a word), not wanting to offend the
feminists by overstating the changes brought by the war, but, on the other
hand, forced to admit that some changes did take place. (It may be noted
here that, with respect to Italy, Tannenbaum, *The Fascist Experience*, 1972,
p.323, declares roundly that 'the active role played by women in the
Resistance helped to change the status of women as a whole in the post-war
period').

2   There is actually no explicit mention of women, but the point is implied in
the first clause ('universal suffrage') and the last ('equality of all citizens') of
paragraph 4. (Maurice Larkin, in *France Since the Popular Front* (1988)
argues that the absence of explicit mention of women was deliberate,
because both the Radical Party and trade unionists feared that women
naturally leaned towards Catholicism; I prefer Bédarida's version.)

3   Worries about the low birth-rate and the destruction of life in the war. □

Formally, equal rights for women were more a reality in Russia than anywhere in
the west. Paul Dukes (in his paper in *Total War and Social Change*, 1988) has
noted an increase in the percentage of women in the Communist Party, from 15
per cent in 1941 to over 19 per cent in 1942. However, he also points out that in
the latter year only two out of 125 full members of the Central Committee were
women.

Germany

Again I'm going to bring in the excellent collection of documents edited by
Jeremy Noakes. Here is an extract from a Wehrmacht High Command (OKW)
Directive of 22 June 1942:

> Increasingly, nowadays, women have to replace soldiers who are needed at
> the front in the service of the Wehrmacht. It is the Führer's fullest wish that
> all German women, particularly when they are acting as Wehrmacht
> auxiliaries, far from their parents and homeland, should be provided with
> care and supervision to protect them and facilitate the fulfilment of their
> duties. However, the measures which are necessary to implement the care
> and supervision must be appropriate to their feminine natures and must on
> no account lead to a militarization of women which might tend to happen
> within the Wehrmacht. The 'female soldier' does not accord with our
> nationalist socialist view of womanhood.
>
> (Noakes, *Nazism 1939–1945*, 1998, p.341)

Earlier, on 28 October 1939, Himmler had instructed the SS:

> Beyond the limits of bourgeois laws and conventions, which are perhaps
> necessary in other circumstances, it can be a noble task for German women
> and girls of good blood to become even outside marriage, not light-
> heartedly but out of a deep moral seriousness, mothers of the children of

soldiers going to war of whom fate alone will decide when they will return or die for Germany ...

(p.369)

Himmler added that the SS would look after the mothers and the children.

Now, feminists attack attitudes in all countries at this time as sexist. But, this really is sexist, and certainly a little different, I would argue, from attitudes in Britain (but see what you think when I move on to discuss some British films).

Noakes offers (p.367) this brilliant summary of the situation in Germany:

> The war had a major impact on relations between the sexes. The absence of the majority of the male population for long stretches of time combined with brief periods of leave often produced tensions between husband and wife as heightened expectations of their relationship often failed to be realised because of the difficulty of re-adjustment to being together again under conditions of great stress for both partners. The strain on marriages was increased by sexual frustration and increased opportunities for new relationships. The mobilization of large numbers of women into various forms of employment, the increased mobility produced by conscription and evacuation tore them out of their existing social networks and facilitated the creation of new liaisons which could be conducted without the customary supervision of family and neighbours. The continued awareness of the fragility of such relationships, which could easily be ended by relocation or death, encouraged an intensity which removed inhibitions. Marriage breakdowns, precipitate marriages and illegitimate births were the frequent result.
>
> In fact, the Germans created a system of post mortem marriages for unmarried mothers: that is to say, mothers would be declared to be the wives of the fathers of their children, even though these fathers were already dead.

(p.383)

If you turn to Document II.27 in *Primary Sources 2: Interwar and World War II* ('Germans in industrial labour force 1939–44') you will see that the numbers of women in employment went through minor fluctuations, but did not show any large or steady increase, even though, because of military requirements, the total labour force was declining. The table as a whole says a lot about the inefficiencies of the German war effort. One might well conclude overall that the new responsibilities women had to assume as home-makers were as important as the taking on of new jobs. The absence of men, the dislocation of war, the strident intrusions of government (particularly of the Nazi government) may well have made family life seem more precious.

R. J. Overy, 'Mobilization for total war in Germany', while not disputing the accuracy of the statistics in Document II.27, has written:

> While it is certainly true that the number of German women employed between 1939 and 1945 hardly increased at all, it would be quite wrong to conclude from this that women were not mobilized for war work. The fact is that by 1939 women already constituted a very much larger part of the workforce than in other industrialised countries.

(1988, pp.627–8)

Jill Stephenson in *Women in Nazi Germany* (1975) points out that '37% of the German labour force was female even before the outbreak of war' (p.123). If we compare Britain and Germany, we find that the proportion of women in the German workforce *in 1939* was already higher than the proportion of women in the British workforce at the very height of the British war effort in 1943. In 1939 women made up 25.7 per cent of the labour force in Britain, but 37.4 per cent in Germany. The corresponding figures for 1943 were 36.4 per cent in Britain and 48.4 per cent in Germany. More women were brought into the workforce in Britain because there was a much larger pool of non-employed or unemployed women before 1939, as might be expected given the great difference in British and German unemployment levels. The high 1939 figure reflects the large part played by female labour in the German countryside, which continued during the war as women were forced to cope with family tasks usually carried out by conscripted men. However, Noakes, in his own contribution to a valuable collection he edited, has insisted that in Germany there was a lower level of mobilization of women than in any other belligerent country ('Germany', 1992).

Italy

Feminists at the beginning of the century believed that the absolutely vital objective was winning the vote. I believe that too. If women were ever to achieve equality the idea that somehow the man, the husband, could represent them politically had to be destroyed; if women were to put their case forward, they would have to have a voice in politics equal to that of men. I have suggested (purely as a matter for discussion and debate) that events have played a bigger part than fundamentalist feminists would like to believe. I have also explained the combination of circumstances which prevented women in Italy, as well as in France, from winning the vote at the end of the First World War. At the end of the Second World War there were no debates, no votes. Liberation governments in both France and Italy, in 1944, simply granted votes to women as if it was the most obvious thing in the world: it was, but it had again taken the circumstances of war to make the decision an irresistible one. The Italian Constitution of 1948 formally declared men and women equal, but it also enshrined some of the traditional ideas about the family. And women did not secure equal pay for equal work any more than they did in other countries. Many women in Italy, and France, and all other countries, made it clear that what they really wanted to do above all, after the horrors of war, was to settle down and raise a family.

I think that the events of the two total wars did significantly affect the role and status of women, but I certainly have no wish to exaggerate. There is a profoundly moving account of women's war experience, based on archive materials and personal reminiscences, by Miriam Mafie. I am going now to print quite a long extract, discussing the Liberation. Taken at face value, it is saying 'nothing changed'. I think, if you read it carefully, taking the unwitting testimony into account, you will see that it is rather like the Anna Bravo chapter in your Course Reader – two steps forward, but only one step backward. Judge for yourself.

> In many cities basic supplies were lacking: gas, milk, bread, water. But now, in contrast to a few weeks previously, we knew that the problems could find

a solution, but the solution depended on local authorities in power. But now new authorities were in power, different from those of the past.

The Liberation was not the sudden change which many had hoped for: the return to normality was marked by new and old injustices. On 5 May [1944] there was granted to all workers a 'Liberation Award'. It was 5,000 lire for each head of family and 3,500 for those who were not heads of families. There was equality, as between men and women. But when, at the end of June, it was agreed that there should be a national emergency payment even the trade unions agreed that while men should get 120 lire per day, women should only get 100. In Turin this decision was not accepted. The women workers joined together, protested, went to the union, to the prefect, and to the Allied Command, putting this question: 'Perhaps women pay less for bread and wine than men? Surely the high cost of living for essentials is the same for all?' At the Chamber of Labour, the union leaders didn't want to know. The original agreement was signed in Rome, creating a national policy governing everyone. But the women workers of Turin were not going to accept defeat. They had led strikes against the Germans and they could strike against the unions. A strike, therefore, was declared. Thousands and thousands of women came out on the streets, protesting and demanding equality with regard to the emergency payments. The Chamber of Labour hesitated, the Industrial Union could not make up its mind. In the end, through the intervention of the UDI (Union of Italian Women) and of the Committee of National Liberation, a provincial agreement was signed: in Turin male and female workers would have the same emergency payments.

But this agreement in Turin remained an isolated instance. The return to normality signified also the return to the old discriminations: women got lower wages than men, as had always happened. It was not a question of fascism or antifascism: this was the way things had been and would be ... And so also with women.

The most audacious and courageous, those who understood perfectly well that this was not fair, slowly but surely resigned themselves to it. There was no work, and the women were awaiting the return of the soldiers, of the prisoners, of those who had been interned. Work was given back to them: this also was normality.

In Milan the prefect was a socialist, Riccardo Lombardi ...

(*Pane Nero: Donne e vita quotidiana nella seconda guerra mondiale* (Milan, 1987), (*Black Bread: Women and Daily Life during the Second World War*)

Think about it. War creates tragedy not miracles. But *I* think I detect the consequences of the new (often horrific) experiences undergone by women, and a new spirit, a new willingness to protest. And don't forget the vote, which, interestingly, is never mentioned in this account. Nobody writing in Britain, of course, would mention bread and wine as the two essentials!

Women in British wartime films

Now I want you to consider the attitudes about the role of women being transmitted in British wartime films, and also other issues discussed throughout these units.

Item 6 on Video 2 consists of the last quarter-of-an-hour or so of *The Gentle Sex*, a British World War II film which, through the device of a narration by its director Leslie Howard, explicitly sets out to follow the experiences of seven young women (fictional, of course) who enlist in the ATS. Item 5 comes from quite early in another British wartime film, *Millions Like Us*, and runs continuously for about twenty minutes (we have made a few minor cuts in the sequence showing people coming to work).

One feature film might be dismissed as unrepresentative; with two similar films we can be on more solid ground in identifying certain images and representations as being characteristic of popular films of the time. Little in a fictional film can be taken as fact; however, our attention may be drawn to issues which we would then wish to follow up in other more reliable sources. In the next exercise I have deliberately selected fairly long extracts so that, among other things, you can relax and enjoy them.

I also want you to set down some of your reactions. As these are bound to be very varied, I shan't be able to anticipate all of them. At the same time there are particular points that I do want to be sure you have noted. Therefore I am going to put some questions in the usual way, hoping that they will help you to relate what you see in the films to what you have learned elsewhere in the course.

Exercise   I suggest you read through my questions first, then sit back and enjoy the two film clips. Then write down answers where you can. After that, if necessary and if you have time, go back through the films trying to find answers to any remaining questions.

1   What is the main subject matter of the two films?

2   What do you feel about the tone of the two films?

3   What responses, relative to the war effort, are the films intended to arouse in audiences? *Millions Like Us* seems to try to allay worries some viewers might have – did you notice this?

4   Both main plots take the form of girl meets RAF boy (a sergeant in one case, a commissioned officer in the other); they fall in love; boy is killed in action. Why do you think the plots took this particular form?

5   Try to pin a class label on each of the women – Celia, Gwen, Jennifer and Annie – in *Millions Like Us*. Try also to pick out precise examples, or symbols, of class or (alleged) class behaviour. Would you agree that the general message in both films is of the mixing of classes (cite precise examples)? What, in *Millions Like Us*, seems to conflict with the views of Penny Summerfield in the Course Reader? What had Jennifer done before coming to the factory? Any comments?

6   Would you agree that both films suggest that social reform and social change will, or should, come after the war? Give examples. These films form a very different type of evidence from, say, the Beveridge Report: what significance do they have in the discussion of war and social change?

7   Finally, a very precise question on *Millions Like Us*: where were the machine tools you see made? Is there any wider significance to this? ∎

Specimen answers and discussion

1   Women's part in the war effort: military in *The Gentle Sex*, civilian in *Millions Like Us*.

2   *The Gentle Sex*, particularly at the end, is perhaps rather patronizing; yet the intentions, and the goodwill, are (I think) genuine. Perhaps *Millions Like Us* seems a little patronizing too. I am not sure, but you must decide for yourself.

3   To encourage women to participate enthusiastically in the war effort, and to encourage acceptance of this among men. The harsh conditions feared by Celia and Gwen (in different ways) do not materialize.

4   In 1940–43 (the films were both released in 1943) the air war was the most immediate one for civilians – hence both young men being in the RAF. Many in the audience would have lost loved ones: both films have the function of trying to reconcile such people to their losses. More mundanely, there had to be a story-line to maintain interest (*The Gentle Sex* becomes dangerously documentary-like at times).

5   Celia: lower middle class ('middle class' would be fine; the 'lower' is clearer when you have seen the whole film). Gwen: upwardly mobile working class (her father is a miner, but she has been to college). Jennifer: upper class or upper middle class (clearly, in all sorts of ways, she is intended to be a cut above all the other girls; note her accent and compare it with those of the others). Annie: working class (sleeping in her underclothes is intended as the clear symbol here).

I certainly detected signs of mixing (common, but by no means universal in British films of the time): Jennifer does clearly become less snobbish and tries to integrate herself with the others; in *The Gentle Sex* Maggie (subject to the snide comment about Glasgow docks) makes an accommodation with the snooty corporal (however, differences here may be more personal and psychological than social). Penny Summerfield argued that upper-class figures were not generally to be found in factories (however, that does not mean that Jennifer's situation was a completely unlikely one). Jennifer had been canteening in the West End – among rich officers, the film implies. Actually canteen work could often involve the very mixing of classes which Summerfield tends to deny.

6   Again, I think 'yes'. The most obvious example in our clip from *Millions Like Us* is in the speech by Gwen when she first meets up with Celia (play it again if you are in doubt). I wonder what you made of the exchange between Annie and Mrs Sheridan in *The Gentle Sex*? Women had served in France in the previous war, yet that was apparently forgotten: perhaps service in war does not lead to gains for women. However, the film is saying, both here and in later words by the narrator, that this time things will be different – women are now clearer about what they want, and, indeed, the influence of women will be felt not only in the new position of women, but in social reform generally.

The Beveridge Report is an actual plan for reform; attitudes expressed in the films are not actuality. However,

(a) film-makers are themselves influential people and come from a privileged group in society: these attitudes may be seen as representative of an important section of middle- and upper-class opinions;

(b) films were watched by large audiences who may well have been encouraged to believe that the war must result in social change (perhaps they were even influenced to vote Labour in 1945).

7   America, as the label Cincinatti indicates. Some commentators, in particular Correlli Barnett in his *The Audit of War*, have argued that the much vaunted British war effort was a sham, because it was so dependent on the US (I don't agree with him, but it's worth thinking about). □

Finally, let us consider Simone de Beauvoir's massive *The Second Sex*, published in France in 1949, which has become the Bible of feminism. It is worth noting what she wrote in the historical chapter of the book, entitled 'Since the French Revolution: the job and the vote'; she has just been describing the activities of the British suffragettes:

The war intervened. English women got the vote with restrictions in 1918, and the unrestricted vote in 1928. Their success was in large part due to the service they rendered during the war.

(*The Second Sex*, 1961, p.155)

How, if at all, does this book relate to the study of total war and social change? To speak of the book as a 'consequence' of the war would, of course, be absurd. However, de Beauvoir does rank with the group of Liberation writers who achieved popularity with the reading public in the post-war years. In the words of Maurice Crouzet:

The literature that found most favour with a public disappointed in the conventional variety was that of the liberation, whose most impressive representatives or interpreters were Albert Camus, Jean-Paul Sartre, Simone de Beauvoir and Maurice Merleau-Ponty. It was these philosophers and writers who, inspired by the ideas of Heidegger, Jaspers and Husserl, made existentialism fashionable. Their works offered the pessimistic picture of an artificial, absurd, incomprehensible and useless world in which man feels frustrated and cheated, for 'It is a suspended death' and 'every society creates its own hell'.

(*The European Renaissance Since 1945*, 1970, p.139)

Simone de Beauvoir, to put matters as concisely as possible, was part of an intellectual and literary movement which was itself part of the concluding phase of the war in France. *The Second Sex* is not an existentialist work, but a very powerful analysis of the position of women in contemporary society, drawing upon Hegel's concept of self and other, and upon anthropology, sociology, biology and psychoanalysis. Clearly it relates to European society as it was in the immediate post-war years, but references to World War II, direct or indirect, are very rare. Quite obviously the book owes most to de Beauvoir's own experience and intellect: in the philosophy degree she took at the Sorbonne in 1929 she came second to Jean-Paul Sartre, who was to be her life-long companion. But the book is of central relevance to total war and social change in that it both offers evidence for the status of women in the aftermath of World War II and is a key text in the modern feminist movement, given that the old question of the relationship of war to the changing status of women and to feminism remains a legitimate subject for discussion and debate. In so far as *The Second Sex* persuasively and convincingly identifies the disabilities still affecting women, it is evidence that whatever changes have been brought about by two world wars must have been quite limited in character; but then the manner in which de Beauvoir identifies the nature of these disabilities, and the remedies which she proposes, may well suggest that there could be no possibility that the sort of experiences which wars bring could affect these disabilities.

These points are offered as guidance on how you can relate the extracts from *The Second Sex* printed as Document II.28 in *Primary Sources 2: Interwar and World War II* to the major themes of this course (and it is along these lines that I shall be setting the questions in the exercise that follows shortly). We have printed less than half a dozen pages from a book which runs to two volumes, each of about 400 pages, but even these few pages are immensely rich, and may well provoke very individual responses from different readers. As a primary source this is obviously very different from the ones we studied earlier in this unit.

Both de Beauvoir and Sartre, it is useful to know, were supporters of the French Communist Party. In estimating the significance of *The Second Sex*, it is also helpful to know that the original French edition of 1949 was translated for American publication in 1953 and, later in the same year, for British publication. The book has been continuously in print in both French and English (and many other languages) ever since. Extract (a) comes from the historical chapter early in Book One, shortly after the comment I have just quoted on British women and the First World War. Extract (b) comes from the last main chapter in Book Two, in Part VII, which has the general title 'Towards Liberation', while the chapter itself is entitled 'The independent woman'. Extract (c) is from the conclusion.

Exercise   Now read the extracts from *The Second Sex* printed as Document II.28 (*Primary Sources 2: Interwar and World War II*). You may well wish to write down other points that particularly strike you, but I want you to note down answers to the following questions:

1   What indications are there that women have recently made considerable advances?

2   What indications, if any, are there that these are in any way directly or indirectly related to the Second World War?

3   What are the basic disabilities that women still suffer from?

4   How does de Beauvoir propose that these be removed? Are wars relevant, or irrelevant, to such proposals?

5   Extract (c) presents an idea – related to one of the approaches to history that I discussed in Book 1, Unit 1, and perhaps also to de Beauvoir's politics – which has been central to most feminist writing since. Identify, discuss and critically evaluate this idea. ■

Specimen answers   1   Extract (a) seems to end very optimistically with its reference to the United
and discussion   Nations Commission on the status of women: 'the game is won'; 'The future
                     can only lead to a more profound assimilation of woman into our once
                     masculine society.' Of course, this quotation recognizes that this assimilation
                     is far from having taken place at the time de Beauvoir is writing (in fact, the
                     remainder of this chapter goes on to qualify the optimism). Soviet women,
                     who anyway are 'in a singular [or exceptional] condition', having made great
                     advances, have now suffered set-backs. French women, in theory at least,
                     now have the main civil liberties. Today, according to extract (b), it is less
                     difficult for a woman to assert herself.

2   Simone de Beauvoir refers to the 'masculine' and, indeed, 'military' activities
    of Russian women in World War II. Perhaps there is an implicit connection
    here with the aspects of the status of Russian women de Beauvoir admires,
    but certainly no explicit connection is made. The major reference, really, is
    to the United Nations Commission, if we follow the train of thought that the
    United Nations, and the various commissions associated with it dealing with
    economic, cultural and social matters, were products of the war. I would
    certainly see the United Nations Commission on the Status of Women as
    representing both the 'psychological' desire for a new beginning
    engendered by war, and also the recognition of women's participation in
    the war effort; but that is not an argument that would command universal
    support. The connection is not made explicitly, but you would certainly be
    expected to be able to comment in an exam that the French woman's right
    to vote came only in the concluding stage of the war. On the whole I think
    one has to conclude that de Beauvoir does not provide very powerful
    testimony in support of the thesis about the connection between advances
    in the status of women and war.

3   Women's biological role in the family was clearly what lay at the heart of the
    set-backs in Soviet Russia. But the main point made at the beginning of
    extract (b) is women's lack of economic independence. However, as extract
    (c) makes clear, although the economic factor is the basic one, there remains
    a fundamental problem in the way in which society socializes females into
    being different from males.

4   The emphasis throughout is on positive, interventionist or 'guided' action by
    the state. In the first extract it is clear that de Beauvoir greatly admires the
    interventionist action on behalf of women taken by Lenin. In the last extract
    she refers to changes in laws, institutions, customs, public opinion, and the
    whole social context, and goes on to indicate the necessity for a total
    transformation in the way in which children are brought up and educated.
    Individual initiatives will be no good: 'The forest must be planted all at once'
    – that is, complete and comprehensive reforms must be enacted. De
    Beauvoir's emphasis, it seems to me, is very much on positive, intentional
    action, which is rather different from the unintended consequences of war
    that I have been discussing from time to time throughout this course. On the
    other hand, I would argue that the necessities of war sometimes did entail
    the near obliteration of gender differences. Possibly this is implied in the
    references to the Russian experience in extract (a); on the whole, however,
    de Beauvoir's text does not lend great support to this line of argument.

5   I wonder what you made of this difficult question. This time there definitely
is a 'right' answer, but to get it you probably either have to be acquainted
with recent feminist writings, or, like me, very interested in those
approaches to academic study and life in general which in Book 1, Unit 1
I described as 'Marxist/sociological/linguistic' and which are most evident in
contemporary cultural theory. If you are in tune with all that, then you will
have identified the critical phrase as: 'in human society nothing is natural
and ... woman, like much else, is a product elaborated by civilization'.
Woman, in other words, is made not by biology but by society. It is out of
this theory that the word 'gender' was created to replace the old word 'sex';
using the word 'gender' implies that the differences between men and
women, once believed to be fundamentally sexual, are no more than what
is decreed by society. De Beauvoir (like many other feminists, of course)
does not go as far as this, recognizing elsewhere in her book characteristics,
biological and physiological, particular to women. But the notion of woman
as 'a product elaborated by civilization' has been an enormously influential
and liberating one.

Now, I asked you to evaluate this idea critically. With respect to historical
significance, which is what this course is about, it has undoubtedly had great
influence on the development of the general movement of feminism (though
after 1955, rather than before – I shall return to this). To discuss whether it is
'correct' or not would take us right back into the conflict over approaches to
academic study, which I discussed in Book 1, Unit 1. For myself, I shall simply
say that I find nothing to quarrel with in Simone de Beauvoir's magnificently rich
and complex development of this fundamental idea. I do happen to believe that
it has, in some quarters, been pushed to absurd extremes. Think about it, and
decide for yourself (the way one looks at this issue will affect the way one looks
at historical issues in general). I would put it like this: because the roles and
attributes of men and women manifestly are *influenced* by society (or
civilization), that does not mean that they are *determined* by society. There is,
in my view, a balance between social and biological factors. As I say, in this
question is encompassed a whole debate about how one should look at society
and history. □

High and popular culture

Although the characteristic features of modernism in the arts were already
clearly apparent well before 1914, it would be widely accepted that the
catastrophe of the First World War did have profound effects on the subject
matter, beliefs and modes of expression of artists and thinkers. The Second
World War came to a much less naïve world, and therefore did not have the
same effect in transforming modes of thought and expression. It was,
nonetheless, an experience of enormous intensity, and resulted in the
production of a considerable body of work related directly to that experience.
It can indeed be argued that while the trauma of World War I turned intellectuals
in on themselves and towards the esoteric modes of modernism, World War II,
as a war of peoples and partisans, induced a turning back to realism. The least
significant work, I think it can be safely said, emanated from Germany, the guilty
country, ultimately humiliated, ruthlessly controlled, and from whom most of

the truly distinguished figures in all spheres of culture had emigrated in the 1930s. Many years had to pass before works of true distinction – works that had digested the experiences of war, as distinct from works of immediate emotional intensity or graphic experience – were produced. One of the greatest, Günter Grass's *The Tin Drum* (1959) was a ferocious and rumbustious allegory on the more recent German experience, pre-war, wartime and post-war (an extract from *The Tin Drum* is reproduced as Document II.29 in *Primary Sources 2: Interwar and World War II*).

Before you turn to your music and art audio material I want to make some general points about the relationship between war and the arts and how one studies that relationship.

1   I'm going to take that last point first. Students and tutors tend to be terrified of art and music (and sometimes even novels, plays and poetry). I want to argue that while we can't expect historians and history students to understand, say, the technicalities of musical notation, of tonality and atonality, or of brushwork, chiaroscuro, perspective, etc., we can all approach pieces of music, or paintings as we would approach other primary sources, asking the same questions. I also believe that just as we should be interested in war's possible effects on geopolitics, on women, on welfare, we should also be interested in its possible effects on the arts.

2   As with all questions about war's effects on society and culture, we have to ask: do we just look at changes happening *during* the war, or do we also look at changes *after* the war? I hope you will agree that with the arts, as with everything else, we have to look at both. What we are interested in is *lasting* change. The last piece of music on audio 2, section 1, which you will be playing in a moment, was performed in 1962 – but with a title like *War Requiem* it must be relevant.

3   Now the big issue. If war had any effects at all on the arts does it affect music as a whole, does it affect art as a whole, does it, in short, change musical *language*, change artistic *language*, or does it just affect individual museums and artists? Is it the case that the most we can say is that this piece of music, or this painting, was affected by the war, but that *across the board* there were no really profound changes? That is the key issue to think about.

4   In my own work on the changes the experience of total war brings about (and, of course, does not bring about) one of my key points is that changes take place in all sorts of different areas, which may seem unrelated, but that these changes in fact interact with each other, creating a kind of 'multiplier' effect. What I want to look at here is a couple of changes in technology, and one development in the transmission of news, which actually had great effects on the way music was distributed – no mystery: I'm basically thinking of gramophone records and radio, both enabling people to listen to classical (and other!) music in their own homes.

(a)   Early in the war, RAF Coastal Command approached the British Decca Record Company, requesting that they make a training record which would illustrate the differences in the sounds made by German and British submarines. Existing gramophones and recording techniques could not meet the challenge. However, intensive work under the supervision of Decca's Chief Engineer, Arthur Haddy, led to full frequency range reproduction (ffrr) for a specific war purpose, and then at the end of the war, for manufacturing purposes, led to brilliant, incisive, full-range recordings of concert and operatic classics. Remember Stravinsky's *Rite of Spring?* Well the first 'ffrr' record ever, was Stravinsky's *Petrushka,* released by Decca in June 1946 (Roland Gelatt, *The Fabulous Phonograph 1877–1977,* 1977, pp.282–3).

(b) To enhance the possibilities of radio propaganda during the war, the Germans developed a form of magnetic recording which ensured that pre-recorded broadcasts had all the freshness of live ones, making particular use of the pioneer commercial station Radio Luxemburg, which they had captured in 1940. On 11 September 1944 the Allies recaptured Radio Luxemburg. The secret was out, and was taken up by the commercial record companies. After the dead end of magnetic tapes on huge spools, the perfect modern LP appeared in August 1959. Britain's Decca had done it again, with a truly European production (recorded in Vienna) of Wagner's *Das Rheingold,* with soprano Kirsten Flagstad (Austrian), conductor George Solti (Hungarian, later British) and the all-important English producer, John Coulshaw (Gelatt, pp.286–7, 317).

(c) Civilians everywhere, not least in occupied Europe, suddenly found 'wireless' absolutely indispensable for keeping up with genuine news about the war, as Resistance groups found it essential for basic communication. By the end of the war, a new world offering instant news, and instant entertainment, had come into being (Arthur Marwick, 'Print pictures and sound: the Second World War and the British experience', 1982, pp.135–55). This development was very important for the transmission of classical music, live or recorded.

5   We hope that by the end of this course you will be in a good position to determine which was the greater force for change (bad as well as good), the First World War, or the Second. I've just suggested that, as an unsuspected, unprepared-for catastrophe, the First World War had the greater impact. Yet there is an argument that music changes more slowly than other art forms (romanticism in music came later than in painting). In Audio 2 I'll be suggesting that certain composers, led by Pierre Boulez, felt there had to be a complete break after the Second World War in a way there had not been after the First.

Let us do as all historians do, and consider the primary sources.

Exercise   1   Play section 1 of Audio 2, entering fully into the spirit of my discussions with you.

2   Play section 2 Audio 2, again entering fully into the spirit of my discussions with you. ∎

In the rest of this section I am going to look in turn at Germany, France, Italy, Britain and Russia, taking high culture and popular culture together.

Germany

It is significant that two of the writers who were among the first in the post-war years to try to come to grips in literary form with the Nazi and war experience were both exiles from Germany during the war period itself. One is our old friend Erich Maria Remarque, whose *A Time to Love and a Time to Die* (1951) is generally considered to be a much more contrived and less satisfactory work than his truly heartfelt *All Quiet on the Western Front*. The first serious engagement with the Nazi war experience was that of Carl Zuckmayer, who in the 1930s had fled to Austria, then to Switzerland, then to France, then finally to the US, but who returned to Germany at the end of the war, and whose play *The Devil's General* was produced in 1946. In essence the play is about Hitler and his entourage. A central character is a flying ace named Harras, who has enjoyed professional and personal success all his life without any help from the Nazi Party. Party members, as his girlfriend points out, envy him his successes, particularly his successes with women. In that area they are 'way below zero'. For them, joining the party was a way to setting things right (Frederick Harris, *Encounters with Darkness: French and German Writers on World War II*, 1983, p.104).

In the 1920s German film-making had been one of the most imaginative and innovative in the world. With the advent of Hitler, advances came almost to a total stop. But, as almost everywhere, during the war visits to the cinema became more widespread and popular than ever; in bombed areas open-air cinemas were set up, and film vans turned out to remote villages (there was partly a desire to meet the needs of hard-pressed civilians, partly a desire to continue to pump out forms of Nazi propaganda). By the closing stages of the war, long queues were forming in the early afternoons outside the Berlin cinemas. Many cinemas, of course, had been put out of action by bombing raids, and a considerable black market in tickets developed. Throughout the war soldiers (of whom there were not many around) had been granted the right to go straight to the head of queues, but as the front line came closer and closer to the capital, this privilege was revoked. The enormous wartime audiences provided the basis for the two greatest box office successes of the entire Third Reich, *The Great Love* and *Request Concert*. The first of these:

> focused on the solidarity of suffering of women separated from their men folk at the front. Characteristically omitting any reference to the events or the background of the war, it made wartime separation seem to be a form of alchemy whereby the gold of marital love could be purged of all dross.
>
> ... of sympathetic magic, the film gave married soldiers a more favourable statistical rating than single ones by implying a wife's loving concern for her husband at the front could – like some incorporeal bullet-proof vest – shield him from harm.
>
> (Richard Grunberger, *A Social History of the Third Reich*, 1971, p.87)

Request Concert took its name from a weekly radio programme linking soldiers and their families through musical requests. Artistically these films were of no merit, but they do bring out both the importance of family in wartime Germany, and that critical significance of radio to which I have already referred.

With respect to radio, there was a two-and-a-half-hour Sunday afternoon programme of 'request concerts', incorporating a medley of requests by soldiers for their families, and by families for their serving men. The new and unique power of radio is highlighted in Hitler's crucial broadcast after the attempt on his life in July 1944: the broadcast reassured the public as no other medium then could have done.

Many, but by no means all, of the great musicians, composers, performers and conductors had fled from Nazi Germany. The most popular excerpts from the great German classics were exploited for Nazi purposes. Wagner's great opera house at Bayreuth became a kind of culture centre for the deserving, convalescent soldiers, hyper-industrious munitions workers, nurses, and so on. Hitler had always been hostile to western dance music, and the war meant that Germany was practically cut off from this influence. The playing of such music, and dancing to it, was an activity indulged in at great personal risk by youthful rebels.

France

The intellectual and literary scene in post-war France was dominated by Jean-Paul Sartre and Albert Camus. In no way, however, can one talk of the war as 'creating' existentialism. Camus rejected the label, and Sartre's purely existentialist works date back to before the war. What their wartime and post-war writings implied was, within a broader perception of the irrationality and absurdity of the world, the affirmation of social and political commitment. Later, Paris was the home of the 'new novel' (Alain Robbe-Grillet is mentioned in the Reader article by Josipovici – 'The birth of the modern: 1885–1914', pp.56–71), which went far beyond the stream-of-consciousness techniques of James Joyce and completely destroyed the narrative structure of the traditional western novel. It is not easy to detect any direct links between this development and the disruptions of war. The best generalization one can make about the most significant developments after 1945 is that writers and artists were responding to an entire twentieth-century crisis, of which World War II was one major symptom, rather than to the war as such. In any case, I propose here to concentrate on two examples of more immediate, and therefore more limited, responses to the war (and ones which tend to support the contention that, in contrast to World War I, World War II provoked a reaction towards realism).

Exercise   Turn to Document II.30 in *Primary Sources 2: Interwar and World War II*, the extract from the short novel *Le Silence de la Mer* (*The Silence of the Sea*). This was the first in the clandestine series *Editions de Minuit* ('Midnight Editions') published in France by supporters of the Resistance, and smuggled out to Britain. The novel was completed in October 1941 and published in February 1942. In a moment I want you to consider this novel in relationship to the poetry of Louis Aragon, who in 1939 was editor of *Le Soir*, a left-wing evening paper with a circulation of nearly half a million. Aragon served with great distinction in the French army, winning several medals and being evacuated from Dunkirk, prior to the capitulation. He published one volume of heavily coded poetry (poetry lends itself naturally to coding) under the Vichy regime, before it was banned by the Germans; subsequently, as an active Resistance organizer, he published four more volumes through the clandestine Resistance press, and then one volume at the time of the Liberation. In reading (now) the extract from 'Vercors' (Document II.30) and (in a moment) the poems by Aragon (Document

II.31) you might wish to bear in mind the words of Paulhan, the distinguished French critic of the time: 'art benefits by being clandestine and subversive'. 'Vercors' was the pseudonym of Jean Bruller, an artist and writer of hitherto modest distinction. In his novel a German officer is billeted with an old Parisian (the narrator) and his niece. The old man warms to the officer, but the niece treats him with unrelenting silence. Only at the end, when the officer is called to the eastern front, does the old man hear her mutter to him 'Adieu'.

Now write a commentary on the extract, commenting on any significant or difficult points in it, and saying what you think is its significance. ∎

Specimen answer and discussion   The first part of the extract informs us that the German officer is a man of high culture, and indeed of tolerance. He recognizes the great French authors, and also the English one, Shakespeare. When he turns to music, his obvious implication is that German and French civilization complement each other: France has the literature, but Germany has the music. His ideas, apparently genuine, are those which the Nazis put forward, of France and Germany coming together in a greater civilization in the 'New Order'. The officer suggests that it is a tragedy that there should have been a war at all, and expresses a view that this must be the last one: 'we will marry each other!'

The phrasing here indicates that the novel is operating on several levels: the relationship between Germany and France, the relationship between the officer and the niece (who, it later becomes apparent, is in the room), and the later discussion of the story of Beauty and the Beast.

The novel becomes more politically pointed when the officer refers to his initial entry into France at the border at Saintes. First he had thought the population genuinely welcomed the Germans, then, when he realized that they were simply acting out of cowardice, he felt contempt for France. Thus he actually rejoices in the stern silence of the niece, who is seen as upholding the honour of France. The niece, accordingly, is seen as a metaphor for the Resistance, however cultured and seductive some German claims might be. The next part concerns the conflict between national necessities and personal sentiments (we must bear in mind that this is a novel, fiction, and that although much of this extract is in the form of comments by the German officer, the whole thing has been created by a French writer). It is apparent that the niece is in fact attracted to the officer. The officer then recalls the Beauty and the Beast story which, of course, symbolizes both Germany's relationship with France and the officer's relationship with the niece.

The novel is saying three things:

1   Whatever the temptations, we in the Resistance must be, and are, unflinching.

2   Doing one's duty, in time of war especially, brings personal pain.

3   We in the Resistance are not brutal and ignorant propagandists – we can recognize that there are civilized Germans, even if it is our duty totally to resist them.

The historical significance lies in the very circumstances of the production of this work, the way in which it was both distributed in France and smuggled over to Britain (without being translated). It is a symbol of cultural life, in its most noble-spirited and least partisan sense, being continued in occupied France. □

Now I want you to turn to the two poems by Louis Aragon (Document II.31). the stanzas of the second poem, about a quarter of the total length of the poem, are very clear, and may even, in English translation, seem slightly banal. The first poem, 'Tears are alike', is more in the spirit of *Le Silence de la Mer*, and indeed of the famous film *La Grande Illusion*. It may not be immediately clear to you, but what the speaker is referring to in stanzas 1–3 is his experience as a soldier occupying the German Rhineland in 1922. Stanza 4 is the key stanza: he did not know then about how he would feel when his own country was occupied, as it now is: the reference to 'false prophets' is to the Vichy regime and the French collaborationists, in whom most Frenchmen (though not Aragon) found 'hope'. The next stanza takes us back to the narrator's experience in the Rhineland and the signs he could not decipher. Stanza 6 is also a critical one, linking the tears of the Rhinelanders with the tears of France in 1942. Stanza 7 is again memory, of the 'blank looks' of the 'vanquished' Rhinelanders. Aragon has been termed *the* poet of western resistance in the Second World War. He was a Communist, but an independent-minded one; despite the Nazi–Soviet pact, he was an enthusiastic soldier for France. Aragon can be seen as representing the bringing together of the spirit of resistance and the spirit of reform, the impulse towards a genuinely better post-war world. If we go back to the imagery of Beauty and the Beast in the novel, we may see that as a kind of anticipation of the movement for European union which in fact developed after the war.

The German occupation of France saw the creation of the German company *La Continentale*, which was intended to be the Hollywood of Nazi Europe. Many leading French film-makers remained in France, there being some argument among historians and film critics as to how far they expressed 'coded' resistance through their films. *Symphonie Fantastique* (1942) attempted some kind of nationalist statement through the life of the great French composer Hector Berlioz. Goebbels was not amused:

> the French must content themselves with light films, empty, even a little stupid, and it is our business to give them such films ... Our policy must be identical to that of the Americans with regard to the American continent. We must become the dominant power on the European continent. We must prevent the creation of any national cinema industry.

(Quoted by Georges Sadoul, *Le cinéma français*, 1962, p.91)

What French film-makers did do, in the view of Sadoul, the greatest authority, was to take refuge in what he calls 'stylism' – beautifully made films without any obvious message. The three greatest box office successes of wartime French cinema were *La Nuit Fantasque, Les Visiteurs de Soir,* and *L'Eternal Retour.* The second of these, made by Marcel Carné with a screenplay by Pierre Laroche and Jacques Prévert, was originally set in the contemporary era, then was prudently switched to the Middle Ages. It is possible that the chained and tortured lovers are meant to represent France, while the devil may represent Hitler. The third of these films, made by Jean Cocteau, was based on the famous theme of Tristan and Isolde. Since this theme had its most celebrated incarnation in Wagner's *Tristan und Isolde*, the film was denounced by the British as being collaborationist: Sadoul points out that the original legend originated from Brittany, so that the film could be seen as expressing a form of French nationalism. Sadoul, incidentally, doesn't think much of it, speaking contemptuously of 'gratuitous baroque episodes'. The 'stylistic' tendency of the occupation reached its culmination in *Les Enfants du Paradis*, made by Carné and Prévert under the most difficult conditions in the later stages of the occupation, with the Germans not being at all clear exactly what the film was all about. This is (in my opinion) one of the greatest films of all time, an allegory of good and evil, of reality and representation, of different kinds of love, of the existentialist agent Lecaneur, who in the perfect gratuitous act, assassinates the arrogant, all-powerful nobleman (symbol of the occupation?), all set in the Paris of Balzac. I simply recall the words of Paulhan: 'art benefits by being clandestine and subversive'.

Italy, Britain and Russia

Of *Les Enfants du Paradis* one thing can be said with absolute certainty: it betrays not the slightest whiff of Americanization. The same I believe could be said of the one great creative outburst of wartime and liberated Italy, that of neo-realist cinema. This is a topic fully explored in the Open University course AA304 *Politics, Culture and Society in France and Italy 1943–1973*, and one which cannot be taken further here, though I would like you to reflect on the proposition that the realism of such films as *The Bicycle Thieves* is the realism of a war of peoples (as is maintained, for example, by Tannenbaum in his *The Fascist Experience*, 1972, p.337, where he also contrasts the neo-realism of the painter Guttuso with the surrealism of de' Chirico developed at the end of World War I). Similar points – national, non-American, self-expression and 'democratic' realism – could be made about the great efflorescence of British film-making which accompanied the war (though such films were often very conscious of continuing class distinctions). With the great concentration of effort and resources on national survival, British film-makers who in the 1930s had too often been confused through aiming at US standards and attempting to reach US audiences, developed a genuinely British tradition, examples of which you have already seen in *Millions Like Us* and *The Gentle Sex*. However, the issue of the extent of Americanization (as of Sovietization) brought by World War II is a contentious one, on which, as with other such issues in this course, you should seek to develop your own views.

Finally, I come to Russia. Because of the way in which literature had been politicized in Soviet Russia, the impact of the war was enormous, with the efforts of Soviet writers between 1941 and 1945 being almost completely devoted to the war. Brown comments on a process which we have already seen at work in other spheres. In the middle stages of the war, writers had more freedom than usual, and were able to draw on the reserves of Russian historical traditions. But as the war came to an end, official control returned. Literature then became as debased as ever it was in Nazi Germany, being almost entirely confined to celebrating the glories of Stalin. In assessing the consequences of war we have always, as noted several times, to be aware of other constraints (dictatorship, occupation by a foreign power, etc.) which may contain or terminate forces released by war itself. While creative artists in France had to beware of the alien regime imposed by Germany, artists in Russia had to beware of their own regime. Sergei Eisenstein was able to exploit Stalin's admiration for the historic Russian figure Ivan the Terrible in making his film of that name; at the same time he was able to hint at a parallel between the 'gang of degenerates' (as a critical Communist Party Central Committee later put it) surrounding Ivan and the Communist Party bureaucrats.

The horrific, powerful and sometimes uplifting experiences of World War II were deeply etched into cultural artefacts at all levels, but there was no significant general shift in direction, such as it is possible to associate with World War I. However, as noted before, one contrast that can be made, though it should not be pushed too far, is that intellectuals, 'scorched' or 'traumatized' by the cataclysmic collapse of civilized values after 1914, sought isolation and the new modes of modernism, whereas some intellectuals in the Second World War, seeking an identification with struggling peoples, turned back towards naturalism and realism.

Political institutions and values

Exercise on four French newsreels

These newsreels, items 7–10 on Video 2, are dated respectively May 1940, April 1944, May 1944 and June 1944. We discovered the first one by accident, having actually asked the Imperial War Museum for another issue from 1944. It occurred to me immediately that looking at the four items together gives a very good sense of the beginning and ending of the war for France, and of some of the particular ways in which the war impacted on French society. I shall talk you through each item separately (because of shortage of space we have made cuts in all of these; item 9, which is in the condition in which we found it, starts rather abruptly), but you should try to find time (perhaps when revising for the exam) to play the four items together to get a general overview of certain important developments in France. The aims of this exercise, then, extend beyond the single topic of political institutions and values:

1   Film material can make vivid to you (as it made vivid to audiences at the time) events and developments (which you already know about from your written course material; you, of course, are in a position to make a detached historical analysis, knowing how events unfolded – a position not open to film audiences at the time).

2   You can see the uses that were made of this particular form of mass communication, a subject to which Tony Aldgate and James Chapman will return shortly.

3   You can see (and hear) some of the political, social and ideological responses to invasion (two rather different ones) and occupation.

4   You can see directly and physically something of the impact of the war on civilian life.

Exercise   Play item 7 on Video 2, noting down answers to the following questions:

1   What military stage of the war is being reported here?

2   Against whom is the commentary directed, and for what in particular?

3   The film shows two of the most characteristic tragedies inflicted on civilians by twentieth-century war: what are they?

4   What device is used by the film-makers to heighten the sense of tragedy?

5   Do any scenes strike you as obvious clichés, possibly deliberately set up, presumably to impress French audiences? (I have in mind a scene near the beginning of the extract.)

6   Had you been a French person of the time would you, overall, have found this film reassuring? Give reasons. ∎

Specimen answers   1   The German blitz on Holland, Belgium and Luxembourg, which, of course,
and discussion   preceded the invasion of France itself. There are references to Allied troops having been thrown in, but a month later there came the evacuation from Dunkirk.

2   The Germans, particularly for the barbarity of bombing civilian targets.

3   The flight of refugees (note the reference to the horrific memories of the Belgians of the previous war), and bombing.

4   Music.

5   Maybe you noticed other things as well, but I was struck by the civilians welcoming the 'rescuing' Allied troops (here French) – particularly the girl giving the soldier a bottle of beer and the little boy offering cigarettes.

6   I would think not, despite the scenes of 'rescue' first mentioned. The film does reveal that French civilian targets had been bombed. It is often held that newsreel film was always exploited to maintain morale, but here, I suspect, the naked actuality may well have contributed to the mood of defeatism in France. □

Exercise   Now play item 8, and then answer the following questions:

1   Note the date of this newsreel: what is the general military situation at this time; what indications come through in the film? Which major primary source that you have already studied dates from exactly this time?

2   Look back to question 2 of the previous exercise: what comments occur to you this time (reflect a little on the horrible ironies of war)?

3   The bombing of civilians and the question of evacuation (particularly of children) are much in evidence. Are there any signs (however limited) of a stimulus to social welfare? What, according to Hoffmann, is the significance of Bichelonne in this context?

4   Pay very careful attention to the world of politics sequence referring to the Milice (you may have to play it two or three times). What has happened? What is the attitude of the commentator? What do you learn about the internal situation in France? ∎

Specimen answers   1   The Germans are in slow retreat on the Russian front. British and American
and discussion   bombing raids on France are intensifying in preparation for the invasion of France, which the Germans know to expect, but don't know where to expect it. The only direct manifestations in our example are the Allied bombing raids. The primary source is the programme of the National Resistance Council.

2   Again, the barbarity of aerial bombardment is being denounced, however the evil perpetrators this time are not the Germans but the British and the Americans!

3   The Workers' Committee for Immediate Assistance (COSI) is a direct response to bombing; however, since it obviously depends on voluntary contributions it is rather limited as a social welfare organization. Bichelonne was credited by Hoffmann as being one of the Vichy ministers who pioneered social welfare policies later adopted by the Liberation.

4   A policeman has been killed (obviously by the Resistance). The commentator, inevitably, takes the government line in speaking of the bravery of the police in the face of what he calls 'crime and banditry'. It is clear that by this stage the Resistance is having an impact which even an official newsreel cannot conceal. □

Exercise   Now play both items 9 and 10.

1   At what stage do we realize that a new turning-point in the military war has been reached? In what sense does it echo the first item you looked at?

2   What characteristic feature of this war, evident in both of the previous items, is again central to these two issues? (Did any particular details stand out this time?)

3   The opening titles for item 9 are missing. The opening shot is a hoary old, and very phoney, film cliché. Explain.

4   What three symbols of French patriotism are exploited in the film? Did you learn anything about popular French support for the occupation regime?

5   What impression was the sequence on the Russian front at the end of item 9 intended to give French audiences?

6   What does item 10 do to try to keep up the morale of audiences: for example, what does it concentrate on in portraying the Allied invasion? What about other sequences?

7   I have spoken from time to time of workers' participation. Did you see any hints of this? ■

Specimen answers and discussion   1   Where item 10 begins to discuss 'the war in France'. We begin with the German invasion of the Low Countries; now we have the Allied invasion of German-occupied France.

2   The bombing of civilians (note the similarities of music and moral indignation expressed by the commentaries). I noted the indignation on the destruction of the library at Chartres (the Nazis, of course, were the great burners of books), and the chalked messages on bombed houses (all of these were optimistic – were the cameraman, editor, etc. secretly pro-Allies? Do we again see the 'constructive' response to bombing?).

3   Bombs issuing from planes is one of the oldest tricks in the business. They can never, of course, be the same bombs as do the damage, and anyway a French cameraman could not have got such shots of *enemy* planes.

4   Joan of Arc (sword blown off by the wicked Allies); Marshal Pétain, hero of World War I, here represented as France's only true leader; the 'Marseillaise'. There does seem to be popular support for Pétain – it's not faked; on the other hand, the persuasive powers of the Milice, the Gestapo, etc., were considerable. The evidence in general is that Pétain *was* popular.

5　One of cheerful German soldiers prepared to fight to the death against Bolshevism, contrasted with (this at least was the intention, though we are perhaps less susceptible to such racism) very Slavic-looking Russian prisoners, made to appear as *'Untermenschen'*.

6　Apart from the emphasis on destruction and the deaths of Frenchmen, the invasion sequences featured burnt-out American tanks and anti-aircraft defences against Allied planes. The penultimate sequence (the Milice again – referred to as the 'forces of order' – and Laval) is on the theme of 'Life Goes On'; the last item tries to wring 'Hope' out of the launching of a civilian ship.

7　I don't want to press this, but, while grossly exploited, workers were essential to all aspects of the war effort: we *see* them at work in this final launching scene. □

Comparative study of institutions and values

I shall start with political institutions.

Clearly, the ten areas of social change that I have identified for study throughout this course overlap each other. There is, in any case, considerable dispute over what exactly constitutes the 'political'. Some people argue that everything is in essence political; others that, compared with broader economic and social forces, politics are relatively unimportant. Even if I limit myself here to changes in forms of government, electoral laws, prevailing political ideas (liberal, collectivist, democratic, etc.) and political parties, it will quickly become clear that much of this had already been covered in our discussions of other areas of change. So also has a major question for debate: were political institutions and values in 1945 and after shaped more by war experiences (the participation of labour, Resistance ideas, etc.) or by whether or not countries fell under Russian influence or that of, say, the western occupying powers in Germany? Certainly the establishment of one-party dictatorships (similar to that of Russia, different from those of Hitler and Mussolini) was a major political consequence of the war.

You will probably remember the chart I asked you to construct when you were working on Book 1, Unit 4 (simply a country-by-country list of headings under which you could note down changes in political institutions and values).

I want you now (a) to read Roberts from p.459 ('This prolongation ...') to p.462 ('... entered the war') and then (b) to reflect on what you have learned about political change so far in this book. Take the UK, France, Italy and Germany (I am taking it that the *broad* developments in eastern Europe are essentially similar to each other – the detail will be examined in a later unit) and note down the main changes of 1945 and after (of course, *during* the war countries often had to make temporary changes in their political organization). Note how, if at all, the changes relate to the war experience.

Instead of providing an extensive answer, I am simply going to highlight certain points that may not have come out clearly from Roberts or from your earlier reading in this book.

Britain

In its essentials the political system did not change ('victory' in war was taken as a vote of confidence in the system). This time, for instance, there was no striking reform of the franchise (the Labour government did, however, improve democracy by abolishing the second vote which businessmen could cast). Most historians (see, for example, Paul Addison, *The Road to 1945*, 1975) would agree that as a result of the war experience there was a general shift towards a political consensus in favour of collectivism and the welfare state. Some middle-class voters moved left, and more workers than ever before felt a clear commitment to voting Labour. Thus the election of a Labour government had much to do with changes touched off by the war.

France

It is a commonplace that the spirit of Resistance evaporated quickly and that although some of the forms of the Fourth Republic were different from those of the Third, France continued to be governed by shifting middle-of-the-road governments, as in pre-war years. Crucially, however, the whole French civil service was renewed (the 'regeneration of élites' of Bédarida, product of the 'test' of war, as I would put it) and provided France with the kind of leadership and planning initiatives, and reconstruction of the economic infrastructure, which turned out to be so lacking in Britain. The complete proportional representation system with large constituencies, closely identified with the failed politics of the interwar years, was replaced by a two-round system with low-scoring candidates being eliminated in the first round.

Italy

After the brief and not very competent government of Ferrucio Parri, who, in the words of Martin Clark (*Modern Italy*, 1996, p.317), 'symbolised the values of the Resistance', Italian politics was dominated by the Christian Democrats. However (remember the golden rule: look at what a country you are assessing was like *before* the war), Italy before 1914, unlike France, had not had a secure democratic system imbued with democratic values; hence, in part, the ease with which Mussolini came to power. The moderately progressive democratic system of the years after 1945 was something different, and its spirit was essentially that of the anti-fascism and community welfare politics stirred up in the war years (see Tannenbaum, *The Fascist Experience*, 1972, pp.325–39). Attention must also be given to the special position obtained by the Italian Communist Party (PCI), largely through the leadership it provided during the Resistance the PCI was also helped by the split in the Socialist Party (PSI) in 1947. Though kept out of central government, it had great prestige throughout the nation, most notably in agricultural areas (in part at least because it was able to assert its independence from Moscow); it was a great social influence in many communities, and a power in local politics in such important cities as Bologna. There was a new balance of political forces, committed to democracy and tending towards community welfare. Many writers see only a lost revolution (consider that argument carefully); I, however, believe that, with Germany, Italy underwent the greatest political change of all western countries.

Germany

Post-war forms of government emerged more quickly in Italy than in Germany, where the occupying power spent more time nurturing a new German democracy, eventually also dominated by Christian democracy. You will recall the arguments so well expressed by Roseman. I shall add only one thought. It is hard ever to assert that the appalling carnage and suffering of war is worthwhile. At least World War II did obliterate Nazism and the peculiar 'liberal' and nationalist political values which, in part, lay behind it.

A final reflection on eastern Europe

'Europe divided' was not an instant consequence of war. The situation of Czechoslovakia, in particular, is worth reflecting on. Although many Czech political leaders at the end of the war looked warmly towards Russia, there was a widespread belief in the west that Czechoslovakia could become a new showcase of progressive democratic government. The *coup d'état* which clamped Soviet rule on a country till then governed by a coalition government and operating democratic elections (one was due in May 1948) did not come till February 1948. Even then some historians have blamed the Democratic ministers who walked out, rather than being pushed out, of government, as much as Soviet machinations. In the post-war political history of Czechoslovakia we see different sorts of forces released by war taking effect at different times.

Religion and the family

The experience of war induced something of a revival of religion as a factor in politics. With notable exceptions, Protestants and Catholics were now more able to work together, and generally positively in favour of social reform. In Italy, Christian democracy was exclusively Catholic, but on the whole, while resolutely opposed to communism, was a moderately progressive force. The war was immensely disruptive of 'normal' family relationships. At the same time, the reformed and strengthened Christian democracy/Catholic Church was a very strong force in support of the traditional family, as seen, in particular, in the new Italian constitution. Trends, as so often, go in different directions. The long-term ones everywhere were those of decline in religious observance and in the traditional family. However, contrary to a commonplace but little examined assertion, wars do not necessarily 'accelerate' existing trends. They can produce all kinds of hiccups and counter-trends.

Two final documents exercises

To give you practice in the kinds of document exercise you will have to do in the examination, and, of course, to give you some guidance on how to do them, I am now setting the exercises I mentioned earlier.

Exercise   Turn to Document II.20 in *Primary Sources 2: Interwar and World War II*, the report of *L'Unità* on the Turin strikes of 1943. Imagine that in front of you in an examination is printed the third, fourth and fifth paragraphs, that is to say from 'What are they striking for' to 'the profiteers and the party leaders'.

Write a commentary on this extract, saying what the document is, setting it in its historical context, commenting on specific points in the text, and summing up the extract's historical significance for the study of total war and social change.

In order to make a really serious attempt at this you may find it desirable to refer back to my discussions of Italy, particularly in the section on class. Please do make a serious effort to write out an answer to this question, then compare your answer with mine. ■

Specimen answer   This extract is from the Communist paper *L'Unità*; that is to say, it is a newspaper report from a very politically committed newspaper. While we might expect left-wing bias, we would also expect this source to be closely in touch with events affecting the working class. Mussolini's Fascist regime was being severely tested by the war, and found to be seriously wanting. By early 1943 discontent with the regime was openly breaking out. *L'Unità*, banned along with the Communist Party by the Fascists, had been revived the previous year and was now coming out as a clandestine monthly. RAF bomb attacks on northern Italy had been especially disruptive, and particularly affected the workers in the industrial areas. Although the incomes of workers, essential to the war effort, had held up reasonably well, they were now deteriorating rapidly. The extracts are from *L'Unità's* report on the strikes which broke out in Turin on 5 March 1943, known as 'internal strikes', since the workers simply downed tools at 10.00 a.m. for short periods, rather than going continuously on strike. The *L'Unità* article begins by giving a very colourful account of the strikes, and of the way in which Fascist officials have been unable to do anything about them. The report now turns (in the extract in front of us) to the reasons for the strikes.

The extract explains that the first demand is that the evacuation allowance (equivalent to 192 hours or one month's wages) should be paid to all workers. Although the bombing raids had caused widespread distress, the government was trying to limit these allowances to those who could prove incontrovertibly that they had to take up a new residence. In part, of course, the claims were simply a means towards increasing earnings. But they do also show the real effects that the bombing raids were having. The second claim is for a straight rise in wages to meet the considerable rise in the cost of living. The third claim is for an increase in basic rations. (Italy, of course, had had to impose basic food rationing, the workers generally doing better than other ordinary people, but by this time rations had severely deteriorated.) The remainder of this second paragraph expresses most accurately the general feelings of frustration, war-weariness, and the determination to protest which lay behind the strike. It may be noted that in time of war the Italian Communist Party developed a policy of very precise, realistic demands (as distinct from the call for revolution); it continued this position in the post-war years.

The next paragraph begins with the more fundamental Communist Party principle, that of the power of the working class, provided it is united. There is a triumphant tone about the first sentence, which was justified since the government did give way to the workers' demands. The remainder of the paragraph is about the need to extend the Turin strike to other areas of Italy. Again, what is spoken of did come to pass: there was a series of strikes in other industrial areas.

The significance of the document is that it demonstrates the power workers can have in time of war because of the desperate need for their participation in the war effort. It has the particular significance of describing, as Martin Clark (1996) has put it, the first open workers' protest against fascism. The fact that the strikes spread, and that the government had to make concessions, demonstrate both the potential of the working class and the weakness of the Fascist regime exposed by war. There was much suffering and repression still to come, particularly when the Germans took over all of northern Italy, but events presented in the document (with very little ideological or propagandist exaggeration) can be seen as marking a stage towards the defeat of fascism and the emergence in Italy of a more equal and democratic society. The document also indirectly reflects the fact that British bombing raids on northern Italy, unlike many other bombing raids, did achieve some of their objectives.

Discussion   There is no absolutely right answer, of course, but I hope you were able to make some of these points and, more important, can now see the sorts of points you should be making. Let me just summarize a few guidelines.

1   In stating what the document is, any indicators of its reliability, likely biases, etc., will be welcomed.

2   In setting the context you have to refer to wider knowledge derived from secondary sources (particularly the course units) and you also have to show how the extract fits into the document as a whole, or even, in some cases, into a group of similar documents. The date of the document will almost certainly be of great significance.

3   Note the way of working through line by line, making any appropriate comments (for example, explaining the '192 hours'), commenting on wider significance (there *were* other strikes), on reliability (especially, as compared with your general comment at the beginning). This is a reliable document, though the opening paragraphs of the report, not used in my exercise, are rather rhetorical and highly coloured.

4   The historical significance can be at several levels. The point about bombing, though important, is obviously less important than the point about the place of these events in the development of the Italian war experience. ☐

Exercise   I want you now to turn to Document II.32 in *Primary Sources 2: Interwar and World War II*, 'An average French town in 1950'. Just note for your own general information, with regard to changes in class structure, the social composition given at the beginning. Then read the rest of the document carefully. I want you to note down what it tells you about such questions as Americanization and the effects, or lack of them, of World War II, and about social distinctions and social snobbishness. I suggest you just note down your comments as you work your way through the document: that is the way I am going to give my comments in the specimen answer below, rather than structuring them into an organized exam-style commentary. Then I'd like you to speculate a bit as to how representative this document would be for the rest of France, and then for other parts of Europe. ■

Specimen answer and discussion

After the table the very first sentence makes the comment that people's leisure activities are differentiated by social class (or 'social strata' as the authors put it). The next two sentences are equally positive: the cinema takes first place. Is this just the normal development of modernization, or mass society, or is it a result of the war experience, or of Americanization? There are arguments that in difficult wartime conditions people tended to take refuge in, and therefore developed a taste for, the cinema. On the other hand, we do know that the cinema was already growing rapidly in popularity before the war. At this point, the document does not provide any definitive answers. What the next paragraph repeats is that people from different social backgrounds go to different cinemas. Most interesting are the comments on the *Select*. The religious influence is clear in that the cinema was built by a Monsignor in the Catholic Church, and it is part of a chain directed by the organization 'Familia' in Paris. All this seems to date back to pre-war times, though it is noteworthy that the cinema was reconstructed in 1948. We do then get an answer to the Americanization question: according to this document the public favour French films, while success for American films, it is said, depends on their being shown in conjunction with publicity in the film journals. (Note the detail of preferences, which may well be useful to you in answering other questions; they do not relate to the specific questions I have asked.)

The argument for the war having popularized radio is probably stronger than that for the war popularizing film, though again the document does not make the connection. The figures are certainly worth noting.

Now we learn that reading in fact shares first place with film-going. The origins of this activity clearly go back well before the war. Yet the jump in books borrowed between 1939 and 1945 is quite considerable: it can be argued that in the restricted conditions of wartime, people do turn to reading (this is certainly demonstrable in Britain). Again we find some class distinctions in reading habits. Detective stories were widely popular, and, on the evidence from bookshops, translations from English. Now whether this indicates a growing popularity for American-style crime novels is impossible to say. It is known from other sources that British books were quite popular. Thus there is no positive support for the Americanization thesis. Does one, in any case, think of the Americans as rating reading among their top two leisure activities?

It is significant that the Auxerre Stadium was built in 1942, since this would suggest a link with Vichy policies of encouraging sport. Again we must note the influence of the same Monsignor, which this time goes back even before the First World War. Football, if anything, betrays a British influence, but perhaps basketball betrays an American one. In general, I hope you agree, this is an interesting document with a fascinating range of information.

Now, before speculating on how far it is representative of the rest of France, or the rest of Europe, one really ought (as a basic first question) to have asked how reliable it is for Auxerre itself. If you look at the end of the document, you will see that what we have here is a social survey. It has been carried out, though you would not know this, by two distinguished academics; so although there may have been room for the expression of some slightly snobbish opinions, we can on the whole take it as being as reliable as such a survey could be in 1950. (One could reasonably argue, incidentally, that the idea of systematic social surveys was very much a product of American universities.)

What other areas of France are there? Well, there are big cities and there are purely agricultural areas. In so far as this comes, as it were, 'in the middle', it might be considered as representative as any single document could be. One could reasonably speculate that the biggest variations would come in Paris, but perhaps also Lyon and Marseilles.

As for the rest of Europe, this is probably going to be more typical of the west than the east, though perhaps the activities specified would not be all that different: great emphasis will certainly be given to sports and to youth in the eastern countries. No document can possibly be representative, and certainly not over a wide range of regions and countries, but I feel that this gives you as good a single insight as you could get. Maybe what strikes us most today is the relative lack of sophistication of the activities and attitudes listed. Whatever changes the war may have brought, there were still many other transformations to come, with the further advances of modernization, mass society and, above all, the advent of consumer affluence. □

3   FILM AND RADIO PROPAGANDA DURING WORLD WAR II

In Unit 18 we considered how the mass media, and, more especially, film and radio, were used by the governments of the Soviet Union, Nazi Germany and Britain to present political propaganda to the masses. The word 'propaganda', of course, has often been used in a pejorative sense. An American social scientist, writing in 1935, observed that 'the word propaganda has a bad odor. It is associated with the war and other evil practices' (Leonard W. Doob, *Propaganda: Its Psychology and Technique*, 1935, p.374). In the democracies, especially, the very idea of propaganda was regarded with suspicion and distaste. One British woman, for example, after seeing the first propaganda feature film of the war, a patriotic tribute to the fighting power of the RAF called *The Lion Has Wings* (1939), produced by Alexander Korda, commented that 'I think it un-British to stuff propaganda down your throat like that' (quoted in Jeffrey Richards and Dorothy Sheridan, *Mass-Observation at the Movies*, 1987, p.319). But for all the negative connotations that have been attached to it, governments in democratic countries as well as those of the European dictatorships were alert to the desirability of utilising propaganda to present their case to publics both at home and abroad. This was already evident during the interwar period, as Unit 18 showed, but it became even more necessary during the Second World War. In this section we are going to consider the role and nature of film and radio propaganda during the war, focusing in this instance on Germany and Britain. We'll be referring to an abundance of primary source material on both video and audio, and we've set exercises on much of this material in order that you may get a taste of what sort of messages the German and British publics were presented with by their official propaganda agencies. In order fully to understand the nature of propaganda, however, it is necessary to have some contextual knowledge of the organization of the propaganda machinery in both countries.

Propaganda and the state

Propaganda is an attempt to influence the opinions and behaviour of others. The nature of propaganda depends in large measure on who or what the propagandist is – propaganda might be carried out by an individual (Hitler's *Mein Kampf,* for example, could be considered propaganda in that it was an attempt to persuade others of the doctrines of national socialism), or by a political party (remember the newsreels of Stanley Baldwin's election address that you looked at in Unit 18). The German and British propaganda of the Second World War was what we might call state propaganda – propaganda designed by the government in the interests, or so it was claimed, of the nation as a whole. In both Germany and Britain there were state institutions, in the form of government departments, responsible for the formulation of propaganda policy and the widespread dissemination of propaganda through all available channels of communication.

This is not to say, however, that the organization of propaganda in the two countries was the same. As you would probably expect, there were significant political and ideological differences in the ways in which the state propaganda apparatus operated between democratic Britain and totalitarian Germany. Any comparison of propaganda in Britain and Germany should take into account the following points of difference:

1   *Propaganda in peace and war.* In Germany a state propaganda machinery existed during peacetime, whereas in Britain it did not. The Ministry of Popular Enlightenment and Propaganda, under Joseph Goebbels, had been established shortly after the Nazis came to power in 1933, meaning that when war broke out the Germans were already up and running with their propaganda activities. In Britain, however, a Ministry of Information (MOI) was created only upon the outbreak of war, and although plans had been made for this during the late 1930s they were piecemeal in nature and quickly proved to be ineffective when the time came to implement them. The failings which commentators detected in some early British attempts at propaganda were attributed to Germany's head start in this regard. For example, the British Ambassador in Washington, Lord Lothian, reported to the Foreign Secretary, Lord Halifax, on 28 September 1939, 'there is no doubt that after three weeks of the war the general impression is that the Germans have handled their propaganda better. They have done so because they have studied the art more clearly and are more efficient at it.' And in an internal memorandum of November 1939, Charles Peake, a senior civil servant at the Foreign Office, lamented, 'Germany's tremendous start over this country in respect of film propaganda'.

2   *The relationship between the state and political parties.* Consider the following point by Professor Frederick Bartlett of Cambridge University, who was commissioned by the MOI to write a monograph entitled *Political Propaganda,* which came to inform much of the ministry's thinking:

> What is democracy? To this question all kinds of answers can be given. From the present point of view, however, one consideration overrides all others. In the modern world, political propaganda may be said to have been adopted as a weapon of State, but very nearly everywhere it has been adopted as the tool of a single political party within the State.

This is precisely what cannot happen, except in a very incomplete way in a democratic country. A democracy differs from every other form of government in that it must always contain at least two main political parties, each treating the other with a very considerable degree of respect. Although each party may develop its own political propaganda, neither can violently suppress that of the other without destroying the spirit of democracy itself.

(*Political Propaganda*, 1940, p.16)

While this might seem a rather unusual definition of 'democracy' (it's probably not one that would spring immediately to most people's minds), it does highlight a fundamental differencein the role of propaganda between democracies and dictatorships. In Germany state propaganda meant Nazi propaganda, and all the key posts in the Ministry of Popular Enlightenment and Propaganda were filled by party members. In Britain, however, it was soon realized that if the MOI was to command the respect of the public then it should not be seen as an instrument of a single political party. There was much sensitivity at the beginning of the war over the fact that many key positions initially were filled by people sympathetic to the Conservative Party. The first Minister of Information, Lord Macmillan, was a Tory peer, while the first Director of the Films Division was none other than Sir Joseph Ball, whose name you might remember from Unit 19 as Director of the Conservative Research Department. Clement Attlee, for one, remarked that he 'was not satisfied that the Ministry of Information was not part of the Conservative machine' (as told to Sir John Reith, and reported by Reith in his memoirs, *Into the Wind*, 1949, p.370). This situation did not persist, however, especially following the formation of Churchill's coalition government in May 1940, when members of the Labour Party were brought into senior ministerial positions in Cabinet. The perceived Conservative bias within the MOI was remedied by the appointment of people like Joseph Reeves, the former Secretary of the Workers' Film Association (a film education body set up jointly by the Labour Party and the TUC), and Sidney Bernstein, a cinema exhibitor who was a prominent Labour supporter, who both joined the Films Division. Indeed, the MOI went so far in appeasing its critics by recruiting prominent members of the intellectual left (including for example, George Orwell) that it was later said in some quarters that the ministry helped to win the 1945 general election for the Labour Party. This was especially so in respect of some of the films produced under official auspices which held out the promise of the 'New Jerusalem' (we'll be looking at an example of one of those, *Tyneside Story*, later in this section).

3   *The relationship between the state and the media industries.* This is an important difference. In Germany, when the Nazis came to power, the film and newspaper industries were still privately owned, though broadcasting had been state regulated since 1925 through the Reichsrundfunkgesellschaft, the Reich Radio Company. Goebbels moved to bring the other media within his orbit. The press was brought under state control through the Nazi Party acquiring ownership of the majority of German newspapers and through the establishment of an official press

agency, the *Deutsches Nachrichtenbüro*, which oversaw the content of newspapers through daily press briefings and directives. Even tighter control was established over the film industry through the cinema law of February 1934 which instituted the compulsory censorship of all scripts before production, as well as encouraging films favourable to the Nazi ideology through a system of distinction marks (*Prädikate*) awarded to 'worthy' films. State control of the media industries, combined with rigorous exercise of censorship, effectively meant that only ideas and themes of which Goebbels and his colleagues approved could find expression through film, radio and the press. Both Goebbels and Hitler saw this control to be essential to their cases. In his diary entry of 20 June 1941, for example, Goebbels wrote:

> The Führer praises the superiority of our system compared with the liberal-democratic ones. We educate our people according to a common world view [*Weltanschauung*], with the aid of films, radio and the press, which the Führer sees as the most important tools of popular leadership. The State must never let them out of her hands.

In Britain, however, the state did not assume direct control of the media industries, and the MOI was without any powers of censorship: censors were installed at source to oversee the dissemination of news from Reuters and the Press Association, and radio broadcasters had to contend with the presence of an official in the studio who could cut them off the air if they strayed too far from the script. But there was no question of the MOI in any sense 'taking over' the press or BBC. While film newsreels were subject to security censorship, film censorship remained in the hands of the British Board of Film Censors, not the MOI. Indeed there is a case to argue that film censorship relaxed during the war, for example with the British Board of Film Censors (BBFC) allowing the production of a film of Walter Greenwood's *Love on the Dole* in 1940, a project that had been blocked during the 1930s. The MOI had no powers to instruct film-makers in what sorts of film they should make, preferring instead to make informal contracts through an Ideas Committee, set up in 1941, which kept film-makers informed of what subjects the ministry thought desirable. Unlike in Germany, however, there was scope for the expression of dissenting opinion within British propaganda. This was most famously exemplified by the film *The Life and Death of Colonel Blimp* (1940), made by Michael Powell and Emeric Pressburger, inspired by the cartoon character created by David Low. The film told the story of an officer in the British army who had become out of touch with the realities of modern warfare. In the opening scene he is shown as an impotent and backward-looking commander when he leads the Home Guard in an exercise against the regular army which the regulars win by seizing headquarters before 'war' is declared. A furious Winston Churchill intervened personally when he heard about the film, telling his Minister of Information, Brendan Bracken, that 'I am not prepared to allow propaganda detrimental to the morale of the Army' and asking him to 'propose to me the measures necessary to stop this foolish production before it gets any further' (Public Record Office, PREM 414/15 Churchill to

Bracken, 10 September, 1942). Bracken's reply provides an insight into the political limitations placed upon democracies at war:

> I am advised that in order to stop it the Government would have to assume powers of a very far-reaching kind. These could hardly be less than powers to suppress all films, even those based on imaginary stories, on the grounds not of their revealing information to the enemy but of their expressing harmful or misguided opinions. Moreover it would be illogical for the Government to insist on a degree of control over films which it does not already exercise over other means of expression, such as books or newspaper articles. Nothing less, therefore, than the imposition of a complete censorship of opinion upon all means of expression would meet the case, and I am certain that this could not be done without provoking infinite protest.
>
> (Ibid., Bracken to Churchill, 15 September, 1942)

Bracken realized, therefore, that to suppress the film would have been a politically insensitive move, as it would have involved adopting an extensive censorship apparatus on a par with that exercised by Germany, and would have contradicted so much British propaganda which was about democratic ideals and values. In the event Churchill was persuaded to let the matter rest and the film was allowed to go ahead.

These three areas are the main points of difference in the organization of German and British propaganda. The other important difference, of course, is in the content of propaganda – what the propagandists of each country were saying, and to whom.

In the remainder of this unit we shall be looking at several examples of wartime propaganda. We are going to concentrate on German and British sources, an approach which has several distinct advantages. First, it allows you to familiarize yourself thoroughly with a manageable amount of propaganda material and to explore the nuances in the methods and techniques applied. Second, the propaganda organizations in Germany and Britain set up bodies to record and assess public responses to their output, so one is able to judge their effectiveness with a good deal more confidence than is sometimes the case. Third, it is still possible for you to compare the propaganda emanating from a 'closed' and tightly controlled form of government, of the sort traditionally associated with the totalitarian states, with that in a more 'open' society of the liberal democratic variety. Fourth, it permits comparison between two systems imbued with distinctly different and opposing ideologies: one, as in Germany, which was committed to the 'revolutionary' task of re-educating the people for a new society based on a drastically restructured value system; the other, as in Britain, with the relatively simpler and more 'conservative' role of building on the general acceptance of a just and necessary war in defence of existing values. Those at least are the terms in which the function of wartime propaganda in Germany and Britain has often been construed, in both contemporary and historical accounts. There are many historians who continue to categorize the difference between German and British war aims and propaganda in terms of a divide between 'revolutionary' and 'conservative' objectives. It remains to be seen whether the terms hold good at the end of our survey.

Germany

Exercise   Now listen to items 2 and 3 on Audio 4, and watch the three extracts from the 1941 film *Ohm Kruger* (Uncle Kruger) to be found on Video 2 as items 11, 12 and 13. Read both Document II.33 in *Primary Sources 2: Interwar and World War II* (the SD report on the audience response to *Ohm Kruger*) and the synopsis for the complete film, which you will find below, and answer the questions that follow.

> Gold is discovered in the land of the Boers, the Transvaal, and Orange Free State. The English decide they must acquire this land: Cecil Rhodes and Joe Chamberlain try to provoke them into war; Paul Kruger, the leader of the Boers, goes to England and signs a treaty which provides the English with many advantages but retains the Boers' independence. Returning home, however, Kruger starts to prepare for what he knows is an inevitable conflict. The English start the war but the Boers repel them, London changes its tactics and appoints Kitchener Supreme Commander. He decides not to engage the Boer Army but the helpless civilian population. Their homes are burnt, their herds are destroyed, their wells are poisoned, the Negroes are armed, and women and children are forced into concentration camps where they are brutally treated, starved, and infected with diseases in an attempt to break down the morale of the Boer men still fighting. Thousands of men and women are killed in this way whilst Kruger travels around the capitals of Europe imploring help. English diplomacy assures his failure, and while the Boers are finally forced to sacrifice their independence and become part of the British Empire, a broken Kruger finds asylum in Switzerland.

> (Extract from *Aktuelle Filmbficher,* Berlin, 1941, reprinted in David Welch, *Propaganda and the German Cinema 1933–1945,* 1983, pp.271–2)

1   Who were these examples of German propaganda directed at?

2   What was their purpose?

3   How were they meant to achieve their desired effect? ∎

Specimen answer   1   The radio items were clearly intended for overseas broadcast and foreign consumption, i.e. by British listeners, whereas the feature film was straight anti-British propaganda and obviously aimed at the domestic market and the population in Germany.

2   Put bluntly, the former was meant to sap the enemy's morale, and to undermine the confidence of the British people in their leaders; the latter was meant to denigrate the British further in the eyes of the German people, to paint a 'historically valid' picture of the enemy they were confronting, and thereby boost their resolve and determination to continue the conflict.

3   By simple propagandist techniques. Thus 'Lord Haw-Haw' (William Joyce) mentions the damage done to the British cruiser *Exeter* in an engagement with the *Admiral Graf Spee* though he noticeably fails to add that the final

result of the battle of the River Plate was the scuttling of the German pocket battleship in December 1939 – one of the few British successes in the early months of the war. This decidedly partial and highly selective broadcast harps upon the British losses, while from the German point of view it goes out of its way to accentuate the positive aspects of the episode and to eliminate those negative aspects which were considerable, though short-lived. To substantiate his point William Joyce resorts to information gleaned from a neutral source, the *New York Times*, which purportedly lends greater credence to his overall account. The story on tin hats is more trivial, even eccentric, and serves merely to emphasize the everyday inconveniences of war while allowing for a sly gibe at the expense of the 'Ministry of (Mis)Information'. □

The New British Broadcasting Station (NBBS) item was a piece of 'black' propaganda purporting to come from within Britain itself. It supposedly represents the voice of alternative opinion which is increasingly disenchanted with the official version of wartime events, as reported by such organizations as the BBC, and, indeed, which is altogether unhappy with the British system of government. (NBBS professed, Asa Briggs records, to be 'entirely run by British people who put their country above their own interest and are resolved to speak the truth for their country's sake'.) There is much stress on 'the grievances of ordinary people' which are obscured by the mainstream media, at government instigation, and the fact that 'the masses of the people have never had any real heart in the war since it began'. 'Social injustices' such as 'the shocking state of poverty' are highlighted, and leading church and civil campaigners are applauded for their efforts to rid the country of slum conditions and the like. The broadcast is meant to provoke discontent with the existing system by playing upon social divisions and by giving vent to oppositional arguments on what should obtain in a fair and just society. It seeks, in short, to undermine British morale by posing the question whether the war is worth fighting for the values represented by the country's governing élites.

Ohm Kruger (Uncle Kruger) uses the full array of cinematic techniques to depict Britain as the brutal enemy of any kind of order or civilization. That much is evident from the first extract you see, with its heavily ironic juxtaposition of imagery and soundtrack, as Bibles and guns are given out to the natives in equal measure against a backdrop of missionaries singing the national anthem. The *Illustrierter Film-Kurier*, incidentally, commented on this scene as follows: 'When England realizes that even with cannon and rifles she cannot crush the little nation whose heroic struggle is jubilantly acclaimed by the whole world, she decides to commit one of the most obscene acts in the history of the world.'

The full obscenity of Britain's role during this war is revealed when the spotlight is turned on the harsh treatment meted out to defenceless Boer women and children, culminating in the dramatic and emotional massacre in the concentration camp (which was closely modelled on the Odessa steps sequence at the climax of Sergei Eisenstein's *Battleship Potemkin,* a film that Goebbels privately admired). The message, plainly, is that Germany has a mission to rid the world of such an enemy and to restore peace and stability under the Nazi 'New Order'. It is reinforced with Kruger's words at the end of the film, when he declares: 'One day, great and powerful nations will resist the British tyranny, and then the way will be clear for a better world ... There can be no coming to terms with the British.'

To lend an air of impartiality and objectivity, however, the film is set in a historical context, some forty years earlier, and omits any direct reference to Germany. Talk of this film being objective is perhaps difficult to imagine now. The British characters seem grossly caricatured, even comical (in addition to the obvious caricature of Churchill as the camp commander, there is an earlier caricature of a whisky-drinking Queen Victoria, which you do not see). Furthermore, the Nazi propaganda emphasis on the British invention of concentration camps (with the possible implication that the camps in Germany were somehow different and less brutal) becomes, with the benefit of hindsight, loaded with tragic irony.

The Security Service (SD) summary of audience reactions to the film gives you a better idea of how it was received in its day. Such reports have to be treated with some degree of caution, since people were always capable, as the Nazi authorities well recognized, of saying one thing in public and quite the opposite in private. But historians still consider that they provide a reliable indicator of public opinion and that they were characterized by an honesty which was uncommon in the Nazi state. Note, in the SD report on *Ohm Kruger,* the repeated emphasis on the film's 'plausibility' and 'historical authenticity'. Apart from the inevitable reservations about occasional scenes being 'too heavily loaded' with propagandist intent, the film does appear to have been a considerable success. It seems also genuinely to have fulfilled its function in helping to stiffen anti-British sentiment and resolve.

Discussion   The Nazi leadership certainly held *Ohm Kruger* in great esteem. Emil Jannings, who came up with the original idea for the film and played the leading role of Kruger, was presented by Goebbels with the 'Ring of Honour of the German Cinema' for his achievement. The film was also the first to be awarded the accolade 'Film of the Nation', and it went on to win the Mussolini Prize for the best foreign film at the Venice film festival. In terms of its success at the German box office, the film did very well, with receipts amounting to RM 5.5 million, as against box office figures of RM 8 million and 7.5 million for *Die Grosse Liebe* (*Great Love,* 1942) and *Wunschkonzert* (*Request Concert,* 1940), the two top hits at the German box office during these years. Despite *Ohm Kruger's* popular success, however, it did not make a profit for the state, since Goebbels had invested more than RM 5.5 million in its production.

Judging the success of Nazi radio propaganda on British public opinion is difficult, since it was, by definition, intended to be a covert operation. The best estimate from informed sources (see Asa Briggs's *The History of Broadcasting in the United Kingdom* for the war years, vol. 3, *The War of Words,* 1970, pp.140–59) is that 'black' German radio stations like NBBS could only be picked up by 38 per cent of British listeners with powerful enough receivers. Nor, it seems, did other stations such as Radio Caledonia, which sought to play on nationalist sentiment in Scotland and Wales and even reported the news in Gaelic, fare much better. Anti-British nationalist fervour, incidentally, found its echoes in many German films, with titles like *Der Fuchs von Glenarvon* (*The Fox of*

Glenarvon, 1940), *Mein Leben für Irland* (*My Life for Ireland,* 1941) and *Das Herz der Königin* (*The Heart of a Queen,* 1940), about the life of Mary Queen of Scots and starring the immensely popular Zarah Leander.

Lord Haw-Haw, by contrast, built up a regular audience for a short while in the late autumn of 1939 and the early months of 1940. The opening announcement to his programmes, 'Germany calling, Germany calling', quickly became a catch-phrase and a ready stand-by for comedians up and down the country. He was variously dubbed 'the Humbug of Hamburg' and 'the Comic of Eau-de-Cologne' (and worse) in popular songs and jokes of the period. But his broadcasts caused genuine fear and alarm in the Ministry of Information and the War Office because of the likely effects and potential of his 'socially subversive message'. The BBC was prompted to conduct an enquiry into the extent and impact of 'Hamburg Broadcast Propaganda'. An interim report, in January 1940, found that of the 16 million people (over 50 per cent of the listening public) listening to a typical 9 p.m. BBC news bulletin, some 9 million would stay tuned to the BBC if the news was followed by a talk. Six million, however, would switch over to the Hamburg station and listen to Joyce. Among this 'Hamburg audience', as the final report confirmed in March 1940, there was a distinctly strong interest in current affairs. The report concluded:

> The blackout, the novelty of hearing the enemy, the desire to hear both sides, the insatiable appetite for news and the desire to be in the swim have all played their part both in building up Hamburg's audience and in holding it together. The entertainment value of the broadcasts, their concentration on undeniable evils in this country, their news sense, their presentation, and the publicity they have received in this country, together with the momentum of the habit of listening to them, have all contributed towards their establishment as a familiar feature in the social landscape.

Haw-Haw's appeal soon diminished, however, when popular programmes such as *Band Waggon* were switched to compete directly with his slot and when, shortly after, the *Postscripts* series was evolved with the express aim of projecting 'reasonable explanation' rather than 'exaggerated propaganda'; the series was to be presented by speakers who 'should not hesitate to admit our own shortcomings'. When speakers like J. B. Priestley were invited to the microphone, the BBC found it had commentators who could do all that was required of them, and more besides. □

Exercise   Now watch the extract from *Der Ewige Jude* (*The Eternal/Wandering Jew*) (1940), to be found on Video 2 as item 14; read the translation of the extract's commentary (Document II.34 in *Primary Sources 2: Interwar and World War II*), and the SD report on audience reaction to the film (Document II.33); and read the synopsis of the complete film which follows. It is the synopsis that accompanied the film on its initial release.

> The film begins with an impressive expedition through the Jewish ghettoes in Poland. We are shown Jewish living quarters, which in our view cannot be called houses. In these dirty rooms lives and prays a

race, which earns its living not by work but by haggling and swindling. From the little urchin to the old man, they stand in the streets, trading and bargaining. Using trick photography, we are shown how the Jewish racial mixture in Asia Minor developed and flooded the entire world. We see a parallel to this in the itinerant routes of rats which are the parasites and bacillus-carriers among animals, just as the Jews occupy the same position among mankind. The Jew has always known how to assimilate his external appearance to that of his host. Contrasted are the same Jewish types: first the eastern Jew with his kaftan, beard and sideburns, and then the clean-shaven, western European Jew. This strikingly demonstrates how he has deceived the Aryan people. Under this mask he increased his influence more and more in Aryan nations. But he could not change his inner being.

After the banishment of the Jews from Europe was lifted, following the age of Enlightenment, the Jew succeeded within the course of several decades in dominating the world economy, before the various host nations realised, and this despite the fact that they made up only 1% of the world population. An excerpt from an American film about the Rothschilds, made by Jews, reveals to us the cunning foundations of their banking empire. Then we see how Jews, working for their international finance, drive the German people into the November Revolution. They then shed their anonymity and step out openly on to the stage of political and cultural life. Thus the men who were responsible for the disgraceful debasement of the German people are paraded before us. Incontestable examples are shown of how they robbed the country and the people of immense sums. As well as gaining financial supremacy they were able to dominate cultural life. The repulsive pictures of so-called Jewish 'art' reveal the complete decline of cultural life at that time. Using original sequences from contemporary films, the degrading and destructive tendency of Jewish power is exposed. For hundreds of years German artists have glorified figures from the Old Testament, knowing full well the real face of Jewry. How the Jew actually looks is shown in scenes shot by Jews themselves in a 'culture film' of a Purim festival, which is still celebrated today to commemorate the slaughter of 75,000 anti-Semitic Persians, and the doctrine with which future Rabbis in Jewish schools are educated to be political pedagogues. We look into a Jewish 'Talmud' class and experience the oriental tone of the ceremony in a Jewish synagogue, where Jews conduct business deals among themselves during the holy services.

However, the cruel face of Judaism is most brutally displayed in the final scenes, in which original shots of a kosher butchering are revealed. These film documents of the inhuman slaughter of cattle and sheep without anaesthesia provide conclusive evidence of a brutality which is simply inconceivable to all Aryan people. In shining contrast, the film closes with pictures of German people and German order

BOOK 4 THE IMPACT OF WORLD WAR II

which fill the viewer with a feeling of deep gratification for belonging to a race whose Führer is fundamentally solving the Jewish problem.

(Extract from *Illustrierter Film-Kurier*, no.3152, reprinted in David Welch, *Propaganda and the German Cinema 1933–1945*, 1983, pp.292–3)

An opening title to *Der Ewige Jude* (*The Eternal/Wandering Jew*) states it was intended as 'a film contribution to the problem of world Jewry'. As you will be aware by now, it is a particularly virulent and repulsive example of Nazi propaganda. Indeed, after the war, the Allied Commission's *Catalogue of Forbidden German Film* concluded that it was, 'One of the most striking examples of direct Nazi anti-Semitic propaganda, probably the vilest and subtlest of its kind ever made for popular consumption by the masses'.

What methods were being employed in this instance to convey the film's meaning and to what effect? ■

Specimen answer   The film-makers adopted the documentary format, utilizing actuality film for the most part, but also feature film extracts (ironically using Alfred Werker's 1934 American film *The House of Rothschild,* a thinly veiled statement against Nazi anti-Semitism, yet turned cleverly here into an indictment of Jewish financial practices), along with maps, animated inserts, statistics and the like, to build up an apparently factual piece of reportage on the so-called 'Jewish problem'. The commentary reinforces the visual impact of the images by equating Jewish migrations into Europe with the spread of disease brought by rats; by marshalling an array of 'facts and figures' designed to prove that these 'parasites' were involved in every aspect of international crime; and by highlighting the process whereby Jews had been assimilated into various national cultures and had insinuated themselves into positions of financial power, thereby having a supposedly deleterious effect upon the course of social, political and economic events everywhere. The message throughout was that the Jews remain an essentially alien race, a pernicious influence, and a threat to western civilization and culture: an odious message for an odious film.

In assessing the film's impact, as no doubt you have spotted, the SD report noted that an extensive advance publicity campaign provoked 'great interest' in it and 'remarkably high audience figures' after its first release. Subsequently, audiences seem to have fallen off somewhat except among the 'politically active sections of the population'. Two reasons are given for this reaction. First, the feature film *Jud Süss,* which had been released just two months earlier and had already enjoyed huge success, clearly captured a lot of its potential audience – that film, too, displayed a vitriolic anti-Semitic slant, though more attractively couched in the trappings of costume drama. Second, word-of-mouth reports about the ritual slaughter scenes at the climax of *Der Ewige Jude* simply put a good many people off – a point anticipated by the Nazi authorities, who approved two versions for release. One, without the slaughter scenes, was exhibited at afternoon showings. The other, complete with slaughter scenes, was shown in the early evening. Advertisements announced that 'those of a sensitive disposition are recommended to see the 4 o'clock performance'.

The slaughter scenes are, indeed, gruesome. But it is perhaps revealing of both the Nazi regime and Nazi society that it was these scenes which compelled attention and required careful thought to be given to avoid placing undue 'strain on the nerves' of 'those of a sensitive disposition' in the cinema audience, while the rest of the film openly espoused racial hatred of the most virulent kind. 'The repulsive nature of the material' is a judgement that could be made on the whole film and not just the scenes of ritual slaughter, which really depend for their effectiveness upon public antipathy towards cruelty done to animals – a factor acknowledged in the official synopsis of the film. Interestingly, by contrast, no comments are to be found in the SD report which even begin to question 'its starkly realistic portrait of the Jews'. The most frequent reaction there, you will note, is one of complacency and indifference – 'a Jew is always a Jew', 'We've seen *Jud Süss* and we've had enough of Jewish filth'.

Discussion Apparently, then, the German cinema-going public was growing increasingly tired of anti-Semitic propaganda of the sort found in *Der Ewige Jude*. That, though, did not invalidate its purpose as far as the film's director was concerned. Two days after his film was released on 28 November 1940, Fritz Hippler wrote:

> I can envisage that film audiences may feel they have had enough of this subject. I can hear the comments: 'Not another film about the Jewish problem'. But I must reply to this and it is the intention of the film to stress the fact that the Jewish problem only ceases to be topical when the last Jew has left the *Volkisch* fabric of all nations.

Consequently, and unsurprisingly, *Der Ewige Jude* was dubbed and distributed to all Nazi-occupied countries. It attracted very large audiences, not least in France, where free exhibitions ensured its success despite the proven popularity, once again, of *Jud Süss*. Furthermore, a specially edited and adapted French version was released ten days before the round-up of some 13,000 Jews in preparation for their mass deportation to the east. The film was clearly intended to prepare public opinion for such an event, and it is in this regard that the importance of such films to the Nazi regime can be seen. As David Welch has concluded:

> By the late 1930s the increasingly fanatical tone of propaganda reflected the growing radicalisation of the regime's anti-Semitic policies. Not only had racial propaganda convinced the population that a 'Jewish Question' existed (a point acknowledged by Sopade [The Social Democrats' exile organization] as early as 1935), but Jews were now being openly driven from public posts and their property confiscated. The Jewish stereotype depicted in Nazi propaganda served to reinforce anxieties about modern developments in political and economical life, without the need to question the reality of the Jewish role in German society. The massive increase in the circulation of the obnoxious and virulently anti-Semitic *Der Sturmer* was an indication of this trend. It may well be true that the 'Final Solution' did not follow a more or less 'programmed' development and that Hitler was not its prime mover, but what remains unchallenged is that the culmination of such a policy resulted in a network of concentration camps where thousands were confined without trial, and eventually [led] to the slaughter of six million Jews during the Second World War. At precisely the time that Jewish persecution was being intensified and

final details of the 'solution' arrived at the SD reports were noting either boredom with or massive indifference to the 'Jewish Question'. Such indifference proved fatal. From the Nazis' point of view, the Jew provided an important escape valve from serious political and economic problems. The 'image' of the Jew portrayed in the mass media as 'self-seeking' and 'parasitic' was outside the range of serious intellectual analysis, and that was its strength. In this way, racial propaganda was able to rationalise any doubts that may have existed, minimise possible dissent, and at the same time provide the emotional basis for a totalitarian solution to the 'Jewish problem'.

('Propaganda and indoctrination in the Third Reich: success or failure?', 1987, p.415) □

Britain

Exercise   Listen now to items 4–6 on Audio 4, watch item 15 (*Miss Grant Goes to the Door*) on Video 2, and read Document II.35 in *Primary Sources 2: Interwar and World War II* (transcript of commentary to *London (Britain) Can Take It*).

We do not want to set a full-scale exercise on this particular selection of material, but you might care to note down what you think were its various aims and what differences you can spot in emphasis and approach between the individual items. ■

Clearly, the two initial broadcasts are examples of straightforward exhortatory ministerial announcements. In the first talk, Ernest Brown, the Minister of Labour, was seeking to recruit the additional workers required to meet the engineering industry's needs for the war effort. Despite his emphasis on the non-compulsory nature of the appeal ('You are free men' compared with those in 'the totalitarian states') and the complacent assumption by the ministry that the million and a quarter unemployed at the war's outset would provide a ready reservoir of labour, Brown found he had his work cut out during the early months of 1940 to meet the targets fixed for the expansion of employment in the wartime industries. It was only with the appointment by Churchill in May of Ernest Bevin, who concocted a very personal mixture of conscription and voluntarism born of his experience as General Secretary at the TGWU, that the Ministry of Labour was sufficiently revitalized to start seriously on the urgent task that was required of it. It was Bevin, of course, who enthusiastically supported the idea for *Workers' Playtime,* despite some reluctance on the part of the BBC, calling it 'a great work for great people'. The first edition, on 31 May 1941, came from a factory in Wrexham, and by the end of that year three programmes were being broadcast each week. It continued for many years after the war.

The appeal by Lord Woolton, newly arrived as Minister of Food (MoF) by the time of this broadcast, was directed at 'the housewives of Britain' – 'the army that guards the kitchen front'. Woolton, a former social worker in the slums as well as head of a large chain of department stores, was a philanthropic businessman who proved more than keen to learn the art of broadcasting. Angus Calder comments on this speech in the following passage:

The philanthropist radiated goodwill towards all. At his very first public appearance as minister, in the phoney war period, Woolton's homely phrasemaking had marked him out as a man on the people's side, when he had urged housewives, not, in so many words, to make weaker tea, but to give only 'one spoonful for each person ... and none for the pot'. Woolton had been to Manchester University, not to Oxford or Cambridge; he was a man of the provinces, not a slick metropolitan personality; his somewhat potato-like face was suffused with earnest sympathy. In the words of one citizen (whose comments were passed on to Woolton by the postal censors), 'When he harangues us on the radio, as he does now and again, we fancy we are back at dame school. He speaks, with the firm precision of a talented school marm and we all sit quiet and say, "Yes, teacher".'

(*The People's War,* 1971, p.441)

Woolton was certainly 'media-conscious', and after his appointment there was an immediate speeding up and strengthening of Ministry of Food propaganda. By May 1941 his ministry was the second largest spender on advertising, investing well over half a million pounds on press and poster publicity alone. The major theme of leaflets issued to every household and thousands of 'Kitchen Front' exhibitions was the difference between the three main kinds of food groups - energy, protective and body-building – and by September 1941 roughly two-thirds of London housewives claimed to have a pretty good idea of what foods they should take to represent those groups. MoF literature advised on everything from how to make Christmas puddings without eggs, to preserving fruit without sugar, and improvising such 'delights' as pilchard layer loaf and corned beef rissoles. The results, if a jingle from *Housewife* for June 1941 are to be believed, were significant:

Pat-a-loaf, pat-a-loaf
Baker's man,
Bake me some wheatmeal
As fast as you can:
It builds up my health
And its taste is so good,
I find that I *like*
Eating just what I should.

Furthermore, from April 1940, an experimental series of nightly five-minute broadcasts after the 6 o'clock news, given by the popular comediennes 'Gert and Daisy' (Elsie and Doris Waters), convinced both the MoF and the BBC that there was an audience for regular radio talks dealing with domestic cooking problems and dispensing useful recipes. They were an undoubted success, though the time of broadcast proved unsuitable, not surprisingly, for many housewives. From June, it was placed in the more convenient slot of 8.15 every weekday morning. *The Kitchen Front* series 'on what to eat and how to cook it' was to command close on six million listeners by October 1940, and more when it included such contributors as 'the Radio Doctor', Dr Charles Hill. His 'vulgarity' while talking of Christmas Day over-indulgence or referring to 'the belly' and the like, did not exactly recommend him to everybody. But then, as Wilfred Pickles was to find when he started reading the news, the new 'stars' of wartime radio could not hope to please all listeners all the time, even in the changed circumstances of war. Besides, as we shall shortly hear in the case of Pickles, some listeners were plainly inclined to write in and complain on the merest pretext. In that regard, nothing had changed.

Wynford Vaughan Thomas's documentary interview with 'women at the benches' is, I am sure you will agree, similar in spirit to the scene you saw in Launder and Gilliat's 1943 feature film, *Millions Like Us,* where Eric Portman is introducing the latest band of 'mobile' women to the Castle Bromwich factory front. Portman, though, never patronizes the new recruits quite so much as Vaughan Thomas, with statements like 'the lady who is regaling that technical information so confidently was only a few months ago only interested in housewives' work'. You might also have noticed that Vaughan Thomas's piece of reportage was being broadcast around the time when the MOI's Home Policy Committee was deliberating on the need to give more publicity to women's work in the factories and the services as the nation was fully mobilized. The BBC could act faster than the film-makers, of course, at putting into effect official policy on where the latest propaganda push should be directed. Janet Quigley, a talks producer who had pioneered *The Kitchen Front,* was moved over to work on programmes mainly for women in the forces by the autumn of 1941. She came up with *Women at War,* with a format that included 'brainteaser's trust' as well as the predictable spot for advice on 'beauty hints'. We shall hear more of the role allotted to women in BBC output when we come to the end of Audio 4 and listen to extracts from a very popular woman on British wartime radio, Vera Lynn.

Women were very much to the fore in the British Ministry of Information short film of *Miss Grant Goes to the Door,* which you have just seen. Made by the feature film director Brian Desmond Hurst, with screenplay and dialogue provided by Rodney Ackland and based upon a story by Thorold Dickinson and Donald Bull, the film was given a cinema release in August 1940 and put on the non-theatrical circuit (that is, it was shown by 16 mm mobile film units) in October 1940. It was meant to boost British morale by assuaging some of the home front's fears about invasion which were keenly and justifiably felt early in the summer of 1940. There was considerable emphasis, as you must have spotted, on the simple precautions people might take in order to thwart enemy infiltration, and the film was clearly intended to be instructional as well as reassuring and entertaining. Along with other films of a similar nature, though on a different theme – *Now You're Talking, Dangerous Comment, Albert's Savings, The Call for Arms, Food for Thought, Salvage With a Smile* and *Miss Know-All* – it formed part of a series initiated by the MOI. As Sir Kenneth Clark put it during a radio broadcast in October 1940, the series was intended to 'help people to remember government messages by putting them in a dramatic form'. They were small-scale feature films which were often enjoyed, perhaps not surprisingly, more for their dramatic than their instructional content.

In the case of *Miss Grant Goes to the Door,* which proved especially popular among the first wave of MOI films, the organization monitoring the public reception of the films on behalf of the MOI, Mass-Observation, found that audiences liked the 'strong story'. By contrast, the instructional elements were unfavourably received, not least because of some improbable features. For example, success in dealing with live spies, so it was implied, lay in having a dead German parachutist conveniently to hand, with a revolver on him. The class base of the characters was also picked up – you may have noticed it in the distinctly middle-class flavour of the Grant household – with comments noting that Miss Grant lived in 'a big house' (a point also noted about *Miss Know-All* and other films, particularly the early 'Careless Talk' ones, where unfortunately the spy or gossiper causing untold if inadvertent damage was usually working class).

In the main, however, *Miss Grant Goes to the Door* was adjudged a success and was well liked. It was felt that the film registered with audiences in significant ways and that, for example, 'The sight of this untrained hand wielding the weapon, however ineffectively ... was incidental propaganda for a "people's war".' The film did show the people dealing resourcefully with the problems that confronted them. It at least advocated action, which was a good deal more than was advocated in some of the other MOI material related to the prospect of invasion. 'Stay put and do nothing' seemed to be the basic message emanating from the official leaflet of instructions *If the Invader Comes,* which was issued to all households throughout the country in mid-June 1940. Alfred Duff Cooper, Minister of Information at the time, reported that the leaflet had 'a good reception' but acknowledged that it left people 'expecting further instructions' and guidance, not least about such essential matters as '(a) whether they, the civilians, are to fight, or (b) whether they might even take steps to protect themselves'. *Miss Grant Goes to the Door* suffered no such shortcomings. Far from it. The two sisters living alone in the country deal resourcefully in the main with the danger that threatens them.

This film did suffer, however, from the problem that beset much propaganda, especially film propaganda, namely that it was tied to and used in conjunction with particular campaigns. In these instances, of course, timing was of the essence. It was vital to get material out in time to be relevant; and doubtless the credibility of a film like *Miss Grant* was undermined slightly because of the time it took in production and before release. In fact, the film-makers worked quite speedily on this production. It was completed on 2 July 1940 and released on 5 August 1940. But in between, at the end of July, the Local Defence Volunteers referred to in the film had been renamed the Home Guard. Also, as Ian McLaine recounts, 'from mid-July onwards reports showed people passing from acceptance of the possibility of invasion through to a tendency to doubt its imminence and then, with the exception of people living near the eastern coast, to a stage late in August when expectation of invasion seemed to have almost receded' (*Ministry of Morale*, p.77). There was a sense of widespread relief with the passing of those dates that were popularly held to be of particular significance – 19 July, when it was thought the invasion would start, and 15 August, the date it was believed Hitler had chosen for his arrival in Britain. (Mass-Observation confirmed these peaks of expectation, as its various 'morale' reports indicate, throughout July and August.)

Though also made for the MOI, *Britain Can Take It* was quite a different proposition to *Miss Grant Goes to the Door,* as I am sure you could tell from a reading of the script alone. (This film, and other British documentaries made during the war, will be available for viewing in your week at Residential School.) Directed by Harry Watt and Humphrey Jennings, with a commentary written and narrated by Quentin Reynolds, the London war correspondent for the US magazine *Collier's Weekly,* it was released to cinemas in October 1940 and put on the non-theatrical circuit in December 1940. It was made in two versions: a five-minute film for domestic consumption (the script for that runs to the bullet points in Document II.35), and a longer version (with the complete commentary) for exhibition in the US under the title *London Can Take It* and with a running time of ten minutes. Its theme is expressed in the latter title, suggested by Reynolds, and its story is of London in the blitz. The story is related in a deadpan and underplayed style, with the emphasis on a seemingly straightforward and factual narration of events. It is not dramatized at all, nor does it use actors; it was plainly intended as a piece of descriptive reportage and was meant to convey the impression, 'this is how it is in wartime London'.

'These are not Hollywood sound effects', Reynolds points out as he proceeds to show the devastation caused by 'the nightly siege of London'. Actuality is everything ('I am speaking from London'), and there is an insistence upon objectivity ('I am a neutral reporter'). It is a highly personalized account, but the message is one of quiet confidence and continued hope among the people ('London raises her head', 'London looks upward'), and there is repeated reference to the moulding of a new 'people's army' and to the high morale of the population despite its tribulations. The film was greeted with much critical acclaim in Britain – even the generally jaundiced *Documentary News Letter,* voice of the documentary film movement, reviewed it kindly in its issue for November 1940 – and it went on to enjoy considerable success with cinemagoers. As Mass-Observation assiduously reported to the MOI, this film 'received nothing but praise', and it topped their popularity poll of official films. Audiences felt it was 'factual, honest, and to many of them it was part of an actual experience they had gone through ... People were delighted to see themselves recognized as fully involved in the war and not in any way being spoken down to.'

Britain Can Take It, then, was a popular success because it recognized and acknowledged the role of the population at large in the war effort. It should be said, though, that one or two of the other major cities across the country took it mildly amiss that London should have been chosen to represent Britain as a whole. The Co-operative Wholesale Film Company in Manchester, for instance, produced its own variation on the same theme, entitled proudly *Manchester Took It Too* (1941), which included an impressive array of footage showing the effects of the blitz on that city during Christmas of 1940.

It was *Britain Can Take It* of course, that Quentin Reynolds took with him to America to show on a lecture tour he was engaged to deliver there. The film was shown without any British credits, and only Reynolds' name appeared on the titles, as war correspondent for the American *Collier's*. Thereafter, it was booked by the prestigious Warner Brothers corporation for nationwide release in their cinemas. Once more, it proved to be immensely popular. The MOI was delighted and commissioned both Reynolds and Watt to do a follow-up, *Christmas Under Fire,* this time about London during the Christmas of 1940, and again for American as well as British distribution. In all, Quentin Reynolds wrote and narrated the commentary on three documentaries for the MOI, and appeared as himself in the 1942 Ealing feature film *The Big Blockade*. In addition, he penned a series of personal messages in the radio *Postscripts* series entitled 'Dear Dr ...' (Goebbels) and 'Dear Mr Schickelgruber' (addressed to Hitler). Churchill was not very pleased when Reynolds persisted in trying to reinstate a censored reference to Rudolf Hess in one of his broadcasts, after Hess had landed in Britain on 11 May 1941. Churchill, like Hitler, had placed an embargo on mention of him. But for every one person against Reynolds' talks, Mass-Observation found, there were thirty in favour. Furthermore, along with Edward R. Murrow, Eric Sevareid, Vincent Sheean, Alastair Cooke, and a band of like-minded commentators, Quentin Reynolds proved an invaluable ally to Britain's cause in the US. (I have included items 10–12 on Audio 4 as examples of British radio propaganda directed specifically at audiences in the United States and broadcast over the North American Service. They are intended as a resource, but are well worth listening to since they bear out many of the points made already with regard to *Britain Can Take It*. There is an Ed Murrow broadcast on London in the blitz and broadcasts by Lord Lothian and Leslie Howard, which show how the BBC sought to promote Anglo-American relations.)

Exercise   Listen to items 7–9 on Audio 4; watch items 16 *(The Dawn Guard)* and 17 (extract from *Tyneside Story*) on Video 2; and read Document II.36 in *Primary Sources 2: Interwar and World War II* (the J. B. Priestley broadcasts of 5 June and 21 July 1940). Please note that Document II.36 (a) transcribes the first part of audio item 8, which was missing from the sound archive recording.

There is a distinct difference in purpose, I would suggest, between, on the one hand, the Priestley talk on the 'Epic of Dunkirk' and the extract from Churchill's 'finest hour' speech, and, on the other, the remaining pieces of film and broadcast propaganda. What differences do you detect, and what would you say they were trying to achieve? ■

Specimen answer   The simple division I would make in the first instance is between plain inspirational propaganda, which tries to turn moments of undoubted national disaster into something approaching success, and propaganda with a larger ideological and idealistic purpose, which relates to wider sea changes in society brought about by the country's wartime experience generally.

Priestley's talk of 5 June 1940, his first in the *Postscripts* series, and Churchill's broadcast to the nation on 18 June 1940, both seek 'to snatch victory from the jaws of defeat' and turn the setbacks they refer to into reflections on the strength of the national character (very much along the lines of what the film *Britain Can Take It* was to do during the blitz). They extol the virtues of the British people as a prelude to exhorting them to expend greater effort in continuance of the war, if the nation is to survive. The extract from Priestley's 'A New "English" Journey' (a radio follow-up to his 1934 book of the same name) and his *Postscript* of 21 July 1940 are more ruminative in character; they require the people to deliberate on the reasons why the war is being fought, and to consider what sort of world they would like to see emerging at the end of it. For his part Priestley believes there can be no going back to 'the old days'. The war has brought about social and economic changes in British society and the only thing to do is to capitalize on them with the aim of producing a new and better order. There is a good deal of homespun philosophizing – much more so, as you would expect, than is evident in Churchill's impressive and eloquent report on the state of affairs for this nation, given the imminent fall of France. But it is not so difficult to spot why Priestley also proved popular. His talks are powerfully persuasive, simply and succinctly expressed. They are evocative but have no recourse to party political rancour, though clearly they are arguing for change and 'no going back', which implicitly suggests no return to the Conservative rule of before the war (a point not lost on some people at the time who complained that his talks were decidedly 'leftish'). BBC listener research soon reported that Priestley was second to Churchill in size of audience: two out of every three adults on average listened to Churchill's broadcasts, one out of three to Priestley's.

The two films you have just watched echo the same themes evident in Priestley's 'new world order' broadcasts. Roy Boulting's *The Dawn Guard* (released to cinemas in January 1941 and the non-theatrical circuit in March 1941) and Gilbert Gunn's *Tyneside Story* (given a non-theatrical release in January 1944 but not released to cinemas) harp upon the idea of war as 'the midwife of social progress'. Both vividly contrast 'the bad days' of the 1930s, with the potentially beneficial changes wrought by war, and argue that these should point the way to a better planned, more rational, fair-minded and equitable society in the future. In the former case, the overall effect is rather benign and beneficent, perhaps because of the idyllic rural imagery and the resort to the use of Bernard Miles and Percy Walsh as typical country yokels. In the latter, the effect is definitely hard-edged and sharper, doubtless because the film is brought to an abrupt and peremptory halt with the interjection of an actor from the People's Theatre Company of Newcastle-upon-Tyne, who consciously disturbs any hint of complacency that might possibly have crept in, with his remarks: 'Ay, but wait a minute. Tyneside is busy enough today ... but just remember what the yards looked like five years ago ... Will it be the same again five years from now?' □

As you will be well aware by now, historians disagree about the question of whether World War II was a catalyst for change and about the extent to which it altered British society. As you saw earlier in this book, they continue to engage in a debate over how profound the changes were and how far the war was responsible for them. Some, like Henry Pelling (in *Britain and the Second World War*, 1970) and Angus Calder, contend that 'The effect of the war was not to sweep society on to a new course, but to hasten its progress along the old grooves' (Calder, *The People's War*, 1969, p.20). Arthur Marwick, of course, is one of the proponents, indeed an architect, of the view that war causes change, and has repeatedly outlined what he sees as the social consequences of the war for Britain.

Similarly, Paul Addison has charted the significance of the war in effecting political change. After the fall of France, and especially after the setback at Dunkirk, there was a distinct swing to what might loosely be called 'the left' in Britain. This tide of popular feeling was not necessarily of a political character, nor indeed was it always channelled along Labour Party or socialist lines, though clearly Labour was to be an immediate beneficiary in 1945. But it was 'directed against the Conservative Party' in so far as this represented, despite Chamberlain's departure and his replacement by Churchill, 'the so-called "Men of Munich", "the old gang", "Colonel Blimp" and similar diehard types' (Addison, *The Road to 1945*, 1975). It manifested itself, furthermore, in a feeling of revulsion against 'vested interests' and 'privilege', and in a general agreement that 'things are going to be different after the war'.

In addition to the movement in popular opinion, there was a change in thinking at the top. 'A massive new middle ground had arisen in politics', Addison continues, and a new political consensus evolved which was quite unlike the species of consensus that existed before the war, when Baldwin and MacDonald adopted 'safety first' policies and resolved 'to prevent anything unusual from happening'. 'The new consensus of the war years was positive and purposeful', and there was a convergence of opinion in favour of 'pragmatic' economic reform and social amelioration. Beveridge and Keynes inspired those 'socially concerned professional people' who lent their weight to the reform programme, and though little was actually achieved during the war in the way of new laws, except on family allowances and education, nevertheless much of the ground was prepared by the time the Labour Party came to power in 1945 (ibid., pp.14–15, 162–5, and 276–7).

As you would expect, the evidence provided by the British media and by sources such as the films and broadcasts you have just been examining, does not provide an easy or obvious answer to the overarching question of war and change, any more than does the evidence put forward by other historians in the debate. But it does bear eloquent witness, I am sure you will agree, to the fact that many people felt profound changes were afoot in society, born largely of the country's wartime experiences, and that these changes could prove beneficial. It also provides abundant evidence of the desire and commitment to build 'a better world' once the war had been won. It is clear that cinema and radio played a positive and purposeful role in their own right in generating adherence to the new-found consensus of the war years.

This did not happen overnight, of course. Films such as *Ships with Wings* and *The Demi-Paradise,* in 1941 and 1943 respectively, continued throughout the war to purvey the conventional image of gallant officers doing heroic deeds or to project the traditional image of the nation as a class-bound, hierarchically structured society (and proved very popular). But there was increasing emphasis on the idea of 'the people's war', in such films as *Britain Can Take It*, and the contribution made by 'ordinary' people in films like *The Foreman Went to France* (1942). Working-class figures were given a fuller and more rounded characterization, not least in *Millions Like Us.*

Furthermore, subjects were broached in the cinema, as on radio, that had been barely touched upon before. For instance, the director John Baxter could now contemplate making a film of Walter Greenwood's 1933 novel *Love on the Dole.* This had not been possible in the 1930s you will recall from my reference to the matter in Book 3, Unit 18, because the British Board of Film Censors had informed would-be producers that they felt it could only show 'too much of the tragic and sordid side of poverty'. Significantly, no such objections were made in 1941, and John Baxter turned the novel into a serious and moving film. Its message for a Britain at war was enhanced by a postscript caption at the film's end, which was signed by A. V. Alexander, the Labour MP and First Lord of the Admiralty. It read: 'Our working men and women have responded magnificently to any and every call made upon them. Their reward must be a new Britain. Never again must the unemployed become forgotten men of peace.'

John Baxter's next film, *The Common Touch* (1941), also evoked the new consensus. This time, he began his film with a caption that proclaimed: 'This picture is dedicated to the humble people of our great cities whose courage and endurance have gained for us all the admiration and support of the free countries of the world.' Thereafter, Baxter treated audiences to a whimsical social fantasy in which a young toff experiences life in a doss-house as well as at the top of the firm he has just inherited. His adventures teach him a lot about human nature and the values of life. He leaves the doss-house 'better fitted to start on the work of rebuilding', and the film ends with an exchange of dialogue between two of the doss-house characters:

> *Tich*: All this talk about better things, homes and all that. Do you suppose they really mean it or will they forget?
> *Ben*: No, I think they really mean it this time, Tich.
> *Tich*: Blimey, it'll be like heaven on earth.
> *Ben*: And why not?

Such sentiments were neither uncommon nor incidental. For his part, Baxter reiterated them endlessly in his later films like *Let the People Sing* (1942, based upon J. B. Priestley's novel of the same name which had actually started life as a BBC radio serial) and *The Shipbuilders* (1943, from George Blake's 1935 novel of the Clydeside during the depression). The sentiments were as much in evidence in the work of other film-makers – everything from Roy Boulting's short film *The Dawn Guard,* made for the MOI and which you have seen, to the Ealing Studios feature film of J. B. Priestley's allegorical play *They Came to a City* (1944), which ends with the following exchange between Googie Withers and John Clements as they leave their 'ideal' city:

> *Alice*: Goodbye, my lovely city. I don't know when I'll ever see you again.
> *Joe*: Now, Alice, take it easy kid.
> *Alice*: I don't want to go. And if it'll seem worse than ever when we get back.
> *Joe*: No, it won't. Because, to begin with, we'll remember. That's why we've got to go back – because we're the ones who've been, and seen it all ... And then we'll hope. And keep on hoping. And every time we find a spark of hope and vision in anybody, we'll blow it into a blaze ... They will tell us we can't change human nature. That's one of the oldest excuses in the world for doing nothing. And it isn't true. We've been changing human nature for thousands of years. But what you can't *change* in it, Alice – no, not with guns or whips or red-hot bars – is man's eternal desire and vision and hope of making this world a better place to live in. And wherever you go now – up and down and across the Seven Seas – from Poplar to Chunkink – you can see this desire and vision and hope, bigger and stronger than ever beginning to light up men's faces, giving a lift to their voices. Not every man, not every woman, wants to cry out for it, to work for it, to live for it and if necessary to die for it – but there's one here, one there, a few down this street, some more down that street – until you begin to see there are millions of us – yes, armies and armies of us – enough to build ten thousand new cities.
> *Alice*: Like our city?
> *Joe*: Yes, like our city. Where men and women don't work for machines and money, but machines and money work for men and women – where greed and envy and hate have no place – where want and disease and fear have vanished for ever – where nobody carries a whip and nobody rattles a chain. Where men have at last stopped mumbling and gnawing and

scratching in dark caves and have come out into the sunlight. And nobody can ever darken it for them again. They're out and free at last. I dreamt in a dream I saw a city invincible to the attacks of the whole earth, I dreamt that was the new city of Friends. *(They look back to the city)*
Alice: Come on, Joe, let's get going.

(Priestley, *They Came to a City,* 1944, pp.64–5)

All these films were imbued with the same vision of a 'brave new world' arising from the ruins of the old, and of the war as a harbinger of social progress. It was a message that was especially suited to Britain's wartime circumstances. C. G. H. Ayres, who wrote the original story on which the screenplay of the film *The Common Touch* was based, expressed it simply but effectively in 1942 when discussing with the director, John Baxter, some ideas for their next project together: 'The political outlook for our type of stuff was never more promising.' There was among these film-makers something of a 'mild revolution', to borrow producer Michael Balcon's phrase. Balcon described its nature in the following terms:

> We were middle-class people brought up with middle-class backgrounds and rather conventional educations. Though we were radical in our points of view, we did not want to tear down institutions ... We were people of an immediate postwar generation, and we voted Labour for the first time after the war; this was our mild revolution.

With hindsight, then, Balcon qualified the nature of the 'revolutionary' impulse which reportedly inspired him and others like him, and concluded that its 'radical' import was really quite 'mild'. It did not necessarily appear so during the war. Though many shared the feeling that change and reform ought to be an inevitable outcome of the harsh experiences of war, and though questions of post-war expectations and reconstruction were definitely on the agenda for public discussion as far as official bodies such as the MOI were concerned, these matters, in fact, were not always easily aired. Churchill, in particular, was of the opinion in January 1943 that 'Ministers should, in my view, be careful not to raise false hopes as was done last time by speeches about "Homes for Heroes", etc.' 'The broad masses of people face the hardships of life undaunted but they are liable to get very angry if they feel they have been gulled or cheated', he continued, and 'It is for this reason of not wishing to deceive the people by false hopes and airy visions of Utopia and Eldorado that I have refrained so far from making promises about the future.' Churchill was adamant that winning the war was the priority, and he was opposed to anything which he felt might detract from that purpose.

Nor did talk of reconstruction pass unchallenged. When Priestley returned with a second series of *Postscripts* in January 1941, his tone was decidedly more aggressive and political over war aims. The listening figures for that second series were the highest ever. But the Conservative 1922 Committee protested about the 'socialist' tendencies in the talks and Priestley was forced off the airwaves for a while as far as Britain was concerned (though he continued broadcasting successfully on the North American Service and returned to domestic radio in 1943). Furthermore, despite the unprecedented public acclaim which greeted publication of the Beveridge Report on 1 December 1942, that too was the cause of much dissatisfaction in cabinet circles. It was also included in Churchill's January 1943 ban on the ventilation of post-war topics by government speakers (except for overseas, where, 'It was proudly broadcast through the world as an advertisement of our Democratic accomplishments and aims'). Arthur Marwick has already discussed the implications of the report in considerable detail. We want to deal with it along with the final items which make up our compilation of wartime broadcasts. They have been chosen to spotlight the changes in style and content of radio programming and the BBC's reaction to the conditions of wartime broadcasting generally, to highlight its strengths and its limitations. We have appended commentaries to help contextualize the individual broadcasts.

Exercise   Listen to the remaining items of Audio 4, extracts 13–18, and read Document II.37 in *Primary Sources 2: Interwar and World War II* (transcript of the Dimbleby broadcast of 19 April 1945). Refer to the notes below before you listen to or read the appropriate item. ■

Item 13: 'War with Japan', Wilfred Pickles (1 p.m. News, 8 December 1941)

The [news] readers up to September 1939 had performed in evening dress. This consorted with the fact that their voices, while pleasant, were all southern English and impeccably upper middle class. In mid-war, this convention was broken when a Yorkshire character actor named Wilfred Pickles was called south from the BBC's northern headquarters in Manchester to become a regular 'front line' newsreader. There was a press furore over the prospect of a reader who pronounced his 'A's' short in the northern manner. Excitement increased when he ended the midnight news by saying a special 'Good Neet' to all northerners. Though his voice was very popular (especially in the south), Pickles himself asked to return to Manchester.

(Calder, *The People's War*, 1971, p.415)

Item 14: 'Operations against Pantelleria', Lt Cmdr Anthony Kimmins (22 June 1943)

... it is all too easy to forget the astonishing wartime growth in the function of broadcasting. Such was the novelty of eyewitness descriptions of scenes of combat that there was angry criticism of a recording made at Dover in 1940, during the battle of Britain. Many people felt that an eyewitness's account of a dogfight overhead between RAF fighters and the Luftwaffe was not a proper thing to broadcast. The contention was that an incident in which men were losing their lives was being treated as if it were a cricket match or a horse-race.

Public opinion had changed radically by 1943 ... It would be ludicrous to suggest that there is any equivalent to direct experience of the hardships and hazards of battle. But at least broadcasting does help to diminish the gap between the combatant and the civilian – and not merely in the details of battle but also in their lesser items of song, of slang, of tone of speech, which are a not inconsiderable part of the measure of an army's exile from the homeland. If Caen and Arnhem seemed less remote psychologically than were Mons or the Somme thirty years earlier, it was largely because of the power of broadcasting to act as an immediate link between the battlefront and home. Every fireside could entertain the voices, the personalities, of men in action, of men stepping out momentarily from the smoke and confusion of battle to talk in those intimate terms of informality – as between two or three people – which are peculiarly the gift of radio.

(Desmond Hawkins, War Report, 1985, p.21)

Items 15 and 16: 'Report on Social Insurance and Allied Services', Sir William Beveridge (2 December 1942) and 'The Story of a Thirty Years' Fight', Sir William Beveridge (28 December 1942)

This short feature programme [item 16] was a potted biography made to celebrate the great man after his Report. Within two weeks of its publication (1 December 1942) a Gallup Poll found that 19 out of 20 people had heard of it, and 9 out of 10 believed its proposals should be adopted ... At first the Ministry of Information intended to give the Report the widest possible publicity, but shortly afterwards that decision was reversed. From dawn on 1 December the BBC broadcast the details in 22 languages. It was yet another proof for the rest of the world, enemies and allies alike, that democracy was still alive and flourishing in England if nowhere else in Europe. Beveridge gave a short talk about his proposals to the home audience on the next day [item 15]. But after that there was virtually nothing. The feature programme you hear is about the only thing, in the wake of the Report, to refer to it direct – and most of the programme is about Beveridge himself. There is very little reference to the social and political implications of the Report in the programme.

The government was taken aback by the enormous popular interest in, and support for, the Beveridge Report. Churchill did not want to arouse 'false hopes and airy visions of Utopia'. The cabinet sat on the Report, which was not discussed in the Commons until late February 1943. The official line was to welcome the proposals in principle, while declaring that no firm commitments could be made.

(David Cardiff and Paddy Scannell, 'Radio in World War II', 1983)

Document II.37: transcript of Richard Dimbleby war report (19 April 1945)

Richard Dimbleby was the first British correspondent to reach a camp. He broadcast a report, 'The Cesspit Beneath', from Belsen, on 19 April 1945. Belsen, he wrote, was 'the first of these places to be opened up. He had only gone to Belsen with the advance team of medical services to follow up a story of an outbreak of typhoid. But they expected nothing different from the many POW camps they had already been through. He described the horrific conditions that he saw and, like [Richard] Crossman, the surreal otherworldly nature of life in the camps, where apparently all order and all rules had broken down. Dimbleby emphasised the appalling shock: 'No one could have imagined a scene like this, no one even hinted at what I was to see.' He broke down five times while he was recording the broadcast. But when the recording was received at the BBC, he wrote, it was queried. The broadcast was delayed by over a day, 'and the BBC kept coming back to him to check the authenticity of the account'. Apparently the Corporation was anxious. 'When they heard it some people wondered if Dimbleby had gone off his head or something. I think it was only the fact that I'd been fairly reliable up to then that made them believe the story.' Dimbleby, who was to return to Belsen several times later, emphasised that he had no idea of the role of the camps and that he had been totally unprepared for what he saw. No briefing had dealt with it ...

Thus the dominant theme in eyewitness accounts of the opening of the camps was one of shock and unpreparedness. This was obviously an attempt to deal with the appalling things they saw. Almost unanimously the eyewitnesses claimed that they had not known what they were going to see. In the spring of 1945, when the full horror of the camps was revealed, the problem crystallised into one of why more was not known ...

Some people had knowledge, other people did not. Knowledge was not uniformly available. Some people believed what they knew. Others did not. Many perhaps could not. The disbelief was subtly structured. It was as if the most accurate and vivid accounts were often undercut by a refusal to focus on the consequences if the accounts were real. That information about what was happening to Jews was widely available and widely broadcast is clear. But its focus did not encourage campaigning or action. More was not done because, rightly or wrongly, it was felt that nothing could be done except win the war. The BBC might have taken independent action – but it saw the world with government eyes in the war. When the camps were opened, it seemed like the unveiling of an obscene evil, of which nothing had been known, yet one which proved a final, irrefutable justification for the anti-German war. Yet our conclusion must be, in some way, grimmer than the secret that was disclosed. It was a secret known by some, understood at least by some, but over which there was no political will to act.

(Jean Seaton, 'Reporting atrocities: the BBC and the holocaust', in Jean Seaton and Ben Pimlott, *The Media in British Politics*, 1987, pp.57 and 179)

Item 17: *ITMA* (13 April 1944)

By 1945 the Corporation had apparently become less aloof. Programmes like *ITMA, Hi Gang* and *Workers' Playtime* introduced a more vigorous tradition of speech and humour to broadcasting, one that was closer to the music hall tradition than the well mannered 'variety' of pre-war programmes. They were part of a feeling that the British war, unlike that of the prudish Germans, was taken seriously, but never solemnly ... Humour was part of the protective self-image with which the British faced air attacks and the possibility of invasion. It was an image that the BBC helped to create, and was determined to encourage. Harold Nicolson even broadcast talks on the subtle superiority of English humour to that of the status-conscious Germans.

There was, of course, another war which did not get much broadcasting time. This one of apathy, and dingy making do rather than cheerful resilience. Life in shelters was not always a protracted east End party; it was squalid, with inadequate sanitary arrangements, little food and chaotic overcrowding. Novels of the period document the dreariness and austerity of life in England after several years of war, and newspapers campaigned against the pettymindedness of official regulations and bureaucracy. The BBC did not campaign for the public on any of these issues.

However, the Corporation succeeded in producing a dignified but humorous image of what kind of people the British were. It was not that the BBC 'came closer to the people'. Rather it represented them as a liberal, compassionate, reforming administrator might have seen them. Subsequently, it has been argued that there was a significant change in public mood during the war. The people became determined that there would be greater social justice after it. Certainly the war changed the BBC, and it changed public taste.

(James Curran and Jean Seaton, *Power without Responsibility*, 1981, pp.189–90)

Item 18: *Sincerely Yours* (8 March 1942)

Sincerely Yours deplored, but popularity noted.

(BBC Board of Governors, minutes, 4 December 1941, quoted in Asa Briggs, *The War of Words*, 1970, p.578) ☐

Propaganda and morale

What, then, can be said about the role and nature of propaganda in Germany and Britain respectively? Both governments were confronted with much the same problems – to mobilize their populations for the continual effort required in waging total war, and to maintain civilian and military morale at a level sufficient to help achieve a successful outcome. The governments in both countries, furthermore, set about that task with similar ideas on the power of propaganda as a significant force and basically the same views on the malleability of the masses in the face of sustained propaganda. Both, however, shared an essentially pessimistic vision of the likely effects on society of such new-found methods of destruction as mass bombing. How many of these assumptions remained intact by the end of the war?

Mass bombing did not result in a complete collapse in civilian morale in Germany or Britain, but it did not necessarily result in a wholesale stiffening of civilian morale, either. Clearly, the scale of personal loss and hardship suffered was the initial factor in determining how people reacted to bombing raids. Thereafter, however, the success of official propaganda in mitigating these effects depended on the extent to which individual sacrifice was recognized and merged into a sense of group unity with the feeling that all parts of the community were sharing the burden. This required of the propagandists, of course, a willingness to change their approach and to extend their horizons to accommodate somewhat different reactions than expected.

When the time came, Goebbels proved slow off the mark in acknowledging frankly that German cities endured any bombing at all, and he was unable to prevent Germans so afflicted from feeling resentment towards 'the good fortune of their countrymen who had not been bombed'. To compound his errors, Goebbels proceeded to indulge in exaggerated and early promises of a retaliatory response which only materialized in June 1944, when the first V1 long-distance missiles landed on London. If the German population's will to fight was strengthened during late 1942 and 1943, as there is reason to believe it was, it owed little to Goebbels' propaganda on the matter of Allied bombing and more to such factors as the increasing threat from Russia and the fear of bolshevization. (For a detailed study of these issues see Gerald Kirwin's articles, 'Allied bombing and Nazi domestic propaganda', 1985, and 'Waiting for retaliation – a study in Nazi propaganda behaviour and German civilian morale', 1981.)

Britain, of course, had to deal with the problem of bombing before Germany. As we have seen, its propagandists proved capable of revising their pre-war opinions about the people when actually suffering from the onslaught of aerial bombardment. They recognized their role, not least during the blitz, as being 'fully involved in the war'. 'The British public as a whole shows a very high degree of common sense', observed Dr Stephen Taylor of the MOI's Home Intelligence Division. 'Given the relevant facts,' he concluded, 'they will listen to and accept explanations when they will not accept exhortations.' His comments seem sensible and straightforward enough, but they were a long way away from the disdainful and elitist view of the British people that obtained in the 'official' mind during the 1930s. The war had changed that.

Nazi propaganda definitely scored some notable successes. It was effective during the first phase of the war in painting Britain as the major obstacle to peace and order. 'Building on a store of traditional anti-British feeling,' Ian Kershaw has argued:

> enormous hostility to Britain was whipped up in the summer of 1940, though Goebbels realized that this was engendering a dangerous impatience and optimism about Germany's ability to steamroller Britain as it had done the rest of Europe, and the protracted build-up to the German offensive against Britain and the inability to force a victory again put strains on the confidence in German propaganda.
>
> ('How effective was Nazi propaganda?', 1983, p.195)

Clearly a film like *Ohm Kruger* sought to capitalize on this store of anti-British feeling and consolidate it.

Yet again, as Kershaw has stated, German propaganda was effective 'in spreading the conviction that there was such a thing as a Jewish Question (p.191). However, he does not believe the film we have seen, *Der Ewige Jude,* to be a key factor. The 'successes' on this front, he maintains, were mainly achieved before the onset of war; furthermore:

> despite an increasing rather than diminishing volume of anti-Jewish propaganda during the war, anti-Semitism was for most Germans now so abstract and so routine that there was apparently difficulty in keeping alive a real interest in the 'Jewish Question'.
>
> (p.192)

(You should remember, though, that David Welch feels differently about this matter. For him, the continual reinforcement that such films offered was significant.)

Kershaw is also less sure about the revised propaganda policy that Goebbels was compelled to adopt after the momentous German setback at Stalingrad. He states:

> Though the new 'realism' as portrayed in Goebbels' 'total war' speech in February 1943 and in related propaganda was in the short term effective, and though in the remaining period of the war there were still propaganda successes ... the final two years were in general a period of decreasing propaganda effectiveness and culminating sense of failure.
>
> (p.198)

Certainly, as all commentators agree, propaganda success was exceedingly difficult in those final two years of the war when the circumstances had turned so decidedly in favour of the Allies.

It may be, indeed, that Nazi propaganda had reached its peak by 1939. Fear of war was as pervasive in Germany by 1939 as elsewhere in Europe. Ironically, as Kershaw continues, 'an important feature of [Nazi] propaganda success lay not so much in its militarism as in its bolstering of the Hitler image in such a way that, perversely, the Führer appeared to act as a guarantor of peace, not a bringer of war' (p.187). Thus the onset of war was a test of the Hitler myth which the propaganda machine had helped to create, of the German people's genuine trust in their leader, and of the credibility of Nazi propaganda.

From the start of the war Hitler delivered immediate results, but that allowed Goebbels no respite – quite the contrary in fact. 'It could also be argued', suggests Richard Overy, 'that the easy victories of the early years of war created an unfortunate psychological climate.' He elaborates further:

> In the summer of 1940 and again in October 1941 the popular feeling was that the war was over, and all the propaganda effort before 1939 directed at preparing the population for sacrifices and privation seemed curiously inappropriate.
>
> ('Mobilization for total war in Germany 1939–1941', 1988, p.635)

What price the propagandist's job when it is popularly thought victory has been won? Perhaps it is no surprise that Ian Kershaw is prompted to the following conclusion:

> The anxieties of war made Germany keener than ever for reliable information. Yet the 'closed' and tightly-controlled information provided by the propaganda agencies gave rise in such circumstances – to a far greater extent than in wartime Britain – to the construction of a frequently powerful counter opinion which contributed significantly to the growing general scepticism about the reliability of 'official' information. The part played by rumour – often started by foreign broadcasts which, despite draconian penalties found ready listeners – in forming resilient counter opinion and prompting scepticism about the 'official' version, was extraordinary. And stories told by eyewitnesses – soldiers home on leave or bombed out evacuees – often conflicted directly with optimistic press reports and were listened to eagerly. The veracity of German propaganda was in these and other ways increasingly called into question, and general confidence in official information gradually undermined. Of course, there were certainly phases of propaganda success and themes which were

undoubtedly highly effective, but the general picture of wartime propaganda which can be gleaned from sources such as press directives and especially SD reports is one of growing and eventually almost total propaganda failure long before the end of the war. The more propaganda seemed to conflict with reality, the more discredited it became. The process began even in the 'triumphant' phase of the war, before the invasion of the USSR.

('How effective was Nazi propaganda?', 1983, pp.194–5)

Kershaw, you will note, uses the word 'closed' to describe the German context. It is a word we used earlier in this unit to contrast totalitarian Germany with 'open' liberal democratic Britain. Do the terms really have any meaning in the attempt to distinguish between one system of social and political organization and another when engaged in total war? What also of the suggested divide between 'revolutionary' Germany and 'conservative' Britain? If the descriptions are relevant for the onset of the war, how might they be applied by its end?

We think by now you must have enough sources and arguments at your disposal to answer questions like those for yourself. Just in case you feel otherwise, we shall direct you to the one remaining document for these units and the last two pieces of film. Document II.38 in *Primary Sources 2: Interwar and World War II* is the transcript of a newsreel extract covering Goebbels' 'total war' speech of 18 February 1943. Ian Kershaw referred to it earlier as marking a point of departure in Goebbels' propaganda approach with the adoption of a new-found 'realism'. You should really be watching the film of this speech, and our apologies for the fact that you are not. Ironically, though, the printed extract fulfils my purpose. Notice the well-orchestrated nature of the proceedings. The audience of party members had been rehearsed beforehand and knew exactly what was expected. It shows in the exhortatory question-and-answer sequence which elicits the appropriate amount of 'spontaneous' consent for Goebbels' message. Little had changed, in fact, from the propaganda techniques used years earlier in *Triumph of the Will,* and, as far as we can judge, the relationship between the leaders and the led had changed little. One was still exhorting the other and urging greater sacrifice.

Contrast that approach with the one adopted in the second story of item 18 on Video 2. Here we see Field Marshal Montgomery talking to factory workers. Again, you will doubtless note, there is the same sense of the proceedings being well orchestrated, with the appropriate amount of careful editing to convey a feeling of 'spontaneous' rapport between 'Monty' and everyday folk. Despite the editing, however, some things cannot be hidden. Notice the distinctly autocratic air and the patriarchal tone. Monty and the workers ('and women too') were one 'big happy family', yet they remained classes apart. But it is surely not insignificant that Monty was appearing on the factory front. Furthermore, there is little exhortation, just explanation (however limited in scope). I wonder if you feel that despite the obvious manipulation this newsreel does still convey a sense of genuine agreement and unity? Is this a sign of change between the leaders and the led in Britain, do you think, resulting from the conditions of war? The purpose of item 19, should be obvious.

Exercise   Now read Document II.38 in *Primary Sources 2: Interwar and World War II* and watch items 18 and 19 on Video 2. ∎

Film and post-war reconstruction

In view of the considerable amounts of attention and consideration given over to the use of film as a medium of propaganda during the war, and the ongoing belief in its powers of persuasion, it is perhaps no surprise that the victorious allies employed it once again in the cause of post-war reconstruction for a devastated Europe. To conclude our study of the media, then, we shall consider briefly both feature film and documentary examples of its application in the aftermath of war. To start, we want you to look at an extract from one of Roberto Rossellini's films. Rossellini is often considered the founding father and a leading exponent of the Italian neo-realist cinema which emerged at the end of the war. In such films as *Roma Città Aperta (1945)* and *Paisa (1946)* he explored the nature of the Italian reaction to the wartime experience (these films are discussed in considerable detail in AA304 *Politics, Culture and Society in France and Italy 1943–1973,* where the whole question of neo-realism and its impact on post-war Italian culture is broached). For the third film in his war trilogy, *Germania Anno Zero* (*Germany Year Zero,* 1947), Rossellini concentrated on Germany at the moment of defeat.

Set in 1945, *Germany Year Zero* chronicles the experience of a 12-year-old boy among the rubble and ruins of bombed-out Berlin. His father is ill, his brother, an ex-soldier, is in hiding from the authorities, and his sister is compelled to drink with Allied soldiers for cigarettes which can then be bartered for food to eke out the family's precarious existence. Falling under the influence of his former schoolteacher, an unrepentant Nazi who dutifully trots out such catchphrases as 'The weak are always eliminated by the strong', the boy administers poison to his ailing father. The extract you are about to watch comes from the very end of the film.

Exercise   Watch item 20 on Video 2 now, bearing in mind the following questions:

1   What does this film convey?

2   Why do you think the film turned out to be a commercial failure? ■

Specimen answers   and discussion

1   It conveys the extent of the destruction and devastation of Berlin at the end of the war. The city is destroyed and so too are its people, with the family unit disintegrating under the pressures of everyday survival. It is a bleak picture with an added note of personal despair. The boy is lost, alienated and defenceless. Christianity can offer no solace (the symbolic meaning, surely, of the scene by the roofless church), and the only guidance he has been given comes from the warped mentality of a former member of the Nazi educational establishment. Death is now a commonplace in the city (notice the casual loading of his father's coffin on to a lorry already heaped with coffins). The boy is oblivious to the calls of his sister, who seems remote as he looks down from a vantage point in the ruined buildings opposite, and the only way out is suicide. There is a lot of critical debate, as you can imagine, about the meaning of the boy's suicide. Rossellini maintained the intention was to show that the 'Flame of morality is not extinguished in him'. He commits suicide to escape the 'malaise and contradiction' of 'an erroneous education', 'the false morality which is the very essence of Nazism', and which leads the child 'to perpetrate a crime

while he believes himself to be carrying out an heroic act'. Whatever moral dilemmas the film may highlight, to my mind it reveals an essentially nihilistic vision of the world.

2   Though, of course, any answer to this question must be largely speculative, I cannot help but think that the film failed simply because it was too bleak and too pessimistic People did not want to see this sort of thing. German cinemagoers were no more inclined to watch their own film-makers' rendition of the problems that beset them. Wolfgang Staudte's *Die Mörder Sind Unter Uns* (*The Murderers Are Among Us*, 1946, produced in East Berlin) and Helmut Kautner's *In Jenen Tagen* (*In Those Days*, 1947, made in West Germany) are often cited as examples of the native '*Trummer*' (rubble) films, the German efforts that most closely parallel the concerns of the Italian neo-realists. Yet they too did badly at the German box office. The British film of *The Wicked Lady* (1945), a costume melodrama starring James Mason and Margaret Lockwood, epitomizes the sort of film that did well in Germany, west and east alike, in the immediate aftermath of the war. Escapism was, unsurprisingly, very much the order of the day. The audience for neo-realist films throughout most of Europe was generally confined to the realms of élite art-house cinemas. Even in Italy, neo-realism proved a short-lived movement whose concerns and forms were increasingly seen as being far removed from the interest of the masses. □

Now let us turn to instances where documentary and newsreel film were put to use in furthering postwar reconstruction.

Exercise   Documents II.39–II.41 in *Primary Sources 2: Interwar and World War II* are the transcripts of commentaries to four official government films. The first is an American documentary made late in 1944 and shown from April 1945, just before the end of war in Europe. The second is a British Crown Film Unit documentary made in the summer of 1945 and released at the outset of 1946. The third and fourth are from the Anglo-American newsreel. *Welt im Film*, which was compulsorily screened in Germany between 1945 and 1950. Read them now, and then answer the following questions:

1   Who were these films aimed at?

2   What points of emphasis do you detect and what were the intentions?

3   What would you say they generally reveal? ■

Specimen answers   1   The first was clearly an indoctrination exercise intended for American troops
and discussion   and discussion in Germany. The second explains the government of the British zone of occupation and was obviously meant for domestic audiences in Britain. The third and fourth were plainly examples of newsreel stories primarily intended for exhibition to the occupied German population.

2   The American film is somewhat vindictive in tone and urges vigilance as the troops embark on full-scale occupation. After a potted history of German militarism, it emphasizes the collective guilt of the German people for the war and cites this as a reason for non-fraternization. While equally intent on conveying the message of collective German guilt, the British film is really more concerned with showing how some of the principles agreed among

the Allies for the reconstruction of Germany – de-Nazification, democratization and re-education – are being put into practice. The 'get tough' attitude
advocated before war's end had noticeably softened into a more
conciliatory note once the actual process of reconstruction got underway
and the sheer size of the problems was revealed. (The extent to which there
was genuine disagreement among the Allies over their approach to
reconstruction is outlined in Unit 26). The Potsdam agreement essentially
settled on the so-called 'Four Ds' – demilitarization, de-Nazification,
democratization and de-industrialization – though not without considerable
debate, as you have seen. Nicholas Pronay has argued, however, that Britain
saw re-education as the paramount issue throughout and central to all
objectives, plans and propaganda on the matter. (See his introduction in N.
Pronay and K. Wilson, *The Political Re-education of Germany and Her
Allies,* 1985.)

The first *Welt im Film* newsreel from June 1945 shows much the same sort of
emphasis on the complexity of reconstruction, with stories on returning
prisoners of war, the recovery of stolen artworks, the rebuilding of
democracy through the restoration of a free press and the establishment of a
new education system (under Allied control and supervision, of course),
and the investigation and execution of war criminals. It concentrates,
predictably, on the German defeat and Allied power, with some space
reserved, you will note, for an item stressing the efforts of Russian and
American forces alike in the liberation of Czechoslovakia. By June 1948,
however, *Welt im Film* has clearly become a mouthpiece for the western
Allies alone. Now the Soviet Union is the enemy and Berlin 'the symbol of
the new democratic order in a Germany that hungers after peace'. The Cold
War is engaged and the Americans, British, French and Germans are
working together to break the Soviet blockade of the city which 'serves only
to intensify the determination of democratic peoples everywhere'.

3   Perhaps the most obvious feature about these items is the extent to which
they reveal, once again, a belief in the power of propaganda and the
malleability of the subjects chosen as its target. In the event, little of this
official propaganda appears to have achieved its desired effect. *Your job in
Germany,* for instance, argued a policy which, as David Culbert has pointed
out, was 'abandoned well before the film completed its original run' (see his
essay 'American film policy in the re-education of Germany', 1985, p.180).
Non-fraternization proved, as Culbert states, 'a totally unenforceable
regulation'. Similarly, the policy stressing collective German guilt was soon
abandoned. 'The futility of such feelings became apparent', Culbert notes,
when occupation forces discovered that 'The physical destruction of so
much of the country ... meant that practical matters relating to food and
housing obviously took precedence' (p. 175). Indeed, if anything, official
films like *Your job in Germany* could prove counter-productive to the
urgent task of reconstruction when given a general release to civilian
audiences. 'While everyone directing occupation policy in the American
zone turned to the practical matter of feeding a starving German populace',
Culbert concludes, 'groups in America learned emotional responses to
oppose such largesse' (p.190).

Audience reaction to the British Crown Film Unit's A *Defeated People* was always likely to be similar: why help a people we have spent so long trying to overcome? (Hence, perhaps, the attempt to offset such questions with its obvious *vox populi* introduction.) The Crown Film Unit was disbanded in 1951. The endless stream of commercial feature films made between 1946 and 1958, which gloried in the war and evoked traditional stereotypes of the enemy, might provide a more accurate picture of the way in which the British preferred to view their former foe. □

Welt im Film fared little better, it appears, when it came to the considerable task of re-educating German cinemagoers. Official surveys reveal some measure of animosity towards these Allied newsreels. Their impact can be judged from anecdotal and impressionistic sources. One German schoolboy, for instance, remembers that the tune which accompanied the newsreel titles was invariably greeted by a chorus of young voices singing a home-made verse:

Haut sie'raus, den Tommy	(Chuck'em out, the Tommies
Haut sie'raus, den Ami	Chuck'em out, the Americans
Haut sie'raus, den Russki	Chuck'em out, the Russians
Haut sie'raus, das allierte Pack	Chuck'em out, the Allied rabble)

(Quoted in Roger Smither, *Welt im Film 1945–1950*, 1981)

The official surveys highlighted certain salient, if unsurprising, features – not least the finding that 'The Germans have been filled to overflowing with propaganda, and will reject in disgust any output which tastes even faintly of an attempt to propagandise.' Little wonder, then, that the re-education policy proved difficult to implement, especially given that the wartime ideals on which it was based – the ideals that had been marshalled to inspire the British and Americans to fight 'the Good War', 'the Justified War', 'the Necessary War – were hardly likely to recommend themselves to a nation imbued with its own ideology but now defeated and on the receiving end. Inevitably, the successful reconstruction of Germany owed less to Allied propaganda espousing the cause of re-education, albeit highly-minded and laudable, than it did to the provision of such essentials as economic help and support. By contrast, when it came to 'selling' the Marshall Plan, more sensible and pragmatic opinions prevailed about the wartime propagandist ideals. 'These ideas all revolved round the notion of *raising living standards everywhere,* of economic well-being as the key to social and political stability', David Ellwood states '... of Fascism and Communism as roughly the mirror image of each other, produced by backwardness, underdevelopment and misery' ('From re-education to the selling of the Marshall Plan in Italy', 1985, p.232). Thus, the operating principles applied to Italy, as elsewhere, agreed that:

> ERP is a unique chance offered to European nations toward reconstructing their economy, raising the standard of living among the masses, and attaining by the year 1952 an economic stability which is the foundation of political independence ... Every worker, every citizen is bound up in their rebirth. The future and the peace of Italy and Europe, the general well-being of all, depend on the will and the work of each single one of us.
>
> (Ellwood, 1985, p. 232) □

Thereafter, the campaign set out to 'Carry the message of the Marshall Plan to the people. Carry it to them directly – it won't permeate down. And give it to them so that they can understand it' (p.229). The people could hardly fail to get the message when the Marshall Plan Freedom Train bore the slogan 'Prosperity makes you free' while distributing gifts, aid and comfort. 'This was the meaning of the Marshall Plan', Ellwood concludes, 'a vision of consensus and prosperity conveyed by a programme of action which brought material aid and propaganda together as never before' (p. 220). Clearly, in the final analysis, propaganda was at its most effective when it was accompanied by the realistic prospect of peace, prosperity and personal benefit rather than merely empty promises of the same.

References

Addison, P. (1975) *The Road to 1945: British Politics and the Second World War*, Cape.

Aldgate, A. and Richards, J. (1986) *Britain Can Take It. The British Cinema in the Second World War*, Blackwell.

Baker, G. W. and Chapman, T. E. (1962) *Man and Society in Disaster*, Basic Books.

Barnett, C. (1986) *The Audit of War. The Illusions and Reality of Britain as a Great Nation*, Macmillan.

Bartlett, F. C. (1942) *Political Propaganda*, Cambridge University Press.

Bartlett, Frederick (1940), *Political Propaganda*, Cambridge University Press.

Bédarida, R. (1988) 'World War II and social change in France' in A. Marwick (ed.) *Total War and Social Change*, Macmillan.

Bielenberg, C. (1968) *The Past is Myself*, Chatto and Windus.

Briggs, A. (1970) *The History of Broadcasting in the United Kingdom*, Vol.3, *The War of Words*, Oxford University Press.

Brooke, S. (1992) *Labour's War: The Labour Party during the Second World War*, Clarendon.

Calder, A. (1969) *The People's War: Britain 1939–1945*, Granada.

Cardiff, D. and Scannell, P. (1983) 'Radio in World Star II', U203 Popular Culture, Broadcast Notes, The Open University.

Carr, W. (1987) *A History of Germany 1815–1945*, 3rd edn, E. J. Arnold.

Childs, D. (1988) *The GDR: Moscow's German Ally*, Unwin Hyman.

Childs, D. and Johnson, G. (1981) *West Germany: Politics and Society*, Croom Helm.

Clark, M. (1996) *Modern Italy 1871–1982*, Longman.

Crosby, T. L. (1986) *The Impact of Civilian Evacuation in the Second World War*, Croom Helm.

Crouzet, M. (1970) *The European Renaissance Since 1945*, trans. S. Baron, Harcourt, Brace, Jovanovich.

Culbert, D. (1985) 'American film policy in the re-education of Germany' in N. Pronay and K. Wilson (eds) *The Political Re-education of Germany and Her Allies after World War II*, Croom Helm.

Curran, J. and Seaton, J. (1981) *Power without Responsibility: The Press and Broadcasting in Britain*, Fontana.

Dahrendorf, R. (1968) *Society and Democracy in Germany*, London, Weidenfeld and Nicolson.

Davies, M. (1996) *Europe: A History*, Oxford University Press, (first published 1949, France).

Davies, N. (1981) *God's Playground: A History of Poland*, Vol.2, *1795 to the Present Day*, London, Oxford University Press.

de Beauvoir, S. (1961) *The Second Sex*, New English Library.

Dockrill, M. (1988) *The Cold War 1945–63*, Macmillan.

Doob, L. W. (1935) *Propaganda: Its Psychology and Technique*, New York.

Dukes, P. (1988) 'The social consequences of World War II for the USSR' in A. Marwick (ed.) *Total War and Social Change*, Macmillan.

Ellwood, D. (1985) 'From "re-education" to the selling of the Marshall Plan in Italy' in N. Pronay and K. Wilson (eds) *The Political Re-education of Germany and Her Allies after World War II*, Croom Helm.

Ellwood, D. (1985) *Italy 1943–45*, Leicester University Press.

Fitzgibbon, C. (1957) *The Blitz*, Wingate.

Gelatt, R. (1977) *The Fabulous Phonograph 1877–1977*, Cassell.

Grunberger, R. (1971) *A Social History of the Third Reich*, Weidenfeld and Nicolson.

Hardach, G. (1977) *The First World War 1914–18*, Allen Lane.

Harris, F. (1983) *Encounters with Darkness: French and German Writers on World War II*, New York, Oxford University Press.

Harris, J. (1977) *William Beveridge: A Biography*, Clarendon Press.

Hawkins, D. (ed.) (1985) *War Report. D-Day to VE-Day*, Ariel Books.

Hockerts, H. G. (1981) 'German post-war social policies against the background of the Beveridge plan' in W. Mommsen (ed.) *The Emergence of the Welfare State in Britain and Germany 1850–1950*, Croom Helm on behalf of the German Historical Institute.

Horne, A. (1988) *Macmillan*, 2 vols, Macmillan.

Howard, M. (1976) 'Total war in the twentieth century: participation and consensus in the Second World War' in B. Bond and I. Roy (eds) *War and Society. A Yearbook of Military History*, Croom Helm.

Iklé, F. C. (1958) *The Social Impact of Bomb Destruction*, W. S. Hall.

Jefferys, K. (1994) *War and Reform: British Politics During The Second World War*, Manchester University Press.

Johnson, P. (1983) *A History of the Modern World*, Weidenfeld and Nicolson.

Keenan, E. L. (1986) 'Muscovite political folkways', *The Russian Review*, no.45.

Keller, S. (1963) *Beyond the Ruling Class: Strategic Élites in Modern Society*, Random House.

Kennedy, P. (1988) *The Rise and Fall of the Great Powers*, Unwin Hyman.

Kershaw, I. (1983) 'How effective was Nazi propaganda? in D. Welch (ed.) *Nazi Propaganda. The Power and the Limitations*, Croom Helm.

Kirwin, C. (1981) 'Waiting for retaliation – a study in Nazi propaganda behaviour and German civilian morale', *Journal of Contemporary History*, vol.16.

Kirwin, G. (1985) 'Allied bombing and Nazi domestic propaganda, *European History Quarterly*, vol.15, no.3, July.

Klein, J. (1965) *Samples from English Cultures*, Routledge and Kegan Paul.

Kosinski, L. (1970) *The Population of Europe: A Geographical Perspective*, Longman.

Kreici, J. (1976) *Social Structure in Divided Germany*, Croom Helm.

Laqueur, W. (1972) *Europe Since Hitler. The Rebirth of Europe*, revised edn, Penguin.

Larkin, M. (1988) *France Since the Popular Front: Government and the People 1936–86*, Oxford University Press.

Linz, S. J. (1985) *The Impact of World War II on the Soviet Union*, Rowman and Allanheld.

Loth, W. (1988) *The Division of the World 1941–55*, trans. C. Krojzlova, Routledge and Kegan Paul.

Maier, C. S. (1975) *Recasting Bourgeois Europe: Stabilization in the Decade after World War I*, Princeton University Press.

Maier, C. S. (1981) 'The two post-war eras and the conditions for stability in twentieth-century Western Europe', *American Historical Review Forum*, vol.86, no.2, April.

Marwick, A. (1967) 'The Labour Party and the welfare state in Britain, 1900–1948', *American Historical Review*, vol.73, no.2, December.

Marwick, A. (1974) *War and Social Change in the Twentieth Century*, London, Macmillan.

Marwick, A. (1976) *The Home Front: The British and the Second World War*, Thames and Hudson.

Marwick, A. (1982) *British Society since 1945*, revised edn 1990, Penguin.

Marwick, A. (1982) 'Print, pictures and sound: the Second World War and the British experience' in *Daedalus*, vol.III, no.3, Fall, pp.135–55.

Marwick, A. (1986) *Class in the Twentieth Century*, Harvester Press.

Marwick, A. (1988) *Total War and Social Change*, Macmillan.

Marwick, A. (1990) *Class, Image and Reality in Britain, France and the USA since 1930*, revised edn, Oxford University Press (first published 1980, Collins).

Marwick, A. (1991) *The Deluge: British Society and the First World War*, Macmillan.

Marwick, A. (2000) *A History of the Modern British Isles 1914–1999: Circumstances, Events and Outcomes*, Blackwell.

Mason, T. (1971) 'Some origins of the Second World War' in E. M. Robertson (ed.) *The Origins of the Second World War*, Macmillan.

Mayne, R. (1970) *The Recovery of Europe. From Devastation to Unity*, Harper and Row.

McCauley, M. (1983) *The German Democratic Republic since 1945*, Macmillan.

McLaine, I. (1979) *Ministry of Morale. Home Front Morale and the Ministry of Information in World War II*, Allen and Unwin.

Michel, H. and Mirkine-Guetzovitch, B. (1954) *Les idées politiques et sociales de la Résistance*, Paris.

Milward, A. (1977) *War, Economy and Society 1939–45*, Allen Lane.

Milward, A. (1984) *The Reconstruction of Western Europe 1945–51*, Methuen.

Morgan, K. (1984) *Labour in Power 1945–51*, Oxford University Press.

Nicolson, H. (1967) *Diaries and Letters 1939–45*, ed. Nigel Nicolson, Collins.

Nish, I. (1977) *Japanese Foreign Policy 1869–1942*, Routledge and Kegan Paul.

Noakes, J. (1992) 'Germany' in J. Noakes (ed.) *The Civilian in War: The Home Front in Europe, Japan and the USA in World War II*, Exeter University Press.

Noakes, J. (1998) *Nazism 1939–1945*, Vol. 4, *The German Home Front in World War II: A Documentary Reader*, Exeter Studies in History, University of Exeter Press.

Nove, A. (1972) *An Economic History of the USSR*, Penguin.

Overy, R. (1988) 'Mobilization for total war in Germany 1939–41', *English Historical Review*, vol.ciii, no.408, July.

Pelling, H. (1970) *Britain and the Second World War*, Collins.

Perkin, H. (1989) *The Rise of Professional Society: England since 1880*, Routledge and Kegan Paul.

Priestley, J. B. (1944) *They Came to a City*, Samuel French.

Pronay, N. and Wilson, K. (eds) (1985) *The Political Re-education of Germany and Her Allies after World War II*, Croom Helm.

Reith, John (1949), *Into the Wind*, London, Hodder & Stoughton.

Rhode, G. (1973) 'The Protectorate of Bohemia and Moravia 1939–45' in V. S. Mamatey and R. Luza (eds) *A History of the Czechoslovak Republic 1918–1948*, Princeton University Press.

Richards, J. and Sheridan, D. (eds) (1987) *Mass Observation at the Movies*, Routledge and Kegan Paul.

Rioux, J-P. (1987) *The Fourth Republic 1944–58*, trans. G. Rogers, Cambridge University Press.

Sadoul, G. (1962) *Le cinéma français*, Flammarion.

Sandford, J. (1976) *The Mass Media of the German-speaking Countries*, Oswald Wolff.

Seaton, J. (1987) 'Reporting atrocities: the BBC and the holocaust' in J. Seaton and B. Pimlott (eds) *The Media in British Politics*, Gower.

Smith, A. (1976) *The Shadow in the Cave*, Quartet.

Smith, H. L. (ed.) (1986) *War and Social Change: British Society in the Second World War*, Manchester University Press.

Smith, H. L. (ed.) (1996) *Britain in the Second World War: A Social History*, Manchester University Press.

Smither, R. (1981) *Welt im Film 1945–1950*, Microfiche Film Catalogue No.1, Imperial War Museum.

Stephenson, J. (1975) *Women in Nazi Germany*, Croom Helm.

Summerfield, P. (1998) *Reconstructing Women's Wartime Lives: Discourse and Subjectivity in Oral Histories of the Second World War*, Manchester University Press.

Suvorov, V. (1990) *Icebreaker: Who Started the Second World War?*, Hamish Hamilton.

Tannenbaum, E. R. (1972) *The Fascist Experience: Italian Society and Culture 1922–1945*, Basic Books.

Thomas, H. (1986) *Armed Truce: Beginnings of the Cold War 1945–46*, Hamish Hamilton.

Walter, G. (1963) *Histoire des paysans de France*, Flammarion.

Weinberg, G., (1994) *A World at War: A Global History of World War II*, Cambridge University Press.

Welch, D (1983) *Propaganda and the German Cinema 1933–1945*, Clarendon Press.

Welch, D. (1987) 'Propaganda and indoctrination in the Third Reich: success or failure?', *European History Quarterly*, vol.17, no.4, October.

Werth, A. (1964) *Russia at War, 1941–45*, Barrie and Rockliff.

Wheatcroft, S. G. and Davies, R. W. (1994) 'Population' in R. W. Davies, M. Harrison and S. G. Wheatcroft (eds) *The Economic Transformation of the Soviet Union 1913–45*, Cambridge University Press.

Further reading

Addison, P. (1985) *Now the War is Over: A Social History of Britain 1945–1951*, BBC and Jonathan Cape.

Aldgate, A. and Richards, J. (1994), *Britain Can Take It: The British Cinema in the Second World War*, second edn, Edinburgh University Press.

Armes, R. (1971) *Patterns of Realism,* Tantivy Press.

Balfour, M. (1979) *Propaganda in War 1939–1945. Organisations, Policies and Publics in Britain and Germany*, Routledge and Kegan Paul.

Briggs, A. (1979) *The History of Broadcasting in the United Kingdom*, Vol. 3, *The War of Words*, and Vol. 4, *Sound and Vision*, Oxford University Press.

Calder, A. and Sheridan, D. (1984) *Speak for Yourself: A Mass-Observation Anthology 1937–1949*, Oxford University Press.

Cardiff, D. and Scannell, P. (1981) 'Radio in World War II', Unit 8 of U203 *Popular Culture*, The Open University.

Chapman, J. (1998), *The British at War: Cinema, State and Propaganda, 1939–1945,* I. B. Tauris.

Ehrlich, E. (1985) *Cinema of Paradox: French Filmmaking under the German Occupation*, Columbia University Press, 1987.

Ellwood, D. (1985) *Italy 1943–1945*, Leicester University Press.

Forgacs, D. (ed.) (1986) *Rethinking Italian Fascism, Capitalism, Populism and Culture,* Lawrence and Wishart.

Gerner, K. (1986) *The Soviet Union and Central Europe in the Post-War Era,* Gower.

Guess, G. M. (1987) *The Politics of United States Foreign Aid,* Croom Helm.

Harper, J. L. (1987) *America and the Reconstruction of Italy 1945–1948*, Cambridge University Press.

Hayes, N. and Hill, J. (eds) (1999) *Millions Like Us? British Culture in the Second World War*, Liverpool University Press.

Kershaw, I. (1987) *The 'Hitler Myth'. Image and Reality in the Third Reich*, Clarendon Press.

Kris, E. and Speir, H. (1944) *German Radio Propaganda*, Oxford University Press.

Landy, M. (1986) *Fascism in Film: The Italian Commercial Cinema 1931–1943* Princeton University Press.

Leiser, E. (1968) *Nazi Cinema*, Secker and Warburg.

Nicholas S. (1996) *The Echo of War: Home Front Propaganda and the Wartime BBC 1939–45*, Manchester University Press.

Pollard, R. A. (1986) *Economic Security and the Origins of the Cold War 1945–1950*, Columbia University Press.

Priestley, J. B. (1967) *All England Listened. The Wartime Broadcasts*, intro. by Eric Sevareid, Chilmark Press.

Pronay, N. and Thorpe, F. with Coultass, C. (1980*) British Official Films in the Second World War: A Descriptive Catalogue*, Clio Press.

Reeves, N. (1999) *The Power of Film Propaganda: Myth or Reality?*, Cassell.

Richards, J. and Sheridan, D. (eds) (1987) *Mass-Observation at the Movies*, Routledge and Kegan Paul.

Short, K. R. M. (ed.) (1976) *Western Broadcasting over the Iron Curtain,* Croom Helm.

Short, K. R. M. (ed.) (1983) *Film and Radio Propaganda in World War II,* Croom Helm.

Short, K. R. M. and Dolezel, S. (eds) (1988) *Hitler's Fall: The Newsreel Witness,* Croom Helm.

Smith, A. (1978) *The Politics of Information. Problems of Policy in Modern Media,* Macmillan.

Smith, A. (ed.) (1979) *Television and Political Life. Studies in Six European Countries,* Macmillan.

Taylor, P. M. (ed.) (1988) *Britain and the Cinema in the Second World War,* Macmillan.

Taylor, R. (1998) *Film Propaganda: Soviet Russia and Nazi Germany,* revised edn, I. B. Tauris.

Thomas, R. (1976) *Broadcasting and Democracy in France,* Bradford University Press/Crosby Lockwood Staples.

Welch, D. (ed.) (1983) *Nazi Propaganda. The Power and the Limitations,* Croom Helm.

Welch, D. (1983), *Propaganda and the German Cinema, 1933–1945,* Clarendon Press.

Welch, D. (1993), *The Third Reich: Politics and Propaganda,* Routledge.

Williams, A. (1976) *Broadcasting and Democracy in West Germany,* Bradford University Press/Crosby Lockwood Staples

Zeman, Z. A. B. (1973) *Nazi Propaganda,* 2nd edn, Oxford University Press.

Unit 26 EUROPE DIVIDED

BILL PURDUE, CLIVE EMSLEY AND MARK PITTAWAY

(Introduction and sections 1, 2, 3, 7 and 8 by Bill Purdue; sections 4 and 5 by Clive Emsley; section 6 by Mark Pittaway)

Open University students of this unit will need to refer to:

Primary Sources 2: Interwar and World War II, eds Arthur Marwick and Wendy Simpson, Open University, 2001

Maps Booklet

INTRODUCTION

This unit looks at the division of Europe in the aftermath of World War II. Its aims are to help you to understand:

1   the way in which political divisions were made and evolved in post-war Europe;

2   the relative importance of ideology, contingency and pragmatism in this division.

The Cold War determined the major structures and essential characteristics of international relations for nearly half a century. It was a world war involving the Asian, American and African continents, and indeed its greatest crises and drifts into 'hot war' occurred outside Europe. Its centre, however, was Europe, and it was there that its freezing effects were most clearly demonstrated.

A perverse historiographical effect of the Cold War was that it imposed a perspective upon the conflict which preceded it. Concentration was focused upon the breakdown of the alliance against Hitler but little upon the circumstances in which that alliance was created. The Allied victory cast a long shadow most graphically illustrated by Berlin in the late 1980s, which in some respects resembled a time warp of 1945, still divided between and garrisoned by the victorious Allies and symbolic of both the grand alliance of the Soviet Union and the western powers and their subsequent enmity. Thus, continuity between the international rivalries of the 1930s and those of the post-1945 era was understated, and it was as if the grand alliance, if not in place from 1939, had always been imminent. Yet the immediate circumstances of the outbreak of war in 1939 had their part to play in the origins of the Cold War, as did the mutual suspicions which from the beginning underlay cooperation between the USSR and the western Allies. The Cold War was apparently a clash of ideologies, while in its later stages World War II was presented as a war against an ideology – fascism – rather than as a war between states wedded to different ideologies and systems. Thus, the years of the Cold War saw histories of its origins which consistently underestimated national rivalries and nationalism itself.

Our concern in this unit is with the origins and early development of the Cold War, but the west's eventual 'victory' in that war inevitably affects the way we view the events of the 1940s and 1950s. As you will know, the position or date from which one views the past has much to do with one's interpretation of it. Viewing the Cold War from the beginning of the twenty-first century, a decade after the fall of the socialist regimes of eastern Europe, the reunification of Germany and the dissolution of the USSR, provides a very different perspective from that of the 1980s when the divide between east and west seemed immutable. It reminds us of the degree to which all historical judgements, especially those made about the recent past, are provisional. It should, perhaps, also remind us of the fallible nature of expertise in the social sciences, for very few of the established experts on eastern European politics or society appreciated the weakness of the Soviet empire and almost none forecast its imminent demise.

Throughout this unit we would like you to bear in mind the following central questions:

1   Was it always probable that the alliance against Hitler's Germany would fall
     apart and end in mutual hostility given the histories, ideologies and
     ambitions of the partners?

2   Was Stalin impelled by Marxist conventions, opportunism or the traditional
     ambitions of Russian foreign policy?

3   Was the Soviet Union intent, even before the end of World War II, upon the
     imposition of uniform political systems based on the Soviet model and
     ultimately subject to the Soviet Communist Party within the Soviet sphere of
     influence?

4   Did Stalin have more extensive ambitions and hope for a socialist Europe or
     world?

5   Could different western policies have averted post-war divisions or,
     alternatively, pushed the dividing line further eastwards?

6   Was the situation in both western and eastern Europe relatively fluid
     between 1945 and 1948, and the polarized outcome far from determined but
     rather the result of an interaction of Soviet and western policies and mutual
     suspicions within specific circumstances?

7   As with 6, do we need to consider not just the divide between east and west,
     communist and liberal capitalist, but the individual circumstances and
     histories of particular states in both western and eastern Europe and the way
     in which factors such as class, culture and nationality determined the
     specific nature of the regimes and societies that had emerged by 1948?

1   YALTA AND THE SHAPE OF THINGS TO COME

The fluidity of international relations until June, even December, 1941 was based
on the essentially triangular nature of the conflicting ambitions of the
democracies, the Soviet Union and the Third Reich. Thereafter for the
duration of the war, there was an uneasy pragmatic alliance between two
corners of the triangle who fought to destroy the third, the German state and its
allies, but the verbiage of cooperation could not for long conceal conflicting
ambitions as to the shape of the post-war world once victory over Hitler's
Germany was assured. The big question was, therefore, what Europe would be
like without Germany; the second was how long you could have a Europe
without a powerful and united Germany. Further questions were how to
reconcile the Soviet Union's demands for security, hegemony or dominance in
the areas it had conquered with the aspirations of the occupied states, and
whether western European states like France and Italy could be reborn as stable
liberal democratic (or, as contemporary Marxists put it, 'bourgeois') societies.

As we have seen in Units 21–5, Roosevelt was not prepared to align military
strategy to political goals. The consequence of this was bound to be that Soviet
influence in central and eastern Europe would increase. The problem was that
such a result was incompatible with the Wilsonian aims of the end of power
blocs and spheres of influence and the inauguration of a liberal capitalist world
where nations would enjoy self-determination. 'It is better that Russia should

dominate eastern Europe than that Germany should dominate western Europe,' argued Sir William Strang, British representative on the newly formed Inter-Allied Armistice Commission in May 1943 (quoted in Mazower, *Dark Continent*, 1999, p.229). Given America's lack of interest in anything that smacked of aligning prosecution of the war with provision for spheres of influence as its end, Strang's view may have been brutal but realistic. The Inter-Allied Armistice Commission was set up on the suggestion of Anthony Eden so that the three Allied powers could coordinate policy in the territories that came under their control. There is at least circumstantial evidence, however, of an acceptance of a free hand for occupying powers in their respective spheres of influence. There were muted protests from the western Allies when the Soviet Union withdrew recognition of the Polish government in London in April 1943, and rather more voluble protests from the Russians when they were excluded from the negotiations for Italian surrender a few months later – but were such words a mere smokescreen? As Mark Mazower has put it: 'Was there not then, at the highest levels, a tacit quid pro quo here regarding Poland and Italy?' (p.230).

Once the decision had been made that Britain and America were to put their strength into an invasion of France and were not to invade the Balkans from Italy, it was clear that the Soviet Union would be in a position to dominate eastern Europe, though different military decisions by Eisenhower in late 1944 and 1945 might have found Anglo-American forces deeper into central Europe. A *de facto* division into spheres of influence was thus emergent, but the sharpness of the eventual division was far from certain. Spheres of influence could well have simply meant a privileged influence for certain powers able to exercise an informal hegemony, and this could have been quite compatible with a degree of pluralism within states subject to such hegemonies. Coalition governments were, after all, to be the norm in both eastern and western Europe in the immediate post-war years. Arguably, it was such a view that Churchill, and perhaps even Stalin, took of spheres of influence when they made the Percentage Agreement (see Units 21–5).

This puts the question as to Stalin's plans firmly in centre place. Was he pragmatic as to the nature of the states within the Soviet sphere, provided only that their governments were compliant to the needs of Soviet foreign policy, or was he determined that within a few years all such states would be effectively under the control of communist parties themselves subject to Moscow? We will return later to the question of Stalin's and the Soviet Union's long-term aims, but for the moment let us accept the view that, for whatever reasons, both the western Allies and the Soviet Union were, in 1944 and 1945, prepared to see Allied cooperation extend into the post-war world and were also prepared to allow a degree of political pluralism within their (as yet) not totally separate spheres. There were to be two major obstacles to such a scenario, the first already plain, the second to be revealed. The first was Poland and the second was Germany.

It was apposite that the first serious differences between the USSR and its allies came over the fate of the country France and Britain had in 1939 overtly gone to war for and Stalin had, by helping Hitler dismember it, gone to war with. As Adam Zamoyski has written, 'The Poles were the nation who really lost the Second World War' (*The Polish Way*, 1987, p.371). Stalin is supposed to have said that to make Poland communist would be 'like putting a saddle upon a cow'. He then went on to prove that cows can be forced to wear saddles but that they have to be severely beaten first.

Britain may have gone to war in defence of Poland, but Chamberlain had been careful not to guarantee Poland's frontiers. There was thus always an escape clause. In 1941 and 1942 the Russians pressed the west to accept that the eastern frontiers of Poland would have to be redrawn in the USSR's favour, and Churchill and Eden began to put pressure on the Poles to accept a loss of territory in the east in exchange for gains at Germany's expense. No doubt if the Poles had accepted this, relations between the Polish government in London and the Soviet Union might have temporarily eased, but the Russians were determined on nothing less than a Poland completely subordinate to Moscow. Britain, with very few cards to play, faced the choice between an ethical policy which was unlikely to enjoy much success and a pragmatic acceptance that in Poland and most of eastern Europe the USSR would get its way.

For a brief period in 1939 Neville Chamberlain had succumbed to the illusion that east-central Europe was a sphere in which Britain could effectively intervene. In so doing and in handing out guarantees to Poland and Romania, he had abandoned his policy of appeasement and had paved the way for the Nazi–Soviet Pact. By 1945 the long-term consequences of that illusion were evident: east-central Europe was a Soviet sphere of influence and Poland was to be abandoned to one of the two powers that had partitioned the country in 1939.

Was British and American policy towards Poland perfidious or merely brutally realistic? Britain had in reality gone to war not so much for Poland but to prevent further German expansion based on force or the threat of force, while the US had joined the war in Europe because Germany had declared war on it. Neither was prepared to contemplate war with the Soviet Union, and to help the Poles get the best terms available and persuade them to accept them seemed the only practical path. If this policy was realistic it was, however, carried out with hypocrisy. From 1941 both Britain and the US knew of the massacres of Polish officers at Katyn in 1940, but went along with the fiction that the Germans rather than the Russians had been responsible. There was little public criticism by the western Allies of the way that the Polish Home Army was encouraged by Radio Moscow to rise as the Soviet forces approached Warsaw in August 1944, after which, having set the trap, the Russians denounced those who rose as a gang of criminals and the Red Army halted, allowing the Germans to reinforce and brutally put down the rising, killing some 240,000 Poles. It was not until the following January that the Red Army entered what remained of Warsaw. To the western Allies the Poles were inconvenient, stubborn and in the wrong place.

The future of Germany did not, at first, seem such a contentious question. All the Allies were agreed that Hitler's expansion of Germany would be reversed, and there was a tacit consensus that the old east Prussia would no longer be German. As during the First World War, the possibility of totally dismembering Germany was also considered by all the Allies, but by 1945 all the 'big three', though not the French, were agreed that the unity of Germany should be preserved. If Poland was a problem from the very beginning of the alliance, Germany, in the long run a more important factor in the Cold War, only became a cause of contention after its defeat.

When the leaders of the three principal Allied powers met at Yalta in the Crimea in February 1945, the war in Europe was as good as won and the broad outline of a Europe divided into two spheres of influence already visible. The sharpness of the final post-war divide was, however, not yet apparent nor, perhaps, inevitable. Yalta maintained a façade of harmony, largely because it combined real concessions by Britain and the US *on behalf of* Poland and an agreement on Germany, which provided for four Allied zones of occupation (what Stalin termed the *arithmetic* of the agreement), with more lofty innovations and sentiments: the inauguration of the United Nations, foreshadowed at the 1944 Dumbarton Oaks Conference, and the Declaration on Liberated Europe, which bore witness to a verbal adherence to democracy and self-determination (to Stalin the *algebra* of the agreement). The real problem with Yalta was that the algebra, the high-flown sentiments of the Declaration on Liberated Europe, obfuscated while they contradicted the 'realism' of the arithmetic, the provisions for Poland.

Exercise   Read the Declaration on Liberated Europe, article 5 of the Crimea Declaration (Document II.7 in *Primary Sources 2: Interwar and World War II*).

1   Can you find any contradictions or loopholes in this article which might enable the power actually in control of a liberated country to evade its apparent intentions?

2   What were its essential weaknesses? ∎

Specimen answers   1   I suppose a purist might wonder whether destroying the last vestiges of Nazism and fascism and the holding of totally free elections might not have been incompatible. What if electors wanted to vote fascist? In the circumstances of 1945 few would have thought it permissible to allow fascist parties the right to exist. Yet parties that were not fascist could be so defined in order to justify their banning: thus the National Democracy, Poland's largest pre-war party, was banned under a very broadly defined anti-fascist policy, as were the largest pre-war Czechoslovakian parties, the Agrarian Party (Czech) and the People's Party (Slovak). The formation of interim governments 'broadly representative of all democratic elements' left plenty of room for subjective or self-interested interpretations: what was 'democratic' and who were 'broadly representative'?

2   The essential weakness was that this was simply one of those 'solemn and binding declarations' that bind no one because they cannot be enforced and on whose meaning everyone disagrees. The 'Allies' were not in control of the liberated countries: America and Britain were in control of some, and the Soviet Union was in control of others. ☐

At Yalta the two western powers not only agreed to changes in Poland's frontiers that ran directly counter to the Atlantic Charter (the Anglo-American declaration of August 1941 – see Document II.5 in *Primary Sources 2*) and, in Britain's case, to a Foreign Office note of July 1941 on the non-recognition of any territorial changes in Poland since August 1939; by accepting Stalin's proposal that the communist-controlled Lublin Committee should become the basis of Poland's future government, they also repudiated the government-in-exile for which Britain had ostensibly gone to war. Yalta was indeed Churchill's Munich. Yet Norman Davies is almost certainly correct in saying that 'At Yalta and Potsdam, there was no way that Churchill or Roosevelt, *by diplomatic means*, could have deflected Stalin from his chosen solution' (*God's Playground*, vol.2, 1981, p.15; emphasis added). British and American public opinion, nurtured on a wartime propaganda diet of amity with the Soviet Union, would have taken much persuading that any other than 'diplomatic means' should be employed. Yet that same public opinion would have been aghast at a frank exposition of the reality that Poland and east-central Europe were to be placed under Soviet hegemony whatever their own wishes. So, as Davies goes on to argue, 'matters were not decided at the conference table, but by the situation on the ground and by the men who held the reins of practical power' (p.15).

Yalta, which attempted a temporary resolution of Allied differences, can thus be seen as the position from which the 'Cold War' and the division of Europe developed. By the time the victorious Allies met at Potsdam in July 1945, not only was Roosevelt dead and replaced by Truman, but American distrust of the Soviet Union had grown. By May the Soviet Union had tightened its control over its east-central European sphere of influence by marginalizing all anti-Soviet forces. How important the change was from Roosevelt to Truman is debatable. The contradictions in Roosevelt's policy were becoming evident, with a gap opening between his Wilsonian faith in a liberal post-war world with self-determination for all and the reality of Soviet determination to dominate east-central Europe. British leadership changed, too, with the defeat of Churchill and the Conservatives at the 1945 election, but the new Labour government proved staunchly anti-communist, with incoming Foreign Secretary Ernest Bevin declaring that it was important to prevent the substitution of one form of totalitarianism by another. That the Americans had successfully tested their atomic bomb may have encouraged Truman to take a firm line with the Soviets, and preliminary discussions were cantankerous: Truman turned down a Russian list of demands which included putting the Black Sea Straits under Soviet control and being given the trusteeship of the Italian colony of Libya. That Potsdam did not end with hard words and confrontation was largely due to the fact that it decided nothing of importance. There were compromises over German reparations to the USSR and over Polish acquisition of ex-German territory, but the contentious issue of the composition of east-central European governments was left to future meetings of a Council of Foreign Ministers. In the end at these meetings the western powers could do little but accede to what had been implicitly determined at Yalta. The Soviets would decide.

To put Yalta into context we need to return to and continue our discussion from section 1 of Units 21–5 of the war aims of the Allied powers, their hopes and fears for the post-war world, and the interaction between military and diplomatic strategy.

Exercise   What do you consider were the main aims of each of the principal Allied powers? How did they align their diplomatic and military strategies to further their ambitions for the post-war world? ■

Specimen answers   In the case of the Soviet Union, the main aim from 1941 to at least 1943 was survival. Thereafter, there was no incompatibility between the military aim of advancing through east-central Europe and on to Berlin and the expectation that this would enable them to dominate the states they occupied in the post-war world. This would provide at the least security and (this depends on how we assess Stalin's intentions) the potential for further advances for the Soviet Union or world communism. Of course, Stalin kept the diplomatic options open, was suspicious of the western Allies, and didn't rule out a new understanding or compromise with Hitler until late in the day. His calls for a second front – by which he meant an invasion of France – were designed to take pressure off Russia and to ensure that the western Allies didn't advance instead into east-central Europe from Italy. An example of his aligning military tactics to diplomatic ends is his halting of the Soviet Army before Warsaw while the Germans put down the Warsaw Rising. On the whole, the Soviets closely integrated military and diplomatic strategy, being well aware that at the end of the war whose army occupied which territory would be of crucial importance.

Of all the powers, the USA was the least interested in aligning its military tactics to post-war ambitions. It concentrated on winning the war, though it was concerned to limit US casualties, and trusted that a general post-war settlement would provide for a United Nations, national self-determination and a free trading world.

Britain was concerned about its position in the post-war world. It had special interests in the Mediterranean, was concerned at the prospect of Soviet hegemony in the areas that the Soviet Army conquered, and was worried about the balance of power in Europe. To this end Churchill had supported plans for an advance from Italy into central Europe and urged that the British and American armies should attempt to reach Berlin before the Russians. The 'Percentage Agreement' was Churchill's attempt at damage limitation.

Discussion   Debate over the Soviet Union's aims tends to be dominated by the question of whether Soviet policy was based on an overarching desire to further world communism or a traditional Russian perception of national self-interest. The interests of both could be served by a domination of east-central Europe, with the bounds of that dominion set as far west as circumstances and opportunity made available. As the war drew to a close, the success of the Soviet forces made circumstances more favourable and opportunities greater. Whatever long-term and far-reaching plans Stalin had for the spread of communism outside east-central Europe, there can be no doubt that that zone was his first priority. He was prepared to be pragmatic over spheres of influence, as the 'Percentage Agreement' with Churchill shows.

America had no territorial ambitions in Europe, disapproved of plans for the allocation of territory after the war, and disliked the idea of spheres of influence. The military strategy of the USA was just that – a military strategy unaffected by diplomatic considerations or worries about where its armies might be positioned when Germany surrendered.

Britain was attempting to play realistic politics with a weak hand. Its aims were to safeguard the empire, preserve a sphere of influence in the Mediterranean and achieve as favourable a balance of power in Europe as possible, but Britain was already aware that its economic and military strength were limited. ☐

All the above is basically true, but is it the whole truth? Did America's lack of concern for spheres of influence, and its apparent refusal to adopt Clausewitz's dictum of war as the continuance of diplomacy by other means, in fact disguise ambitions so far-reaching that they made the territorial boundaries and the political complexities of European states seem unimportant? Was the US seeking to use its military and economic might not to make short-term gains in east-central Europe but to impose a '*pax Americana*' upon the world? The thesis can be put in either the Machiavellian or missionary modes. The Machiavellian version, put forward not surprisingly by Soviet historians and by a revisionist school of Americans, sees a United States reaching towards the peak of its economic and military strength and determined to extend its power throughout the world. As the end of the war would inevitably bring with it a crisis of overproduction, the US sought to turn the whole world into a free market that it could dominate and in which it could find new markets and investment opportunities. The missionary version sees a conjunction between traditional American values – liberty, democracy, constitutionalism – on the one hand and America's new-found military and economic power on the other. Thus, as Michael Dockrill has argued, 'Before 1941 the United States did not have the power to project her ideology beyond the shores of the continent (except in Latin America which the United States had long claimed as her special sphere of interest)' (*The Cold War*, 1988, p.4). By 1945 the US felt it had that power.

It could well be argued that, even had American politicians possessed no strong views on the shape of the post-war world and its political or economic structure, its enormously favourable economic and strategic position would have ineluctably led it to become the actively dominant world power. Paul Kennedy, in his study of *The Rise and Fall of the Great Powers*, has seen the US as to some extent in thrall to its power and the position in which the world-wide success in war had placed it: 'Like the British after 1815, the Americans in their turn found their informal influence in various lands hardening into something more formal – and more entangling; like the British too, they found "new frontiers of insecurity" wherever they wanted to draw the line' (1988, p.359).

At the time of the Yalta Agreement, the US was unaware of the consequences of its new-found power and the degree to which the implementation of its vaguely formulated plans for a world economic and political order would involve it in a continuous and active political and military involvement overseas. Nor did the Americans realize that they would have to adopt many of the traditional stratagems of the other great powers they saw as morally inferior. US foreign policy sought a post-war world much like that envisaged by Woodrow Wilson in 1918: a community of self-governing nations existing on the basis of self-determination within an international constitutional framework. At the same time, its political liberation was to be accompanied by an economic liberation, at once self-serving and idealistic, in which free convertibility of currencies and open competition would open up overseas markets to American goods and capital. Yet the illusion persisted that these goals might be achieved without great opposition, armies overseas, alliance commitments or the embracing of the 'corrupt' methods and the 'old' diplomacy used by the great powers of the past.

Thus, in pursuit of great goals the US felt it could remain aloof from the undignified jostling for position in the post-war world that marked Soviet and British policy. Where armies met, questions of frontiers and the political complexion of regimes in east-central Europe were of minor importance because the post-war world would exist within an international, democratic and liberal economic structure. Such an inclination was reinforced by the determination both to bring about Woodrow Wilson's aims and to avoid his fate of losing political support at home: the aims must be achieved without embarrassing commitments.

The result of this policy was that the United States denied itself or failed to use the weapons and strategies that might have furthered its aims and improved its post-war position. A fundamental misreading of the nature of Stalin and the Soviet Union led Roosevelt to believe that the Soviet Union would see the benefits of an essentially liberal capitalist post-war system and would not stand clear of it. American policy therefore failed to subordinate military to diplomatic considerations. It also failed to use economic loans to gain influence with the USSR, and US–Soviet discussions on new loans to replace lend-lease came to nothing. Nor were US policy-makers prepared to countenance the notion of spheres of influence.

The uncertainty and ambivalence of the Yalta Agreement, uplifting in its Declaration on Liberated Europe, cynical in its treatment of Poland, and vague as to the future of Germany thus reflected the uncertainty and ambivalence of US foreign policy. With the Truman Doctrine and the Marshall Plan, 1947 saw the US utilize some of the weaponry it could have employed at Yalta but in a far less favourable context.

One can downgrade the importance of the Yalta Agreement on two counts. First, what really mattered was the absence of either clear or united strategic thinking on the part of the western Allies during 1941 and 1943 when things were still in a state of flux (Tehran had first revealed the likelihood of the Soviet Union becoming the dominant power in east-central Europe – see Units 21–5). Second, the significant point was what Yalta did not do: namely, come to detailed agreements for tripartite control of all occupied territories. Yet much can be traced to Yalta. The decisions on Poland convinced Stalin that he had a free hand in east-central Europe, and he was not slow to act on this. Immediately afterwards he sent Vishinsky to Romania with an ultimatum to King Michael to instal a communist-controlled government, and when a Polish delegation representing the Home Army resistance went to Moscow it was arrested on arrival and, after months of interrogation, given long terms of imprisonment. The lack of a detailed agreement for Allied government of Germany did much to ensure that all zones were treated differently and that distinctions between western and Soviet zones of occupation foreshadowed the division of Germany. The period 1945–7 saw a progressive hardening of the divide between east and west as the Soviet Union tightened its grip on east-central Europe, the delineations of the future west and east Germany appeared, western and southern Europe were securely bound to the liberal capitalist world, and the propaganda war between the Soviet Union and its erstwhile allies increased in volume and bitterness.

2   EXPLANATIONS

Inevitably, historians have disagreed about interpretations of this period and the reasons for the Cold War. What may be termed the classic or orthodox theory and its antithesis, usually known as revisionism, are as follows:

1   The Soviet Union with its Marxist ideology, which insisted on world-wide revolution and the victory of international communism, was entirely to blame for the division of Europe and the Cold War. See, for instance, Herbert Feis, *Churchill, Roosevelt and Stalin: The War They Waged and the Peace They Sought* (1957).

2   The fundamental hostility of capitalism, and particularly American capitalism, to socialism and the Soviet Union was to blame. The Soviet Union's policies were primarily defensive. The USA was determined to impose a *pax Americana* involving economic and political domination on the world. An example is J. Kolko and G. Kolko, *The Limits of Power: The World and United States Foreign Policy 1945–54* (1972).

If the second of these explanations has found few recent defenders of its full-blown version, there have been, both before and since the demise of the Soviet Union and the end of the Cold War, a host of alternative theses, often termed 'post-revisionist'. They tend to be characterized by a perception that both the original thesis and its antithesis were too crude, that they were born in the heat of the Cold War, that both overemphasize ideology, that it is necessary to look at the causes and events with a more objective eye, and that the Cold War needs to be seen in a longer historical context.

One such approach is to bring what may be called the 'cock-up' theory of history as a counterweight to the ideological or conspiratorial theories. It can be persuasively argued that both the western Allies and the Soviet Union misunderstood each other, read each other's signals wrongly, and responded inappositely to the actions of the other side. The Cold War was thus a product of miscalculation.

Another, related approach is to argue that the role of ideology has been much exaggerated and that it played a minor part, save as justification for policies that were intended to further the interests of the great powers and especially of the US and USSR.

We have already outlined a further view, which is to emphasize the importance of not starting from 1941, 1943 or 1945 but considering the Cold War in a longer framework of international relations. If at its beginning Bolshevik Russia was to the west a revolutionary regime to be destroyed, it had become by the 1920s a power to be contained. For its part the Soviet Union saw itself as alternatively the exporter of world revolution and as a quarry that the capitalist world strove to kill. If Viktor Suvarov is right, Stalin welcomed the coming of Hitler because he saw him as the 'ice-breaker' who would facilitate Soviet expansion (*The Icebreaker*, 1990). The Nazi–Soviet Pact can be interpreted from the Soviet Union's point of view as either impeccably in line with Marxist-Leninism (as it enabled the Soviet Union to stand aside while 'capitalist' powers destroyed each other) or an agreement between two outsider powers to carve up Europe. Hitler's invasion of Russia nearly resulted in his being Stalin's nemesis rather than ice-breaker, but by 1945 Hitler was defeated and the ice was well broken. For the US and Britain, the USSR was a necessary, if not the most desirable, ally in the war against Germany. However, as victory neared, it was obvious that the price to be paid was the threat from an equally unpleasant, unpredictable and very powerful state. As Martin McCauley has written:

> Containment, the term usually used to describe US policy towards the USSR after 1945, may be regarded as a series of attempts to deal with the bargain struck during the Second World War. The object of this policy was to restrain the Soviets from re-shaping the international order in a way that would have been as dangerous to western interests as that which would have been implemented by Germany and Japan had they won the war,
>
> *(Origins of the Cold War,* 1995, p.15)

Recent research suggests that in the Cold War's epicentre, east-central Europe, the Soviets did have every intention of interfering directly in the internal affairs of the countries within their orbit and were determined to have compliant regimes (see section 6). It also suggests, however, that until the summer of 1947 there was no insistence that such regimes needed to be single-party dictatorships and that the Soviets were content with manipulated popular front governments where key posts were held by communists. An exception to this was the eastern zone of Germany, where what was in effect a single-party system was created in April 1946. The most common approach was to ensure communist control of the interior and defence ministries and the establishment of a political police dominated by the party. In former enemy states like Hungary, the Soviet occupiers would interfere through the Allied Control Commissions.

We have to ask, therefore, why it was that by 1947 such forms of control were considered insufficient and the Soviets felt it necessary to move to what were in effect single-party dictatorships. Explanations include:

(a) a reaction to the policies of the US, particularly the Marshall Plan, and the worsening international situation;

(b) a realization that even a semblance of democracy was dangerous in that it could expose the extent of anti-communist and anti-Soviet feeling and make countries difficult to manage;

(c) a reaction to the greater stability of western European states and to the increasingly evident division of Germany.

Stalin was rather more aware of the Soviet Union's weaknesses than were the western powers. The Marshall Plan offering aid on western capitalist terms to countries within the Soviet sphere of influence was something he could not afford those countries to accept. In 1945, despite knowledge of Soviet weaknesses, Stalin had seen great opportunities: a social revolution was occurring in east-central Europe as land seizures took place as the Axis forces withdrew and workers attempted to take over factories; at the same time, communist partisans in western Europe seemed to exert considerable influence, and he could hope that communist parties would wield great influence in France and Italy. This was a time to appear moderate and flexible and to play for bigger stakes than a communist east-central Europe. By 1947–8 there was evidence that in much of eastern Europe even partial democracy had its risks, while communist parties were no longer making headway in the west. It was apparent that popular conservatism in eastern Europe in the shape of smallholders' and peasants' parties posed a formidable obstacle to Soviet hegemony and that in the west the dominant political force was likely to be neither communism nor even social democracy but Christian democracy. Ever the realist, Stalin had few illusions about communism's dwindling appeal or the ability of the Soviet economy to compete with that of the US. The decisions to tighten control and impose uniformity within the Soviet sphere and to cut off east from west sprang not from confidence but from fear.

There is, however, a strong case for looking in some detail at some individual countries, as we do in section 6. Post-war international relations may have been fundamental in determining the division of Europe, but though they explain why division occurred, they do not explain how. An explanation of how helps us to understand why states, within the limits set by great powers' policies and interests, established the political settlements they did after 1948. It allows us to see how the Titoist state developed as it did in Yugoslavia. Such a perspective can also help us appreciate how a state like Italy staved off the threat of its strong Communist Party and remained within the western camp.

Such a concentration on individual case studies informs rather than contradicts the broader debates which stress the foreign policy interests of the great powers, the disposition of military forces and the clash of ideologies, and draws attention to the interaction of such dimensions with political and economic developments in individual countries and changes in the climate of popular opinion. It is this interaction which sections 4 and 5 will address. Before this we will discuss the role of ideology, which, after all, is what the Cold War is supposed to have been about.

3   THE ROLE OF IDEOLOGY

Do the causes of the division of Europe and the Cold War lie primarily and inescapably in ideology, in the clash between liberal capitalism and Marxist socialism? Or are they more accurately to be located in a conflict between great powers with opposed geopolitical ambitions who happened also to have conflicting political ideologies? It is often difficult to see whether ideology was the servant or master of the policies of states.

This is particularly so in respect of the Soviet Union, in whose foreign policy aims so many historians have detected a continuity with Tsarist policy: the desire to regain for the state territory lost at the end of World War I; the drive for hegemony in east-central Europe with its overtones of pan-Slavism; the push into Manchuria in 1945 recalling the eastward expansion of the Russian Empire; the attempt to detach the province of Azerbaijan from Iran, which similarly seemed a continuance of the long Russian advance down the shores of the Caspian Sea; and Stalin's demands at Potsdam for a base on the Dardanelles (control of the Straits had been a major aim of nineteenth-century Russian foreign policy). A Red Tsar seemed to want much the same things as his White predecessors. Yet if Soviet policy-makers were convinced that a future world communism depended on the Soviet Union and that the revolutionary struggle for socialism was synonymous with the security and advance of Soviet power, the ideology and the traditional great power aims of Russia could go hand in hand.

If it would be wrong, even ridiculous, to see the kaleidoscopic changes in Soviet policies and rhetoric between 1939 and 1948 as led by Marxist-Leninist ideology, it would be a mistake to see the explanations that justified policy changes as so much window dressing. It was always possible, by diligent searching in the books of the socialist sages, to find a theoretical justification for any policy, but it *was* significant that such a justification had to be found.

Exercise Consider the following three descriptions of World War II by Stalin:

(a) 'A struggle of predatory imperialist nations over the control of world markets' (20 June 1941).

(b) 'A great patriotic war of freedom-loving nations against fascism' (3 July 1941).

(c) 'An inevitable result of the development of world economic and political forces on the basis of modern monopoly capitalism' (9 February 1946).

(Quoted in Thomas, *Armed Truce*, 1986, pp.38, 92)

Now answer the following questions:

1   What do you think might explain the difference between (a) and (b)?

2   What distinguishes descriptions (a) and (c) from (b)? ■

Specimen answers 1   On 22 June 1941 Germany attacked Russia.
and discussion
2   Essentially (a) and (c) identify the war in terms of laying stress on its supposed economic origins. They both to some extent impart blame on two sides, the first directly and the second implicitly, for if monopoly capitalism was responsible, then the US and Britain as leading capitalist states were presumably impugned. We can clearly distinguish (a) and (c) from (b), which talks of freedom-loving nations, presumably Britain and the Soviet Union, engaged in a war against fascism.

The war can thus be seen from the Soviet Union's point of view as involving an opportune and temporary alliance with what was perhaps regarded in the long term as the major enemy, the western capitalist powers, against Germany and fascism. Once that conflict was over, fundamental antagonisms based on a Marxist reading of historical development reasserted themselves. □

We may well ask how important fascism was in all this. Was it a full-blown ideology in its own right? Was there a triangle of the three 'isms', so that when two corners had drawn together to destroy the third, the conflict between the remaining two was resumed? Was fascism instead a late freak of world capitalism? With its corporatism and elevation of the state over civil society, fascism can, of course, alternatively be seen from a liberal capitalist viewpoint as a socialist heresy which replaces the struggle of classes with the struggle of nations. There can be little doubt, however, that by the time of Stalin's speech of February 1946 the Soviet analysis of fascism had swung back to the dicta that had prevailed before Hitler's invasion of Russia. Hugh Thomas has described Stalin's remarks as signifying 'the view that capitalism and Nazism were at the same "last stage of capitalism" as Communists had conceived them to be in the early 1930s' (*Armed Truce*, 1986, p.38).

Stalin's and the Soviet Union's change in attitude and policy was sudden and harsh. During the war Marxist-Leninism had given way to Russian nationalism as a means of encouraging or cajoling the Soviet population. The *Internationale* was replaced as the national anthem by a hymn glorifying Russia. Old Tsarist heroes once more became national icons. Eisenstein's film *Alexander Nevsky* had been made as a warning to the Germans at the end of the 1930s; it celebrated the achievements of its eponymous hero, the Prince of Muscovy, who had defeated the Teutonic Knights in 1242. Stalin kept portraits of Nevsky and the great generals of the French Revolutionary and Napoleonic Wars, Suvorov and Kutuzov, on the walls of his study. Little was heard of the Party, of communism or of the class struggle, but a great deal was heard of Russia, the motherland and patriotism. Even the leaders of the Orthodox Church were wheeled out to help fan Russian resistance. Britain and then the US were for the duration not capitalist or imperialist predators but 'freedom-loving nations' and allies in a common struggle. The reversal of these policies began to be discernible early in 1945, and Stalin's speech of February 1946 marked their final burial.

For the reasons behind the shifts in policy we have to look at the Soviet internal situation as well as the burgeoning dissension with the western Allies. The Soviet Union adopted the stance of the patriotic war in the circumstances of a German invasion which not only was at first worryingly successful in military terms but shook the Soviet system of government. Vast areas of the state (about 4 million square miles and about 65 million people) were for some years under German occupation. Had the Germans, who in some areas were greeted with relief, been prepared to win over the subject population and play on the separatist desires of many of the non-Russian regions, then they might have found valuable allies. Even in purely Russian regions there was no great enthusiasm for a war for communism: hence the appeal to Russian patriotism. Nor should we imagine that in the circumstances of a relaxation of doctrine there was any parallel relaxation of the state's grip on the populace, for the police state tightened its grip, especially as it encountered difficulty in restoring order in former occupied territories (Ukrainian nationalists, for instance, were to mount a partisan struggle until 1947). Once the war was clearly won, there was not only the problem of reinstating the state's control over all its territory but the necessity of reinstating the Party's control over the state. During the war the Party had kept a low profile and the power of generals and industrial managers had grown apace. With victory it became once more ubiquitous. The role of the generals was quickly downgraded and the great heroes of the victory parade of 24 June 1945, Zhukov and Rokossovsky, were soon sent to quite junior commands. 'Our victory means', said Stalin in his speech of February 1946, 'that our Soviet system has won': not, Hugh Thomas comments, Russia, nor the Allies (*Armed Truce*, p.38).

The return to a more overtly Marxist foreign policy was reflected in economic policy. If the peoples of the Soviet Union had hopes that after the war was over they might have a higher standard of living, they were quickly disabused. They were told not to expect more consumer goods after the sacrifices of the war, for, said Stalin, under communism heavy industry must continue to have priority.

Foreign and economic policy reinforced each other. An aggressive foreign policy required an economic policy geared to armaments, while a low standard of living required a repressive state and repressive states need enemies.

The harder line towards the western Allies and the increased emphasis on their capitalist and anti-Soviet natures thus coincided with, and was to some extent part of, the same process by which Stalin and the Communist Party sought to overcome internal problems and redirect Soviet society along Marxist-Leninist lines. The Soviet Union desired security for its borders, which meant control of all adjacent, strategically sensitive areas. That desire by itself was increasingly creating tensions with the west, but the Soviet Union also desired security for its system, a system that would be imperilled by too close co-operation with its erstwhile allies and could wither in any world system dominated by American economic might. If Soviet policy was straightforward in regard to exercising a strict hegemony over areas under the occupation of the Red Army, which controlled North Korea as well as east-central Europe, it was more pragmatic elsewhere, in the Mediterranean and in western Europe. In the former, as we shall see, it was for a while prepared for a British sphere of influence, while in western Europe if communist parties were seen as arms of Soviet influence under tight control from Moscow, Moscow's orders until the founding of the Cominform (Communist Information Bureau) in 1947 were that they should co-operate with 'bourgeois' forces and assist with national recoveries rather than act as a force for overthrowing capitalism. Here Stalin was concerned to support almost any elements in western Europe, even indigenous capitalists, who appeared independent of US influence.

It can indeed be argued that Stalin would have been happy to accept in 1945 more or less what he wanted from Germany in 1940. In 1940 he had the fruits of the Nazi–Soviet Pact of 1939: the return of the Baltic States, eastern Poland and the Romanian provinces of Bessarabia and northern Bukovina, and Molotov was instructed to demand in November 1940 a maximum share of influence in east-central Europe as a whole. There is a case for seeing considerable continuity in Soviet ambitions.

Stalin's essential pragmatism can be demonstrated by the very different degrees of control he was prepared to exercise over the nations of eastern Europe: incorporation into the USSR (the Baltic Republics); a veto over foreign policy (Finland); and what was essentially a compromise with nationalism and a recognition of what the west would wear (the thinly disguised control of Poland and Hungary).

If it's difficult to decide where ideology ended and pragmatism or traditional Russian aims began with the Soviets, the policy of the west presents a more complex problem. Marxism does seem to fulfil all the requirements of an ideology: a system of ideas or beliefs, attitudes or ideas which form a set. Confusingly, Marx himself used ideology to refer to almost every system of ideas but his own, considering ideologies to be beliefs which were distorted or false, but we shall use the word in the former sense. We may ask whether, as there were two sides in the Cold War, there were two ideologies involved. Robert Conquest for one would deny that the west had an ideology: 'The Western culture had, in a general way, a view of politics which included political liberty and the rule of law. It did not have a universal or exclusively defined mind-set' (*Reflections on a Ravaged Century*, 1999, p.155). Certainly it can be argued that the anti-communist side in the Cold War can best be defined as just that – *anti-communist* – and that it was a broad church encompassing conservatives, liberals, social democrats (some of whom considered themselves Marxists), and even a few dictators. Pluralism may best describe the west's attitudes, but does pluralism constitute ideology? Nevertheless, it was the US which led the west, and a number of beliefs, ideas and attitudes are characteristic of American political life and have usually been claimed to imbue its foreign policy: liberal capitalism for shorthand or associated ideas such as a rule of law which is more than the will of the government of the time, representative democracy, property rights and a maximum degree of individual freedom. Most of the states which eventually made up the NATO alliance did, with different emphases, largely share this outlook. This bundle of attitudes may not fit a strict definition of ideology, and perhaps we should refer instead to a set of principles, not always adhered to. The tradition of Woodrow Wilson, influential for so long in US foreign policy, comes somewhat closer to an ideology.

The role of ideology or of political principles in US policy was in many ways more ubiquitous than it was in Soviet policy. As we have seen, some historians (for instance, Joyce and Gabriel Kolko, *The Limits of Power*, 1972) have seen US policy as inspired by the aim of world-wide economic domination, but if this is so, it seems odd that the Cold War originated primarily in east-central Europe, an area of limited economic interest to the United States. On the whole, the missionary rather than the Machiavellian view of US policy seems to make more sense. There was an altruistic urge to reform the old world in the image of the new; the resemblance between Roosevelt and Woodrow Wilson is striking, while President Truman was a convinced Wilsonian who at first followed the main outlines of Roosevelt's policies. If the Atlantic Charter, the United Nations Organization, and the plans for a new economic order agreed at Bretton Woods (the economic conference of 1944 which among other things provided for the International Monetary Fund and the World Bank) added up to a blueprint for a liberal world, the American isolationist impulse that destroyed Wilson was still strong. Roosevelt's announcement that American troops would be withdrawn from Europe within two years of the end of the war compounded the mistakes of Yalta. A Wilsonian stance was not only attractive to Roosevelt and Truman in its own right, but was probably essential for US domestic consumption. US politicians could not gain domestic support for a war with realistic aims but only for a war for 'one world' with liberal democratic principles. Yet the only realistic policy, given the nature of America's Soviet ally, lay in the acceptance of a Soviet sphere of influence in which liberal principles would not hold. Yalta and Potsdam saw the gap grow wider between the foreign policy for domestic consumption and the necessary compromises with the USSR if the alliance was to continue. As the gap became more obvious, it became imperative that the US should either seek to make the rhetoric fit the practical policies or change the practical policies in line with the rhetoric. Faced with the difficulty of changing an imperfect world after World War I, the US had moved towards isolation, but in 1945 America was far more conscious of its military and economic might. Political beliefs were in the final analysis a central factor in the slide towards the Cold War, but they were a factor more determinant of US policy, responsible to an idealistic electorate, than of Soviet policy. American policy was to a considerable extent led by liberal democratic principles but was leavened by expedience and empiricism. Soviet policy tended to be *justified* by Marxism.

It is noteworthy that the policy adopted by the United States towards the perceived Soviet threat was one of *containment*, a term which suggests a fundamentally defensive posture. The genesis of this policy is attributed to George F. Kennan. Previously Counsellor in the US Embassy in Moscow, Kennan was chosen by the European Division of the State Department to write a comprehensive appraisal of Soviet policy. His famous 'Long Telegram' of 22 February 1946 provided the diagnosis of the nature of the Soviet regime and its intentions which were to guide US foreign policy.

Exercise   Read the extract from the 'Long Telegram', Document II.42 in *Primary Sources 2: Interwar and World War II*, and answer the following question: what does Kennan see as the fundamental factors behind Soviet policy? ■

Specimen answer   He sees the two major factors as being a traditional Russian sense of insecurity and Marxism. The two are seen as connected as he argues that Marxism took hold in Russia because of Russian historical experience and insecurity while it gave ideological justification to fear of the west, the need for intensive armament and for dictatorship. The Soviet outlook is determined by a synthesis of paranoid nationalism and Marxism or by nationalism clothed in Marxism. □

The Long Telegram has been seen as having a decisive influence on the Truman administration, leading to a policy of greater firmness in dealings with the Soviet Union. Essentially Kennan was explaining Soviet behaviour, but the acceptance of his analysis led to a new policy: containment. The aim was not to roll back Soviet power but to demonstrate to the Soviets that the US would be pushed no further. This might persuade Stalin to negotiate and compromise.

4   BRITAIN AND FRANCE: 'GREAT POWER' STATUS AND US AID

World War II had left two genuinely 'great powers', the US and the USSR, on the flanks of Europe. Yet there were two other powers, Britain and France, both on the winning side in the war, both with a tradition of being 'great powers', and both keen to maintain this position.

Exercise   Using common sense and your recollection of material from earlier in the course, answer the following questions:

1   How do you suppose British and French politicians could justify their country's claims to 'great power' status? What, if any, was the difference between their respective claims, given the situation in 1945?

2   Given the experience of the previous six years, what problems do you suppose impeded these great power aspirations?

3   What factors made it most unlikely that they could seriously challenge the dominance of the US and the USSR? ■

Specimen answers   1   The British had the better claim to continuing great power status; they had, after all, been the most consistent enemy of Hitler since 1939, whereas France had been occupied and, even if de Gaulle and the 'Free French' had continued fighting, the government of the Third Republic had surrendered in June 1940 and the new Vichy regime had been created. The claim to being a great power rested partly on tradition – Britain and France were the only European powers to have survived two world wars more or less intact and with regimes not greatly different from those of 1914. It rested also on the fact that they were on the winning side in 1945, and that they had empires spread across the globe; the British Empire was still the largest in the world, and the French Empire was the second largest.

2   Both countries had been severely weakened economically by the war. France had the greater problems as it had been plundered during the German occupation and had been a battlefield for several months following the Allied landings in June 1944. Britain had not been fought over by land armies, but had suffered from aerial bombardment and, in spite of US aid and the lend-lease agreement, had been compelled to spend enormous sums on armaments and campaigns.

3   Britain and France had neither the manpower nor the economic resources to challenge the two enormous powers on the flanks of Europe. Of course, it was possible that the US would opt for isolation as it had done at the end of World War I, thus enabling Britain and France to fill something of a vacuum; but Russia in 1945 was in a very different situation from that in which it had found itself during the negotiations at Brest-Litovsk and Versailles. Russia had suffered enormous losses of men and material in the war against Nazi Germany, but there was no reason to suppose that it would now opt for isolation. □

I hope that you found it possible to make a stab at those questions, and to get somewhere near my specimen answers. If not, think about the answers in the light of the questions. I want to move on now to develop the answers with some more detailed information.

Since the beginning of the twentieth century, the task of British foreign policy-makers had been the management of decline. Neville Chamberlain had fully appreciated that a major war – and especially one involving Europe and the Far East – would lead to economic disaster, the dissolution of the empire and the end of great power status. Britain emerged on the winning side in 1945 but at great cost. America's entry into the war and the subsequent Anglo-American alliance made victory possible but at the cost of eventual subservience to the US. Churchill never fully appreciated the price Britain would have to pay for the alliance.

Attention to the quarrels and disputes between the western Allies and the Soviet Union can distract from the tensions between Britain and the US. The 'special relationship' existed mainly in the mind of Churchill. If Britain had some supporters in Washington, it had many enemies. Admirals King and Leahy were hostile, Irish-American politicians and diplomats tended to be almost automatically anti-British, while Roosevelt himself continuously sought the end of the British Empire and of the sterling area and imperial preference.

Britain was forced by its need for lend-lease to open up its traditional markets to American competition, and the US seized the chance offered by the war to replace Britain in Latin America and to compete with British oil interests in the Middle East (see John Charmley, *Churchill's Grand Alliance*, 1995).

A major difference between Britain and France and the US during the war concerned their approach to France and to General de Gaulle and the Free French. Anthony Eden, struggling to find opportunities for an independent British foreign policy, ascribed great importance to the rapid return of France to the circle of great powers. He saw de Gaulle as essential to this aim. The Americans had to the contrary appeared to support Admiral Darlan in 1942 and, after his death, General Giraud. The Americans were tardy in recognizing the Free French as the government of France in 1944, and it was British pressure which brought France its zone in conquered Germany.

One supporter of Eden in his insistence on the recognition of de Gaulle was Ernest Bevin, who was also concerned that British interests should not be subordinated to American policies. From 1945 it was to be Bevin who was Foreign Minister and who had to take over managed decline in even less favourable circumstances than Eden's or Chamberlain's. To refer to a man whose time at the Foreign Office was associated with a sharp decline in British power and influence as one of the great Foreign Secretaries may seem a contradiction, but by Bevin's time the mistakes had been made and all that could be done was to preserve the maximum power commensurate with rising pressures and reduced resources. As Paul Kennedy has written:

> Attlee's administration, with Bevin as its Foreign Secretary, faced a horrific concatenation of problems: Europe in ruins, Palestine in turmoil, India on the brink of civil war, seething discontents in Egypt and other parts of the Arab world, insurrection in Malaya, an alarming decline in relations with Russia, communist pressure from Berlin to Hong Kong, American indifference and then, as it seemed, excessive American belligerency, and all this at a time when the economic pressures upon Sterling were both ominous and persistent.
>
> (*Realities Behind Diplomacy*, 1985, p.362)

With Bevin's guidance and a fair amount of good luck, many of these problems were solved and others ameliorated. Bevin attempted to maintain as much British power and influence as possible but, as a realist, saw that this could only be done in the context of reduced commitments and an acceptance of American leadership.

As we have seen, it was of considerable importance to Britain that France was reborn as once more a great power. Otherwise Britain would have felt even more squeezed between the emerging superpowers of the US and USSR. Unsurprisingly, this was the main aim of Charles de Gaulle. 'To rebuild our power: that is what is henceforth the great cause of France,' he told the provisional Consultative Committee in Algiers in November 1944 (quoted in Robert Gildea, *France since 1945*, 1996). In the interests of such rebuilding, France was to oscillate between a perceived need for American protection and aid and overtures towards the alternative, an understanding with the Soviet Union. As in Britain there was hostility and resentment on both the left and right in politics towards the US, but this was much more pronounced in France, where there was also a general resentment of 'Anglo-Saxon' influence. French policy was also characterized by ambivalence towards Germany. Should France continue with its traditional stance of seeking to thwart a German recovery, or had defeat in 1940 been a defining moment, proving once and for all that France could not compete on economic and military power with Germany and must therefore seek to bind Germany to it by close economic ties? At first the former course was followed, but by 1950s it had become French policy to work as closely as possible with West Germany, gain from its increasing economic strength, and hope that the French jockey could keep its seat on the German horse.

Fading empires

The war had affected the colonies as much as the metropolis. In Asia many of the British colonies and all of the French colonies had been overrun by the Japanese, something which struck a devastating blow at the image of the white man's superiority. The war had brought a new infrastructure to those colonies and dependencies that had been battlegrounds or close to battlegrounds; modern war required roads, railways, airfields, port facilities, and so forth. It also brought economic development in areas encouraged to produce foodstuffs, raw materials, or even military equipment for wartime needs. When Malaya fell to the Japanese, for example, British west Africa became a centre for rubber production, and in India the British Raj began encouraging indigenous entrepreneurs in the production of chemicals and light tanks rather than just consumer articles. All of this, in turn, contributed to the development of nationalist consciousness, notably among educated members of the indigenous communities, many of whom had looked to the colonial bureaucracies for employment, but who now saw their living standards eroded by wartime inflation and the profits acquired by local landowners and business leaders.

When the Labour government came to power in Britain in 1945, it was already prepared to negotiate some kind of withdrawal from India, partly for ideological reasons and partly because of increasing difficulties with the nationalists; Indian independence was granted in 1947. In the following year, unable to solve the problem of Jewish demands for a homeland in a land claimed by Arabs, Britain gave up its mandate in Palestine. But Britain's Labour government had no intention of a complete withdrawal from empire, and considered that overseas development, especially in Africa, would be a means of helping the sterling area in general and the British economy in particular. The French, similarly, had no intention of any withdrawal from empire. They were keen to get back into Indo-China, hoping to play off Ho Chi Minh's communist guerrillas (who, though largely confined to the north-east of the country and few in numbers, could claim to have been fighting the Japanese since 1941) against other factions. Before 1946 was over this policy had embroiled the French in the opening skirmishes of the first of their savage wars of colonial independence. The French reluctantly recognized that there would be no restoration of their mandated territories in the Middle East, but they did not yield claims to their colonies in equatorial Africa, Madagascar, Morocco and Tunisia. Algeria, with its one million white settlers, was considered a part of metropolitan France.

These continuing imperial roles may have been the marks of great powers in the eyes of the governments of Britain and France, and in the eyes of many in their populations. But in terms of production, gross national product and share of world trade, neither country was any longer in the first rank, and great power adventures and postures were expensive. In addition to their imperial role, the British were also prepared to take on other international tasks to check what were perceived as threats to the peace of Europe. Both Britain and France maintained armies of occupation in defeated Germany, and in March 1947 they signed the Dunkirk Treaty, promising mutual support in the event of renewed aggression by Germany – something which still worried the French but which the British Foreign Office described as 'rather academic', increasingly perceiving the real threat to Europe as coming from the Soviet Union. The demands of empire, occupying Germany, and sometimes playing world policemen meant that the British used military conscription in peacetime, and thousands of young national servicemen found themselves deployed in distant garrisons, sometimes being shot at.

It was believed that the shortage of manpower, given the imperial and international commitments, could be partially made up by building an atomic bomb, but there were also other reasons for this. British scientists had been involved in developing the weapon with the Americans during the war; the Labour government was furious when the Americans elbowed them out of the research and development of these weapons and determined to build their own. Moreover, Labour ministers reasoned, what better mark of great power status could there be than possession of this weapon? In the mid-1950s a French government under Pierre Mendès-France followed similar lines of reasoning: an atom bomb would demonstrate that France was still a great power and it would help to compensate for its lack of manpower. The idea was taken up with even more enthusiasm by de Gaulle when he became the first president of the Fifth Republic in 1958. But imperial and international roles, which involved the deployment and maintenance of troops around the world, and the development of atom bombs and their delivery systems cost vast amounts of money, and this was in short supply even among the victorious European powers.

The war had cost both Britain and France enormous sums, and as armaments became more sophisticated and more dependent on complex, changing technologies, so they were becoming more costly to develop and then to produce. It was not just the new nuclear technology that was expensive; so too, for example, were radar and electronics, both of which had been extensively developed and deployed in World War II. In 1945 there was the need to replace destroyed, damaged or worn-out production equipment, as well as roads, railways, bridges and so on. The French transport system had completely broken down at the end of the war. Imports and exports were non-existent. There was no stock of foreign currency, and the franc was weak: in 1944 the official exchange rate was 50 francs to $1, but on the black market a dollar could fetch four times that sum. At the end of 1945 the franc was officially devalued by almost 60 per cent, to $1 to 116 francs, and a further devaluation followed in 1949.

Britain had fought the war by increasing taxes (taxation, both direct and indirect, rose from £1,007 million in 1938–9 to £3,411 million in 1945–6 in cash terms), by disinvestment abroad which raised some £4,198 million, and by leaning on the burgeoning US economy. As a result of the war, Britain's internal debt rose from £7,247 million to £23,372 million. Britain was not prepared for peace when it came; it had anticipated the struggle against the Japanese continuing into 1946 and perhaps into 1947, and was relying on lend-lease continuing during this period, which, it was hoped, would enable some restructuring for peace. But when, following the attacks on Hiroshima and Nagasaki, the Japanese surrendered in September 1945, so lend-lease also came to an end. Already, in July, the Labour government had received a memorandum from John Maynard Keynes warning of a 'financial Dunkirk' and stating starkly that, without help, 'a greater degree of austerity would be necessary than we have experienced at any time during the war'. Remember, too, that this Labour government wished to finance a new welfare state as well as maintain Britain's international role as an imperial and a 'great' power. Keynes negotiated a long-term loan from the United States of $3,750 million, but during 1946 this began to be spent at an alarming rate, far faster than anyone had anticipated. The situation was aggravated by a determination to prove that nothing had changed with respect to the British economy and financial system, and this led to the British exchange rate being set ridiculously at the 1939 level of $4 to £1; not until 1949 was the more realistic rate of $2.8 to £1 established.

The crunch came in 1947. The winter of 1946–7 was terrible; in both Britain and France the bitter cold was aggravated by fuel shortages, factories were forced to close, and the beginnings of a European economic recovery that had appeared in 1946 disintegrated. On 21 February 1947 the United States government received two *aides-mémoires* from its British ally. These are printed as Documents II.43 and II.44 in *Primary Sources 2: Interwar and World War II*.

Exercise Read the documents now and then answer the following questions:

1   What are the problems identified by the two *aides-mémoires?*

2   What remedy is proposed by the British government? ∎

Specimen answers 1   The *aides-mémoires* describe internal problems in both Greece and Turkey: the former has acute economic difficulties and a military emergency caused by 'bandits'; the latter is not able to finance its necessary military reorganization or any extensive programme of economic development. The key problem highlighted in these documents, however, is that the British government feels itself incapable of continuing, let alone increasing, its financial assistance to Greece and Turkey.

2   The solution to these problems in the eyes of the British government is for the United States to take over the British role. □

The specific problems of Greece and Turkey will be addressed later in the unit; the financial difficulties of the British government outlined in the *aides-mémoires* and its decision to end its aid to Greece and Turkey led, as it had hoped and suggested, to the United States taking over these tasks. Just three weeks after the receipt of these documents, President Truman outlined to a joint session of Congress what has become known as the Truman Doctrine:

> To ensure the peaceful development of nations, free from coercion, the United States has taken a leading part in establishing the United Nations.

The United Nations is designed to make possible lasting freedom and independence for all its members. We shall not realise our objectives, however, unless we are willing to help free peoples to maintain their free institutions and their national integrity against aggressive movements that seek to impose upon them totalitarian regimes. This is no more than a frank recognition that totalitarian regimes imposed upon free peoples, by direct or indirect aggression, undermine the foundations of international peace and hence the security of the United States.

(Quoted in J. M. Siracusa, *The American Diplomatic Revolution*, 1978, p.227)

Exercise   Turn now to Document II.45, a memorandum by William L. Clayton, the US Under Secretary of State for Economic Affairs, and to Document II.46, the extract from a speech made by General George C. Marshall, the US Secretary of State, in *Primary Sources 2: Interwar and World War II*. Read the two documents, and answer the following questions:

1   What are the problems and dangers outlined in these documents?

2   What are the remedies? ■

Specimen answers   1   The problem identified by both Clayton and Marshall is the destruction and disruption of the European economy that had been caused by war and the preparation for war. Clayton suggests that if the situation deteriorates much more, then there could be revolution; Marshall foresees the possibilities of 'disturbances', but also believes that the problems might have a demoraliz-ing effect on the whole world.

2   The remedy is seen as coming from large-scale American aid over the next three years or so. □

Planning for the economic recovery of Europe by means of American aid began in both Europe and the United States almost immediately after Marshall's speech. Britain took the initiative in Europe, where representatives from a dozen different countries came together in the Committee for European Economic Cooperation (CEEC, later the Organization for European Economic Cooperation, OEEC). In December 1947 the CEEC presented a report to the United States recommending a four-year programme of aid. A series of committees studying the matter for the United States government presented similar reports at roughly the same time. In April 1948 Congress ratified the European Recovery Program Bill, commonly known as Marshall Aid, and from June 1948 until June 1952 some $13,150 million in American aid was given to Europe. The largest amounts were forwarded to Britain ($3,176 million) and to France ($2,706 million); then came Italy ($1,474 million), West Germany ($1,389 million), the Netherlands ($1,079 million) and a dozen other smaller nations. Most of the money was spent in the United States itself, providing at first food, animal feed and fertilizers for the immediate problems, and then raw materials and semi-finished products, together with fuel, machinery and vehicles. By the end of the aid programme agricultural output in western Europe was 10 per cent above its pre-war level and industrial output was 35 per cent above (though the outbreak of the Korean War in 1950 also had some impact in boosting European industrial production, particularly related to military needs).

Exercise   1   From what I have said in the preceding paragraphs, does Marshall Aid appear to you to have been directed at any particular part of Europe; if so, which part?

2   Is there anything in the two documents by Clayton and Marshall that expressly denies aid to the Soviet Union or those states within its sphere of influence?

3   Can you think of any reason why the Soviet Union might reject the kind of aid offered under the Marshall Plan? ■

Specimen answers   1   The countries noted in my list of those receiving aid are all in western Europe.

2   There is nothing in Clayton's memorandum or in Marshall's speech which specifically says that aid should be confined to the west of Europe. Neither differentiates between eastern and western Europe, and while the only countries mentioned by Clayton are in the west and he is concerned about 'revolution', he also writes about the need to save Europe 'from starvation and chaos' (not from the Russians).

3   Given the increasing ideological split between the Soviet Union and the United States, it was unlikely that the former would be keen to open up to investment by the latter. This might weaken Russia's increasing hold on eastern Europe, and it would also be boosting the very capitalism that the Soviet system was out to replace. □

President Truman saw Marshall Aid as part and parcel of the ideological struggle and as fulfilling the promise of support for free people outlined in the Truman Doctrine. Initially, American aid was promised for all those European states prepared to participate in the programme. Shortly after Marshall's speech a meeting was held in Paris involving the foreign ministers of Britain, France and the USSR to discuss the proposal. The talks rapidly broke down and the Russian delegation left. In some ways, given the points raised in specimen answer 3 above, the Russian walk-out was predictable, but this is not the whole story. It seems likely that the western powers expected that the Russians would refuse the offered aid; and there was some justification for fearing that, if the Russians accepted it, then the strongly Republican Congress would, in the context of the increasing ideological split, refuse to ratify an aid Bill. Ernest Bevin, the British Foreign Secretary, and Georges Bidault, his French opposite number, also presented Viacheslav Molotov with a blueprint for the integration of the European economies which he would have had great difficulty in accepting, since it proposed that each nation should produce what it currently produced best; this suggested to Molotov that eastern Europe was to be maintained as a relatively backward area providing food for the industrial west.

5   A 'RED MENACE' IN THE WEST?

It was noted in Unit 20 that communists throughout Europe played an influential role in the resistance movements during World War II. The largest and most significant partisan armies may have been in the east, but once, following the Nazi invasion of Russia, the communists began to participate in resistance movements in the west, so these movements became stronger and more effective.

Exercise   What do you suppose the communist resistance fighters hoped to achieve in western Europe following the defeat of Fascist Italy and Nazi Germany? ■

Specimen answer   If not socialist revolution, the communist resistance fighters hoped for significant economic, political and social change at least. □

Exercise   Bearing in mind the military situation in western Europe at the end of World War II, can you think of any physical restraints on, for example, Belgian, French or Italian communists in carrying out a socialist revolution in 1945? ■

Specimen answer   Each of these countries contained large numbers of British and American troops, and it is doubtful whether these troops would have stood aside and let such revolutions happen – recall that Unit 20 describes the British action against the communists in Greece in December 1944. Moreover, the countries of western Europe did not have common borders with the Soviet Union, and the Russian army was too far away to offer much assistance even had it wanted to. □

The Soviet Union was a further restraining influence on west European communists. It took the view that communists must work with 'progressive', anti-fascist groups to complete the bourgeois revolution before any proletarian revolution or peaceful takeover would be possible. Even in eastern Europe this was the initial Soviet strategy and the advice or orders given to the communist leaders returning from the Soviet Union. Both France and Italy witnessed the return of communist leaders from the Soviet Union as the countries were liberated. Maurice Thorez and Palmiro Togliatti each acted as restraining influences on rank-and-file party members who had fought in the resistance and who wanted immediate and significant changes.

In military terms the resistance movements in western Europe made little difference to the outcome of the war. By the spring of 1945, however, they seemed in a position to make a difference to the outcome of peace. To the men on the ground who helped liberate their locality, the power of the resistance, and of their faction within the resistance, probably seemed considerable. In northern Italy around 230,000 people were engaged in some form of partisan activity at different times following the overthrow of Mussolini; it was partisan units which, in the spring of 1945, liberated some of the great towns of the north (admittedly helped by the progressive German collapse and by the advance of Allied troops), and it was partisans who captured and shot the *Duce* himself. There was less fighting by resistance units in France; often all that French armed resisters had to do in the summer of 1944 was to enter a town as the Germans pulled out, and declare it liberated. But in both countries the resistance liberators established their own organizing committees, their own local administrations, and often their own system of justice. Often arbitrary and retaliatory, these could be seen as the model for the new society; they posed a threat to the authority of the new central governments, and they were viewed with suspicion by the British and the Americans. If revolution, or at least the potential for armed insurrection, was to be prevented, then the central governments had to disarm these groups and dismantle their local power structures. In Belgium the Communist Party objected to the disarming of the resistance and resigned from the coalition government in protest. In France and Italy, in contrast, where the parties were proportionately much larger, both Thorez and Togliatti supported the disarming of the resistance and the re-establishment of the power of central government.

In Belgium, France and Italy there was a feeling that the unity of the struggle against Nazism and fascism should be reflected in the governments established at the time of liberation. In consequence, the new governments were coalitions that embraced all of the anti-fascist parties, including the communists; even though it walked out of government when the resistance was disarmed in December 1944, the Belgian Communist Party was happy to rejoin in the following February. The influence and popularity of the communists in all three countries were manifested by their successes in the elections of the immediate post-war years. In France the communists won the largest number of seats in the Constituent Assembly in the election of October 1945, but not an overall majority. In February 1946 the Belgian communists secured just under 13 per cent of the vote and won 11 per cent of the seats in the Chamber of Representatives. In Italy the following June, the communists secured about one-fifth of the vote and one-fifth of the seats. In each election the communists sought an alliance with the socialists, and in each case this gave the two parties around half of the total seats in the respective assemblies. In no instance did the communists and the socialists form a government on their own, but they both continued to hold ministries in different coalitions. While they did not satisfy the aspirations of the extreme rank-and-file militants, these governments, with their communist membership, supervised significant reforms and political and economic change. In all three countries women were granted the vote. New constitutions were drafted for both France and Italy, and in Italy a popular referendum voted away the monarchy. France particularly experienced a massive extension of state ownership during 1945 and early 1946: railways, coal mines, gas and electricity, leading financial institutions and some large manufacturing concerns were all taken into public ownership.

Probably a preponderance of informed opinion in western Europe in the immediate post-war years would have considered that some form of socialism was the likely future. Nationalization and central planning were popular with bureaucrats, intellectuals and powerful trade unions. The main political development was, however, to be the rise of Christian democracy. Communist parties in Italy and France were to maintain some 20–25 per cent of the vote for many years but not to advance from this, while social democratic parties, even though they began cautiously to abandon their traditional Marxism, were to find themselves marginalized.

Several factors accounted for the strength of Christian democracy. These new parties, notably the Democrazia Christiana in Italy and the German CDU, inherited many of their voters from the old pre-war Catholic parties, but they were not confessional parties as their predecessors had been, so were able to widen their appeal. Their support for property and for the family proved popular, as did their economic policies, which rejected economic liberalism and state planning alike in favour of a socially committed market economy. They were aided by the essential continuity of the state apparatus, a general desire for a concentration upon recovery rather than contention, and a slow but steady economic resurgence in the late 1940s which was to accelerate in the 1950s.

The increased influence of the centre-right in coalition governments was aided by the Cold War, by American support and, as we shall see, by reactions to changes in communist tactics. One must not, however, push relativism too far. As Robert Conquest has commented: 'in the west the Communists were not "eliminated" from legal opposition, while in eastern Europe the non-Communist opposition was crushed and its democratic leaders executed or jailed' (*Reflections on a Ravaged Century*, 1999, p.158).

By the spring of 1947 the strains in successive coalition governments were beginning to show. Initially, the French communists had revealed themselves almost as concerned as General de Gaulle about France's standing as a great power. However, in the early months of 1947 communist deputies criticized the behaviour of French troops in suppressing nationalist disorder in Madagascar, and voted against credits for the war in Indo-China; communist ministers abstained in the vote. In May 1947 communist ministers went so far as to vote against the government on the issue of a strike over the rising cost of living by workers at the recently nationalized Renault works. They were sacked from the government, and in spite of their continuing popularity at the polls, they were never to return in the lifetime of the Fourth Republic. In Belgium and Italy the internal differences between the coalition partners were, of course, different, but the effects were the same, and by the early summer of 1947 the communist parties were no longer in government.

Exercise   What events in international affairs do you think may have made the positions of the western communist parties even more difficult in the spring and early summer of 1947 and in 1948? ■

Specimen answer   The worsening relations between east and west, manifested particularly by the Berlin blockade, the Czechoslovakian crisis, and the declaration of the Truman Doctrine. There was also the problem of how to respond to the offer of Marshall Aid, since, although it would obviously be of benefit to the recipients, the Soviet Union was critical of it. □

The Americans had been growing increasingly suspicious of communists in western governments during 1946 and early 1947. Less than a week after the Americans received the British *aides-mémoires* on Greece and Turkey, Dean Acheson, the Under Secretary of State, was warning congressional leaders of Soviet attempts to encircle Germany by infiltration and subversion:

> In France, with four Communists in the Cabinet, one of them Minister of Defense, with Communists controlling the largest trade union (the CCT) and infiltrating government offices, factories and the armed services, with nearly a third of the electorate voting Communist, and with the economic conditions worsening, the Russians could pull the plug at any time they

chose. In Italy a similar if less dangerous situation existed, but it was growing worse.

(Quoted in J. M. Jones, *The Fifteen Weeks*, 1955, p.140)

This actually says rather more about American fears than Soviet intentions, since it appears that in the early months of 1947 the western communists were receiving little direction from Moscow. For several months, for example, they received no advice on how they should respond to Marshall Aid. The French communists went so far as to welcome the offer, provided that it was administered by a United Nations agency. The central committee of the French Communist Party restated its positive approach to the aid programme in the first week of September 1947. Within a month, however, it was forced to adopt a different position.

In May 1943 the Communist International (Comintern) had been dissolved on the grounds that it no longer served the interests of the working class in the different countries; at that moment the principal aim of all communist parties was the defeat of fascism. In September 1947 the Soviet leadership summoned the party leaders from both eastern and western Europe to a meeting in Poland. The gathering heard a keynote address from Andrei Zhdanov, then Stalin's chief theoretician, and the meeting resulted in the formation of the Communist Information Bureau (Cominform).

Exercise   Document II.47 in *Primary Sources 2: Interwar and World War II* is an extract from Zhdanov's address. Read it now and then answer the following questions:

1   How does Zhdanov represent the developing world situation?

2   How does the Marshall Plan fit in with Zhdanov's interpretation?

3   How does Zhdanov's view of the international situation compare with that of Truman and his advisers?

4   According to Zhdanov, what did the dissolution of Comintern demonstrate, and what has experience subsequently shown?

5   What do you suppose the creation of Cominform meant for the communist parties of western Europe, particularly with reference to the Marshall Plan? ∎

Specimen answers   1   Zhdanov sees the world developing into two armed blocs: on the one hand the USSR, 'the stronghold of anti-imperialist and anti-fascist policy', with its supporters in 'the new democracies'; and on the other Britain and especially the United States, uniting 'all the enemies of the working class without exception'.

2   The Marshall Plan is simply a part of the American attempt to create a bloc of states bound to the United States and in opposition to the USSR.

3   Zhdanov's interpretation of developments, however much one may query some of his facts, is, to my mind, the mirror image of the Truman view of the 'free world' under threat from international communism.

4   The dissolution of the Comintern demonstrated that Moscow was not interfering in the internal politics of other countries and giving directions to their respective communist parties. However, experience has demonstrated that the isolation of communist parties is 'unnatural'.

5   The implication at the end of this document is that the communist parties of
     Europe (and elsewhere) will start receiving directions from Moscow once
     again (this time via Cominform), and that they will be expected to criticize
     and condemn the Marshall Plan as part of the American imperialist
     conspiracy. □

Zhdanov's address was followed by criticism of the French and Italian parties for
'unrevolutionary' behaviour. The Yugoslav delegates to the conference, Edvard
Kardelj and Milovan Djilas, led the attack, declaring that by opportunism, the
pursuit of bourgeois democratic policies, and retaining government portfolios,
the French and Italian parties had missed the chance of power that was offered
in 1945. It mattered little that Moscow had favoured their working within their
bourgeois democratic systems at that time, and that a theoretical justification had
been found for this. From now on the communist parties were to encourage
strikes and disorder which, it was hoped, would make the Marshall Plan
unworkable and bring about the elimination of independent socialist, labour
and peasant parties. The wave of strikes that began in France and Italy towards
the end of 1947 had traditional economic causes, but they were seized upon and
encouraged by the two communist parties. The division of Europe and the Cold
War thus became as much an expression of internal as international politics.

6   EASTERN EUROPE FROM WORLD WAR TO COLD WAR

Introduction

By the middle of 1945 the Red Army had 'liberated' virtually all of eastern
Europe. Soviet troops were present in Bulgaria, Czechoslovakia, Hungary,
Poland and Romania. In addition, they controlled one zone in eastern Austria,
while communist partisans – who could be expected to be sympathetic to
Moscow – gained power as a result of the war in Yugoslavia and Albania. By
1949 all of these countries save Austria were ruled by communist dictatorships.

Interpretations of Yalta which suggest Stalin's solemn undertaking to permit
free elections in eastern Europe were believed by Churchill and Roosevelt are
naive. All parties knew that the agreement meant a sphere of influence for the
Soviet Union and that it was up to Stalin to determine what happened in Poland,
Hungary, Romania, Bulgaria and Czechoslovakia. Churchill and Roosevelt could
simply not admit that they knew this.

However, there is still some room for debate as to what the western Allies and
even Stalin understood by a Soviet sphere of influence or expected it to be like.
Was the eventual satellite status of much of eastern Europe inevitable and
foreshadowed at Yalta? Was it not possible in 1945 to believe that the Soviet
Union might be content with something short of socialist dictatorships, provided
foreign policies were aligned to Soviet wishes? After all, the Soviet Union was
just emerging from a period of war. Could it not be hoped at least that Stalin

might preserve a façade of democracy while he ensured that pro-Soviet governments emerged?

Coalition governments were maintained for some time. Some historians have argued that Stalin only created dictatorships in the states concerned amidst the burgeoning Cold War, that it was the rhetoric of Truman – who was no more prepared to use force than Roosevelt in order to prevent the Soviet domination of eastern Europe but complained more loudly about it – which led to the destruction of pluralism.

Yet there are good reasons for believing that Stalin was determined to go beyond a traditional idea of spheres of influence towards complete political control in the countries that had been 'liberated' by the Soviet army. As he explained to the Yugoslav communist, Milovan Djilas: 'This war is not as in the past; whoever occupies a territory also imposes his own system as far as his army can reach; it cannot be otherwise' (quoted in Rupnik, *The Other Europe*, 1988, p.72). This is not to allege that Stalin was inflexible but that he was inflexible in the areas where Soviet forces were firmly in control. Elsewhere Stalin was prepared to probe or retreat, to compromise and even to order communist parties to support existing regimes, or – as in Germany – to continue a limited co-operation with the western powers.

Exercise Can you think of a country that was occupied by the Red Army but was allowed to continue as an independent and non-communist country? ■

Specimen answer Part of Austria was occupied by the Red Army, and indeed this occupation closely mirrored that of Germany with its separate Allied zones and the joint occupation of Vienna. It was only after the death of Stalin in 1953 that negotiations between the Soviet Union and the western powers allowed the Allied occupation to end, and the country was allowed to move towards independence in 1955. □

This introduction has focused on the debate about Soviet intentions towards the region. Eastern Europe, however, was far from monolithic. The timetable to which communist rule was established differed enormously across the region. Furthermore, the dictatorships that were established in the late 1940s were, despite their institutional similarities, never uniform, even if this diversity did not become obvious until at least the mid-1950s. These factors have provoked considerable debate above and beyond that about Soviet intentions. Before we turn to outline this debate, let us consider the basic differences between the states of eastern Europe.

Exercise What major differences can you distinguish between the eastern European states in 1945? ■

Specimen answer 1 Some had fought alongside Germany. Hungary, Romania and Bulgaria had been allied with Germany, although Bulgaria had not declared war on the Soviet Union. Poland, by contrast, had been occupied by Germany. Czechoslovakia had been dismembered. Bohemia-Moravia was governed as a German protectorate, while Slovakia was given independence under a collaborationist government.

2   Some were by tradition and inclination pro-Russian in their outlook (Bulgaria and Czechoslovakia), while others (Hungary, Poland and Romania) were anti-Russian.

3   The pre-war regimes varied enormously. Czechoslovakia was the only state in the region to remain a democracy until 1939. Pre-war regimes in Romania, Bulgaria and Yugoslavia could be described as autocratic monarchies.

4   The economies varied between the largely peasant-based agrarian economies of Bulgaria, Romania, southern Yugoslavia and Albania at one extreme and the industrialized economy of western Czechoslovakia on the other. □

These basic differences between the individual states of the region should be borne in mind as we move on to consider the debate about the imposition of communist regimes in the region and later focus more closely on some of the countries.

The debate on the imposition of communist regimes in eastern Europe

However fragile post-war democracies in eastern Europe were, their dissolution in the late 1940s came as a severe shock to the vast majority of western observers. The creation of socialist dictatorships was accompanied by the creation of prison camps designed to house political opponents and by waves of show trials that brought dissident elements in the new ruling parties into line with Stalin's policies. With the onset of the Cold War most observers of the region looked on with alarm. It was in this climate that the first analyses of how the new systems were created were written.

In 1950 Hugh Seton-Watson published the first edition of *The East European Revolution*, in which he identified a pattern for the communist seizure of power across the region; this book has remained influential in historians' thinking up until the present day. Political scientist Zbigniew Brzezinski, in his book *The Soviet Bloc: Unity and Conflict* (1960), identified a similar pattern. Brzezinski argued that the Soviet Union intended in 1945 to create 'totalitarian' regimes across the region, that where limited democracy existed this was simply a charade masking real Soviet intentions. Communism was imposed on the region according to what Brzezinski describes as 'the Polish pattern', which had 'Bulgarian, Romanian and Hungarian variants' as well as 'Yugoslav and Czechoslovak extremes' (*The Soviet Bloc*, pp.3–21). According to this pattern the Red Army eliminated alternative centres of political and military power as it moved west; it ensured that the new police and armed forces were under communist control, while the Soviets built up the communist parties. By skilfully combining popular social reforms with the use of undemocratic tactics against other parties, the communist parties quickly became strong enough to assume absolute power.

Brzezinski raised the question of how the transitions differed from each other. He argued essentially that every transition was a variant of the same pattern set down in a blueprint drawn up in Moscow. One can draw a parallel between the arguments of Seton-Watson and later Brzezinski and Cold War ideology. Both arguments assume that the Soviet Union's intentions were aggressive and expansionist – that Stalin used the opportunity accorded by the Red Army's advance to hasten the victory of world communism. They both assume also that the diverse states and societies of central and eastern Europe had to conform to a uniform vision of the future, and that similar tools were used to realize this vision across the continent.

Exercise   Using the knowledge that you have just gained, briefly identify several points which might lead you to doubt these arguments and some of the assumptions on which they are based. ■

Specimen answer   1   Soviet intentions cannot be so easily assumed, and as you will have noticed from the previous section are themselves subject to considerable debate among historians.

2   The case of Austria supports arguments that suggest there were limits to Soviet expansion.

3   Not all countries that were subsequently ruled by socialist dictatorships were occupied by the Red Army in 1945. Yugoslavia, for example, was 'liberated' by Tito's communist partisans. Yugoslav-supported partisans played a decisive role in Albania also. It is much more difficult to make the case for Soviet control in these instances. □

The timetables of communist takeover were very different in each of the states. One might divide the states of eastern Europe into several different groups to demonstrate the differences between the transitions that occurred:

1   Albania and Yugoslavia, where communist rule was achieved through partisan victory and not through Soviet occupation.

2   Bulgaria, where in September 1944 the combined actions of partisans, popular protest and Red Army intervention led to the installation of a government controlled by the communist-dominated Fatherland Front.

3   Poland and Romania – in both cases the Red Army and the Soviets built up a strong parallel state dominated by the communists, while the communists themselves relied on extensive Soviet support to dominate governing coalitions.

4   Hungary and Czechoslovakia – in both countries free multi-party elections were held. Popular front coalitions existed until 1948, though democracy was limited due to extensive communist control of the security forces.

The fact that the timetable of takeover in the states of eastern Europe was different does not in itself prove that Moscow had no plan. Brzezinski's notion of variations depending on national circumstance could account for the differences in the timetable and the nature of the transition to dictatorship. Some historians argue that in fact there were different 'national roads to socialism'. According to the authors of one textbook that takes such a view, 'the evidence clearly suggests ... that between 1945–7 Stalin had no overall blueprint for Eastern Europe' (Swain and Swain, *Eastern Europe since 1945*, 1993, p.54) They are supported by historians and commentators, particularly of events in Hungary and Czechoslovakia. The American political scientist Charles Gati argues that the coalition years in Hungary between 1945 and 1947 should be seen as a period of 'democratic interlude'. This, he says, was made possible by both a desire among the population for social change and the fact that Stalin's aims in Hungary were limited until the onset of the Cold War (Gati, *Hungary and the Soviet Bloc,* 1986). In the case of Czechoslovakia Martin Myant has argued similarly that the creation of a one-party state in the Czechoslovak case can only be attributed to changes in the political climate in 1948. According to Myant, the Communist Party led a popular movement in 1945 that aimed at 'a synthesis of parliamentary democracy and socialism' (*Socialism and Democracy in Czechoslovakia,* 1981, p.3).

These arguments fit some countries better than others. They do have one advantage in that they stress the degree to which a desire for radical social change after the stagnation of the interwar years and the catastrophe of World War II created the social climate in which socialist dictatorships were institutionalized. The importance of the social consequences of war for the dictatorships that emerged in eastern Europe has only recently been recognized by historians. In 1989 the US-based historian of Poland, Jan T. Gross, argued in a seminal article that without 'an analysis of the social consequences of the Second World War in these societies ... understanding the mechanisms of postwar imposition of communist regimes in this region is impossible' ('Social consequences of war', 1989, p.198). Gross started from the diversity of the region's interwar experience. He argued that 'different national roads to socialism' began with the outbreak of war rather than its end. He identifies several factors that spanned the war years and the immediate post-war period that were to help pave the way for socialist dictatorship:

1   The creation of war economies, whether under Nazi occupation or by governments that were allied to Germany, necessitated both an enhanced role for the state and a shift towards economic autarky – in other words, a drive for self-sufficiency. In the post-war period this statist model continued to meet the demands for economic reconstruction and laid the ground for the imposition of planned economies throughout the region.

2   Population losses and population movements represented another factor. It has been estimated that Poland lost around 17 per cent of its pre-war population and Yugoslavia 10 per cent. Jewish populations in the region were all but eliminated during the war years. Post-war border changes and the expulsion of ethnic Germans following the war further reshaped societies. The region entered the post-war period with relatively ethnically homogeneous nation states. These huge changes generated unprecedented opportunities for social mobility from below, and allowed states to remould societies from above.

3   The brutality of World War II with its mass murder, rape, enforced deportations and the confiscation of property brutalized society. It also smashed traditional hierarchies. This brutalization and upheaval created a political vacuum that a determined political movement could use.

With the advent of albeit fragile liberal democracy across the region since 1989 and the consequent improvement in the access to records about the post-war period, historians have begun to examine the effect of the experience of 'total war' on the creation of post-war dictatorships. Historians have begun to examine the deportations of civilians and the mass rapes conducted by members of the

Red Army in 1945, as well as the creation of communist-dominated police forces. Cold War political histories are being complemented and questioned by those who examine the relationship between gender, ethnicity or class, and the transition from war to dictatorship in eastern Europe.

The questions raised by these competing interpretations and approaches can only be addressed by examining several of the countries in a comparative perspective. We are therefore going to look at the post-war histories of Poland, Czechoslovakia, Hungary and Yugoslavia.

Poland

Poland was central to Soviet strategy in post-war eastern Europe. There is considerable consensus among historians and other observers that for Stalin control over Poland was the key to establishing a Soviet presence in central Europe and a buffer between the Soviet Union and any future German state. Furthermore the eastern regions of pre-war Poland had been incorporated into the Soviet Union in 1939, and the Soviets continued to be keen to force Poland westward. For the Soviets the need to guarantee their new western border necessitated a degree of political control over any post-war Polish state. As the Red Army moved westward, it became clear that the Soviet Union would 'liberate' the country from Nazi occupation, and this enhanced the importance of communists among the anti-Nazi forces and diminished that of the government-in-exile based in London.

Poland's Communist Party, known as the Polish Workers' Party (PPR), was refounded in Warsaw in January 1942. For most of the next two years it was a marginal group within the anti-Nazi resistance, attracting little support outside a small communist minority – a year after its foundation it claimed 8,000 members. It had little prestige among the resistance when compared to the London government-in-exile, which claimed 350,000 Home Army troops in 1944. The PPR aimed to break out of its isolation by detaching sympathetic parties such as the Peasants' Party and the Socialists from the London government and by creating a popular front of its own – the so-called Homeland National Council. These attempts met with little success. It was only the arrival of the Red Army in summer 1944 that changed the situation. The Red Army crossed the eastern border of interwar Poland in June 1944, re-occupying territory originally taken in 1939. On 23 July the city of Lublin was taken – the site of the attempt to create a People's Republic after World War I (see Units 11–13, section 9). Here the Homeland National Council, renamed the Committee of National Liberation, formed a government dominated by the PPR.

As the Red Army entered Poland, the London government-in-exile sought to regain the initiative from the communists. Throughout the first half of 1944 the Home Army had been active in much of Poland, desperately attempting to establish the authority of the government-in-exile in the country before the Soviets arrived. On 31 July, in the face of Red Army advance, the Home Army led an uprising in Warsaw, anticipating taking the capital as the Germans were beaten back by the Red Army. The uprising failed, the Red Army advance was stopped in its tracks by the Germans, while Stalin failed to provide air support or arms to the uprising – preferring instead that the London government take no credit for the 'liberation' of Poland. The uprising was brutally crushed by the Germans. Warsaw was finally 'liberated' by the Red Army on 12 January 1945.

Despite early attempts to win over non-communist forces such as the Peasants' Party and to gain a measure of support from both the London government-in-exile and its supporters in the Home Army, the Lublin government ruled on the basis of repression, relying heavily on the Red Army. Throughout the autumn of 1944 conditions of near civil war existed in those parts of Poland governed from Lublin. During this period both a new army was created and the foundations of a police state were laid.

During January 1945 the Red Army swept across Poland, reaching the western borders of the interwar state by the end of the month. The Soviet-backed regime resorted to repression in order to establish its authority in newly 'liberated' territory. It set up a network of internment camps for members of the Home Army and other political opponents. Repression split those sections of the underground that supported London, thus weakening the authority of the government-in-exile, but it also was counter-productive in that it increased guerilla activity, making some areas of rural Poland all but ungovernable. The behaviour of Red Army soldiers towards the civilian population did little to pacify the population. Near civil war in the countryside combined with unrest in the cities. The industrial workforce, reduced to penury by food shortages and collapsing real wages, resorted to strikes and open protest. This was exacerbated by the attempts of the PPR to gain tighter control over the factories and the trade unions. Faced with the almost complete collapse of the state, the PPR shifted from a strategy of confrontation to one of compromise in May 1945. A multi-party system was created with the PPR, the Peasants' Party or PSL, the Socialists or PPS, a Catholic Party of Labour and a middle-class Democratic Party. A limited democracy was created: the PPR recognized limits on its power by participating in a coalition government with the other legalized parties, but excluded the nationalist right from politics and maintained tight control over both the army and the security forces.

The new popular front government faced a formidable task. 17.9 per cent of Poland's pre-war population had died during World War II, including the bulk of the country's Jewish population murdered during the Holocaust. According to one historian the brutalizing effects of German occupation had led to the 'disintegration of social life' (Gross, *Polish Society under German Occupation*, 1979, p.166). Two-thirds of Polish industry had been wiped out by war. The new government not only faced huge demands for national reconstruction but had to manage the consequences of post-war border changes. The new borders determined at the Potsdam Conference shifted the country westward, granting the Kresy region of what had been eastern Poland to the Soviet Union, and moving Poland's western borders to the Oder and Neisse rivers. Much of the ethnic German population of pre-war Poland was deported; according to the most recent estimates, 6.3 million Germans resident in Poland in 1944 had left for Germany by 1948. The deserted regions of western Poland were resettled with 3 million Poles who went west in search of jobs and land during the same period. At the same time, 2.1 million Poles were moved from the eastern territories into Poland proper.

Enormous population shifts generated opportunities for social mobility and considerable social tension at the same time. Radical land reform – implemented from 1944 onwards – generated class conflict in the countryside between its poorer beneficiaries and existing peasants allied to larger landowners. In the factories the policies of the communist-controlled Ministry of Industry met with the mistrust of industrial workers. Political tensions about Poland's future and especially the role of the PPR were superimposed on to these social tensions, which manifested themselves in strikes, other demonstrations, continuing political violence in the countryside, and most notoriously in the Kielce pogrom of 4 July 1946, when a community of 400 Holocaust survivors were attacked by a mob that accused them of the kidnap and murder of a Christian boy. Forty-one Jews were killed. It was the most significant incidence of anti-Jewish violence in post-war eastern Europe. There were reported pogroms elsewhere in Poland, in Hungary and in Slovakia in 1946. All the incidents were in some way related to tension between returnees from Nazi death camps and local populations, as well as to post-war political instability.

Political tension was fuelled by the imminence of elections – due during the first half of 1946 – and the power struggle between the PSL and the PPR over the leadership of the coalition. PSL leader Stanislaw Mikolajczk was determined to wrest control of the government from the PPR. He steadfastly refused to accept a united list for all members of the governing coalition, insisting instead on competitive elections that he believed would lead to the PSL becoming the largest in the government. In the country he began to organize the anti-communist majority of the population into his party in order to acquire the political strength to dominate the popular front government. The PPR sought to restrain the PSL by making it part of a unified electoral block – the failure of Mikolajczk to agree to such a block's formation led to the postponement of elections and a return by the PPR to the politics of confrontation.

The PPR concentrated on its alliance with the PPS and began to move against the PSL. The remnants of the Home Army became the subjects of intervention by the PPR-controlled security services during early 1946. Political violence against PSL members also increased, as party activists were subject to routine arrest and generalized intimidation. PSL members of local councils were replaced by central government appointees. Mikolajczk continued to resist PPR pressure to enter a unified electoral block. In a climate of political polarization the government held a referendum on 30 June 1946, supported by the left, on the issues of constitutional reform, nationalization and the new borders. Though the referendum resulted in 'yes' votes on all three counts, fraud disguised the degree of hostility among ordinary Poles towards the PPR.

Despite the attempts of the PPS to broker a compromise on the distribution of seats on a unified list, the PSL concluded from the referendum result that it could defeat the PPR in a contested election. The PPR leadership simultaneously came to the same conclusion, and the election campaign took place in an increasingly polarized climate. The PPR and the PPS stood on one side and the PSL on the other; the PPR leadership presented the up-and-coming elections as a struggle between 'democratic' and 'reactionary' camps. The PPR took no risks, waging a campaign of intimidation in the run-up to the elections, which were finally held on 19 January 1947. The elections were far from free and fair; members of the PPR dominated electoral commissions, and in much of the country there was no secret ballot. PSL scrutineers were denied access to the counting of the votes across the country. Officially the Democratic Bloc dominated by the PPR and

PPS won 80.1 per cent to the 10.3 per cent recorded for the PSL. Although the power struggle was settled in 1947, a form of popular front government continued until the creation of dictatorship was begun with the forced merger of the PPR and PPS in March 1948. With that act Poland's Stalinist experience began.

Czechoslovakia

While little support for communism existed in Poland at the end of the war, the same cannot be said of Czechoslovakia. The Communist Party of Czechoslovakia, or the KSČ, had been legally allowed to function and enjoyed a substantial amount of support prior to 1938. The outcome of war could only be expected to strengthen support for the KSČ in the post-war state given the radicalization of public opinion that war brought in train and the prestige the Soviet Union enjoyed in Czechoslovakia in 1945.

Hitler's division of Czechoslovakia into the Protectorate of Bohemia-Moravia, incorporated into the Reich, and the puppet 'parish republic' of Slovakia affected post-war Czechoslovakia. Industrialized Bohemia-Moravia was treated as an integral part of the Nazi war economy. As the tide turned against Germany in 1942, working hours were lengthened, young Czechs were conscripted to work in German factories, the industrial labour force was expanded, factories were turned over wholesale to military production, and living standards declined. Despite growing discontent there was little organized resistance – ordinary Czechs preferred to engage in individual acts of defiance. The KSČ, in so far as it did exist, consisted of isolated groups of activists. Slovakia, however, was not occupied and the collaborationist regime that ruled the country based its appeal in part on its ability to keep Slovakia out of the theatre of conflict. The Slovak state was more tolerant of resistance than its Czech counterpart, and this allowed opposition headed by the Slovak communists to gather strength. Communist partisans backed by anti-fascist politicians and significant sections of the Slovak army formed the Slovak National Council, which mounted an uprising in August 1944 as the Red Army advanced beyond Soviet territory. The Slovak National Uprising was crushed by pro-government forces in September, but its consequences would be important for the new Czechoslovakia. It established communism as the focus of anti-fascist resistance and weakened the authority of the London-based government-in-exile led by Edvard Beneš.

The Red Army crossed into Slovakia in October 1944. Its advance was followed by the creation of 'national committees', revolutionary organs of public administration, often dominated by the Slovak communists. The Soviets recognized the Slovak National Council as the legitimate authority in the country. Soviet strategy in Czechoslovakia was very different, however, to Soviet strategy in Poland. Rather than exclude the London government-in-exile, the Soviets and the KSČ had in 1943 agreed to restore it to power in the event of Czechoslovakia's successful 'liberation'. In March 1945 Beneš, the KSČ and the Slovak National Council were brought to Moscow for negotiations about the formation of a new government. The outcome of these negotiations was a coalition with a unified programme: the Kosice programme, so-called after the Slovak city where the government was proclaimed. Of a total of 17 ministries, 4 and the premiership were held by Communists, 2 by the Democratic Party, 2 by the Social Democrats, 2 by the centre-right National Socialists, 2 by the People's Party and 4 by Independents, some of whom, however, were crypto-communists.

As the Red Army advanced into the Czech Lands, weak and fragmented resistance movements gathered strength, largely operating under the influence of the KSČ. May 1945 was marked by an uprising in Prague, followed several days later by its liberation. On 10 May 1945 the Czechoslovak government returned to the city. The new government faced nothing like the population losses, damage and social dislocation that confronted Poland's new rulers, but it still faced considerable problems. The legacy of Bohemia-Moravia's role in the Nazi war economy left a large industrial sector geared to the demands of armaments production and dominated by the state. Severe food supply problems led to social tensions in the cities.

In addition, the new government implemented a radical programme. The Sudeten German population was declared to be collectively guilty of the dismemberment of Czechoslovakia and the subsequent occupation of the Czech Lands. Initially in 1945 and the early part of 1946, ethnic Germans were required to perform forced labour in industry to alleviate shortages of workers while former Nazis were interned. This was a prelude to the wholesale expulsion of the Sudeten German population: 2.9 million were expelled in 1946 and 1947. People's Courts were set up in 1945 to try those accused of collaboration, bodies that were criticized by the Czech right because of perceived communist domination. The police force was purged, provoking similar criticism. Factory councils were set up in industry to control management. Widespread nationalization, particularly in mining and heavy industry, occurred immediately – strengthening further the role of the state – while in the countryside limited land reform was introduced.

Elections in May 1946 confirmed the KSČ as the country's largest political force with 38 per cent of the vote across Czechoslovakia. Parties committed to socialism won an absolute majority of the popular vote. The elections revealed a deep political split between the industrialized Czech Lands and rural Slovakia. In the former the KSČ took over 40 per cent as against only 24 per cent for the National Socialists (the most conservative of the legal Czech parties). In Slovakia the Communist Party took only 30 per cent as against the 61 per cent won by the conservative Democratic Party, which unified Catholics, peasants and supporters of the collaborationist wartime regime. In addition to the national split, the KSČ enjoyed overwhelming support among working-class voters in industrial areas, while the National Socialists won most support among the urban middle classes.

Coalition continued and was expanded to include Slovakia's Democratic Party. Relations between Slovak Communists and the Democrats, backed by the Catholic Church, remained tense. During 1946 and 1947 industrial workers in the Czech Lands were militant; strikes normally directed against the black market or against the transfer of small factories to their original owners disturbed the functioning of the coalition government in Prague. Students protested against what they saw as undemocratic behaviour by the KSČ, but workers remained solidly loyal to it. Political tension between right and left was increased when KSČ Secretary and Prime Minister Klement Gottwald set himself the aim of winning an absolute majority for the Communist Party in the following elections. Yet this polarization did not prove fatal for the popular front.

The turning point in Czechoslovakia was to come with the announcement of Marshall Aid. By mid-1947 Czechoslovakia's economic performance was still sluggish. In order to expand the country's heavy industrial sector, it required raw materials and machinery only available in the west yet was unable to pay. Consequently, the coalition government expressed its interest in Marshall Aid, but was forced to pull out after Stalin expressed his displeasure to the KSČ and Social Democrat leaderships. This led to a political split and growing hostility between left and right within the coalition. Throughout the second half of 1947 the KSČ began to make a bid for power as the security forces began a purge of public administration in Slovakia and intensified their drive against the black market.

The collapse of Czechoslovak democracy was precipitated by the dismissal of senior police officers who were not KSČ members by the communist Interior Minister in January 1948. In February ministers from all of the non-socialist parties resigned. The communist-dominated unions called for a general strike supported by Prague's workers, while 'action committees' were formed from KSČ activists in the ministries, radio, factories, universities and even within independent social organizations designed to secure party control. Gottwald formed a new government with only the Social Democratic Party as partners; later in the year it was forcibly merged into the KSČ and Czechoslovakia became a one-party state.

Hungary

Hungary was regarded by its Soviet 'liberators' as 'Hitler's last ally', and as such is the only country under discussion to have fought on the German side. Its experience of war from the German invasion of March 1944, the establishment of the puppet regime of the Arrow Cross, the murder of over half a million Jews, and then the forced occupation of the country by the Red Army in late 1944 and early 1945 was deeply traumatic. The war was seen as a national catastrophe of enormous proportions that profoundly discredited pre-war political élites and left economic devastation in its wake. As towns were 'liberated', in industry radical activists among the workforce took over the management of enterprises that had been deserted by management. 'National committees' took over local public administration, and poor peasants on the Great Plain seized land. This popular movement was to some extent supported by the 'liberating' Red Army.

Yet not all Hungarians greeted the Red Army and social change with open arms. Substantial numbers of civilians were rounded up by the Red Army and deported to the Soviet Union as political prisoners or forced labourers, leading to fear and ill-feeling among local populations, which was fuelled by the widespread rape of civilians by Soviet soldiers. Hungarian society by no means universally supported the popular movements that accompanied 'liberation'. The middle classes, disorientated by their loss of social position, were deeply suspicious and fearful of change. This social tension was to have a profound effect on developments in post-war Hungary.

The Soviet Union felt it had a substantial strategic interest in securing the direction of Hungary's future – and as Hungary was a defeated power the

Soviets could directly intervene in domestic politics through the Allied Control Commission until the signing of the peace treaty in 1947. In 1945 the Soviets sought the creation of a multi-party, anti-fascist government on Hungarian soil. This government included a refounded Communist Party and was established in close consultation with the Soviets, who were directly involved in drawing up the new cabinet and its policies. The government set out by acceding to the demands of the popular movement in the countryside and introduced land reform. This destroyed the great estates, redistributing the land in a way that benefited the poorest among the agricultural population. It also created a parallel security state closely allied to the Communist Party and the Soviet occupiers. The police were reorganized; so-called 'fascist' elements were purged and replaced by members of the left-wing parties. The government also created a political police force under the control of communists and the NKVD (the Soviet secret police at the time). It was extraordinarily active in its first year, having detained some 35,000 people by March 1946.

The first post-war elections in November 1945 proved a severe shock to Hungary's fledgling communists. The most conservative of the anti-fascist parties, the Smallholders' Party, won with 57.03 per cent, compared with 17.41 per cent for the Social Democrats, 16.95 per cent for the Communists, 6.87 per cent for the left-wing National Peasants Party and 1.62 per cent for the liberal Bourgeois Democratic Party. The size of the Smallholders' victory concealed many weaknesses: namely, their lack of control over the security apparatus, their poor organization and the fragile social coalition of forces that had delivered them victory. The party was split into several factions: an intellectual left-wing around Zoltán Tildy, the first post-election Prime Minister and later the President, a centre group around Tildy's eventual successor as Prime Minister, Ferenc Nagy, and a right-wing one.

The defeat of the left was greeted with despair and fury by its working-class supporters. They turned their attack on the conciliatory attitudes of the left-wing parties towards private business and the Smallholders' Party, sharply rejecting the 'popular front' approach. These frustrations were sharpened by hyper-inflation which reduced workers' incomes to negligible proportions during the first half of 1946. On the other hand, the election results increased the confidence of the right within the Smallholders' Party. They were forced into a continued anti-fascist coalition by the Soviets inside the Allied Control Commission. They were also obliged to concede control of the crucial security ministries to communist appointees. Throughout the first part of 1946 politics was ill-tempered. Smallholders complained about the communist domination of the security forces, while the left grew increasingly anxious about the open conservatism of many Smallholders' Party deputies, moving to strengthen its opposition to the 'restoration of reaction' by founding a 'Left Block' within the coalition. Left-wing militancy was mirrored by right-wing militancy that occasionally erupted into violence; the murder of two Soviet soldiers and the discovery of links between anti-Soviet activity and a Catholic youth organization led to heavy-handed police tactics.

The combination of high inflation and extremism on both the left and the right created an ugly situation during 1946 that underlined the problems the Soviets faced in creating a genuine 'popular front' government. Despite their weak position within the government, the communists were able to rely on the Red

Army, the Soviets and their control of the parallel security state to continue with radical anti-fascist measures. This was combined in the political sphere with the employment of the now notorious 'salami tactics' by the communists against right-wing politicians within the Smallholders' Party. 'Salami tactics' meant that the radicalism of the left's constituency was mobilized to demand a continuance of anti-fascist administrative measures. The security forces were used to root out 'conspiracy' among right-wing politicians, and the Communist Party Secretary, Mátyás Rákosi, with consummate political skill and Soviet support was able to bully the Smallholders' Party into accepting new ultimatums. 'Salami tactics' were to ruthlessly destroy the political coalition that the 1945 Smallholders' Party represented by initially forcing the leadership to expel its right-wing and then attack its centre in 1947. The was done through the so-called 'conspiracy against the republic', in which Smallholders' Party plans to create a distinctly right-of-centre government excluding the communists after the conclusion of a peace treaty and Red Army withdrawal were represented as a threat to democracy. The Soviets arrested the Smallholders' Secretary-General, Béla Kovács, and forced Prime Minister Ferenc Nagy into exile.

The collapse of the Smallholders' political coalition necessitated new elections that were held in August 1947. Marred by accusations of extensive fraud, the official election results produced a clear majority for left-wing parties including the rump of the Smallholders' Party. The Communists secured their goal of dominance in the coalition by taking 22.3 per cent of the poll; the Smallholders took 15.4 per cent, the Social Democrats 14.9 per cent, the National Peasants Party 8.3 per cent, and two smaller allies won less than 2 per cent between them. The Communists therefore had succeeded in their goal of establishing a stable popular front coalition, albeit through less than democratic means. Right-wing voters had not gone away and the collapse of the Smallholders' 1945 coalition produced a space which right-wing and confessional parties had been able to fill. Though the elections gave the left hegemony within the state, they emphatically did not reflect hegemony within society. The elections were marred by serious fraud, and the evidence suggests that a true picture of opinion would have shown society evenly divided between the popular front coalition and the conservative opposition.

Coalition government continued until 1949 with the gradual dissolution of other parties. The creation of a single-party dictatorship began in response to the deteriorating international climate in late 1947. 1948 marked 'the year of change' in Hungary with mass nationalization, the introduction of Soviet-style labour competition, the announcement of a collectivization campaign and the forced merger of the Social Democrats with the Communists.

Exercise   Looking at the three cases, how far do you think one can discern a coherent Soviet policy towards eastern Europe? ■

Specimen answer   In all three cases the Soviets certainly attempted to interfere in domestic politics. In Poland the interference was most blatant, in Hungary it used the Allied Control Commission to enforce its will, while in Czechoslovakia Soviet interests were ensured both by the strength of the communists and the pro-Soviet orientation of the coalition government. In all countries democracy was constrained from 1945 by communist control of the security services, the military and key ministries – something demanded by the Soviets.

No real intention to create single-party dictatorships in 1945 can be discerned, and it seems that the Soviets sought more direct control in Poland than in either Czechoslovakia or Hungary. The Soviets certainly wanted pro-Soviet governments in all three countries, but the nature and scope of their intervention was conditioned by the particular circumstances of the different states. A marked shift occurred in 1947–8 in Soviet policy in response to the announcement of Marshall Aid and the growing American role in western Europe that led directly to much greater Soviet control in eastern Europe and the formation of dictatorships. □

Yugoslavia

Yugoslavia was different for two principal reasons. First, it was – along with Albania – the only country where communists subsequently came to power which was not 'liberated' by the Red Army but where the communist partisans emerged from the war victorious. Second, the war in Yugoslavia was not just a struggle against Nazi occupiers but had in fact been a bloody civil war initiated by German dismemberment of Yugoslavia in 1941. These two factors were of decisive importance for the creation of the communist regime.

As the Red Army moved west through Romania and Hungary in autumn 1944, it was Tito's partisans who took Belgrade in November. Even with the defeat of Germany, however, the communists had not suceeded in eliminating armed opposition. Opposition from the remnants of the Ustashi and the Croatian Home Army was not overcome until spring 1945. The partisans' campaign was characterized by extreme violence including the massacre of 30,000 Croatian prisoners in May, and later concluded with mass arrests not only of former Ustashi but of priests and Croatian non-communists. The Chetniks were crushed militarily and their remnants were mopped up by the security services in 1945 and 1946. Kosovar Albanians, fearing that communist government would lead to a return to rule from Belgrade, mounted their own uprising in December 1944. This was brutally crushed in the first half of 1945. Tito sought to legitimize communist power in elections in November 1945. Though the communists enjoyed substantial popular support, the victory of their National Front was aided by electoral irregularities and harassment of non-communist parties. They then moved swiftly to create a one-party dictatorship.

The communists attempted to reconcile the peoples of Yugoslavia with consitutional change while implementing a programme of radical social reform – including land reform and nationalization. The 1946 constitution created a federal Yugoslavia to replace the Belgrade-dominated unitary state of the interwar years. Six constituent republics were created: Bosnia-Hercegovina, Croatia, Macedonia, Montenegro, Serbia and Slovenia. Areas populated by substantial numbers of Serbs were included in other republics, particularly Bosnia, Croatia, Macedonia and Montenegro. Furthermore the multi-ethnic regions of Kosovo and Vojvodina were incorporated into Serbia as autonomous provinces. Campaigns of 'Serbianization' were conducted in both provinces; in Vojvodina deported Germans were replaced with Serb peasants during the 'colonization' of 1946. This balance was to cause tension throughout the life of the second Yugoslavia, as communist attempts to create a common Yugoslav identity through the education system foundered.

Communist control was established and social change went further earlier than in any of the other countries. Tito saw Stalin's post-war policies as overly moderate. Tensions between Moscow and Belgrade had been visible over Tito's support for the communists in Greece before 1947; the Soviet Union saw the support given by Belgrade to communist partisans in Greece as a threat to Soviet policy. Moscow also viewed Belgrade's attempts to pursue an independent foreign policy in south-eastern Europe with some alarm. In March 1948 Stalin withdrew military advisors and accused the Yugoslav communists of being 'undemocratic'. Tito rebutted these accusations, and Yugoslavia was expelled from the Cominform.

Exercise   Briefly compare Yugoslavia to the other three countries. What are the differences between both the timetable of communist takeover and the degree of independence of the regime from Moscow? ■

Specimen answer   The communist regime was created in Yugoslavia by domestic partisans and in no way came about as a result of external intervention. This is crucial to understanding both the timetable of the communist takeover and its independence from Moscow. The Yugoslav communists moved for single-party domination and nationalization immediately, while in the areas liberated by the Red Army change was more gradual. It could be said that the Yugoslav regime was better able to resist the Soviets because it in no way depended on Stalin for its existence. □

Yugoslavia initially moved towards a siege economy in response to the split with Stalin, though by 1953 a different model of socialism to that created in the Soviet bloc was emerging underpinned by aid from the United States and greater toleration of market forces if not of political opposition. In the rest of eastern Europe the Tito–Stalin split resulted in series of show trials and purges designed to ensure conformity in the region's communist parties. The early 1950s were years of forced collectivization, industrialization designed to prepare the Soviet bloc for a war with the United States which was expected by the Soviet leadership, declining living standards and considerable political repression. Though such policies resulted in extensive political unrest across the region in the mid-1950s that threatened the collapse of the regimes, they remained in place – though in substantially modified form – until 1989.

7   THE MEDITERRANEAN

As we saw in section 4, Britain in the immediate post-war world was still a great power but was finding it difficult to maintain that position. A searching appraisal would have revealed that Britain's commitments extended beyond its resources, that its armed forces were overstretched, and that its financial affairs were in a sorry state. Yet, though it was obvious that Britain was no longer in the same league as the United States and the Soviet Union, few – at least until 1947 – drew the conclusion that Britain could not maintain its great power role for much longer. The Americans, who were in the best position to judge the strength of their ally, came to no such conclusions. This was why the message delivered in late February 1947 by the British Ambassador to Washington, Lord Inverchapel, to General Marshall, the Secretary of State, came as a shock. The news that Britain could no longer be responsible for economic aid to Greece and Turkey had the most profound implications for American foreign policy.

Britain's continued military and political role as a great power had enabled Washington to avoid full acceptance of the consequences and responsibilities of its new status as the world's greatest power. The delusion that American troops could be brought home from Europe at the end of World War II had stemmed from the conviction that Britain would be there. Such hopes had waned, but although Roosevelt and Truman had had a certain feeling of moral superiority over Britain, had disapproved of the British Empire, and had been prepared to bully their ally and act against its interests, they had relied on Britain to shoulder responsibility for many strategically important areas and to take on tasks that might be unpopular with American public opinion or that they were too squeamish or too irresolute to take on themselves. South-eastern Europe and the Mediterranean were, in particular, areas that had been regarded as a British sphere of influence.

Roosevelt had written in a memorandum of 21 February 1944: 'I do not want the United States to have the post-war burden of reconstituting France, Italy and the Balkans. This is not our actual task at a distance of 3,500 miles or more. It is definitely a British task in which the British are far more vitally interested than we are.' He went on to say: 'our principal task is not to take part in the internal problems in southern Europe' (quoted in H. Feis, *Churchill, Roosevelt and Stalin*, 1957, p.340). Between 1944 and 1948 the USA was to find itself increasingly driven to take on responsibilities and commitments that it had at first baulked at. But until 1947 the problems of Yugoslavia, Greece and Turkey were largely a British concern.

Exercise Why do you think south-east Europe and the Mediterranean should have seemed naturally a British sphere of interest? ■

Specimen answer
1 Britain had traditionally always given priority to the east Mediterranean as the route to India.
2 Partly for that reason Britain had always taken a close interest in Turkey and the Black Sea Straits.
3 As a great naval power Britain had sought to ensure its naval supremacy in the Mediterranean.
4 The British colonies of Gibraltar, Malta and Cyprus supported a British military presence in the Mediterranean.
5 Britain had given a guarantee to Greece in 1939 and had tried to honour that guarantee in 1940.
6 The possibilities offered by the Italian campaign to press on into eastern Europe had always appealed more to the British than the Americans.
7 Support for the Yugoslavian resistance had largely come from Britain.

Although by 1945 the route to India seemed likely to become a less important British preoccupation, British plans to consolidate its interests in the Middle East, because of the increasing importance of the oilfields, pointed to a continued interest in the Mediterranean. □

Churchill's agreement with Stalin in October 1944 as to spheres of influence had recognized Britain's special interest in south-east Europe, so that Britain was given a putative 50 per cent influence in Yugoslavia and a 90 per cent interest in Greece. That agreement, as we have seen, had been the outcome of Churchill's frustration with Roosevelt's refusal to look beyond the end of the war with Germany and was essentially an attempt at damage limitation. Harold Macmillan, Britain's peripatetic minister in the Mediterranean area, and by November 1944 Acting President of the Allied Commission in Italy and in practice the administrator of Italy, found himself also heavily involved with British policy in Yugoslavia and Greece. He noted in January 1945 that he could count less and less on American assistance: 'the Americans want to "liquidate" as soon as possible the whole situation arising from the war in Europe' (quoted in Horne, *Macmillan*, 1988, p.244).

Macmillan's position and that of General Alexander, Commander-in-Chief in Italy and Supreme Allied Commander of the Mediterranean, underlined the major responsibility of Britain in the region. British policy under Churchill's direction was to support and re-establish the monarchies of Italy, Greece, Albania and Yugoslavia. American pressure, influenced by the republican sympathies of New York Italians, was against the Italian monarchy, and only in Greece was Britain to be successful in implementing a monarchical restoration.

Yugoslavia

Mark Pittaway has discussed Yugoslavia in section 6 in the context of the imposition of the communist regime, but here I wish to discuss Yugoslavia largely in terms of British foreign policy and the balance of power in the Mediterranean area. In the last years of the war Britain directed support to the Yugoslavian resistance from Italy. The war in Yugoslavia was both extremely nasty and extremely complex. The German and Italian forces, aided by the fascist Ustashi in Croatia, had ranged against them two resistance movements: the communist partisans led by Tito and the Chetnik royalists under General Mihailovich (Minister of War in the government-in-exile based in London). These two armies fought each other with as much enthusiasm as they fought the Germans and with considerable brutality and cruelty (recall Clive Emsley's discussion of partisan warfare in section 4 of Unit 20).

Considering that the policy of the British government was to restore the royal government, the switch of British support from Mihailovich to Tito late in 1943 seems odd. It is explained largely by the strange enthusiasm for Tito demonstrated by the largely conservative British intelligence and liaison officers who had contact with the partisans. Tito had an expansive personality and convinced Brigadier Maclean in particular that not only were the communists bearing the brunt of the fighting against the Germans, but their success would help produce 'a strong, democratic and independent Yugoslavia' (he was to be proved right about the independence in the long run, but wrong from the beginning about the democracy). British support for Tito helped ensure that the communists emerged as the most powerful force in Yugoslavia, though the Soviet occupation of parts of the country in September 1944 also played a part. The Titoists were able to make a convincing claim to have been the force that liberated Yugoslavia, though in fact no one liberated Yugoslavia: the Germans withdrew because they had been defeated elsewhere.

British policy was thus contradictory; while on the one hand it sought to support the royal government based in London, on the other it provided arms for the opponents of the government. The compromise of December 1944, by which members of the all-party assembly AVNOJ (Anti-Fascist Council of National Liberation) and six representatives of the government-in-exile were admitted to the communist-dominated government, was largely cosmetic. As we have seen in section 6, there was never a genuine coalition and never any real opportunity for anti-communist associations to organize. In November 1945 this government felt secure enough, having terrorized the population and killed or intimidated much of the opposition, to hold elections in which the communists gained 81 per cent of the vote. The consequences of the election were the abolition of the monarchy and the end of the pretence of pluralism.

In the closing stages of the war Tito's partisans moved into Austrian and Italian territory, into Klagenfurt and Austrian Carinthia and into Trieste and other parts of north-east Italy. A considerable responsibility was then thrown upon General Alexander and Harold Macmillan. Should they make a firm stand against the Yugoslavian communist partisans with forces already depleted by the demands of Greece and with American support in doubt? Macmillan wrote on 9 May 1944:

> I feel that we must be very careful. Neither British nor American troops will care for a new campaign in order to save Trieste for the 'Eyeties'. On the other hand to give in completely may be a sort of slav Munich.
>
> (Quoted in Horne, *Macmillan*, 1988, p.247)

Though Alexander and Macmillan at first found it difficult to get clear orders from London or indications of American support, they stood firm, gaining Churchill's and eventually Truman's support. Tito was told that unless Yugoslavian forces withdrew, Alexander would be asked to take matters into his own hands. Tito conceded on 9 June and began to withdraw. It was against this background that perhaps the most shameful episode of Britain's conduct of the war took place: the forced repatriation of Cossacks and other members of Axis military units to the Soviet Union and of refugees from Yugoslavia to the Titoists. The fact that Alexander's army was overstretched and might at any moment find itself at war with the Yugoslav communists goes some way to explaining, if not excusing, the repatriation. British firmness against the Yugoslavs in both Italy and Austria had a considerable impact on Italian public opinion and played a part in increasing support for the western powers in Italy. Clearly, however, it also reduced any remaining British influence on Yugoslavia. Yet Tito was by no means getting unequivocal support from the Soviet Union at this time.

Tito's achievement was to demonstrate that Stalinism could exist without Stalin, and this did not endear him to the Soviet dictator. The Yugoslav communists had already imposed their own administration and security apparatus on two-thirds of the country by the time the Red Army arrived, and Soviet attempts to penetrate these instruments of control were one of the main reasons for Stalin's eventual break with Tito. It may well have been that Stalin would have preferred to satisfy Churchill and allow King Peter to return. Certainly, Stalin showed little enthusiasm for Yugoslavian ambitions in Austria and Italy. But by 1946 relations between Stalin and Tito were already strained as the Soviet representatives attempted to recruit Yugoslavs for their own security services, while Soviet propaganda which exaggerated the role of Soviet forces in the war in Yugoslavia was unwelcome to the Yugoslav communists. The main reason for the split that was to occur in 1948 was the independence of Tito and the Yugoslav Communist Party – an independence which, as we have seen, had already been noted by Fitzroy Maclean.

Albania

As in Yugoslavia, the partisan forces that opposed the Italian and German occupations were split between monarchists and communists. Enver Hoxha and the communists emerged as the victorious force in 1945. As with Yugoslavia, more British arms seem to have gone to the communists there than to the supporters of King Zog, though this may have had more to do with the infiltration of the Special Operations Executive by the communist agent James Klugman than to London's intentions. Subsequent attempts by the British from 1946 on to take advantage of Albania's long coastline and establish a guerrilla movement within the country seem to have been successively betrayed by communists within the secret services. By 1946 Albania was a people's republic and effective resistance was stamped out.

Greece

In the long run British intervention in 1944 was to ensure the survival of the monarchy and the failure of the Greek Communist Party's bid for power. But it was to prove a long and costly battle. There was an essential continuity of policy towards Greece between the Churchill government and the succeeding Labour administration. Churchill had been steadfast in his support for the Greek monarchy and had committed Britain to maintaining in power a succession of unstable coalition governments. British forces were largely instrumental in crushing the rising by the Greek communist partisans, ELAS, in December 1944, and in maintaining the government's position when ELAS resumed the civil war in 1946.

Churchill went so far as to make a personal visit to Greece, flying to Athens in late December 1944 and helping to establish a government under Archbishop Damaskinos. Churchill wrote:

> When three million men were fighting on either side in the Western Front and vast American forces were deployed against Japan in the Pacific the spasms of Greece may seem petty, but nevertheless they stood at the nerve centre of power, law and freedom of the western world.
>
> (Churchill, *The Second World War*, vol.6, 1985, p.269)

Ernest Bevin was strongly committed to maintaining British support for the Greek government until the threat from ELAS, the armed wing of the Communist Party, was over. During the winter of 1945–6 there were 40,000 British troops in the country. Hugh Thomas describes the British as:

not only the most influential foreign power but, in effect, the rulers of the country appointing and dismissing prime ministers, dictating all departments of state from defence to employment plus arranging for the Secretary General of the British Trade Union Congress, Sir Walter Citrine (fresh from similar lectures in Germany), to suggest how to revive the Greek unions.

(*Armed Truce*, 1986, p.545)

It was indeed suggested by the Australian-born British Ambassador to Greece, Sir Reginald Leeper, that Greece should join the British Commonwealth as a dominion.

The agreement between Stalin and Churchill over Britain's 90 per cent influence in Greece remained intact until the end of the war. There was no Soviet support for the Greek communist uprising in late 1944, and the Yugoslav communists, who had supported the rising to begin with, withdrew – probably on Moscow's insistence. By 1946, however, the Soviet Union was supporting ELAS.

Bevin's declared intention was to promote the establishment of a broad-based coalition in Greece, to provide for free elections, and to withdraw British troops. Nothing, however, polarizes opinion better than a bloody civil war, and the series of governments supported by the British were for the most part governments of the right. They were able to control the towns, but the mountains remained mostly in the hands of ELAS.

There was opposition to the British government's policy in Greece from the left wing of the Labour Party, but the most effective opposition came from Hugh Dalton, the Chancellor of the Exchequer, and was based on economic rather than political grounds. Could Britain afford its Greek policy? Until January 1947 Bevin beat off Dalton's complaints, but then, as Britain's financial problems became overwhelming, gave in. On 30 January Bevin endorsed Dalton's view that Britain should cut its losses in Greece, abandon a commitment which was costed at an additional £50 million, and withdraw British forces.

Turkey

In giving Turkey support against a threat from Russia, Britain was fulfilling the familiar role that had characterized its nineteenth-century foreign policy. Turkey had been persuaded to declare war on Germany in 1945, but had in fact been fairly pro-German and anti-Russian during the greater part of the war. In March 1945 the Soviet Union announced that it was not going to renew the Turko–Soviet Treaty of Friendship signed in 1925, and later in June Molotov demanded the revision of the Treaty of Montreux, which gave Turkey control over the Straits, a Russian base in the Dardanelles, and territorial concessions from Turkey to the Soviet republics of Georgia and Armenia. These demands demonstrate an impressive continuity with Tsarist policy towards Turkey; indeed, one of Molotov's complaints concerning British opposition was to wonder why Britain refused to allow the Soviet Union to have that access to the Straits which it had been prepared to give to the Tsar in the secret Treaty of London of 1915. Ernest Bevin was, if anything, firmer than Churchill in his support for Turkey (Churchill at Potsdam had been prepared to accept a division of Montreux in the Soviet Union's favour): 'I do not want', he said to the House of Commons in 1946, 'Turkey converted into a satellite state' (quoted in Thomas, *Armed Truce*, 1986, p.553).

British support for and aid to Turkey in 1945 and 1946 was important for the future. It linked Turkey securely to the west. Since the 1920s the country had been a one-party state, but now it sought to align its political system to that of the western powers, allowing the opposition Democratic Party to be formed. In the post-war world Turkey would need to maintain a large army to confront the obvious Russian designs on its territory, and it would need allies. Turkey's role in NATO was foreshadowed. Indeed, British policy in this period did much to tie two strategically important but mutually antagonistic partners, Turkey and Greece, to the future western alliance.

The last *pax Britannica*

British interest and involvement in south-east Europe and the Mediterranean in 1947 was not, any more than it had been in the nineteenth century, for the sake of that area alone. In the past British concern had centred on controlling the route to India. It was now the Middle East that was Britain's main concern. Bevin, fully appreciative of the importance of the Middle East oilfields and the vulnerability of Iran and the Arab world to Soviet penetration, saw the importance of the Mediterranean in terms of maintaining Britain's position in the Middle East (Britain, the United States and the Soviet Union all had troops in Persia/Iran in 1945, and it was there that the Soviet Union made its only move to seize new territory when it attempted to detach Persian Azerbaijan). A British sphere of influence thus stretched through the Mediterranean to the Middle East. It was a heavy commitment for the medium-sized power that Britain had in reality become.

Richard Mayne has succinctly summarized Britain's position:

> Living on rapidly dwindling credit, Britain was at the same time bearing heavy overseas burdens. Not only Greece and Turkey, but a number of other countries, were dependent on her aid. In 1946 it had spent 60 million dollars on feeding the German people, however inadequately; in the first quarter of 1947 it was to spend 60 million dollars more. Around the globe ... British soldiers were still acting as policemen – against Communists in Greece, against the Zionist *Irgun Zvei Leumi* in Palestine, between Hindus and Muslims in India. Nearly two years after the end of World War II there were still a million and a half men in the services, while at home the available manpower was 630,000 short of Britain's needs.
>
> (*The Recovery of Europe*, 1970, pp.97–8)

The announcement that military and economic aid to Greece and Turkey would have to be suspended forthwith marked Britain's withdrawal from great power status. The implication for the United States was that, if the Soviet Union and communism were going to be contained, they could not rely upon Britain to be in the front line. The atavistic reaction of the United States at the end of the war was to retreat from European commitment; lend-lease was terminated, it was hoped to bring the troops home, and in 1946 a Republican majority in Congress called for cuts in taxes and military expenditure. Such actions, rather like Britain's commitments, were echoes of the past. America's giant economic strength had inevitably to be translated into political and military muscle if it was to further its foreign policy aims and ideological preferences outside the American continent. The chimera of Britain's continued great power status had helped to enable US policy-makers to avoid, at least in public, the full consequences of its foreign policy aims. No doubt the essentials of what became the Truman Doctrine were already implicit in the reality of US policy, but that doctrine, enunciated under the pressure of threatened British withdrawal from Greece, made explicit that the US was now a power with world-wide responsibilities. It also heightened the ideological dimension of the divisions that had taken place in Europe since 1945; it was not possible to convince American public opinion of the necessity for US spheres of influence, but it was possible to enthuse it for a world-wide conflict between expansionist communism and western free democracy. The Truman Doctrine proclaimed on 11 March 1947 was to the effect that the United States would henceforth take over the burden of military aid to Greece, Turkey and other potential victims of Soviet aggression. In fact, a British military presence was maintained in Greece until 1950, but it was clear from March 1947 that not only had the line between two Europes been firmly drawn, but the containment of Soviet expansion was to be underwritten by the United States.

8 THE ICE HARDENS

As we have seen, the need to help Greece led to the wider policy of the Truman Doctrine of support for other potential victims of Soviet penetration: 'I believe that it must be the policy of the United States to support free peoples who are resisting attempted subjugation by armed minorities or by outside pressures' (12 March 1947, quoted in McCauley, *Origins of the Cold War*, 1995, p.138). The Truman Doctrine was followed by the Marshall Plan, proposed on 5 June 1947.

So far US policy had been to rely primarily on economic support and diplomacy to prevent the extension of communist power, though military force and the atom bomb were in reserve. The events of 1948 and 1949 led to a reappraisal and a new emphasis upon the need for defence. The imposition of complete communist rule on Czechoslovakia in February 1948 and the blockade of Berlin during 1948 and 1949 led the western European states (Britain, France, Luxemburg, the Netherlands and Belgium) to conclude the Brussels Treaty of 17 March 1948, which provided for defence against any aggressor, not simply renewed German aggression as had been provided for by the Treaty of Dunkirk of 4 March 1947. It was apparent, however, that American participation was essential to the defence of non-communist Europe. The American tradition of isolationism combined with constitutional problems still stood in the way of the United States entering into a military alliance in time of peace, but this was made possible by the Vandenberg Resolution adopted by the Senate on 11 June 1948. This gave bipartisan congressional support for an American alliance policy within the UN framework to meet any communist threat. It made possible the association of the USA, together with Canada, with the western European states in the North Atlantic Treaty of 4 April 1949.

The actual potential enemy is not named in the North Atlantic Treaty, and the preamble asserts simply the 'determination to safeguard the freedom, common heritage and civilization of their peoples, founded on the principles of democracy, individual liberty and the rule of law', but it was clear enough whom it was aimed at. Article 5 proclaimed that 'an armed attack against one or more of them in Europe or North America shall be considered an attack against them all', while Article 6 deemed such an attack to include one against the 'occupation armed forces of any party in Europe', thus making it clear that the treaty covered the territory of the Federal German Republic and West Berlin (Grenville, *The Major International Treaties*, 1974, pp.335–6).

It was not until May 1955 that the Soviet Union and its satellites formed the Warsaw Pact. If this was a response to NATO, it was a delayed response. In fact, it was rather a response to the crisis in Soviet-controlled eastern Europe in the wake of Stalin's death and to the Paris Agreements of October 1954, by which the western powers agreed to the restoration of sovereignty to the Federal Republic and provided for the entry of West Germany into NATO. By 1949 the Soviet Union had ostensibly defensive treaties with all its satellites, while the Soviet influence in each state made these symbolic rather than legal agreements. Stalin was quite capable of exercising control with or without paper contracts. Comecon (the Council of Mutual Economic Assistance), established in January 1949, was a response to the west's OEEC (Organization for European Economic Cooperation) of April 1948, but as J. A. S. Grenville states, 'was little more than a paper organisation until the death of Stalin on 5 March 1953; it had only met twice before the Dictator's death' (*The Major International Treaties*, 1974, p.354). By 1955 the first in a series of upheavals in the eastern European socialist states had taken place and West Germany was a member of NATO. Although the Warsaw Pact largely formalized existing arrangements as the armies of the east European socialist states had been re-equipped and placed under Soviet command in 1952, its inauguration was an important statement that Soviet control of eastern Europe had outlived Stalin and that the bloc was welded into a military alliance opposing NATO.

Exercise   At which date do you consider we can conclude that the Cold War – as opposed to merely poor and worsening relations between the western Allies and the Soviet Union – can be said to have begun? ■

Specimen answer   Possible answers include:
and discussion
(a) The last years of the Second World War with the increasing divisions between the Allies, especially over Poland.

(b) The period 1945–7, which saw irreconcilable differences over Germany, the strengthening of communist and Soviet influence in states within the Soviet sphere, and in 1947 the Truman Doctrine and the Marshall Plan.

(c) 1948, the year which saw the end of any semblance of pluralism in Czechoslovakia and the beginning of the Berlin blockade.

(d) 1949, the year which saw the establishment of NATO.

(e) 1955, the year which saw the establishment of the Warsaw Pact.

I would plump for 1948. One can certainly point to worsening relations and even irreconcilable differences during the last years of the war, but military cooperation continued and political cracks were papered over. The period 1945–7 certainly saw an embryonic Cold War with mutual suspicions mounting, but the after-glow of wartime cooperation still prevented frost becoming ice. The events of 1947 may have had much to do with the crisis year of 1948, but it is with the end of limited democracy in Czechoslovakia and the beginning of the Berlin blockade that I would see the onset of full Cold War. The formation of the NATO Alliance in 1949 was essentially the recognition by the USA that a Cold War existed, while, as we have seen, the formation of the Warsaw Pact was more a declaration that the Cold War had not ended with Stalin than a new departure. □

References

Brzezinski, Z. K. (1960) *The Soviet Bloc: Unity and Conflict,* Harvard University Press (third edn 1971).

Charmley, J. (1995) *Churchill's Grand Alliance: The Anglo-American Special Relationship,* Hodder and Stoughton.

Churchill, W. S. (1985) *The Second World War,* 6 vols, Penguin.

Conquest, R. (1999) *Reflections on a Ravaged Century,* John Murray.

Davies, N. (1981) *God's Playground: A History of Poland,* 2 vols, Oxford University Press.

Dockrill, M. (1988) *The Cold War 1945–1963,* Macmillan.

Feis, H. (1957) *Churchill, Roosevelt and Stalin: The War They Waged and the Peace They Sought,* Oxford University Press.

Gati, C. (1986) *Hungary and the Soviet Bloc,* Duke University Press.

Gildea, R. (1996) *France since 1945,* Oxford University Press.

Grenville, J. A. S. (1974) *The Major International Treaties 1914–1973,* Methuen.

Gross, J. T. (1979) *Polish Society under German Occupation: The Generalgouvernement, 1933–1944,* Princeton University Press.

Gross, J. T. (1989) 'Social consequences of war: preliminaries to the study of imposition of communist regimes in east-central Europe', *East European Politics and Societies,* vol.3, no.2. pp.198–214.

Horne, A. (1988) *Macmillan, vol.1, 1894–1956: The Making of a Prime Minister,* Macmillan.

Jones, J. M. (1955) *The Fifteen Weeks (February 21–June 4 1947),* Viking.

Kennedy, P. (1985) *The Realities Behind Diplomacy: Background Influences on British External Policy 1865–1980,* Fontana.

Kennedy, P. (1988) *The Rise and Fall of the Great Powers,* London, Unwin Hyman.

Kolko, J. and Kolko, G. (1972) *The Limits of Power: The World and United States Foreign Policy 1945–54,* Harper and Row.

McCauley, M. (1995) *The Origins of the Cold War 1941–49,* Longman (second edn).

Mayne, R. (1970) *The Recovery of Europe: From Devastation to Unity*, Harper and Row.

Mazower, M. (1999) *Dark Continent: Europe's Twentieth Century*, Penguin.

Myant, M. (1981) *Socialism and Democracy in Czechoslovakia 1945–1948*, Cambridge University Press.

Rupnik, J. (1988) *The Other Europe*, Weidenfeld and Nicolson.

Seton-Watson, H. (1950) *The East European Revolution*, Westview Press (reissue of third edn 1985).

Siracusa, J. M. (ed.) (1978) *The American Diplomatic Revolution*, Open University Press.

Suvarov, V. (1990) *The Icebreaker: Who Started the Second World War?*, Hamish Hamilton.

Swain, G. and Swain, N. (1993) *Eastern Europe since 1945*, Macmillan.

Thomas, H. (1986) *Armed Truce: The Beginnings of the Cold War 1945–46*, Hamish Hamilton.

Zamoyski, A. (1987) *The Polish Way: A Thousand Year History of the Poles and Their Culture*, John Murray.

Further reading

Coutovidis, J. and Reynolds, J. (1986) *Poland 1939–1947*, Leicester University Press.

Draper, T. (1988) 'Neo-conservative history', in D. Carlton and H. M. Levine (eds) *The Cold War Debated*, McGraw-Hill.

Loth, W. (1988) *The Division of the World 1941–1955*, trans. C. Krojzlova, Routledge and Kegan Paul.

Oppen, B. R. von (1955) *Documents on Germany under Occupation 1945–54*, Oxford University Press.

Purdue, A. W. (1999) *The Second World War*, Macmillan.

Swain, G. and Swain, N. (1993) *Eastern Europe since 1945*, Macmillan.

Unit 27 THE TWO GERMANIES 1945–55

ANNIKA MOMBAUER

Open University students of this unit will need to refer to:

Course Reader: *Total War and Historical Change: Europe 1914–1955*, eds Clive Emsley, Arthur Marwick and Wendy Simpson, Open University, 2000

Primary Sources 2: Interwar and World War II, eds Arthur Marwick and Wendy Simpson, Open University, 2001

Secondary Sources, eds Arthur Marwick and Wendy Simpson, Open University, 2000

Maps Booklet

CHRONOLOGY

1945

February	Allied conference at Yalta (Crimea)
30 April	Hitler commits suicide in the State Chancellery in Berlin
8 May	VE Day. Germany's unconditional surrender
5 June	Allies assume supreme power in Germany. Allied Control Council established in Berlin
1–3 July	British and American troops withdraw from parts of the Soviet zone
17 July–2 August	Allied conference at Potsdam – agreement on decartellization, demilitarization, denazification and democratization of Germany
7 August	France joins Control Council
3–10 September	Land reforms begin in Soviet zone
20 November	International Military Tribunal opens at Nuremberg

1946

26 March	Allied Control Council agrees industrial plan on level of post-war German industrial production. All excess to go towards reparations. Steel production restricted to 5.8 million tons
21–22 April	Forced fusion of KPD (Communist Party) and SPD (Socialist Party) to form SED (*Sozialistische Einheitspartei* or Socialist Unity Party) in Soviet zone
16 October	Several leading Nazis sentenced to death at Nuremberg

1947

1 January	British and American zones are fused to create the 'Bizone'
10 February	Peace treaties are signed by the Allies with Bulgaria, Finland, Hungary, Italy and Romania
5 June	Announcement of European Recovery Programme (ERP or Marshall Plan)
2 July	Soviet Union declines participation in ERP
28 October	Anti-communist campaign in American zone

1948

1 June	Six Power conference in London. US, Britain, Belgium, France, the Netherlands and Luxembourg agree to establish a (West) German federal state
18–26 June	Currency reform in American, British and French zones; introduction of Deutschmark in the west. Currency reform in Soviet zone; introduction of the *Mark der deutschen Notenbank*
24 June	Soviet Union reacts to western Allies' plan of introducing currency reform in western sections of Berlin with a blockade of all land routes to Berlin. Allies respond with airlift on 26 June. Berlin supplied from the air for almost one year

1949

8 May	West Germany's 'Basic Law' constituted
14 August	Elections for the first German Bundestag (new federal parliament). CDU/CSU (Conservatives or Christian Democrats) 31 per cent, SPD (Social Democrats) 29.2 per cent, FDP (Liberal Democrats) 11.9 per cent of the votes
12 September	Theodor Heuss elected Federal President
14 September	Konrad Adenauer elected Federal Chancellor
7 October	Proclamation of German Democratic Republic's Constitution
12 October	First East German government announced. Otto Grotewohl is Prime Minister, Wilhelm Pieck President
3 November	Bundestag decides on Bonn as the new capital of West Germany

1950

1 March	End of food rationing in West Germany (except sugar)
June	Outbreak of Korean War
12–14 September	Western Allies' foreign ministers meet in New York. Agreement to end state of war with Germany, revision of Occupation Statute, but continued opposition to rearmament
1 October	East Germany becomes member of COMECON (Council for Mutual Economic Assistance)
19 December	West German rearmament agreed to in principle by NATO (North Atlantic Treaty Organization) council in Brussels

1951

6 March	First revision of Occupation Statute. West Germany has conditional right to conduct its own foreign policy
15 March	Adenauer becomes acting Foreign Minister
2 May	West Germany becomes full member of Council of Europe
9 July	Britain formally ends state of war with Germany
24 October	US does the same. However, there is no peace treaty

1952

10 March	'Stalin note' – offered German reunification if Germany did not become member of any military alliance with US. Eventually rejected by western Allies and by Adenauer

1953

5 March	Stalin's death
9 June	Announcement of 'New Course' in East Germany
17 June	Several days of unrest culminate in uprising in East Germany suppressed by authorities

1954

25 March	The Soviet Union recognizes East Germany as a sovereign state
14 June	Four West Berliners sentenced in East Berlin for allegedly organizing the 'fascist putsch' of 17 June 1953
28 September–3 October	London conference. US, Belgium, Britain, Canada, France, Italy, Luxembourg, the Netherlands and West Germany agree on German rearmament within NATO. Restoration of West German sovereignty, founding of West European Union (WEU)

1955

8 May	West Germany becomes formal member of NATO and WEU
8–13 September	Adenauer visits Soviet Union. Release of thousands of German prisoners of war as a result of the visit

INTRODUCTION

On 8 May 1945, the Second World War was over for those fighting in Europe. Nazi Germany was defeated, and the cost of the war had been devastating. Historians estimate that it claimed a total of 60 million lives worldwide (25 million in the Soviet Union alone, 6 million in Poland, and more than 6 million murdered in extermination camps). Germany lost 4 million lives, and the country lay in ruins (*Die Fischer Chronik Deutschland 1949–99*, 1999, p.14). This unit examines the nature of that defeat, and the problems both victors and vanquished faced in the immediate post-war years. On the one hand, the Allies were confronted with inestimable difficulties: how were they to deal with the defeated aggressor, how should Germany be punished, how should its future be constructed? Their task became increasingly difficult in the light of the growing antagonism between the Soviet Union and the western Allies. On the other hand, Germany had to cope with defeat, physical destruction, occupation and partition.

We will examine first of all how Germany came to be divided, how the Allies imagined Germany's future, and how a new democracy developed in the western zones of occupation. At the same time, as will be seen, the increasing tension between east and west – the beginning of what would become known as the Cold War – spelt a very different fate for the eastern zone of occupation: a democracy by name but in reality Germany's second dictatorship of the twentieth century (although some might even argue that the years 1916–18 constituted a further period of dictatorship – see Unit 6 on the nature of the First World War).

In keeping with the overall concerns of the course, the important questions that we will address in this unit concern social change. We will ask what challenges presented themselves to the survivors of the war in Germany, and how they managed to establish a new life out of the destruction left behind by years of fighting. How, if at all, did they address their recent past and deal with the legacy of the war? What were the main social and economic problems that the two new states had to deal with, and what solutions were found? How could a stable democracy develop out of such unpromising beginnings in the west, and how could a communist regime establish itself successfully in the east? How did life in the new Federal Republic in the west differ from that in the German Democratic Republic in the east? Rather a long list of questions, you may think. Many of them are, of course, interrelated and not all of them will be examined in the same amount of detail, but an awareness of the range of issues is essential in understanding the history of the two Germanies.

The period of time under investigation can be divided roughly into two. The first, 1945–9, ranges from Germany's defeat to the formal division and encompasses the time in which Germany was under Allied occupation. The second, 1949–55, is the time when the two Germanies drifted apart and finally became consolidated as separate states. This is also the time of the 'economic miracle' which helped West Germans finally put the war behind them, while for East Germans the establishment of a communist regime led to a recovery along very different lines. However, the themes with which the unit is concerned do not divide so neatly into two periods: while defeat, occupation and partition fall within the first and the consolidation of the two separate states into the latter, a number of the themes span both sections, such as the refugee problem or the difficult task for Germans of coming to terms with their recent past.

The history of post-war Germany is also the history of the beginning of the Cold War, and Germany's important position in between the two rival powers – the US and the Soviet Union – plays a crucial part in the developments that we are examining in this unit. The Allies' early concerns of punishment and retaliation were soon replaced in the west by a desire to ensure that Germany remained a 'western' country, and that the Soviet Union was hindered from expanding westwards. To achieve this goal, West Germany's economic recovery and political stability had to be ensured. From the Soviet Union's perspective, similar concerns about securing its zone of occupation against a perceived threat from the west determined its approach to the 'German question'. As we will see, its policy was also motivated by a desire for reparations for the damage inflicted on the Soviet Union by Germany. By imposing a political system akin to its own, the Soviet Union effected the development of a very different East German state.

The unit concludes in 1955: a date that spelt the end of the transitional period, when both German states were granted full sovereignty. The German Democratic Republic (GDR) became a member of the Warsaw Pact and COMECON, while the Federal Republic of Germany (FRG) became a member of NATO. The division of Germany seemed complete, although it would take until 1961 for the building of the Berlin Wall to spell the end of German reunification dreams, and until the early 1970s for the two Germanies finally to recognize each other. That reunification would eventually be achieved was not foreseeable by the time the two separate Germanies assumed their different identities, nor did those who wished for it to happen anticipate the countless problems that reunification would bring in its wake when it finally became reality following the momentous events of 1989.

At the end of this unit, you should understand:

- the problems faced by the victors vis-à-vis a totally defeated Germany;

- the problems faced by Germans in coming to terms with the effects of defeat, such as occupation, physical destruction, social and economic hardship, and the anguish of discovering the truth about the crimes committed during the 'Third Reich';

- how the recovery of Germany from such unpromising beginnings was achieved;

- how the onset of the Cold War led to the establishment of two separate and ideologically opposed German states.

Exercise   Your first task in this unit is simply to acquaint yourself with the political developments that led from the end of the war to the establishment of two German states. Begin by reading Lothar Kettenacker's second chapter, 'Drifting apart: the two republics', from *Germany since 1945* in your *Secondary Sources*. In addition, I have included a chronology of political events which you can refer to. You should also consult the *Maps Booklet* to acquaint yourself with Germany's new borders, as well as with the division into four zones of occupation. ■

1   GERMANY DEFEATED

In *Mein Kampf* Hitler had prophesied that in future Germany would either be a world power or cease to exist at all. At the end of the Second World War the latter had seemingly come true. His policy of 'all or nothing' had led to the total destruction of Germany (W. Jacobmeyer, 'Die Niederlage von 1945', 1976, p.13). Whereas in 1918 a ceasefire had spelt the end of the war before enemy troops had entered German territory, in 1945 total war ended in Germany's unconditional surrender and was followed by total defeat and occupation. The unprecedented extent of the defeat and of the destruction has rightly been described as 'the absolute low-point of German history in modern times' (R. Hansen, quoted in Jacobmeyer, p.11). The heavily industrialized Ruhr area, for example, appeared to a British observer as 'the greatest heap of rubble the world has ever seen' (quoted in Kettenacker, *Germany since 1945*, 1997, p.5). Such descriptions can hardly capture adequately the misery of the post-war years. To some commentators, this total destruction appeared as the 'zero hour', a tabula rasa from which a completely new beginning would have to be found. The survivors faced the immediate and urgent task of rebuilding their lives, making towns habitable again, literally picking up the pieces and starting from scratch – in that sense, at least, this was the 'zero hour' (*die Stunde Null*) for most Germans. (The end of Video 2 has some footage on this.)

However, the defeat of 1945 did not really amount to such a completely new beginning. There were more continuities and remnants from the previous Germany than the term 'zero hour' suggests. After all, it was mainly the political regime that had collapsed; in many other respects post-war Germany was not necessarily so different, although in the immediate post-war chaos such continuities might have been difficult to identify. There were, in fact, many continuities: for example, in economic and social structures, the arts and the areas broadly defined as culture. German pride in their nation of *Dichter und Denker* (poets and thinkers) was more important than ever in the face of the barbarism committed in Germany's name. Moreover, not everywhere was equally affected by the post-war chaos. Rural areas emerged from the war largely unscathed, and life continued in some places as though nothing had happened (Kettenacker, p.35), though this was not the case in areas where large numbers of refugees were settled.

The real continuity, however, was that of the people themselves. In Lothar Kettenacker's words: 'Of *Führer, Volk und Reich* (leader, people and empire), only the people had survived, though in a state of shock and disarray' (p.1).

Bombed Dresden in 1949. (Photo: Richard Peters, courtesy of Bildarchiv Preussischer Kulturbesitz, Berlin)

These people, the survivors of the Second World War, were the ones who faced the task of rebuilding Germany, of creating a new German state out of the ashes of the old one. But if 'the people' survived the 'Third Reich', so did certain traditions, attitudes and institutions (such as Germany's giant firms and the churches) which had preceded it. In part, at least, it was almost an instinctive reaction to cling to the familiar and to what little one had been able to save in the face of destruction and total defeat.

Historians have debated the role of the Allies in creating such continuities and breaks with the past as a result of their policies. In the western zones of occupation, for example, existing anti-fascist groups were disbanded, and the development of trade unions and social democratic organizations was hindered in favour of employers' associations and right-wing organizations. The failure to carry out denazification fairly and comprehensively (in both eastern and western zones) could be regarded as another way in which continuities were fostered or a clearer break with the past avoided (M. Fulbrook, *The Two Germanies*, 1992, pp.14–15). We will examine the process of denazification in some detail below.

May 1945 – defeat or liberation?

Of course, for many the events following 8 May 1945 – the unconditional surrender and the occupation of Germany in its wake – did not mean defeat but liberation from the National Socialist regime. This was true for political prisoners, resisters to the regime, prisoners of war, forced labourers and prisoners in concentration camps. The end of war was thus simultaneously occupation and liberation, an important point to keep in mind when considering this time in German history.

Exercise Read the following eyewitness accounts of Germany's defeat in May 1945. What information do they contain about Germany at the very end of the war? How do the views of victors and vanquished differ?

C. F. Melville, diplomatic correspondent for the London *Evening News*, writing on 8 May 1945:

This is the first time in history that a Great Power has emerged from a war in such a state of utter disintegration; but it is a condition of affairs inherent in the situation which the German themselves have created.

(Quoted in Martin Gilbert, *The Day the War Ended*, 1996, p.243)

Editorial in *The Times*, 8 May 1945:

In a score of great cities of Germany scarcely a building stands intact; the Russian armies have swept like an avenging hurricane over the shattered avenues and palaces of Berlin. In the factories where, through the length and breadth of the Reich, all the resources of a rich and populous nation were harnessed, even in times of peace, to the making of engines of destruction, the wheels of industry have stopped. The fields are left untilled by the liberation of the foreign slaves upon whose labour German agriculture had come to depend. Famine and pestilence lower over Germany; only by the efforts of her conquerors can she hope to escape or moderate their ravages. More terrible in the perspective of the human story even than the material ruin is the universal execration that the years of domination have earned for the German name. The Third Reich goes down to destruction unmourned, even by those nations which in the time of its prosperity were content to appear its friends.

(Quoted in Gilbert, p.243)

Anna Hummel, a former Nazi, recalls the defeat from a German point of view:

There won't be any more dying, any more raids. It's over. But then the fear set in of what would happen afterwards. We were spiritually and emotionally drained. Hitler's doctrines were discredited. And then the desperation set in of realising that it all had been for nothing, and that was a terrible feeling. Surviving, finding something to eat and drink, was less difficult for me than the psychological emptiness. It was incomprehensible that all this was supposed to be over, and that it had all been for nothing.

(Quoted in Gilbert, p.245)

**A German woman remembers the end of the war as a young girl
in the city of Breslau in Silesia:**

When the Russians were approaching, in the winter of 1944, we couldn't get out of the city. For three months we were under siege, with continuous shellings, and we took shelter in the cellar. Food was scarce. All the women were in favour of surrendering, but women didn't count. On May 2, a local newspaper announced that Hitler was dead, so the demand for surrender increased. The women turned for support to the priests, who promised to speak to the officers. On the morning of May 7, there was complete silence all around. We realized that the fighting was over, and that the Russians would be coming soon.

The Russian soldiers reached our cellar the next morning, May 8. Women of all ages were raped openly, in sight of everyone, including their own small children. A drunken soldier pushed me to the floor and raped me, but he was only the first. The next day the women didn't ask one another, 'Were you raped?', they just asked: 'How many times?'

(Quoted in Gilbert, p.244) ■

Specimen answers and discussion The accounts give a sense of the scale and nature of the devastation that Germans faced in 1945, as well as providing testimony of the serious consequences the end of the war had on certain members of the German population, in this case on women in particular. The foreign observers (the first two commentators) described the state of Germany on the day the war ended. Both found themselves almost unable to describe the scenes in Germany to their readers, and both agreed that Germany only had itself to blame for the condition in which it found itself. You might have noticed the language used in the editorial as being particularly evocative. There is talk of armies sweeping 'like an avenging hurricane over the shattered avenues and palaces', of 'famine and pestilence' descending upon Germany – a truly apocalyptic scene. Interestingly, the author already recognized the importance of the Allies' role in shaping Germany's future: 'only by the efforts of her conquerors can [Germany] hope to escape or moderate' the dangers it faced.

The German perspective, not suprisingly, is different. Their concerns, first and foremost, are about survival. The overwhelming feeling described by the first witness is one of emptiness, of failing even to be relieved that the horrors of war were finally over. Now there was the fear of what the future held, of the almost certain retribution that the Allies would demand, and the realization that all sacrifices had been in vain. Anna Hummel describes her overwhelming feeling as 'psychological emptiness', of being 'spiritually and emotionally drained'. Worse still was the experience of the young Breslau woman, who shared the fate of thousands of German women in the eastern territories who were at the mercy of the Red Army. We have no way of knowing just how many women were victims of such violence, although it is possible that up to two million women shared this terrible ordeal (N. Naimark, *The Russians in Germany*, 1995, p.133). War had brutalized society, and it was by no means just soldiers who suffered the terrible consequences. □

Despite the unimaginable fates of millions of people, they carried on rebuilding their lives in the chaos left behind by war and tried to get along with their new leaders. In the next section we will look at the Allies' policy towards Germany. The most pressing question facing the victors was how to deal with the former aggressor now that the country had been so devastatingly defeated.

Allied plans for Germany's future

During the war, at the Allied conferences of Tehran (29 November–1 December 1943) and Yalta (4–11 February 1945), the Allies had already discussed the problem of what to do with Germany when it was finally defeated. At Yalta, Roosevelt, Churchill and Stalin agreed that Germany would be divided into three zones of occupation. (Later, a fourth French zone would be formed out of the Anglo-American territory.) The establishment of an Allied Control Council in Berlin as a body for governing all of Germany was decided upon. The Allies agreed that National Socialism and militarism were to be eradicated; Germany was to be disarmed, demilitarized and denazified. Its industry was to be strictly controlled to avoid German rearmament. It was further agreed that Germany would have to pay reparations for the damage inflicted by it on other nations. In the summer of 1944, the complete deindustrialization and reagrarianization of Germany was proposed by the US Secretary of the Treasury, Henry Morgenthau. Although the Morgenthau Plan was not implemented following strong objections in the US media and among politicians, the idea of deindustrialization none the less found its way into the Potsdam agreement, as we will see below (K. Hardach, *Political Economy of Germany*, 1976, pp.91ff.).

When Germany was finally defeated in May 1945, it was the victors' task to come to a definite agreement about its future. The realization of the terrible suffering that the war had brought on to soldiers and civilians alike, and the discovery of the full and awful extent of the Holocaust, led to an understandable desire to ensure that Germany would never again be able to unleash a war. When the victorious powers met in Potsdam just outside Berlin for their third Allied conference from 17 July to 2 August 1945 (at that time Berlin was too badly destroyed to allow such a meeting to take place), they defined their views on how to deal with Germany, and they specified their immediate and long-term aims for the country's future. While cooperation between the Allies had still seemed possible at Yalta, by the time they met again at Potsdam in the summer tensions had begun to develop between them. The conference at Potsdam occurred, in a way, in between war and peace, because while the war in Europe was ended politically at the conference, it failed to lay the ground for a lasting peace (C. Klessmann, *Die doppelte Staatsgründung*, 1984, p.31). Unbeknown to the participants, the next, 'cold', war was about to begin. During the course of further Allied conferences (at London, 10 September to 2 October 1945; Paris, 24 April to 16 May 1946; Moscow, 10 March to 24 April 1947), the divisions between the Allies became increasingly unbridgeable, particularly regarding the question of reparations and the nature of the future administration of Germany. The fifth and last conference took place in London (25 November to 15 December 1947). The fate of Germany was by now inextricably linked to the increasing tensions between the powers of east and west, and the partition of Germany into two separate states was the result of this new international conflict.

Britain and America realized relatively quickly that restraint would be needed vis-à-vis the former enemy once victory had been achieved. In fact, as early as August 1941, Churchill had summed up the new policy following a meeting with Roosevelt: 'We now take the view that impoverished neighbours are bound to be bad neighbours, and we wish to see everyone prosperous, including the Germans. In short, our aim is to make Germany "fat but impotent"' (quoted in Kettenacker, *Germany since 1945*, 1997, p.80). In January 1945 a British Cabinet paper advised that 'Germany must be encouraged to aim at being a super-Sweden, better planned and healthier than any other State ever was before, with better social, medical and educational services and a higher standard of living than any State ever had' (quoted in Kettenacker, p.5). Clearly, the authors of this paper realized that the stability of post-war Germany would depend to a large degree on economic and social provisions, and that it would be important to keep the Germans happy. Stability would not grow out of discontent, and the disaster of Versailles should not be repeated. Hence the apparent leniency. Britain was also concerned that it would have to carry the responsibility for keeping a starving Germany alive, a burden it could ill afford. In the event, having to support Germany after the war was a severe strain on Britain, which even had to introduce bread rationing *after* the war.

A policy of revenge would not achieve a lasting peace. However, Russia and France, the two countries of these four which had been invaded and occupied by Germany, were less inclined to think long term and more keen to satisfy their own demands for reparations, as well as ensure (in France's case) that their belligerent German neighbour would never again be in a powerful enough position to be able to endanger European peace. On this point, the other three Allies also agreed. Germany would have to be treated in such a way that war would never again originate from its aggression. To achieve this goal, forces from the three main Allies – Britain, the United States and Soviet Union – would occupy Germany. In February 1945, at the conference in Yalta, it was agreed that France would participate in the occupation and administration of Germany. There was a basic agenda for dealing with the former enemy on which the principal Allies agreed, as laid down by the Protocol of the Proceedings of the Potsdam Conference of 2 August 1945.

Exercise   Examine the excerpts from the Protocol of the Proceedings of the Potsdam Conference of 2 August 1945 (*Primary Sources 2: Interwar and World War II*, Document II.24), and try to work out the Allies' goals in 1945. It is difficult, of course, to approach such a document without the benefit of hindsight. We know that the onset of the Cold War would soon destroy the hopes of cooperation between the Allied powers, but try to ignore what you know about the years following the Potsdam meeting when you look at the document. In studying the document, try to address the following questions:

1   What was the purpose of the agreement, and what were the intentions of the Allies?

2   How long was the period of Allied occupation to last?

3   Thinking back to the Treaty of Versailles, how does this agreement differ? Do you detect any lessons having been learnt from Versailles?

4   How would you sum up the main aims of the Allies in dealing with Germany? ■

Specimen answers and discussion

1   The document affirms that the Allies were in occupation of the whole of Germany. One of the purposes of the occupation was for the Germans to atone for the crimes committed in their name and by them. The purpose of coming to this agreement was to extirpate German militarism and Nazism, the forces that had led to the war. An explicit future goal of the Allies was to ensure that Germany would never again be able to threaten its neighbours or the peace of the world.

2   The treaty states that the aim of the Allies was to allow Germany eventually to reconstruct its identity on a democratic and peaceful basis. It was hoped that it would be able to take a place among other free and peaceful nations 'in due course'. You might have noticed the lack of any specific time-scale given either for the period of occupation or for the time when Germany might be allowed to rejoin the diplomatic community. Indeed, all the aims are formulated in a rather general and imprecise way.

3   Making the Germans realize that they had been completely defeated and that they were responsible for their own fate was seen as another important task. It was considered imperative that the inevitable economic and social chaos following Germany's defeat would be understood by Germans as resulting from their own government's actions. In this way, it was hoped that a repetition of the post-1918 scenario could be avoided. The economic hardship of the interwar years had largely been blamed on the Allies and the enforced reparations, and Germans had been able to ignore or deny their own responsibility in starting the war and in causing the misery they were suffering as a result of it. In 1945 making the Germans realize that they had only themselves to blame for the suffering they were enduring was high on the agenda. The document suggests that the Allies were consciously trying to avoid a repetition of the mistakes of Versailles.

4   Some of the main aims of the occupation are listed under the third point of 'Political Principles'; they included disarmament and demilitarization, and control of Germany's industry to prevent military production. Denazification was another important objective, dealt with in sections 5 and 6 of the document. In 1945 the Allies specified the explicit need to bring to justice war criminals and members of the Nazi Party 'who have been more than nominal participants in its activities'. They had high hopes that they would be able to achieve a widespread purging of institutions and organizations from Nazi Party members. At this early stage in the proceedings, they had not yet worked out a clear strategy for the re-education that would be needed. As we will see, in the event problems occurred that made this point more difficult than anticipated. Denazification was certainly an important aim, but how it should be achieved was still unclear when the Allies met at Potsdam.

The fourth specified aim, democratization, was a more positive one (all the previous ones were concerned with getting rid of remnants of the past). The agreement promised the 'eventual reconstruction of German political life'.

In accordance with the stated intention not to want to destroy or enslave Germany, it was important to spell out what the long-term plans for an independent and presumably eventually unoccupied Germany might be.

The document also ruled under section 14, in rather euphemistic language, that people of German descent were to be transferred to the territory within the new German borders in an 'orderly and humane manner'. This referred primarily to Germans living in Poland, Hungary and Czechoslovakia. This 'transfer' amounted to the expulsion of millions of people from their homes. For these expellees, the suffering of the war continued well into the post-war period, as we will see below.

In this document the Allied powers determined in principle how the occupation of Germany should be organized. Provisional frontiers in the east were also discussed (these sections have been omitted from the excerpts). But there were some inherent contradictions. Although the treaty proposed to treat Germany as an economic unit, it did in fact decide to partition the country. To sum up the main aims of the Allies, historians often speak of the four 'Ds': demilitarization, decartellization, denazification and democratization. □

During the course of the unit, we will examine how successful the Allies were at achieving these goals. As they soon discovered, the practicalities of occupation imposed certain restraints on their intentions. The Allies' views on how to treat their zones of occupation differed and altered during the course of events following the Potsdam conference. Although both Britain and the United States had advocated harsh measures for dealing with Germany, they soon found that they had to focus on rebuilding their zones of occupation if they wanted to unburden themselves of the responsibility of keeping millions of starving Germans alive. Britain could barely sustain its own population, while in the United States concerns over a new potential enemy, communism, took over from the desire to punish Germany. Germany's role soon changed from that of enemy to that of an ally against the Soviet Union. Even French policy, originally keen to effect a dismemberment of Germany and in lieu of this bent on extracting a maximum amount of reparations from their zone of occupation, fell in line with the new policy of Britain and America in 1949. In comparison, Soviet policy in the eastern zone changed relatively little. It intended to adapt its zone to a Soviet style of government, for example by placing communists in key positions. At the same time, the Soviet Union stripped its part of Germany of a significant part of its industry in an attempt to profit from victory. A substantial number of factories were dismantled as early as the summer and autumn of 1945 (N. Naimark, *The Russians in Germany*, 1995, p.179; M. Fulbrook, *The Two Germanies*, 1992, pp.13–14). The increasing rivalries between east and west resulted in a changed status for the two German zones, and ultimately led to the development and adoption of opposing ideological and political views. The eventual success of the new states, and particularly of the new West German democracy, was not necessarily a foregone conclusion, however. The western Allies faced the problem of how to turn their section of Germany into a democratic country, given that democracy had been thoroughly discredited in the Weimar years. For many Germans, democracy was associated with economic hardship and with the defeat of 1918. It constituted an alien form of government with which they associated largely negative experiences, particularly with the Depression of the late 1920s. If democracy were to be accepted and adopted by the majority of West Germans, then the economic problems of the post-war years needed to be addressed urgently.

The Allies' attempts at addressing Germany's Nazi past: the Nuremberg trials and denazification

On 8 August 1945, the victors signed an act on prosecution of the main Nazi war criminals. In their quest for denazification, this was in many ways the simplest part and the one characterized by the most Allied unity (C. Klessmann, *Die doppelte Staatsgründung*, 1984, p.78), although they increasingly defined it in different ways. The resulting war crimes trials began on 18 October in Berlin, and continued from 20 November in Nuremberg, the town so closely associated with Nazi rule as the scene of the NSDAP's party rallies and the passing of the notorious racial laws of 1935. On trial were members of the Nazi leadership, as well as collectively the most notorious Nazi organizations, including the Gestapo, SS, SA, the Reich government and the leadership of the army. On 30 September 1946, twelve of the twenty-two accused individuals were sentenced to death (one *in absentia*), seven received long-term or life imprisonment, and three were acquitted. Further trials followed in all four zones until 1949. Within Germany there was a sense of a sometimes unfair 'victors' justice' being administered, which did not necessarily lead to the establishment of a deep-seated belief in law and justice. On the plus side, however, one of the most important results of the trials was that it made public the extent of Nazi crimes. For many Germans these crimes only became believable in the wake of the much publicized and widely reported Nuremberg trials (Klessman, p.80).

As we have seen, one of the aims specified by the Allies at the Potsdam conference was the denazification of Germany, which was to go hand in hand with a re-education of the German people. The Allied Control Council was responsible for the uniform implementation of denazification in all four occupied zones, although differences in the views on denazification soon emerged, making effective cooperation increasingly difficult.

In the Soviet zone, denazification was a part of a general process of so-called 'anti-fascist democratic revolution', in which the prominence of *Junkers* (East German land-owners) and other members of the élite was to be replaced by members of the working classes. The Soviet occupiers involved Germans (anti-fascists, especially communists and socialists, many of whom had returned from exile) from the beginning in their denazification procedures. Their aims were to effect a quick and thorough break with the Nazi regime and with the old institutions which had enabled National Socialism to come to power, and to establish a new, anti-fascist Germany. For this end, they removed former Nazis from the judiciary, administration, education and the economy. However, the aim of the Soviet occupiers was not only to denazify German society, as Hermann Weber explains: 'The SMAD[1] used this radical step in order to instal German communists not only in administrative powerhouses, but also

---

[1] *Sowietische Militäradministration in Deutschland* – Soviet Military Administration in Germany.

particularly in the police and judiciary' (H. Weber, *Die DDR*, 2000, p.11). For example, 85 per cent of judges were dismissed and replaced by 'people's judges'. In the Soviet zone, a distinction was made early (1945–6) between 'active' and 'nominal' Nazis. Removal focused on Nazi officials and NSDAP members who had joined the party before 1937. Only 'active' Nazis were to be punished or removed from office. In February 1948 the SMAD ordered the end of denazification, which it considered completed, as a result of which 520,734 former Nazis had been dismissed or not re-employed. More than 12,800 people were convicted, including 118 death sentences (A. Königseder, 'Entnazifizierung', 1999, p.114; Weber, p.10). The results of the Soviets' concentration on high-ranking Nazis in their denazification efforts were double-edged. On the one hand, members of the Nazi élite were more effectively removed from positions of power and official posts in the east than in the west. As a part of denazification 'active' Nazis were stripped of their influence by way of expropriation of banks, companies and large estates (areas which had lent crucial support to the Nazis), and leading Nazis were removed from their positions and could not, on the whole, regain employment. However, on the other hand, there was a negative side to this concentration on 'active' Nazis. This type of denazification made it appear as if the huge numbers of so-called *Mitläufer* ('fellow-travellers') had never existed, and led to a denial of the widespread public support that the Nazis had enjoyed. The rest of the population was morally and politically acquitted of the crimes of the Nazi past (in that sense, this constituted a 'denazification' of a different kind). Under these conditions it was easy for Germans to convince themselves that there had been no Nazi supporters in East Germany. Instead, East German propaganda emphasized the importance of the anti-fascist movement in freeing the country from Nazi rule (R.-K. Rössler, *Entnazifizierungspolitik der KPD/SED*, 1994, pp.15–17).

Denazification in the Soviet zone had a peculiar character because it aimed to achieve a socialist change of society which involved a removal not just of former Nazis but also of other political opponents. The practice of using internment camps (so-called 'Special Camps') highlights this. Such camps existed in East Germany until 1950. Used for the internment of former Nazis, they were, at the same time, part of the Stalinist regime's effort to establish itself in the Soviet zone. As well as Nazi criminals, the communist regime also held critics of the new system ranging from social democrats to oppositional communists. About 150,000 Germans were kept in these camps, about which little information is available to this day, and about 70,000 are thought to have died during their imprisonment (H. Weber, *Die DDR*, 2000, pp.11, 158–9).

Denazification was handled differently in the western zones. The American occupying forces regarded denazification as particularly important. They began to dismiss Nazis from public posts almost immediately, and by December 1945, 117,000 people were already kept in internment camps. According to a USFET[2] directive of July 1945, every German who had occupied a key position in public service, or wanted to do so, was forced to fill in a questionnaire comprising 131 questions. This had to be handed over if one wanted a job or a ration card. According to the answers given, individuals were classed in five different

[2] United States Forces, European Theatre.

groups, ranging from 'mandatory removal', 'discretionary, adverse recommendation', 'discretionary, no adverse recommendation', 'no objection' or 'no evidence', and 'retention recommended' or 'evidence of anti-Nazi activity'. In September 1945 denazification was extended to include the economy. By March 1946, 1.26 million of 1.39 million questionnaires had been assessed. A total of 139,996 employees in public services and 68,568 in commerce, trade and industry had been sacked, and some 73,000 applications for employment or re-employment had been denied (A. Königseder, 'Entnazifizierung', 1999, p.115; P. Borowsky, *Deutschland 1945–69*, 1993, pp.20–1).

In March 1946 denazification was put into German hands. As a result, every German citizen over the age of 18 in the Bizone had to fill in a questionnaire. However, the processing of over 13 million completed questionnaires led to considerable delay. Problems also resulted from the fact that the courts wanted to process the less serious cases first, because the evidence was more straightforward. More seriously implicated Nazis were thus able to escape conviction and trial. Denazification was less bureaucratic in the British and French zones. Here, mainly higher-ranking officials were removed from office. In the west the policy of denazification ceased in the early 1950s as a result of both the Cold War and the improved relations that the new Federal Republic enjoyed with the western Alllies. By February 1950 over 3.6 million cases had been examined in the west, but practical considerations led to a reinstatement of many former Nazis. The 1951 Reinstatement Act ensured that many civil servants were re-employed. As a result, many West German officials in the early 1950s were former members of the NSDAP, although they had not necessarily been active Nazis. Denazification had failed to remove them permanently even from prominent positions in the judiciary and politics. And yet a recovery of Germany would have been impossible without re-employing large numbers of skilled men and women. In the long run, a denazification of the minds of Germans would be more easily achieved against the background of economic stability and recovery. As Mary Fulbrook points out, 'the argument can be mounted that the end, retrospectively, might have justified the means: actions which can be criticized on moral grounds might have had consequences which even the critics would applaud' (*Fontana History of Germany*, 1991, p.188). Mark Roseman raises similar questions regarding the 'selective memory' displayed by many biographical accounts published in the post-war years. 'How should we approach this process in the context of West Germany's political stabilization?' he asks. 'Was such selective memory and repression in fact psychologically necessary for the revival of a stable state?' ('Division and stability', 1993, p.387). For many West Germans denazification was discredited because it was felt that the 'big fish' had managed to get away while the 'small fry' had been punished. The issue was to flare up again in the 1960s, when a new generation of West Germans enquired about the personal histories of some of those Nazis who had managed to 'get away with it'.

Re-education went hand in hand with denazification, and aimed at informing Germans about the crimes committed by National Socialism, and at educating them to foster democratic thinking. The term re-education began to appear in official British documents by late 1942, although it seemed to some commentators an unrealistic proposal. One MP attacked the idea in May 1943: 'What a fantastic idea it is to attempt to educate a whole race to be peaceful, a race that for centuries has had an instinct for war deep down in its nature. I believe it would be much easier to educate 80 million baboons' (Cunningham-Reid, MP for Marylebone, quoted in M. Balfour, 'In retrospect: Britain's policy of "re-education"', 1985, p.140).

In an effort to prepare Germany for its new democratic future, schools were closed, most teachers dismissed while their pasts were being scrutinized, and substitute teachers (retired ones or those dismissed by the Nazis) were trained in reorientation seminars. Prisoners of war held outside Germany by the British were quite literally a captive audience for re-education efforts. Of 2.7 million prisoners in British hands, some 400,000 were 'handled', in Michael Balfour's phrase. 'The primary object ... was to make them think and provide them with material for doing so. Every prisoner was required to sit through an American film on the liberation of Belsen' (Balfour, p.149). The press, radio and film were important vehicles of the re-education process (Borowsky, *Deutschland 1945–69*, 1993, pp.23–4). British and American occupying forces jointly produced *Welt im Film*, a newsreel production for compulsory screening in cinemas in their zones of occupation. It devoted its fifth issue entirely to footage from the death camps. Although on the whole film played a minor role in re-education compared to other media, the one exception was its documentation of the atrocities of the death camps, with footage which brought home the true extent of the terror inflicted by National Socialism on countless victims (R. Smith, '*Welt im Film*: Anglo-American newsreel policy', 1985, p.151; D. Culbert, 'American film policy in the re-education of Germany after 1945', 1985, p.171).

German attempts at addressing the Nazi past

In 1990, in the wake of the recent reunification of Germany, the German writer Günter Grass gave a speech to students in Frankfurt which he entitled 'Writing after Auschwitz'. In it he retraced his origins as a writer starting in May 1945, when he was 17 years old, and explained how he confronted the difficult question: 'How was it possible to write – after Auschwitz?' This question had first been voiced by the German philosopher Theodor Adorno in 1948, who asked whether there could be any poetry after Auschwitz. The excerpt from Grass's speech in *Primary Sources 2: Interwar and World War II* (Document II.48) exemplifies the feelings of disbelief, confusion and shame that many Germans experienced after 1945, although they might not always have been able to voice their emotions in quite the same eloquent way. For most, of course, the question was not how to *write* after Auschwitz, but how to have a 'normal life', how to bring up children, work and go about everyday business in the face of Germany's recent terrible history. Most Germans just wanted to rebuild their shattered lives and return to some sort of normality. Rather than address the past, they hoped to forget it. Once the Allies abandoned their denazification measures, blocking out the past would become easier. In fact, one could even argue that the western powers encouraged a repression of Germany's recent history. As Mark Roseman explains:

> One of the costs of post-war stabilization was the failure of most Germans properly to acknowledge their complicity in the Third Reich. In their dealings with Germany, the western powers increasingly allowed the war to go unmentioned, however much they might still be feeling the wounds at

home. The Cold War allowed the Germans to relocate themselves on the side of civilization as co-warriors against the Soviet Union.

('Division and stability', 1993, p.386)

Another German writer, Alfred Döblin, experienced the 'Third Reich' in exile, and recorded his impressions of Germany and the Germans when he returned after 1945. His comments, also in your *Primary Sources 2* (Document II.49), date from 1949, and attest to the impact twelve years of National Socialism had had on Germans.

Exercise   Read Günter Grass's account in *Primary Sources 2* (Document II.48). Then read the impressions of Alfred Döblin (Document II.49). How do both writers describe the legacy of the war and of National Socialism? How do their accounts differ, and why? What particular problems relating to post-war German society do the authors describe? How do they rate the effectiveness of the Allies' attempts at addressing the Nazi past and at getting Germans to address their past? ■

Specimen answers   There are obvious differences in the two accounts given the fact that the first author, Günter Grass, recalls his personal experience of Nazi Germany and the post-war realization of the true nature of that state, while Alfred Döblin describes his encounter with Germans after the war from the position of an outsider. Having lived through the 'Third Reich' and the war, and having sworn an oath of loyalty, Grass found himself a prisoner of war in 1945 at the age of 17. The difficulties experienced by many Germans in 1945 – how to reconcile years of indoctrination and the belief in German superiority, for example, with the defeat and the realization of atrocities – emerge from his account. Grass refused to believe that Auschwitz and the horrors for which it stands could have been true, even when confronted with images of the evidence. Interestingly, he confirms the importance of the Nuremberg trials in making him believe the crimes committed by Germans and in Germany's name.

Alfred Döblin's account attests to a similar unwillingness, and even initial inability, to confront the past by the people he encountered. His account differs from Grass's because the feelings of bewilderment, denial and guilt that he describes are not his own. Having spent the war years in exile, his impressions once he returned to Germany are those of an outsider, an observer, rather than someone who was part of the war, as Günter Grass had been. Döblin's account raises similar concerns to Grass's. The effects of propaganda and of the regime's legacy emerge from his comments. Although in many ways the people he left in 1933 were still the same, they seem different to Döblin, as though they had existed in a vacuum. His impressions echo Grass's account of his own feelings regarding the horrors of the crimes committed under Nazi rule: an inclination to disbelieve the Allies and to consider their education attempts as propaganda, a refusal to discuss 'the guilt question' in favour of wanting to be 'left in peace'. Döblin also outlined a further problem resulting from the fact that many Germans were able to blame post-war suffering on the occupation by the Allies rather than on the war itself. This was a potential danger, especially given the events following the defeat of 1918. □

Whereas Grass, at least according to this account, quickly accepted the truth and attempted to deal with it, many Germans chose to ignore the past. Particularly in what would become the GDR, where fascists were simply equated with capitalists and were thus 'over there', and where the vast majority of people had no cause to address their own Nazi past as a result of denazification procedures, there was no real coming to terms with Germany's recent history. In West Germany, on the other hand, the late 1940s and 1950s were spent building new lives out of the ruins. Germans retreated into a private sphere that enabled many to leave their recent past behind. Consequently, a representative survey conducted in 1952 revealed that 54 per cent of West Germans did not regard themselves as guilty of Nazi crimes or responsible for any compensation (F. Stern, '"Ein freundlich aufgenähter Davidstern"', 1993, p.721). No similar survey results exist for East Germans who, in the light of the official policy, did not identify themselves with the Nazi past and were even less likely to address Germany's recent history than their West German neighbours.

This focus on the domestic sphere and the refusal to address the past led to some interesting, if disturbing, continuities in attitudes, for example in anti-Semitism. Germans had not turned into non-racists overnight, and twelve years of officially sanctioned anti-Semitism and racism were not wiped out after 1945. Anti-Semitism was, of course, no longer official policy and was unacceptable, unlike anti-communism. Communism was an enemy that the FRG shared with its National Socialist predecessor (H. Berghoff, 'Zwischen Verdrängung und Aufarbeitung', 1998, p.110). The West German state accepted responsibility for the Holocaust and the need for compensation, unlike the GDR, where the murder of the Jews was not acknowledged and barely mentioned, and where no responsibility was accepted.

In September 1951 the German Chancellor Konrad Adenauer addressed the Bundestag on the matter of the attitude of the Federal Republic towards the Jews and 'the terrible crimes of the past epoch', in which he publicly accepted Germany's responsibility for 'a moral and material restitution':

> The German government, and with it the majority of the German people, are conscious of the immeasurable sorrow that was brought upon the Jewish people in Germany and in the occupied territories during the period of National Socialism. There was a predominant majority of German people who abhorred the crimes committed against the Jews and did not take part in them. There were many Germans during the time of National Socialism who, at their own risk, showed their willingness to help their Jewish compatriots for religious reasons, in a conflict of conscience, and out of shame because the German name had been disgraced. The unmentionable crimes committed in the name of the German people demand a moral and material restitution. This includes both the damages inflicted on individual Jewish people and on Jewish property for which the individuals entitled to restitution no longer exist. The first steps have been taken in this area. Much more, however, remains to be done. The German government will see to a quick settlement concerning the restitution legislation and its fair implementation. A part of the identifiable Jewish property has been returned; additional restorations will follow ...

(C.-C. Schweitzer et al., *Politics and Government in Germany*, 1995, pp.122–3)

Adenauer aimed to clarify the Federal Republic's attitude towards Jews. The 'Basic Law' guaranteed equality for all German citizens, and equality was thus, at least in theory, laid down by law. In contrast to the widespread public refusal to address Nazi crimes, Adenauer's speech confirmed the official acceptance of the 'immeasurable sorrow that was brought upon the Jewish people', and the 'unmentionable crimes committed'. This was an important public declaration of guilt. At the same time, however, he delivered an easy excuse for the majority of Germans, for according to Adenauer, 'a predominant majority of German people [had] abhorred the crimes'. Germany's public attitude further accepted the need for restitution, an issue that was being legislated and implemented at the time.

However, while the state no longer practised anti-Semitism, its citizens were not all quite as enlightened, as the following figures resulting from representative public opinion polls demonstrate. As late as 1965, 26 per cent of Germans stated they would have preferred not to have any Jews in Germany. In 1961, 73 per cent of those questioned considered Jews to be 'a different race', and 54 per cent stated that they would not marry a Jew. In 1952, only 20 per cent of interviewees disagreed with the statement that it would be better 'not to have any Jews in the country', a figure that increased to 35 per cent in 1956, and 40 per cent in 1963. Even as late as this, however, 18 per cent of West Germans were explicitly in favour of a Germany that was 'free from Jews' (Berghoff, 'Zwischen Verdrängung und Aufarbeitung', 1998, p.110; Stern, '"Ein freundlich aufgenähter Davidstern"', 1993, p.721).

This negative attitude was to some extent reflected in the government's policy towards Jews, for despite Adenauer's claims of tolerance neither the first post-war German government nor subsequent ones made an international appeal to Jews to return to Germany. The result of the Third Reich's anti-Jewish policy was indeed a Germany that was almost 'free from Jews'. Only around 30,000 Jews remained in the Federal Republic after the war. Before the war there had been about half a million Jews in Germany.

2 THE LEGACY OF TOTAL WAR

A huge proportion of Germans were affected by what has been termed a 'typical post-war fate': expellees and refugees, war widows, severely disabled soldiers, prisoners of war who did not return from captivity until the mid-1950s, those who had been bombed and lost their homes and possessions, those affected by denazification who were not allowed to work in their profession, and so on. The total figure of all those adversely affected by the war in West Germany alone has been estimated at 21 to 23 million people, about 30 per cent of the population (M. Niehuss, 'Kontinuität und Wandel der Familie in den 50er Jahren', 1993, p.321). This section examines the social, economic and demographic changes of the post-war years and deals with the problematic legacy of the war for German society. This included millions of refugees who flooded into the destroyed Germany from east to west, and the social and economic problems that accompanied migration on such an unprecedented scale, in addition to the problems of lack of housing, food and other resources, unemployment, and a general disillusionment. In the years following the war, many Germans were simply exhausted, both physically and mentally, from the strain that the war had imposed on soldiers and civilians alike.

   Life for most Germans in the immediate post-war years was primarily dictated by hunger, lack of housing, unemployment, poverty and lack of resources and heating material. The winter of 1946–7 was a time of particular crisis, with temperatures as low as minus 30°C and the population on the brink of starvation. There was no gas, electricity or water for millions of people, and only the help of the western Allies at that crucial time prevented widespread starvation. The food shortages led to severe malnutrition, with adults in Munich, for example, being allocated approximately 1,300 calories per day, 1,000 in Stuttgart and only 700–800 in Essen. By comparison, the League of Nations had estimated in 1936 that an adult working an eight-hour day needed at least 3,000 calories, and even a person at rest needed 1,600. Even in the last, bitter winter of the war, the daily allowance for adults had been 2,000 calories, a rate that was not again achieved in Germany until 1948 (Jacobmeyer, 'Die Niederlage von 1945', 1976, pp.16–17). The shortage of food and other essential supplies made everyday life a constant struggle for survival. Food was grown in public parks throughout Germany, even just outside the Brandenburg Gate in Berlin.

Allotment garden at the foot of the Reichstag building in 1945. (Photo: Bildarchiv Preussischer Kulturbesitz, Berlin)

In June 1946 the first CARE packets (Cooperative for American Remittances to Europe) arrived in the western zones, a relief measure that supplied much-needed food to Germans until 1960. Black-market profiteering flourished in these difficult months, and the most important means of payment for goods was cigarettes. Money bought increasingly less on the black market, and goods were largely swapped for goods – in Wolfgang Benz's words, a return to the archaic state of 'natural economy' (*Naturalwirtschaft*) ('Infrastruktur und Gesellschaft im zerstörten Deutschland', 1998, p.15). It was also a continuation, perhaps even an intensification, of wartime bartering and black marketeering. The problem was finally overcome following the currency reform of 1948, which brought the black-market economy to an end and made goods available again in the shops, although the late 1940s continued to be a time of poverty and deprivation for most Germans. The 'economic miracle' was still in the future.

Malnutrition increased the risk of disease and did not help to combat the general spirit of disillusionment, especially combined with the extreme shortage of housing. Exact figures do not exist to indicate the amount of housing destroyed, and it varied among regions. Cautious estimates speak of between 17 and 19 per cent of housing completely destroyed as a result of the war. Rural areas and small towns were less affected; it was the larger towns and cities that had taken the brunt of the bombing although the invasion damaged even some rural areas, especially following Hitler's 'Nero Decree', in which he ordered the total destruction of Germany in the face of imminent defeat. In many urban areas one-third of all available housing in 1939 had been destroyed. In the worst affected cities, those figures were even higher: 63.9 per cent in Kassel, 70 per cent in Cologne, 74.3 per cent in Würzburg, for example (K. C. Führer, 'Wohnungen', 1999, p.206). In 1946 there were 13.7 million households but only 8.2 million dwellings. The result was extreme overcrowding and cohabitation as well as homelessness and, for many thousands of people, life in makeshift camps, in converted town halls, gymnasiums, barns, etc. that were barely habitable. The problem was exacerbated by millions of refugees flooding into Germany. Due to a lack of building materials and difficulties in transport, the rebuilding of housing was largely impossible before the currency reform of 1948, and even then was slow to get off the ground. A survey of September 1950 showed that 41 per cent of all flats or houses were occupied by more than one family, and larger flats even accommodated several families (Führer, p.208).

The shortages of coal were another cause of crisis: industry depended on it, as did public transport and domestic households. Problems existed both in mining the coal and in transporting it. Allied bombing had destroyed most bridges, tunnels, railway lines and other transport systems, and about 40 per cent of the road network was out of use. In the British zone, for example, only 1,000 kilometres of useable railway track remained of the pre-war total of 13,000; in the French zone, 500 kilometres were left of previously 5,667. When the canals froze in the winter of 1946–7, the crisis in transport reached its peak (Benz, 'Infrastruktur und Gesellschaft im zerstörten Deutschland', 1988, pp.13ff.).

At the end of the war, 11.2 million German soldiers were being kept as prisoners of war by the Allies, two-thirds by the western Allies (7.8 million) and one-third by the Soviet Union (3.4 million). In the first months after the war, prisoners of war in the west suffered particularly harsh conditions. Many died in inadequate camps or even without a roof over their heads in fields, or were forced to labour in reconstruction and mining. Prisoners in Soviet hands fared much worse, however. In total, about one-third of the total number in Soviet captivity died. Although the Allies decided at the Moscow conference of March–April 1947 to release all prisoners by the end of 1948, the Soviet Union did not adhere to this agreement. The last German prisoners of war were finally released from Soviet camps in 1955. After ten or more years in captivity, they returned to a Germany that they could hardly recognize.

In addition, more than 1.5 million soldiers were 'missing in action' when the war was over. The Red Cross took on the task of searching for those who were missing, and continued to reunite families years after the war had come to an end. However, eventually it had to declare a total of 1,086,000 missing soldiers dead in addition to known deaths. Their fate was never established. This staggering figure can scarcely convey the suffering of the individuals and families associated with every one of those soldiers. For them, the war was not really over in 1945 but continued to haunt them (Benz, p.18).

Women and children were particularly adversely affected by the considerable population shift which resulted from the expulsion and murder of almost the entire Jewish population, from the deaths of four million soldiers and half a million civilians, and from the fact that hundreds of thousands of soldiers were still prisoners of war or missing. At the end of the war, there was a surplus of seven million women in all four zones (Kettenacker, *Germany since 1945*, 1997, p.36). For many of them, marriage would be an impossibility. Losses were particularly high among men born between 1910 and 1925, who would have been between 20 and 35 in 1946, when a census in Bavaria revealed that in this age group there were 162 women for every 100 men. The ratio is even worse if one compares unmarried men and women in this age group: for every 100 unmarried men there were 269 unmarried women (Niehuss, 'Kontinuität und Wandel', 1993, p.317). This demographic change resulted in reduced chances for women to get married, a particular grievance given that spinsters traditionally had a difficult position in society. While both world wars led to demographic changes, the Second World War had a much bigger impact than the First World War on the people of western Europe. Germany had one of the highest numbers of loss of life (of course, the Soviet Union had lost many more lives than any of the other combatant nations), and most fatalities had been among males in the 18–23 age group. As a result, the 'unprecedented post-war generation of spinsters was more a feature of German society than anywhere else in western Europe' (A. Sutcliffe, *Western Europe since 1945*, 1996, p.137).

Another demographic consequence, and one which has received little attention from historians, was the steep increase in illegitimate children, resulting partly from liaisons with foreign workers during the war and with Allied soldiers during the occupation period, and partly from the rapes of the immediate post-war era. Although about a quarter of illegitimate children on average would be 'legitimized' by subsequent marriages, a large number of children (and their mothers) had to live with the prejudice and stigma attached to illegitimacy in those years (Niehuss, 'Kontinuität und Wandel', pp.319–20).

War widows and orphans suffered particularly severely in post-war society. The exact number of war widows was not recorded at the end of the war, although we have figures dating from the 1950 census, according to which 1.7 million women aged between 16 and 65 were widowed, 700,000 were separated from their husbands (including those missing or prisoners of war), and 365,000 women were divorced. 2.2 million children received an orphan allowance. These figures demonstrate that approximately every sixth woman lived on her own, and almost every fifth child was without a father (Niehuss, p.320). Young widows with small children were in a particularly difficult economic situation, as the occupying powers reduced or in some cases completely ceased payments to them. A solution to this financial problem was only achieved in 1950 in West Germany when new social legislation regulated payments.

Another large group of people badly affected by the war and in need of financial support and administrative care in the early months after its end were an estimated 8 to 10 million so-called 'displaced persons' (DPs), 2.5 million in the British zone of occupation alone. These were people who had been forcibly kept in Germany during the Nazi regime, for example as forced labour, or who had been interned in concentration camps, and who now had to be returned to their countries of origin. Many Germans lived in fear of these DPs, who had been exploited during the war and now roamed the countryside (Kettenacker, *Germany since 1945*, 1997, p.36). In May 1945 the numbers of DPs in the western zones of occupation alone amounted to over 4 million: 1.5 million Russians, 1.2 million French, 600,000 Poles, 350,000 Italians, 200,000 Dutch, 200,000 Belgians, 100,000 Yugoslavs, 60,000 Czechs, and 10,000 Danes, Norwegians, Greeks and Luxembourgers respectively (*Die Fischer Chronik Deutschland*, 1999, p.35).

The task of looking after them and arranging their repatriation lay with the Allies, who faced numerous problems. Repatriation of DPs from western states was relatively quick and straightforward, but this was much more difficult for DPs from eastern and south-eastern Europe. For these people repatriation was slow, and the DPs had to be kept in camps, prolonging their suffering and continuing the Nazi practice in internment in concentration camps, if only for reasons of practicality. A minority of DPs posed an extra problem by refusing to be repatriated – as Grigor McClelland, a Quaker relief worker in Germany in 1945–6, recorded in one of his letters home on 31 May 1945:

> The most surprising thing is how many people don't want to go home. Very few people I have met from eastern Europe want to go and live under the Russians. Poles think it means death and torture, I've met Latvians who are not forced labour but families who have left their country rather than stay with the Russians, Serbs who don't want to go back to a Tito- or Communist-controlled Yugoslavia, and I'm quite sure that the Balkan states everywhere feel the same. What is to be done?
>
> (G. McClelland, *Embers of War*, 1997, p.16)

By September 1945, 4.6 million DPs had already been repatriated with the help of the United Nations Reconstruction and Repatriation Administration (UNRRA). Despite this impressive achievement, 1.1 million DPs were still in the western zones of occupation in April 1947.

One of the most serious consequences of the war for German society, and a problem of unprecedented scale, was the population movement as a result of the redrawing of the maps of Europe. You will recall that the Potsdam agreement detailed plans to transfer Germans from the east to the new, smaller

German territory. This decision led to one of the worst social problems in post-war Germany. In fleeing from the Red Army and from acts of revenge of populations liberated from the yoke of National Socialism, and with the forcible expulsion of Germans from eastern and south-eastern Europe, an unprecedented wave of migrants added to Germany's social and economic problems. The census of September 1950 showed that of 47.7 million inhabitants of the new Federal Republic, 9.6 million (20 per cent) had arrived during or after the Second World War (R. Schulze, 'Growing discontent', 1989, p.334). The district of Erfurt in the *Land* of Thuringia in the Soviet zone gave shelter to almost 670,000 refugees between 1945 and 1949, and some 2 million refugees passed throught the town during that period. Thuringia itself had about 3 million inhabitants according to census data from 1946. Such figures give a sense of the vast scale of the refugee problem in post-war Germany (M. Allinson, *Politics and Popular Opinion*, 2000, pp.16–17).

Exercise   Table 27.1 indicates the total numbers of 'uprooted' people in Germany in 1947. In studying the table, note the different total numbers of 'uprooted' people in the four zones of occupation, the total population numbers, and the percentages given. What can you say about the influx of refugees and expellees into Germany as a result of these figures? ∎

Table 27.1   'Uprooted' population in Germany (1 April 1947)

Zones	Total population in 1947	Total number of uprooted people	% of total population
British	22,300,000	4,927,000	22
American	17,200,000	4,100,000	24
French	5,900,000	414,000	7
Russian (incl. Berlin)	20,500,000	4,653,000	23
Germany in 1947 borders	65,900,000	14,095,000	21
Same area in 1939	59,600,000		

(Source: C. Klessmann, *Die doppelte Staatsgründung*, 1984, p.355)

Specimen answer and discussion   The table gives a sense of the huge numbers of refugees and expellees that entered Germany. In April 1947 more than 14 million newcomers had arrived in Germany, whose territory had been decreased by the border changes following the war. The French accepted the least numbers of refugees into their zone of occupation. Only 7 per cent of the population in the French zone were recent arrivals in 1947, as opposed to 24 per cent in the American zone. Unlike the other occupying powers, France had closed the borders of its zone to refugees. The percentage figures indicate that almost a quarter of people in the American zone were recent arrivals. On average, that percentage was 21 per cent. This meant that every fifth person in Germany had arrived under more or less unfortunate circumstances since the war had ended. Moreover, in comparing the total population in 1947, you should have noticed that the number had increased by over 6 million, despite the war losses among soldiers and civilians. □

For the Bizone – that is, the combined territories under British and American occupation – the figures are particularly staggering. Despite the war losses, the population in the Bizone had increased by 25 per cent if the October 1946 figures are compared to those of 1936 (Kettenacker, *Germany since 1945*, 1997, p.36). Such figures serve to give a sense of the scale of the population movement, although it is difficult to convey a true sense of the problems that went hand in hand with such large-scale migration. Millions of Germans were forcibly expelled from eastern-central Europe, others had begun their flight in the face of the advancing Red Army for fear of retribution, or simply because they believed the propaganda about the barbarity and brutality of the Russian soldiers. There were indeed cases of retribution, revenge and crimes committed by the advancing armies against the civilian population they encountered, and hearing of them led more people to flee west. When the borders were being redrawn by the victorious Allies, many thousands of Germans were forced to leave their homes in the territories that had been German before the war and were incorporated into Poland and the Soviet Union after Germany's defeat (refer to your *Maps Booklet*). As we have seen in the Potsdam agreement, the intention was to arrange for an 'orderly and humane' transport of these people. In reality, the exodus was chaotic and traumatic, and many people perished during their long marches and arduous journeys in open railway carriages and other inhumane means of transport. It is estimated that up to two million died as a result of the forcible expulsion (*Die Fischer Chronik Deutschland*, 1999, p.35).

Exercise   Try to think of some of the problems that the refugee situation might have caused, focusing in particular on the social and economic difficulties encountered by the resident Germans that have already been discussed. Why might an influx of poor refugees have been especially difficult at that particular time? Draw up a list of points that come to mind. ■

Specimen answer   You might have jotted down:

- lack of food and other essential supplies;
- lack of housing;
- unemployment;
- problems of integration/loss of identity;
- hostility to outsiders/newcomers. □

Exercise   To give you an idea of the refugee problem from a contemporary point of view, read the statement made by Brian Hubert Robertson in February 1949 (*Primary Sources 2*, Document II.50). Robertson was the Military Governor of the British Zone of Occupied Germany from November 1947. What points does he make about the situation in Germany, and what are his concerns for the future of the country? ■

Specimen answer   Robertson is particularly concerned that the newcomers to Germany formed a
new class, which he calls 'property-less' and, moreover, an underclass which
was embittered because of its fate and situation. The document confirms that
many 'native Western Germans' felt hostility towards the refugees. They were
considered filthy and disease-ridden, and their presence was deemed to make
the already cramped conditions worse. In Robertson's eyes, the treatment of the
refugees by the native Germans is in keeping with a 'latent impulses of the
German character' to persecute the underdog. The document includes a clear
warning that the large and underprivileged proletarian group of refugees posed
dangers for the new German society. This 'class apart bearing a stigma' could
only hope to better its position with the passage of time and with a definite
improvement of its physical condition. You might also have noticed that the
document is dated February 1949. The conditions described were obviously not
new, short-term developments, but an ongoing problem that had existed for
almost four years. The tone of the statement is rather pessimistic, especially
given that Robertson anticipated serious problems for the future of German
society if these problems were not overcome and an integration of these
newcomers could not be achieved. □

The influx of refugees was regarded with some hostility by many residents, due
to real and imagined cultural differences and the perceived threat the
newcomers posed to the residents' own social and economic welfare. As
Ulrich Herbert points out, this hostility was also an expression of 'chauvinistic
feelings of superiority' which had been manifest in the way Germans had treated
foreign workers during the war. The refugees arrived in a society that had
incorporated racism as a principle, and the way Germans conceived of
foreigners and dealt with refugees was determined by six years of dealing
with millions of foreign workers (Herbert, 'Zwangsarbeiter – Vertriebene –
Gastarbeiter', 1987, pp.172–3).

Given these elements of continuity, such pessimism as Robertson's
memorandum implies, and the hostility described by Herbert, the obvious
question must be how these problems were overcome. How could a stable
democratic society develop relatively quickly in the Federal Republic from such
unpromising beginnings, and how could an integration of the newcomers be
achieved? Historians have identified a number of factors that aided the
integration of this great influx of refugees and expellees. More than any other
factor, the rapid economic upturn of the 1950s eventually enabled a relatively
smooth integration. The economic boom provided much needed employment
for residents and refugees alike. Acceptance and integration into German society
was aided by the fact that many of the newcomers were fellow Germans. They
might have had different regional accents and customs, but they were none the
less German, sharing the same nationality and language. Their integration was
further aided by the fact their arrival coincided with great population mobility
within Germany. The refugees were simply another group in this society on the
move in the chaotic post-war years, only one group among many who were
'new to the area'. And at a time when most Germans were poor, the newcomers'
poverty did not particularly single them out. Moreover, it was accepted that the
refugees would be unable to return home and required permanent integration,
and for this reason the refugees, too, were more willing to integrate themselves

although many continued to hope for years that they might one day return to their homes, for example to 'German Silesia'. It also worked in the refugees' favour that they were a socially heterogeneous group comprised of all social classes and backgrounds. As a result, they were not doubly underprivileged by being foreign and workers, as had been the case with the foreign labourers during the war. Finally, the fact that the newcomers had the vote ensured that the new post-war parties could not marginalize them, and that they would be taken into account in the political considerations of the parties (Herbert, p.173).

None the less, many refugees continued to live on the periphery of society for some time; some lived in camps and other makeshift accommodation into the late 1950s. The report of Robertson hardly exaggerates the poor treatment the refugees received. They were regarded with suspicion and contempt by the locals, and were on the whole even poorer than the resident population. Most had lost everything – their home, possessions, family, friends. Eventually, their acceptance had much to do with being German, and their integration was thus a lot easier than that of a later wave of newcomers, the so-called guest workers (*Gastarbeiter*) of the 1960s from Turkey, Italy, Greece and Yugoslavia, who were needed when industry began to boom in the Federal Republic and not enough workers could be found within its borders.

Although I have focused above on the fate of refugees in West Germany, newcomers in East Germany were in a similar situation. In December 1945, 1.9 million more people lived in the Soviet occupation zone than had lived in the same territory in 1939. By that time, the female population had risen by 1.9 million while the male had declined by 600,000. Approximately a year later, the population increase in the eastern occupation zone was 3.4 million people (Weber, *Die DDR*, 2000, p.12). In 1948 the East German authorities declared the refugee problem solved. By March 1949, 4.4 million 'resettlers' (the official GDR term for refugees and expellees) were registered in the eastern zone, including 2.57 million women (*Die Fischer Chronik Deutschland*, 1999, p.67). Clearly, the integration of such a large number of newcomers would take time in both German states, and could only be achieved once economic recovery provided better living conditions for the resident population and the new arrivals alike.

An important part in this integration, and in Germany's recovery, was played by the social policies of post-war governments. Given the severe social problems that German society faced in and after 1945, the issue of social welfare provision was a particularly pressing one. In Britain attempts to justify the notion of a 'people's war' led to a reform of the social security system between 1945 and 1948 by way of the Beveridge Plan (as discussed in Units 21–5). During the Allied occupation of Germany, German politicians largely resented what they regarded as attempts to introduce a Beveridge-style system in Germany. After all, Germany had had a long tradition of social welfare provision dating back to Bismarck, and the country was proud of such achievements. At a rally of the Christian Democratic Union in 1946, Konrad Adenauer objected strongly to any imposition of a system from the outside:

> We must hold on to this social insurance. We are proud of it. And as for the proposals Beveridge has recently made in Hamburg, I can only say that we Germans have already had such things these past thirty years.
>
> (Quoted in Hockerts, 'German post-war social policies', 1981, p.318)

During the period of the first West German Bundestag (1949–53), the social security system was restructured largely along traditional lines. However, in addition to social insurance, the government had to focus on specific problems resulting from the war. The 1952 *Lastenausgleichgesetz* (Equalization of Burdens Act), for example, was a programme of redistribution to benefit refugees and people bombed out of their homes; several other acts addressed the needs of invalids, war widows and orphans, while the social insurance system was reinstated along pre-war lines. To a certain extent it could thus be argued that the war brought about social change to post-war German society, although one should not overlook the fact that the problems alleviated by this legislation were almost entirely of the war's making.

Germany's particular post-war circumstances were reflected in the high rate of social expenditure in the Federal Republic. In 1953, 19.4 per cent of its Net National Product was spent on benefits, as compared to 12.5 per cent in Britain and 13.5 per cent in Sweden. Rather than being an indication of the high level of support given to individual claimants, these figures indicate the vastness of the social problems that the German government needed to address (Hockerts, p.321). During the following years, the government attempted to work out a wide-ranging plan to reform the social security system. While the oppositional SPD favoured a Beveridge-style system, the CDU stressed the need for private initiatives and the individual's responsibility for their own security. During Adenauer's time in office, a comprehensive reform was not arrived at, but certain partial reforms were enacted, most importantly the 1957 pension reform, which was 'an attempt once and for all to achieve a break with the traditional cycle of old age and poverty' (Hockerts, p.329). In providing such crucial security and financial support, this was a particularly important piece of social legislation, as Hockerts emphasizes: 'The pension reform of 1957 thus had a strengthening and consolidating effect on the young Federal Republic that cannot be overestimated' (p.329).

3 THE EMERGENCE OF TWO GERMAN STATES

In this section we will examine the reasons for the separation and drifting apart of the eastern and western zones of occupation, which resulted in the establishment of two separate and ideologically opposed German states. To determine why such a division occurred, it is necessary to highlight how Allied policy towards their zones of occupation differed. During and immediately after the war, the Allies had the same intentions regarding the future of Germany: it should be prevented from manifesting bellicose behaviour in the future, a clear break with the Nazi past should be made, and Germany should pay for the damage it had caused. German society was to be transformed in a genuine attempt to create 'a "good" society – a historical experiment virtually unparalleled in history' (Fulbrook, *The Two Germanies*, 1992, p.3). However, their methods and ultimate goals for Germany's future differed, and so did the results. As Hermann Weber argues, 'the ultimate goal of the western Allies as well as the Soviet Union consisted of integrating all of Germany in their respective block and adapting the economic and political system to their own views on values and order' (*Die DDR*, 2000, p.22). Although they failed to impose their respective views on all of Germany, each succeeded in their own zones in establishing a stable German state based on their own ideologies. Given the manifold problems that both German states faced in 1949, such success and relative stability was hardly a foregone conclusion, as Mary Fulbrook explains:

> What is clear is that by the time of the formal foundation of the two Republics in 1949, neither side looked like a promising candidate for future success. There was, it is true, something of an economic upturn on the West German side; but opinion polls reveal that a high proportion of West Germans were still anti-democratic in political orientation, and prone to grumble about the miseries of everyday life and the unfairness of denazification procedures. On the Soviet side, only a minority of the population were committed Communists: most were hoping that present arrangements would prove to be transitory, and in the meantime tried to make the best of things – or left for the West. Given the imposition of new political forms on such apparently unpromising soil, it is all the more surprising that the two German states in the event proved so long-lived and relatively stable.

(*The Two Germanies*, 1992, p.16)

Such stability was a long time coming in the early days of Germany's defeat, and that it would ever be attained seemed almost unimaginable in the chaos of the immediate months and years following the war. This is an important point to remember, as Anthony Sutcliffe explains: 'We know now that western Europe would recover surprisingly quickly ... In 1945, however, no one could be confident that the recovery would be rapid, or even that there would be a recovery at all before some new disaster took place' (*Western Europe since 1945*, 1996, p.1).

The development of two sovereign German states was accelerated by the onset of the Cold War, although ultimately, of course, the cause for the division of Germany lies in the Second World War. Differences between the western powers and the Soviet Union soon developed, and anti-Nazism was quickly replaced with anti-communism among the western Allies. In particular, US policy towards Germany was motivated by the perceived need for containment of the Soviet Union, in line with the Truman Doctrine. Germany increasingly found itself at the centre of a developing antagonism. Punishing the Germans became less important for the western powers in the light of this new enmity, while extending the hold over their zone of occupation gained importance for the Soviet Union as well as the western powers. It is important to realize that both the Soviet Union and the US had clear political and ideological agendas in dealing with their zones of influence. In the developing Cold War, Germany posed a problem to the Allies, because 'neither side could or would take the risk that a united Germany might become an ally of the other' (R. Steininger, 'Germany after 1945', 1989, p.5).

Once economic unity (one of the decisions taken at Potsdam) was no longer a reality following the creation of the Bizone in January 1947, political unity also became impossible. This was an important turning point in Germany's post-war history. A British Foreign Office official noted in July 1946, 'If Germany is to be divided economically, political division will almost certainly follow, though it need not necessarily do so immediately' (quoted in Steininger, p.8). Indeed, it took until 1949 for that division to manifest itself in the formation of two separate states. The German Federal Republic (FRG), consisting of the western zones of occupation, ratified its 'Basic Law' (*Grundgesetz*) on 23 May 1949 and decided on a new capital, the provincial town of Bonn in the Rhineland. The 'Basic Law' was deliberately not called a constitution, being conceived as an interim measure until the unification of Germany could be achieved. In a preamble 'a transitional period' is stressed during which the 'Basic Law' should be in place, until such a time when Germany would be reunited. In August 1949 elections for the first German Bundestag were held. By a very narrow margin, the CDU won the election. In September Konrad Adenauer became the first Federal Chancellor of the new republic in a coalition government, and Theodor Heuss was elected as the first Federal President (details of the election can be found in Lothar Kettenacker's chapter 'Drifting apart' in your *Secondary Sources*, p.137).

The second German state, the German Democratic Republic (GDR), was founded on 7 October 1949 in the Soviet occupation zone, when its constitution was ratified by the provisional People's Chamber (*Volkskammer*). Wilhelm Pieck was elected President; Otto Grotewohl was the first Prime Minister. One of his deputies was Walter Ulbricht, who was elected General Secretary of the Central Committee at the SED (*Sozialistische Einheits-Partei* or Socialist Unity Party, consisting of the SPD and KPD) Party Congress in July 1950, a position which allowed him to shape the politics of the early years of the GDR. The East German state defined itself as anti-capitalist and anti-fascist, and the new republic emphasized the important role that German anti-fascists had played in freeing the country of fascists (National Socialism was not known by that name in the socialist GDR, but only as fascism or 'Hitler-fascism'). Anti-fascism has been termed the 'congenital myth of the GDR' (quoted in Kettenacker, *Germany since 1945*, 1997, p.217). Part of the function of this myth was to demonstrate that a clear break with the past had been achieved, and at the same time to show that the West German republic had failed to achieve such a break. In East German propaganda the defeat of 1945 was transformed into a communist/anti-fascist victory in which every East German citizen had seemingly played a decisive role, and the GDR was portrayed as the only true German state, whereas the Federal Republic was seen as tainted by capitalism/fascism. In fact, Erich Honecker, the future leader of the GDR, summed up the choice East Germany faced in 1949 thus: 'either to strengthen the anti-fascist democratic condition and to carry on the revolutionary change on the way to Socialism, or to give up on the anti-imperial, democratic achievements and to allow a restoration of monopoly capitalist conditions' (quoted in H. Münkler, 'Antifaschismus und antifaschistischer Widerstand als politischer Gründungsmythos der DDR', 1998, p.16).

Exercise Read Document II.51, the German Economic Commission of the Soviet High Commission's 'Announcement of the impending establishment of the German Democratic Republic', in *Primary Sources 2*, and comment on the way the new West German state was portrayed in the GDR. ∎

Specimen answer   The document highlights how the new East German state attempted to portray itself as the true German state, 'the democratic Germany', while discrediting West Germany. The founding of the GDR is portrayed as a first step towards the restoration of 'sovereignty, independence and freedom'. West Germany, on the other hand, was 'the undemocratic Germany at Bonn, the rump Germany of the war-mongers and the dividers', and was placed in direct comparison with Hitler's Germany and as its direct successor. □

In 1949 both new German states claimed to speak for all Germans, not just those within their territories. Thus, the Federal Republic's 'Basic Law' stated 'the German people, ... desiring to give a new order to political life for a transitional period, has enacted, by virtue of its constituent power, this basic law of the FRG. It has also acted on behalf of those Germans to whom participation was denied.' The German Democratic Republic's constitution similarly claimed to speak for all Germans: 'In the desire to guarantee freedom and human rights, to shape the communal and economic life in social justice, to serve social progress, to support friendship with all nations, and to secure peace, the German people have given themselves this constitution' (quoted in K. H. Jarausch and V. Gransow, *Uniting Germany*, 1994, pp.6–8).

The constitutions were formally similar. Both countries were federal states with lower and upper houses of parliament; both had a political leader (a chancellor in the west, a prime minister in the east) and a president who acted as a ceremonial figurehead. In practice, however, they were implemented in very different ways, and were based on a different understanding of democracy. In the west a range of political parties competed for electoral support, while in the east the SED, which came into being in April 1946, dominated and effectively controlled other small parties. Eventually, the communists increased their influence and established party control over what was *de facto* a one-party state. The GDR's federal regions were abolished in 1952, and the upper house of parliament ceased to exist in 1958. In 1960 the Council of State replaced the role of the president, and in the amended constitution of 1974 the separate identity of the GDR as a nation was stressed (Fulbrook, *The Two Germanies*, 1992, pp.28–9).

The 'Basic Law' of the FRG attempted to address some of the mistakes of the Weimar constitution, for example by introducing proportional representation and a 5 per cent threshold for parties, thus avoiding the problems of coalition governments faced during the Weimar Republic. An important feature was the federal nature of the new republic, which led to decentralization and harmonization of regional differences (Fulbrook, pp.30–1; see also Lothar Kettenacker, 'Drifting apart', pp.132–3 in the *Secondary Sources*, on the thinking behind the 'Basic Law'). The secure democracy that would develop in West Germany over time owed its stability in no small part to the 'Basic Law'.

Adenauer's Germany

Although two German states had been established in 1949, it would none the less not have been impossible, in theory at least, to achieve German reunification in the near future. If, for example, an SPD-led government had overturned Adenauer's narrow majority, or if a coalition of the two major parties (CDU/CSU and SPD) had governed the new republic, the result could have led to a completely different development for German history. Instead, Adenauer's desire for German integration with the west determined the fate of the FRG for the next decade. West Germany's foreign policy in the 1950s was defined by his desire to maintain and improve links with the west. 'The price paid for the Federal Republic's rapid economic and political rehabilitation was the jettisoning of fellow-countrymen to their fate in the east – and Adenauer deemed it a price worth paying,' as Mary Fulbrook comments (*Fontana History of Germany*, 1991, p.175).

Tied in with this political premise were security considerations and economic policies. Adenauer was prepared to forego German reunification in favour of achieving West Germany's integration in the western alliance, with the aim of achieving an equal status for Germany among her new allies in the future. He shared the American fears of the threat of the Soviet Union (G. Niedhart, 'Aussenpolitik in der Ära Adenauer', 1993, p.813). Anti-communism had a long tradition among the German middle classes, and had played an important role in the interwar years and during the 'Third Reich'. Given this continuity it was easy to suggest that West Germany faced a 'Bolshevist threat', thus making western integration more attractive to most Germans, even at the cost of ruling out reunification of the two Germanies (Fulbrook, *Fontana History of Germany*, 1991, p.185). As a result of Adenauer's western focus, the infamous 'Stalin note' of March 1952 was rejected as a ploy and not taken seriously. Stalin offered the possibility of German reunification under the condition that Germany did not enter into a military alliance with the western powers. Historians have debated ever since the sincerity of the note, questioning Stalin's motives and asking if a realistic chance of reunification was missed in 1952. Whatever that chance might have been, Adenauer decided against the possibility of reunification and in favour of firm western integration.

Exercise   Read Adenauer's speech of September 1949 in *Primary Sources 2* (Document II.52) and answer the following questions:

1   How did Adenauer sum up the last four years of German history, and what did the founding of the Federal Republic symbolize?

2   How did he evaluate the role of the Allies, and where did he see their future importance?

3   What were his goals for Germany's future? ■

Specimen answer   1   Adenauer summed up Germany's last four years as a time when the country's life had been ruined by the war, economically, politically and socially. Legislative and executive powers had been in the hands of the Allies and had only gradually been regained by Germany. The founding of the FRG marked the beginning of a new chapter in German history.

2   Adenauer acknowledged that Allied help had saved Germans from starvation and made possible the start of Germany's reconstruction. At the same time, he pointed out that Germany was still far from having attained complete freedom. He looked to the Allies to 'hasten the further political development' of Germany on the road to full freedom.

3   The new Germany would 'tackle the great social problems' of the time. Adenauer singled out employment, the integration of refugees and expellees, and housing as necessary prerequisites for inner stability. He

appealed for support in addressing this problem by pointing out that this was not a German but a European problem. Adenauer envisaged Germany's future firmly within a European federation with close economic cooperation, as initiated by the Marshall Plan. His desire for the integration of Germany in the west was emphasized in his advocacy of a European federation to replace nineteenth-century nationalistic conceptions of states. □

How can we explain the success of both Adenauer and his party, the CDU, in the 1950s? Of course, the most important factor must be the economic growth that Germany experienced in the early years of his leadership (the economic recovery is discussed in detail in section 4). After a rocky start, the new democratic system seemed to be working, providing improved living conditions, employment and security for most West Germans. This development benefited the way democracy was regarded in Germany. It became associated with economic success rather than with hardship, as it had been during the Weimar Republic. Political stability could thus develop out of economic stability. Increasing prosperity guaranteed the support of the majority of Germans for the new political system. Interestingly, it would seem that 'the percentages supporting democratic – rather than monarchical or Nazi – political views in opinion polls in the 1950s and early 1960s grew in close correlation with the increase in the average weights of ever more satiated West Germans' (Fulbrook, *Fontana History of Germany*, 1991, pp.181–3, quotation p.183). Churchill's demand for 'fat but impotent' Germans had become reality. In the early 1950s, Germany became increasingly integrated in the west or, in Lothar Kettenacker's words, 'joined every international, preferably European organization going' (*Germany since 1945*, 1997, p.90). These included the Organization for European and Economic Cooperation (OEEC) in 1950, the European Payment Union (EPU) in the same year, the General Agreement on Tariffs and Trade (GATT) in 1951, the European Coal and Steel Community (ECSC/Montan-Union) in 1951, the International Monetary Fund (IMF) in 1952, and the European Economic Community in 1957. Further western integration was achieved when Germany became a full member of the Council of Europe in 1951 and a member of NATO in May 1955, the date when the occupation status also lapsed and the Federal Republic of Germany became a sovereign state.

Ulbricht's Germany

In the GDR, too, things might have been different had it not been for Walter Ulbricht's hard-line communism, which determined the nature of the new state. The new system was effectively a one-party state, in which the SED was a devoted follower of Stalin and practised a leadership cult that culminated in Ulbricht proclaiming at the second party conference in 1952: 'We will win because the great Stalin is leading us.' The 'building of Socialism' in the GDR was not the implementation and realization of new ideas, but amounted to an adaptation to the outmoded system of Stalinism (Weber, *Die DDR 1949–1990*, 2000, p.39).

Like the other 'people's democracies' of Poland, Czechoslovakia, Hungary, Romania, Bulgaria and Albania, the GDR was not allowed to develop an independent foreign policy, although it did have a say in '*Deutschlandpolitik*': the political relations between the two Germanies. Far from being an independent state, its fate was largely controlled by the Soviet Union. Following Stalin's death in March 1953, the new Soviet leadership criticized the GDR's hard-line policies and demanded an economic, although not a political, liberalization of the GDR. Ulbricht and other high-ranking SED officials were given orders from Moscow to change course. Although the result was a slight moderation and slowing down in the transformation process as part of the so-called 'New Course', too little was changed to avert a popular uprising against the oppressive regime in June 1953. The announcement of the 'New Course' on 11 June appeared like a declaration of bankruptcy to large parts of the population, and only increased the people's willingness to fight the system (Weber, p.162).

Exercise Re-read pages 140–2 of Lothar Kettenacker's chapter 'Drifting Apart' in your *Secondary Sources* and answer the following questions:

1 What were the reasons for the uprising of 17 June 1953?

2 What was the official East German line on the uprising, particularly regarding the numbers who took part, the numbers of fatalities, and the kind of protestors who took to the streets?

3 What do recent interpretations, based on previously unavailable documentary evidence, reveal about the uprising? ■

Specimen answers 1 The immediate causes were economic measures imposed by the SED. Productivity targets were raised by 10 per cent to cope with the deteriorating economy or, put simply, the state demanded more work for the same pay. Following Stalin's death, the East German state revealed its status as a puppet state by adopting the new, more lenient course advocated by Moscow, but it did not abandon the new production targets. Workers rose in protest and strikes occurred throughout East Germany on 16 and 17 June. Although the cabinet gave in and agreed to reduce production rates, the stakes had already been raised by the demonstrators, who now demanded free and secret elections, price reductions, free trade unions and no persecution of the strike leaders. These were considered unacceptable demands. The Red Army intervened and tanks were used to disperse the demonstrators, making the uprising 'the most traumatic event in the history of the GDR.'

2 According to SED accounts, the uprising was a counter-revolution instigated by western agents. Rather than accepting that the demonstrations had amounted to a 'people's uprising', it was relegated to a mere 'workers' uprising' (an interpretation that was accepted in the west), while the intervention of the Red Army was justified. It was alleged that 'only' twenty-one people were killed in the uprising, which was 'proof' that the military intervention had been restrained.

3 Since the archives of East Germany have been opened following German reunification, new evidence is available to historians, who have reinterpreted the official East German version of events. They concluded that the events of 17 June were more than a 'workers' uprising' and did indeed amount to a 'people's uprising'. Moreover, they argue that one should consider the overall circumstances in 1953 rather than focusing only on the

events of 16–17 June. Those included the desertion of collectivized farms, the mass exodus of professional and skilled workers to West Germany, general unrest following the regime's sealing of the border with the West, leaving only Berlin as an escape route. Casualty figures have also been revised in the light of new evidence: fifty people were killed in the clashes, twenty demonstrators were summarily executed, as well as at least forty Russian soldiers who had refused to raise arms against the demonstrators, and three SED functionaries were killed. New evidence suggests that without the intervention of the Red Army, the GDR would have collapsed in 1953. □

However, as is often the case, local studies can reveal a different picture. Mark Allinson has studied the district of Erfurt in East German Thuringia, and concludes from his findings that the events of June 1953 were far less 'revolutionary' in the countryside than they are perceived to have been in Berlin:

> Most commentators agree that [the] roots [of the crisis] lay in particular in the implementation of the decisions of the SED's Second Party Conference (July 1952), which resolved to 'build socialism in the GDR', though one can also see the uprising as the culmination of the frustrations born of poor living conditions. The attempt to build socialism was made at the cost of inadequate provisions of consumer requirements. It brought an intensified 'class struggle' against real and supposed opponents of socialism; reduced social welfare payments; the swift establishment of co-operative farms (LPGs) and the associated food shortages when many farmers emigrated in protest; and ultimately the raising of work quotas, which effectively meant that the 'workers' government' cut workers' pay. The overall effect of these measures was the worsening of already low living standards and increasing popular resentment of the SED and of the Soviet Union which seemed intent on deepening Germany's division.
>
> Though Thuringian records confirm this traditional view of the causes of unrest, local materials allow further insights into the class nature of the uprising, which has proved more controversial. While some historians have classified 17 June as principally a workers' uprising, others believe it was a general revolt which crossed class boundaries. In *Bezirk* [district] Erfurt, this was generally not the case. The date has also been seen as marking both the beginning of the GDR's ultimate collapse and the date of the state's effective foundation ... The *Bezirk* Erfurt materials show that events took a somewhat different course in the region than in Berlin. First, the unrest, mainly but not exclusively in the form of strikes, was not restricted to 17 June 1953, but extended for several days afterwards in some provincial towns. Second, however, the level of participation in *Bezirk* Erfurt was surprisingly low. Only a small minority actively demonstrated dissatisfaction with the regime, though this was undoubtedly at least partly due to the presence or rumoured presence of Soviet troops ... Many areas experienced no unusual disturbances at all. Third, the perception of 17 June 1953 as a major watershed in the GDR's history can, perhaps, be relativised given the surprising speed with which 'normal' life resumed. At least in the provinces, the legend which grew around 17 June 1953 was far more substantial than the events of June 1953 themselves.

(M. Allinson, *Politics and Popular Opinion*, 2000, pp.56–7)

On the basis of new primary sources which have only been available since the collapse of the GDR in 1989, historians are now able to revise the orthodox interpretation of such key events as the June 1953 uprising. The evidence presented by Mark Allinson demonstrates the importance of regional studies, for they can often present a very different picture and add significant nuances to historical debates.

Exercise   Now read the official version of the events of 17 June in *Primary Sources 2*, Document II.53, entitled 'Statement regarding the Berlin riots'. Who, according to the government, was responsible for the unrest, and how was the reaction of East German citizens portrayed? What was stressed as the intention behind the government's unpopular decisions? And finally, given what you have found out from Lothar Kettenacker's account, how would you evaluate the validity of the 'Statement'? ■

Specimen answers   The 'Statement' claimed that government measures designed to improve the situation of the population resulted in provocation from 'fascist and other reactionary elements' in the west. The East German regime's good intentions in taking measures to improve the situation of the people were stressed four times in the document. The unrest was portrayed as resulting from the actions of *agents provocateurs*, fascist and capitalist forces that were unhappy about the democratization and resulting improvement of the situation of the population and wanted to hamper a future reunification. The 'Statement' claimed that the uprising met with resistance from large parts of the population and state authority, and appealed to the citizens of the GDR to turn in any *agents provocateurs* known to them. Harsh treatment was threatened for those involved in provoking the uprising. The document advanced a highly dubious version of events. The reasons behind the uprising were not truthfully revealed, and the uprising was blamed on envious and reactionary western capitalists/fascists rather than unhappy East Germans. In the aftermath of the uprising, several West Germans were arrested and sentenced in East Berlin, accused of having been the organizers of the 'fascist putsch of 17 June', and sentenced to long prison terms with hard labour. The statement, which is clearly no more than propaganda for the East German regime and against West Germany, does not mention the violence with which the demonstrators were dispersed. In comparing this document with the recent findings of historians as outlined in Kettenacker's account, one would have to conclude that the version of events described does not amount to the truth about the uprising of June 1953. □

Although Ulbricht's policies were questioned by the time of the uprising of June 1953, he emerged strengthened from the event and continued to shape the East German nation. In the aftermath of the uprising, his opponents were removed from office when the entire party was purged of 'undesirable' members. Parallel to events in the West, the GDR entered economic and military alliances with the Soviet Union. In 1950 it was integrated into COMECON (Council for Mutual Economic Assistance), and in March 1954 the GDR's sovereignty was recognized by the Soviet Union.

4   THE YEARS OF RECOVERY

As we have seen, the legacies of the war inflicted social and economic problems of an unprecedented scale on Germany. After the establishment of separate states, the two German governments attempted to deal with these problems. How recovery was achieved depended to a large extent on the level of support the occupying Allies were willing to provide. In the east there was little such help, as the Soviet Union extracted reparations to a much higher degree and for a longer time than the western Allies. By way of 'fraternal contributions', the GDR was to help rebuild the USSR. West Germany received financial and economic support from its occupiers much sooner, and the help received was significant enough to effect a positive change for West Germany's economy. In this section we will examine the West German 'economic miracle', which led to an economic boom in the 1950s. We will then compare this development to the economic recovery in East Germany. Here, too, living conditions and economic circumstances improved, but the economic principle underlying the East German state encouraged a different kind of recovery.

The 'economic miracle'

The so-called 'economic miracle' of the 1950s is one of the myths of early West German history. In popular memory it appears as if every German had a hand in rebuilding Germany, and could take pride in producing the miracle that seemingly solved most post-war problems. That memory conveniently underemphasizes the role of the Americans in providing support, and falsely links the currency reform directly with economic recovery. In some ways it is perhaps no exaggeration to speak of a miracle, given that a stable and prosperous society developed out of defeat, destruction and occupation, with the added difficulty of taking care of millions of refugees. However, the term is problematic as it suggests an easier process of recovery than had actually been the case, and because it implies that the developments that led to an economic recovery cannot fully be explained. With hindsight, the myth of the 'economic miracle' overshadows much of the difficulties of the early years. However, it was by no means a foregone conclusion that recovery would occur so quickly, and many contemporaries did not think it possible. Nor was it unique to Germany – Europe as a whole experienced an economic upturn at the time. What was surprising about West Germany's recovery was the speed with which the rebuilding of the economy proved possible, given the devastation of the war, the substantial losses of territory, the division of the country and the massive population shifts (Borowsky, *Deutschland 1945-69*, 1993; Klessmann, *Die doppelte Staatsgründung*, 1984, p.223).

The western Allies played an important role in creating this apparent miracle, as did the 'social market economy' of Ludwig Erhard, Germany's new Economics Minister and future Chancellor. It has often been argued that without the help from abroad, and from America in particular, no such miracle would have been possible. Help arrived in the shape of the Marshall Plan, a 'European Recovery Programme' which offered financial aid for reconstruction to Europe (see Document II.46, George C. Marshall's Harvard speech in June

1947). The 1948 currency reform resulted in an economic upturn, although in the short term price rises and rising unemployment resulted from this measure.

In the 1980s and 1990s the Marshall Plan's direct impact on Germany's economic recovery was the subject of considerable debate. Some historians have played down its importance for Germany's reconstruction, while others have questioned whether there was a direct connection between the Marshall Plan and Germany's recovery and stabilization (see, for example, Milward, *The Reconstruction of Western Europe 1945–1951*, 1984, and Maier and Bischof, *The Marshall Plan and Germany*, 1991). Ludwig Erhard himself had always maintained that the Marshall Plan had contributed nothing to recovery, and recent research seems to bear out his claim. In purely economic and material terms, its importance seems to have been overrated by many contemporary observers. The help arrived so late that economic growth was already occurring, Germany's share in the financial aid was constantly reduced, and Germany did not rely on dollars to buy capital goods (Roseman, 'Division and stability', 1993, p.377). Mark Roseman argues that 'the only thing that spared the Marshall Plan more public criticism was the fact that the anti-Marshall Plan position had become so closely associated with the Communists. It was a curious and ironic reversal: a plan supposed to save the West from Communist influence was in fact saved from attack by the strength of the anti-Communist consensus that existed in western Germany' (p.377).

However, the Marshall Plan's political, psychological and institutional impact must also be taken into account, and here lay the real importance of the recovery programme: 'There is little doubt that the ERP played a decisive role in forcing western European acceptance of rapid German revival. It provided a forum and context for discussion of the recreation of an independent Germany. It was the logic of the Plan which persuaded the USA that there must be a West German state; it was the Marshall Plan dollars ... which enabled the USA to sell the idea to France' (Roseman, p.378). At the same time, however, both the Marshall Plan and currency reform intensified the Cold War. The Soviet Union declined to be involved in the ERP and, following the agreement between Britain, Luxembourg, Belgium, the Netherlands and the US to include Germany in the Marshall Plan and to found a West German state, the Soviet Union withdrew from the Allied Control Council. This spelt the end of Germany's four-power administration and the beginning of a division that would last forty years.

Exercise   Read the following excerpt from Mary Fulbrook's *Fontana History of Germany 1918–1990*, and note the motives behind America's changing economic policy vis-à-vis Germany in the late 1940s:

> The western Allies were not initially clear about their economic plans for post-war Germany. Just as in the sphere of denazification there was a switch from drastic notions of collective guilt to an eventual policy of rehabilitation, so in the sphere of economic policy there was a radical change in approach ... However, it was not only for practical reasons (the attempt to prevent mass starvation) but also because of the developing Cold War that western approaches to the German economy changed.
>
> The change was signalled in the speech by US Secretary of State James Byrnes in Stuttgart on 6 September 1946, when the German public learned for the first time explicitly that it was to receive more lenient treatment. In

the spring and summer of 1947 the shift in policy was confirmed. On 1 January 1947 the Bizone was created out of the British and American zones, ostensibly to allow for a more efficient joint economic administration, but to all intents and purposes actually creating a new, West German political unit in which the Economic Council acted as quasi-government. In March–April 1947 the Moscow Conference of Foreign Ministers saw a breakdown in East–West relations and the Truman Doctrine enunciated the American policy of containing the advance of Communism. Associated with this shift in priorities, away from anti-Nazism and towards anti-Communism, was a major shift in economic policy. On 5 June 1947 US Secretary of State George Marshall ... called for a European Recovery Programme. This was rejected in July by the USSR and by the East European states, because it was predicated on a market (rather than state-controlled and centrally directed) economy which would benefit American exports. Effectively the USA was to support the economic recovery of western Europe, and in particular of western Germany, both for the economic benefits it would bring to the American economy which was seeking overseas markets, and for the political motive of seeking a bulwark against the expansion of communism in central Europe. The USA now officially supported the view that 'an orderly and prosperous Europe requires the economic contributions of a stable and prosperous Germany'.

(Fulbrook, *Fontana History of Germany*, 1991, pp.156–7) ■

Specimen answer The initial hostility and desire for revenge towards Germany changed for two reasons. Practical considerations, such as the desire to avoid mass starvation, were significant but, more importantly in the light of the Cold War, the overriding intention was to contain communism and to strengthen Germany against the perceived threat posed by the Soviet Union, as expressed in the Truman Doctrine. For America this policy of supporting European recovery brought benefits for its own economy, and ensured that the western zones of Germany would act as a bulwark against communism. European recovery and stability were now seen to be inextricably tied up with Germany's economic and political stability. As a result economic policy towards Germany could no longer afford to aim to subdue Germany, as had been the intention behind earlier policies (such as the Morgenthau Plan to deindustrialize the country). West Germany's economic recovery was thus in part a product of the increasing antagonism between east and west. ☐

Another important factor which aided West Germany's economic recovery was the extraordinarily high capital investment of the war years, as well as the fact that much of the 'devastation' of productive capacity was in reality merely damage or dislocation. Allied bombing has been less successful in this respect than both sides had claimed. It was the economic recovery of the 1950s that helped to solve many of the social problems of the early days of West German democracy. Following the 1948 currency reform, the apparent instant success suggested by filled shop windows quickly turned sour, with inflationary price rises and a dramatic rise in unemployment (12.2 per cent by 1950, a total of two million unemployed) that led to strikes unprecedented in scale since the 1920s. And yet, just a few years later, full employment was reached and West

Germany's trade and industry were booming. For West Germans the superiority of the market economy was proven, and the message seemed to be that those who did not adopt the system – the GDR – would remain poor and backward (Münkler, 'Antifaschismus und antifaschistischer Widerstand', 1998, p.20).

A number of contributing factors can be identified that help to explain the economic upturn in West Germany, although not all of them were immediately positive. The Korean War of 1950 provided the basis for the so-called 'Korea boom'. Germany was able to revive its economy as the international demand for its exports (such as coal) increased during the war, although initially the results for Germany's economy were not encouraging. The country quickly ran up a trade deficit, and coal rationing had to be introduced. US High Commissioner John McCloy demanded 'a significant modification of the free market economy' (Kettenacker, *Germany since 1945*, 1997, p.87). This measure was greeted with some ambivalence by West Germany's politicians, because on the one hand it led to a boost in production and exports, but on the other hand it constituted a serious challenge to the new market economy through the threat of a reintroduction of state control.

The political and psychological effects of the Marshall Plan also need to be considered in this context. Seemingly being treated as an equal partner in the help offered by the US to Europe gave new confidence to German investors, and aided the general feeling of recovery. In addition, contrary to what one might expect, the war damage to Germany's industries, as well as the reparations and the disassembly of factories to be rebuilt in the victors' country (demontage), contributed to the economic recovery in the long run. In this sense, up to a point, the war was a catalyst for change and for an eventual economic upturn. Completely new construction of industry was necessitated, and consequently received more support from the state than it would have under different circumstances. This enforced modernization favoured German industry in international competition. Similarly, the lost territory in the east was initially regarded as a loss for the West German economy, but in reality many of these areas had been relatively uncompetitive and had relied heavily on state intervention and subsidies. Eventually, when the FRG was able to buy elsewhere the foodstuffs which had formerly come from the east, the economy actually profited from the territorial change. A further advantage for the West German economy was the large numbers of refugees (again, a positive development resulting from initially problematic circumstances). They provided a huge potential of qualified workers, and as such were a great reservoir for industry. They were cheap and were employed and moved to where they were needed, or companies were founded where refugees lived in great numbers. At the same time, the existence of large numbers of unemployed led to moderate wage demands by the trade unions in the beginning of the reconstruction phase, and there were no interruptions from strikes once recovery was under way (Borowsky, *Deutschland 1945–69*, 1993, pp.93–4). In many ways, then, West Germany's economy was at a great advantage in comparison with its competitors. You might want to keep these points in mind when thinking more generally about wars as catalysts for change.

Germany's economic recovery and the partition of the country went hand in hand. The currency reform of June 1948 in the three western zones had a positive effect on the economy, while the Soviet Union's currency reform three days later failed to have a similarly positive impact. When the western powers attempted to introduce currency reform to their sections of Berlin, the Soviet Union reacted with a blockade of the city. The Allies, and in particular the US, rose to the challenge with the Berlin air-lift, flying food and other essential supplies into Berlin to get round the blockade of all land and water routes by the Soviets. For almost a year, the Allies managed to supply the two and a half million inhabitants of Berlin from the air with the so-called *Rosinenbomber* (raisin bombers), flying in essential food, medicine, coal and building materials. For the fate of the two Germanies, the Berlin blockade was of particular significance. Many Germans feared a new war in the near future. The emotional and political consequences in West Berlin and West Germany led to a consolidation of the negative image of the Soviet Union and renewed traditional feelings of anti-communism, while the western powers gained in the estimation of West Germans. The resulting trauma of the threat from the east led to a general acceptance of western integration for the Federal Republic (Staritz, *Geschichte der DDR*, 1996, p.24).

The transformation of East Germany's economy

East Germany's political leaders were faced with very similar social and economic problems to those experienced in the west, although compared to West Germany less attention needed to be given to housing policy and the integration of refugees because refugees were leaving the GDR for West Germany. East Germany was fortunate in that fewer houses had been destroyed, and due to the great exodus of refugees leaving for the west, there was a less urgent need to provide housing. Regarding the substantial economic problems of the post-war years, however, the GDR was in many ways in a less fortunate position than its West German neighbours.

Reparations to the Soviet Union exacerbated the zone's early economic problems Until the end of 1946, more than 1,000 industrial plants were dismantled and taken to the Soviet Union, the second railway tracks on most railway lines were removed, and reparations were also taken from current production, while 200 of the biggest and most important companies were given over to Soviet ownership by being transformed into 'Soviet joint stock companies' (*Sowietische Aktiengesellschaft* or SAG). As a result, the eastern occupation zone contributed far more in reparations than the western zones, with adverse effects on the economic and social problems experienced (Weber, *Die DDR*, 2000, p.12). In addition, the east lost territory to Poland and no longer had access to the produce of West German industry.

In September 1945 land reform was executed in the eastern zone under the motto '*Junkers*' lands into farmers' hands'. 7,000 large estates were expropriated without compensation and the land redistributed to small-scale farmers. This was a radical measure but by no means a communist one, as all four political parties in the zone agreed to it, although the CDU opposed the fact that there should be no compensation. In fact, all four Allied powers had agreed that the East Prussian *Junker* with their large estates had provided support to German militarism and to Hitler, and they had therefore advocated land reform as part of the demilitarization of Germany. For various reasons, such as the cost of compensation and the damage expropriation might do to the vulnerable economy, the western powers did not implement such land reform (Trittel, 'Bodenreform', 1999, pp.105ff.).

In an effort to establish a socialist economy, industries, banks and building societies were nationalized, a measure that had been agreed to by a plebiscite in Saxony in June 1946 (Weber, *Die DDR*, 2000, pp.13–14). However, it is important to point out that these measures were 'sold' to the people not as expropriation of capitalist opponents but rather as the alleged punishment of 'Nazi activists and war criminals' (Staritz, *Geschichte der DDR*, 1996, p.52).

In many ways, the recovery in the east was perhaps more miraculous than that of West Germany, because the GDR managed to rebuild the economy without outside help such as the Marshall Plan. By 1952–3 it had managed to increase its steel and energy production and its chemical industry, although the production of consumer goods lagged behind and the standard of living was lower than in the Federal Republic (Weber, p.37). The concentration on the recovery and expansion of heavy industry did little to improve living conditions in the east. In addition, East Germany's citizens were exposed to political suppression. Particular protest was raised by the persecution of churches by the new regime (80 per cent of East Germans were Protestants). The mood deteriorated because of forced actions against farmers, the self-employed and intellectuals, and because of price rises and the unavailability of consumer goods (Weber, p.38). As a result, a large number of East Germany's population were attracted to life in the west. In 1949, for example, 1,000 people a day fled to the Federal Republic. Between 1949 and 1956, the total figure was in excess of 1.7 million. (The sharply rising figures for emigrants, particularly in 1960–1, were of course the main reason for erecting the wall between the two states in 1961, although East German propaganda referred to it as a 'bulwark against fascism'. In reality the wall was built out of desperation.) East Germans were in an unenviable position, as Lothar Kettenacker argues:

> Since 1933 East Germans [had] not experienced free and liberal public opinion. Through no fault of their own their frame of mind has been shaped into what Adorno and others diagnosed as the 'authoritarian personality'... GDR society was characterized by repression in all walks of life and constant pressure to conform to standards which were defined by those in authority.
>
> (*Germany since 1945*, 1997, p.217)

For all its shortcomings, however, it is important to remember that the GDR lasted longer than the Weimar Republic and Nazi Germany together, and almost as long as the Kaiserreich, a fact that, in Roseman's words, 'reminds us of how successful the post-war arrangements were in engendering stability in Germany' ('Division and stability', 1993, p.390).

Total war and social change in Germany

Exercise   At the end of this unit, and at the end of the course, we return to the question of war and social change. Mark Roseman's essay in the Course Reader, 'World War II and social change in Germany', addresses this question with reference to West Germany. Read the first section of this essay now, keeping the following question in mind:

Which problems specific to Germany does Roseman identify that make an evaluation of the impact of the Second World War on German society particularly difficult? ■

Specimen answer   Whereas in Britain, for example, strict state controls were imposed only during the war years, in Germany twelve years of National Socialism and four years of Allied occupation have to be considered when one attempts to assess the impact of war on society. Germany had experienced, in Roseman's words, a period of 'total' peace before the total war which began in 1939, and the war itself (at least until about 1944) had essentially seen little change from the pre-war years. The problem for historians is to decide to what extent social change was the result of National Socialism, and to what extent it was brought about by the war itself. □

Exercise   As you read the next two sections of Roseman's article, you will be reminded of your reading in Unit 17. When you have read section III, consider the following question:
   What was the effect of the war on West Germany's post-war economic affairs, and how did it differ from other western European countries? ■

Specimen answer   While in many western European countries the wartime precedent of state intervention in the economy led to continued involvement and a more state-managed economy in the post-war years, the opposite was true in Germany, where a free-market economy and the removal of all state intervention were advocated by economic theorists. The wartime experience seemed to underline the negative character of state intervention, which was largely rejected in post-war Germany. □

Exercise   What about the war's impact on social policy? How significant a role did the war play, and how did the experience differ in Britain and Germany? ■

Specimen answer   Of course, the war created new social problems (for example, the influx of refugees or the housing crisis which we have already discussed), and these problems required new answers. However, Roseman points out that 'war did not stimulate or promote innovative solutions or responses to established social problems'. Rather, there was a return to accepted practices. In Britain social change resulted to some extent from demands that those who had been indispensable to the successful waging of the war should be rewarded. Not only could such a demand not openly be voiced in post-war Germany, but before any demands for thorough social reform could even be made, the country had to be completely rebuilt. As a result, familiar and established practices of dealing with social problems were adopted rather than new ones. □

Exercise   Roseman lists a number of post-war social problems that German society faced, most of which you have already encountered in this unit. What does he say regarding long-term problems, and what overall conclusion does he come to regarding 'total war' as a cause of social change in Germany? You need to read sections IV and V to answer these questions. ■

Specimen answer   Roseman suggests that social and economic problems, although extremely severe, were relatively quickly overcome, and that the war did not present German society with problems it could not solve. War was not as decisive in bringing about change as the nature of the regime that had waged the war and the nature of the regime which followed it. You might disagree with Roseman on this, given that the deaths and population movements which you encountered earlier in this unit could be considered to constitute rather a big change. □

CONCLUSION: THE TWO GERMANIES IN 1955

At the end of this unit, and at the end of our period of investigation, it remains to be examined how the two German states had developed by the mid-1950s and how they had consolidated their different political systems. Hermann Weber sums up the GDR's position thus:

> Ten years after the end of the war the SED had been able to consolidate its leadership in the GDR with the help of the Soviet Union, but it had not managed to gain acceptance from the population and thus acquire a solid basis for its power. The radical changes in structure had not brought about a flourishing system, but a society in crisis ... The lack of consensus resulted on the one hand in a fixation of large parts of the population on the economically successful Federal Republic, on the other hand it was based on the rejection of an uncritical adoption of Stalinist dictatorship and bureaucratism by the SED.

> (*Die DDR*, 2000, p.44)

The West German state, on the other hand, had gained in popular acceptance as the economic crisis turned into recovery and even an economic boom and prosperity. By the middle of the 1950s full employment had been achieved, despite the seemingly never-ending influx of refugees from the GDR and expellees from the east. The unprecedented economic growth played a decisive part in making the political order and western integration acceptable, and left little need for social protest in the west (R. Morsey, *Die Bundesrepublik Deutschland*, 2000, p.48).

In 1955 the two German states faced each other as ideological opponents at the forefront of the Cold War in Europe. Mary Fulbrook notes how the condition of the two Germanies had changed from having been regarded as an enemy by Germany's neighbours to regarding each other as enemies:

> By the mid-1950s, far from a united German people being viewed with hostility by Allied Soviet and western powers as a decade previously, a divided German people now faced each other in hostility, with their respective armed forces representing the wider opposition of the western and Soviet blocs. This dramatic transformation had much to do with the changed international system, and in particular the changed interests of the USA and USSR in a Europe which they had divided into spheres of interest; but it also reflected the ways in which domestic politicians in each Germany responded to opportunities and constraints during this period. And, whatever the causes of the failure of reunification attempts, in practice both sides consolidated the division by the institutional embedding of the two partial states into two very different systems and spheres of influence.

> (*Fontana History of Germany*, 1991, p.180)

In conclusion, thinking back to the Allies' intentions in 1945 regarding Germany's future, we can identify both successes and failures. Denazification, for example, could be regarded as a failure. As we have seen, in the west many leading Nazis escaped punishment, and in the east many ordinary Germans were able to deny and forget their own responsibility. After Germany's reunification in 1990, this inadequate understanding of Germany's Nazi past became a troubled legacy for the new 'Berlin Republic'.

None the less, the Allies' determination to ensure that Germany would not again threaten its neighbours was achieved. With the two Germanies securely integrated into alliance systems and militarily dependent on the USA and the USSR respectively, both German states could concentrate on recovery and consolidation and have not posed a military threat to Europe since 1945.

Although West Germany embraced democracy following the Second World War, and the smaller East German state had to do the same in 1990, the fear of a strengthened, reunified Germany has remained a concern, as could be observed when reunification was finally achieved following forty years of division. Four decades of opposing ideologies and of different social structures have, however, divided the two Germanies more thoroughly than one had at first suspected. Even ten years after reunification, the two German states continue to exist in the minds of many Germans. In 1955 an eventual reunification could not have been foreseen, and after the building of the wall, such an event had become increasingly unlikely. In time, Germans east and west of the wall became accustomed to the division, and many no longer continued to wish for reunification. It appeared increasingly as if reunification would not be a practical proposition, given the different ways in which the two Germanies had developed. These years of division have proved a difficult obstacle to overcome now that the two Germanies are one again, not least because of the different post-war histories that we have examined in this unit.

References

Ackermann, Volker (1995) *Der 'echte' Flüchtling: Deutsche Vertriebene und Flüchtlinge aus der DDR 1945–1961*, Universitätsverlag Rasch.

Allinson, Mark (2000) *Politics and Popular Opinion in East Germany 1945–68*, Manchester University Press.

Backes, Uwe, Jesse, Eckhard and Zitelmann, Rainer (eds) (1990) *Die Schatten der Vergangenheit: Impulse zur Historisierung des Nationalsozialismus*, Propyläen.

Badstübner, Rolf (1989) 'The allied four-power administration and sociopolitical development in Germany', *German History*, vol.7, no.1.

Balfour, M. (1985) 'In retrospect: Britain's policy of "re-education"', in Pronay and Wilson (eds).

Benz, Wolfgang (1988) 'Infrastruktur und Gesellschaft im zerstörten Deutschland', *Informationen zur politischen Bildung*, no.259.

Benz, Wolfgang (ed.) (1999) *Deutschland unter alliierter Besatzung, 1945–1949/55: Ein Handbuch*, Akademie Verlag.

Berghoff, Hartmut (1998) 'Zwischen Verdrängung und Aufarbeitung', *Geschichte in Wissenschaft und Unterricht*, vol.49, no.2.

Borowsky, Peter (1993) *Deutschland 1945–69*, Fackelträger.

Culbert, D. (1985) 'American film policy in the re-education of Germany after 1945', in Pronay and Wilson (eds).

Die Fischer Chronik Deutschland 1949–99 (1999) Fischer.

Führer, K. C. (1999) 'Wohnungen', in Benz (ed.).

Fulbrook, Mary (1991) *The Fontana History of Germany 1918–1990: The Divided Nation*, Fontana Press.

Fulbrook, Mary (1992) *The Two Germanies: Problems of Interpretation*, Humanities Press International.

Gilbert, Martin (1996) *The Day the War Ended*, Harper Collins.

Hardach, Karl (1976) *The Political Economy of Germany in the Twentieth Century*, University of California Press.

Herbert, Ulrich (1987) 'Zwangsarbeiter – Vertriebene – Gastarbeiter: Kontinuitätsaspekte des Wanderungsgeschehens in Deutschland', in Schulze *et al.* (eds).

Hockerts, H.G. (1981) 'German post-war social policies against the background of the Beveridge Plan', in Mommsen (ed.).

Jacobmeyer, Wolfgang (1976) 'Die Niederlage von 1945', in *Westdeutschlands Weg zur Bundesrepublik 1945–1949: Beiträge von Mitarbeitern des Instituts für Zeitgeschichte*, Beck.

Jacobmeyer, Wolfgang (1985) *Vom Zwangsarbeiter zum heimatlosen Ausländer: Die Displaced Persons in Westdeutschland 1945–1951*, Vandenhoeck & Ruprecht.

Jarausch, K. H. and Gransow, V. (eds) (1994) *Uniting Germany: Documents and Debates, 1944–1993*, Berghahn Books.

Kettenacker, Lothar (1997) *Germany since 1945*, Oxford University Press.

Klessmann, Christoph (1984) *Die doppelte Staatsgründung: Deutsche Geschichte 1945–1955*, Schriftenreihe der Bundeszentrale für politische Bildung, vol.193.

Klessmann, C. and Wagner, G. (eds) (1993) *Das gespaltene Land: Leben in Deutschland 1945–1990, Texte und Dokumente zur Sozialgeschichte*, Beck.

Klessmann, Christoph, Misselwitz, Hans and Wichert, Günter (eds) (1999) *Deutsche Vergangenheiten – eine gemeinsame Herausforderung*, Ch. Links Verlag.

Königseder, A. (1999) 'Entnatzifizierung', in Benz (ed.).

McClelland, Grigor (1997) *Embers of War: Letters from a Quaker Relief Worker in War-Torn Germany*, British Academic Press and I.B. Tauris Publishers.

Maier, Charles S. and Bischof, Günter (eds) (1991) *The Marshall Plan and Germany: West German Development within the Framework of the European Recovery Program*, Berg.

Milward, Alan S. (1984) *The Reconstruction of Western Europe 1945–1951*, Methuen.

Mommsen, W.J. (ed.) (1981) *The Emergence of the Welfare State in Britain and Germany, 1850–1950*, Croom Helm.

Morsey, Rudolf (2000) *Die Bundesrepublik Deutschland: Entstehung und Entwicklung bis 1969*, Oldenbourg Verlag.

Motte, Jan, Ohliger, Rainer and von Oswald, Anne (eds) (1999) *50 Jahre Bundesrepublik – 50 Jahre Einwanderung*, Campus Verlag.

Münkler, Herfried (1998) 'Antifaschismus und antifaschistischer Widerstand als politischer Gründungsmythos der DDR', *Aus Politik und Zeitgeschichte*, B45.

Naimark, Norman (1995) *The Russians in Germany: A History of the Soviet Zone of Occupation, 1945–1949*, Belknap Press of Harvard University Press.

Niedhart, G. (1993) 'Aussenpolitik in der Ära Adenauer', in Schildt and Sywotteck (eds).

Niehuss, M. (1993) 'Kontinuität und Wandel der Familie in den 50er Jahren', in Schildt and Sywotteck (eds).

Pronay, N. and Wilson, K. (eds) (1985) *The Political Re-Education of Germany and her Allies after World War II*, Croom Helm.

Roseman, M. (1993) 'Division and stability: recent writing of post-war German history', *German History*, vol.11, no.3, pp.363–90.

Rössler, Ruth-Kristin (ed.) (1994) *Entnazifizierungspolitik der KPD/SED 1945–1948: Dokumente und Materialien*, Keip Verlag.

Schildt, Axel and Sywotteck, Arnold (eds) (1993) *Modernisierung im Wiederaufbau: Die westdeutsche Gesellschaft der 50er Jahre*, Verlag J.H.W. Dietz.

Schröder, Rainer (ed.) (1997) *8. Mai 1945 – Befreiung oder Kapitulation?*, Berlin Verlag.

Schulze, Rainer (1989) 'Growing discontent: relations between native and refugee populations in a rural district...', *German History*, vol.7, no.3.

Schulze, Rainer, von der Brelie-Lewien, Doris and Grebing, Helga (eds) (1987) *Flüchtlinge und Vertriebene in der westdeutschen Nachkriegsgeschichte*, Verlag August Lax.

Schweitzer, Carl-Christoph *et al.* (eds) (1995) *Politics and Government in Germany 1944–1994: Basic Documents*, Berghahn Books.

Smith, R. (1985) '*Welt im Film*: Anglo-American newsreel policy', in Pronay and Wilson (eds).

Staritz, Dietrich (1996) *Geschichte der DDR*, Suhrkamp Verlag (2nd rev. edn).

Steininger, Rudolf (1989) 'Germany after 1945: divided and integrated or united and neutral?', *German History*, vol.7, no.1.

Stern, Frank (1993) '"Ein freundlich aufgenähter Davidstern": Antisemitismus und Philosemitismus in der politischen Kultur der 50er Jahre', in Schildt and Sywotteck (eds).

Sutcliffe, Anthony (1996) *Western Europe since 1945: An Economic and Social History*, Longman.

Trittel, G. J. (1999) 'Bodenreform' in Benz (ed.).

Weber, Hermann (2000) *Die DDR 1945–1990*, Oldenbourg Verlag (3rd rev. edn).

Further reading

Fulbrook, Mary (2000) *Interpretations of the Two Germanies: Problems of Interpretation*, Palgrave (2nd edn).

Kettenacker, Lothar (1997) *Germany since 1945*, Oxford University Press.

Roseman, M. (1993) 'Division and stability: recent writing of post-war German history', *German History*, vol.11, no.3, pp.363–90.

Schulze, Rainer (1989) 'Growing discontent: relations between native and refugee populations in a rural district...', *German History*, vol.7, no.3.

Index